W9-BOL-867

T·H·E

A.D.D. BOOK

Also by William Sears, M.D., and Martha Sears, R.N.

The Pregnancy Book
(with Linda Hughey Holt, M.D., F.A.C.O.G.)

Parenting the Fussy Baby and High-Need Child

The Discipline Book

The Birth Book

The Baby Book

300 Questions New Parents Ask

Nighttime Parenting

Becoming a Father

Also by William Sears, M.D.

*SIDS: A Parent's Guide to Understanding and
Preventing Sudden Infant Death Syndrome*

T·H·E

A.D.D. BOOK

New Understandings, New Approaches to Parenting Your Child

WILLIAM SEARS, M.D.,
AND LYNDA THOMPSON, PH.D.

LITTLE, BROWN AND COMPANY

Boston ◆ *New York* ◆ *Toronto* ◆ *London*

First Edition

Drawings by Dennis Dunn and John Marden

The authors are grateful for permission to include the following previously copyrighted material:

Poem from *Full Esteem Ahead* by Diane Loomans with Julia Loomans. Copyright © 1994 by Diane Loomans and Julia Loomans. Reprinted by permission of HJ Kramer, Tiburon, CA.

Library of Congress Cataloging-in-Publication Data

Sears, William, M.D.
     The A.D.D. book : new understandings, new approaches to parenting your child / William Sears and Lynda Thompson. — 1st ed.
         p.   cm.
     Includes index.
     ISBN 0-316-77938-5 hc
     ISBN 0-316-77873-7 pb
     1. Attention-deficit hyperactivity disorder — Popular works.
     2. Parenting.   3. Child rearing.   I. Thompson, Lynda, Ph.D.
     II. Title.
     RJ506.H9S43   1998
     618.92'8589 — dc21   97-29504

10   9   8   7   6   5   4   3   2

MV-NY

Designed by Jeanne Abboud

Published simultaneously in Canada by Little, Brown & Company (Canada) Limited

PRINTED IN THE UNITED STATES OF AMERICA

Contents

Acknowledgments

A book for families could not have been written without the support of our own families. We gratefully acknowledge the incalculable contribution of our spouses at every phase of this endeavor. We also thank our children for their patience. We want to further acknowledge the tremendous contribution made by the work of Dr. Michael Thompson and the late Dr. Paul Patterson to understanding early child development and developing methods for assisting children and their families. These ideas were the basis of many chapters of this book.

The people at Little, Brown and Company have done an outstanding job in terms of polishing this work. Its pleasing format is a credit to them. Editor Jennifer Josephy and copyeditor Pamela Marshall are outstanding. Their patience and guidance were greatly valued.

Finally, continuing thanks to our patients. We cannot help but learn from them and expand our own knowledge as we work with them to find solutions to A.D.D. problems. In this vein, Dr. Bill has a special thanks to Patricia McDonald for her contribution to the book. Helping people with A.D.D. is very much a collaborative effort. This book is thus a reflection of the wisdom of others and not just something newly created by us. We thank all those others for sharing with us and hope we have done justice to their ideas and experience.

A Word from the Authors

A WORD FROM DR. BILL

As a pediatrician and father, I am concerned that each day two million American children go to school under the influence of mind-changing medications. I'm also concerned that while many of these children need medicating, some are misunderstood, misdiagnosed, mislabeled, and mistreated. If Attention Deficit Disorder had been a fashionable diagnosis fifty years ago, I certainly would have been labeled an A.D.D. child and probably would have been drugged in order to fit conveniently into a school system I found boring. On more than one occasion I faked an illness so that I could stay home from school to complete a bridge on my Erector set, which I found infinitely more interesting than learning about which mountain Attila the Hun crossed centuries ago. During grade school I had two "promotions" to higher grades so the teachers could "manage" me. Even during medical school some experts were concerned about my having too much energy and wanted to evaluate me for some disease, from hyperactivity to hyperthyroid. The subtle implication was always that there was something wrong with me, rather than something right. And to every growing

child, being different equals being less. The more I learn about A.D.D. the more I realize that I could very easily have been mislabeled and mistreated for this "disorder" and probably had my energy mischanneled so that I would not have become a hyperproductive adult, authoring twenty-three books and parenting eight children.

My perspective on A.D.D. comes from being a pediatrician for twenty-five years. In my practice, I see three general types of children labeled A.D.D. Some children truly do have a neurobiological quirk, causing them to think differently, act differently, and learn differently. These children merit this diagnosis and need a total management package, including medication, behavioral strategies, and learning strategies. Other children have what I call situational A.D.D. Because of some problem in their environment, possibly a mismatch between child and school, the overall well-being of these children is threatened, and this is reflected in how they act and learn. A third group doesn't have A.D.D. at all. They are just bright, energetic, creative children who act differently and learn differently. These children are exhausting for parents and challenging for teachers, and they are just plain inconvenient for society, especially for a school system that rewards sameness and undervalues difference. These children are just differently abled, not disabled. They have neither a deficit nor a disorder. They are just different. They need a different style of parenting and a different style of learning. They do not need a label.

Our goal in writing this book is twofold: to help parents understand A.D.D., so that they can tell whether or not their child has it and if so, to what degree; and to work out a personalized management program that brings out the best in these children — the positive qualities that make these children shine — rather than emphasizing the inconvenient behaviors they show. We want you to become an expert in your child, because no one else will. We will show you how to become an advocate for your child, making sure your child is accurately assessed and appropriately managed. We will show you how to work with A.D.D. professionals and school systems with the ultimate goal of helping your child's specialness work in a positive way rather than becoming a disadvantage.

Throughout the past, many famous people who have made this world a better place for us all may have had A.D.D., but they learned to use the positive features of A.D.D. to work to their advantage. They learned how to harness their energy and channel their differences into abilities rather than disabilities. We want the same for your child.

A WORD FROM DR. LYNDA

As my plane climbed into the skies above Orange County, California, my job was to write a few words to fellow parents of A.D.D. children, but instead I became mesmerized by the view out the window. As we headed east,

brilliant white cumulus clouds gave way to clear skies over the mountains and desert, and I thought about how getting above things gives one a perspective not possible from the ground. The terrain below looked like a living, large-scale map, the geology and topographic features relating to the human geography of settlement patterns, roads, and railways.

In a similar vein, this book provides a map for parents, lending a new perspective on the territory of Attention Deficit Disorder. It relates the inborn features common to people with A.D.D. to the social landscape they must navigate. If you feel like you are battling in the trenches, it will provide relief by getting you to a vantage point from which to take a new look at the terrain and plan a strategy for attacking the problems. And what a varied terrain Attention Deficit Disorder is! At the A.D.D. Centre in Toronto, we have had clients ranging in age from four to sixty-three, many of whom have been gifted. They range from children struggling with inattention, hyperactivity, and learning disabilities to successful middle-aged entrepreneurs whose spouses want them to improve their listening skills. Obviously, there is no single picture of the person with A.D.D. and no single treatment or solution. But there are basic principles and knowledge that will help you chart a course that is right for your family.

The information in this book reflects Dr. Bill's and my respective backgrounds in Medicine and Psychology. We met more than twenty-five years ago at the Hospital for Sick Children in Toronto. Since then, we and our spouses have shared and developed ideas about parenting while raising a dozen children (four Thompsons and eight Searses). This book is a distillation of that accumulated experience. In addition, we have drawn on the details of hundreds of families who have shared their experiences with either Dr. Bill or me over the years.

My interest in Attention Deficit Disorder stems from my decision in the 1970s to do my doctoral research on hyperactive children treated with medication. A.D.D. was not yet a popular diagnosis, but these children intrigued me. My first encounter with a child with A.D.D. was in Germany, where I had spent a year teaching English after completing my B.A. He was a bright, active, and impulsive student who did not fit the rigid demands of an academic German high school. Later I had a son with attentional difficulties, so I know about parenting the child with A.D.D. from both a professional's and a mom's point of view. I broadened my experience further by working in child and family mental health clinics and as a school psychologist and as the owner/director of learning centers. In the 1990s I entered the field of neurofeedback, an intervention for A.D.D. that involves learning to self-regulate brain wave activity. When I saw the difference that neurofeedback techniques combined with learning strategies could make, I decided to specialize in providing that service. It brought me back full circle to my graduate school fascination with A.D.D.

Watching the meandering Colorado River below reminds me of the twists and turns one faces in raising a child with A.D.D. The course looks calm enough from a distance, but along the way there will be moments akin to white-water rafting! This book provides an opportunity to share with you what Dr. Bill and I have learned about navigating the rapids and shoals. We hope it will help you detour around some of the tricky spots. Information is power. So we have packed as much information as we could into this volume: about A.D.D., child development, family interactions, school success, and effective interventions.

There is rain when we reach Dallas and change planes. It is a reminder that we can control our course but not the elements. In parenting your child, expect some rough weather (from critical family members, teachers, tough situations, for example) but stay hopeful. When we rise above the clouds we find the sun is still there. Sunshine radiates, just as your love for your child does, even when immediate circumstances get clouded by frustrations. The fact that you are reading this book means that you and your child will have an edge in dealing with A.D.D. We hope it helps you fly with as little turbulence as possible.

T·H·E

A.D.D. BOOK

An Introduction to a Different Kind of Book About A.D.D.

M. Barry Sterman, Ph.D.

Professor emeritus, Department of Neurobiology and Biobehavioral Psychiatry, School of Medicine, University of California, Los Angeles

This book is about Attention Deficit Disorder, or A.D.D. It provides the reader with a comprehensive overview of this disorder and a novel perspective from which to view it. The approach taken by Dr. Sears and Dr. Thompson reflects many years of relevant experience dealing with the problems that children face growing up in this complex modern world in general, and the issues raised by A.D.D. in particular. Together they have spent thousands of hours of meaningful face-to-face contact with challenging children and have helped develop some important new approaches to treating them.

Understanding A.D.D. has always presented a challenge to the health-care and educational professions, and certainly to the parents of children afflicted by this problem. Because a diagnosis of A.D.D. is usually followed by the prescription of stimulant medications, as has been extensively reported by the media, the United Nation's Narcotics Control Board has serious concerns. According to recent estimates, more than 5 percent of school-aged boys in the United States are currently taking Ritalin, resulting in the as-

tounding fact that some 90 percent of the annual production of Ritalin, or about 8.5 tons, is used in the United States. Certainly, a new perspective on treating A.D.D. would be helpful.

Stimulant medications have been found to be more or less effective in about 65 percent of children using them. But even in these children, stimulants do not cure the disorder; they merely correct some of its symptoms. They are effective only when taken and must be taken for many years, in some cases indefinitely. And, like all drugs, they can lead to undesirable side effects. So what are the alternatives?

In fact, a number of non-drug alternative programs for the treatment of A.D.D. have been developed. These involve various systematic intervention procedures for environmental structuring and behavior modification. The most recent and unique of these is a physiologically based behavior modification technique called EEG biofeedback, or, as more recently termed, "neurofeedback." This book is the first parents' guide to A.D.D. that includes an extensive examination of this novel treatment approach.

Neurofeedback is a very technical field that spans several different scientific disciplines. It uses advanced electronics and mathematical computations to convert electrical patterns recorded from the brain into images and sounds that are then presented in a video display. Changes in the characteristics of the EEG from a given brain area are expressed as changes in the gamelike components of the display. Since these characteristics directly reflect internal physiological responses related to brain functions, learning to control these components can lead to changes in how the brain functions.

The modification of behavioral responses through the manipulation of feedback reward is, in fact, a well-established principle in the scientific study of the learning process. According to this principle, responses that are followed by positive rewards increase, while those producing negative rewards become less likely to occur.

Neurofeedback can be viewed as a focused exercise program for selected pathways within the brain. Certain physiological characteristics that are common to many children with A.D.D. are reflected in the EEG and can be altered by a neurofeedback program that supports EEG changes that teach the children to gradually increase their attention while sustaining a quiet body. The child's desire for rewards will initially promote transient changes in brain function. However, as normal interactions within relevant circuits of the brain become more frequent, there appear to be also progressive and more permanent changes in both the functional and structural characteristics of the brain. As a scientist who has worked for many years in the field of neurofeedback and who has published numerous papers on this topic in respected scientific journals, I am convinced that this method is as effective as any, and far more benign than most, in achieving improved functional regulation in the human brain.

Today, with continually improving technology and integrated into an overall management package for children, neurofeedback is proving to be an effective therapeutic alternative for thousands of children with A.D.D. Reading about this promising new approach within the context of a sensitive and intelligent book about A.D.D. should prove to be both rewarding and instructive.

I

UNDERSTANDING A.D.D.

Before you can help your child manage the problem of Attention Deficit Disorder, you must first understand it. Is your child super-energetic, or is he truly hyperactive? Is she a creative daydreamer, or is she truly spacey because of an attention deficit? At what point does a neurologically based difference become a disorder for the child? Can A.D.D. work to your child's advantage in the long run? These are questions that parents ask, and we provide answers based on our experiences as a pediatrician, an educational psychologist, and as parents ourselves. We take a helpful and hopeful approach because we have lived with A.D.D. and have found that the two most important ingredients for a successful outcome are accurate information and a positive plan of action. You will notice that we avoid the term "A.D.D. child," because it inaccurately and unfairly focuses attention on the condition rather than the child. Here is what parents need to know so that they can help their children solve day-to-day problems and utilize their full potential to achieve their goals.

A.D.D.: What It Is and What It Isn't

MOST WRITINGS ON the topic of Attention Deficit Disorder (A.D.D.) and Attention-Deficit/Hyperactivity Disorder (A.D.H.D.) stress negative symptoms and frustrations. There are, however, many positive aspects. Indeed, the world would be a poorer place without the contributions from individuals who have been labeled, sometimes retrospectively, with A.D.D. The creativity, energy, spontaneity, and ability to focus intensely, which characterize A.D.D., are qualities that often improve the world for all of us. Thomas Edison, Winston Churchill, and Wolfgang Amadeus Mozart probably all had A.D.D. They learned how to use their A.D.D. traits to their advantage. How dull and different history would be without them!

WHAT A.D.D. IS

Attention Deficit Disorder is a collection of traits that reflect the child's inborn, neurologically based temperament. There is no question that these children are difficult to raise due to the particular cluster of temperament traits that characterize them. There are some

positive traits: spontaneity, creativity, the ability to lock on to and hyperfocus on tasks of the child's own choosing. There are also traits that present potential problems; these include selective attention, distractibility, impulsivity, and, sometimes, hyperactivity. Depending on how they are perceived and shaped, the combination of traits can work to a child's advantage or disadvantage. This chapter presents the characteristics that define and explain A.D.D. This is not a simple task because we are not dealing with a single entity. People with A.D.D. are a very heterogeneous group. They come in many varieties and within each subgroup are children who manifest the symptoms in varying combinations and to different degrees. In order to qualify for a diagnosis, the behaviors must be out of line with children of the same age and they must be causing impairment of functioning at home or school.

WHAT A.D.D. IS NOT

In addition to understanding what A.D.D. is, you should also understand what A.D.D. is not.

The A.D.D. Hall of Fame

Wolfgang Amadeus Mozart

Though he left the world a legacy of brilliant music and is the best-known composer of the classical era, Mozart might well have been described as an underachiever when he died in his mid-thirties in 1791. He was capable of incredible hyperfocus, sometimes composing an entire opera in only a few weeks, yet there were some commissions that he left to the last minute and others that he did not finish at all. He did not handle practical details like finances well, and he died a pauper. His impulsiveness in social situations stood in the way of his being rewarded with major court positions that would have brought greater financial reward.

Sir Winston Churchill

Winston Churchill was not a success in school. He was described as hyperactive and naughty, and he was frequently excused from the classroom so that he could run around the school yard to release his excess energy. In his autobiography *My Early Life,* Churchill described his impulsivity, tendency to be accident-prone, and his painful experiences in school. Although he had been an indifferent student, when he became interested in history as a young army officer in India, he devoured crates of books that were shipped to him from England. His high energy level, creative problem solving, and hyperfocus as prime minister of England during World War II led Britain through the darkest days of the war.

Thomas Alva Edison

Edison presents a classic profile of A.D.D. As an inventor he typifies the creative individual unable to stick with just one thing and constantly heading off in new directions. One biographer wrote of Edison's brief experience in school before he ran away, "He alternated between letting his mind travel to distant places and putting his body in perpetual motion in his seat." Later in life, Edison showed his tenacity in sticking with things that caught his imagination in his many inventions.

A.D.D. is not a deficit in attention. A deficit means "a lack of something," implying less of something. But children with A.D.D. sometimes pay *more* attention to certain topics. What they really show is the two extremes of focus: they are not good at paying attention to things they find boring, but they can focus intensely on things that catch their interest. This can be an advantage when children are creating something. It can be a disadvantage when their hyperfocus in one area prevents them from paying attention to the things other people find important. For example, a child may spend six hours doing an incredibly clever cover page for a project but spend little time on the content; this won't earn a good grade from the teacher.

A.D.D. is not just a problem with attention. A.D.D. includes problems with paying attention, but this is not the whole story. There are also problems with impulsivity, distractibility, and, sometimes, hyperactivity. Academic underachievement is a frequent complaint from parents, and it frustrates the child, too, when she sees others with no more ability doing much better in school. These children are in some ways immature, but in other ways they display creativity and insight beyond their years.

A.D.D. is not a disorder in the usual sense. "Disorder" implies illness or pathology. A.D.D. is not a disorder like a thyroid disorder, for example. It is merely a difference, in the same way as being left-handed is a difference. As with left-handedness, the difference is related to the way the individual's brain works. Like left-handedness, A.D.D. occurs in at least 5 percent of the population, and it affects people to different degrees. Unfortunately, in the minds of some people, being different equals being less. To call this collection of traits a disorder does a disservice to individuals who have these traits, often making them feel handicapped. That may help them access services in some instances, but the cost may be a loss of self-esteem. Later on, this label may have other disadvantages: the time might come, for example, when car insurance rates are higher for people who have ever been diagnosed with A.D.D. When the symptoms are so extreme that a child cannot function in school without major interventions, A.D.D. does merit the term "disorder." But there is much wasted potential in children with less severe A.D.D. symptoms. They are at a *disadvantage* due to their traits rather than having a *disorder* that makes them abnormal.

Another "D" word we want to dismiss is "diagnosis." "Diagnosis" suggests the outcome of lab tests, a box on an insurance form, or, as we discuss on page 272, a tag necessary to qualify for educational benefits. You cannot diagnose A.D.D. with any single test. A more accurate "D" word is "description," which is really a summary of observations from significant people in the child's life. This is why parent and teacher questionnaires are so often used in identifying A.D.D.

A PORTRAIT OF A CHILD WITH A.D.D.

The tag "A.D.D." is not a judgment as to whether a child is good or bad. It is just a term to describe how he thinks or acts. While we feel it's important to look at the positive as well as the negative aspects of A.D.D., it must be said that A.D.D. poses a lot of challenges for the child and the family. Understanding what makes your child behave in a certain way will help you meet these challenges.

Johnny, eight years old, seemed to hear the first instruction given by the teacher but often missed the next two. He had an excellent memory for things that interested him, like baseball players' names or the exact words of a television commercial, but seemed completely unable to memorize his multiplication tables. Sometimes he had trouble getting started on his schoolwork. Once he'd started it, he would abandon it long before it was completed, get up to sharpen a pencil, start on something else, or just sit and play. This seeming inability to attend to an assigned task for any reasonable length of time was quite confusing to his parents, as they had observed time and again how Johnny could play for hours with his building toys or video games. It was a struggle to get him out the door for school each morning because he was easily sidetracked. His mother would find him still in his pajamas, sprawled on his bed with a handheld video game fifteen minutes after he had been sent upstairs to brush his teeth and get dressed.

His report cards said, "More effort needed." His parents felt he was fooling around at school, and they tried taking privileges away to punish him when they got calls from the teacher. Johnny had been examined by the family doctor and tested by a special-education teacher, and neither one had noted any problem with attention span in these one-on-one situations. His parents felt Johnny was the brightest of their four children by far, but he was failing third grade. "He's just so creative," they said. "He comes up with these fantastic ideas! When he gets into inventing something, his energy seems endless, but he won't stick to any of his school assignments unless we really sit on him. He irritates his teacher because he blurts out the first thing that pops into his mind. He jumps from one idea to the next. He just doesn't think things through."

Despite the fact that the family doctor and the special-education teacher said Johnny's attention span seemed fine, there is clearly something different about him. Johnny has A.D.D. His mother supplied all the clues in comments she made about her son. Although Johnny has the collection of traits known as A.D.D., like many children with A.D.D., he does not always display a *deficit* in attention (he is fine one-on-one and can focus on video games for hours), and he does not have a *disorder* in the usual sense of having an abnormality. The two "D"s in A.D.D. would tell more about the problem if they stood for *difference* and *distractible*.

A.D.D. is most easily understood as a variation on normal patterns of behavior. Unlike diseases such as tumors and bacterial infections, which produce abnormal symptoms, A.D.D. is a grouping of *normal* characteristics that appear in some children more frequently, more obviously, and more intensely

than in others of the same age. All children are impulsive, distractible, and inattentive some of the time. Children with A.D.D. are impulsive, distractible, and inattentive most of the time. They think, act, feel, and learn differently. This difference can work for or against them. It is important for parents to recognize and value the differences and for the child to conclude that it's okay to be different. Throughout this book we will show you how to shape these different traits to work to your child's advantage.

A CLOSER LOOK AT THE BIG FOUR

The four main qualities that define A.D.D. are selective attention, distractibility, impulsivity, and, in many children, hyperactivity. Each of these traits helps to explain the behavior of children with A.D.D. and the challenges they face.

Selective Attention

Children with A.D.D. pay attention selectively. Remember Johnny, our first example in this chapter. You may be confused, just as Johnny's mother was, about your child's attention span. Whom are you going to believe if both the classroom teacher and the karate instructor insist that your child has a real problem paying attention, yet you observe that your child can work busily with Play-Doh for hours and be a perfect angel in the doctor's office? Who is right? Probably everyone: children with A.D.D. don't have an attention deficit so much as they have *selective attention*. They operate from one extreme to another, exhibiting either brief attention or intense concentration, depending on the situation. Your child pays atten-

A.D.D. Facts

- Around two million school-aged children in the United States (at least 5 percent) are thought to have A.D.D. or A.D.H.D.
- Boys diagnosed with A.D.H.D. outnumber girls about 3:1, but in A.D.D. without hyperactivity, the overall incidence is similar in both genders. In the younger years, however, both A.D.D. and A.D.H.D. are diagnosed more frequently in males. By adulthood there is gender equality in these diagnoses.
- The genetic component far outweighs the environmental component with A.D.D. Environment influences how severe and persistent the inherited A.D.D. traits will be but does not produce them.
- One large study found that 25 percent of the first-degree relatives of children with A.D.H.D. had the problem.
- If one identical twin has A.D.D., there is an 80- to 90-percent chance that the other twin will also have A.D.D.
- A.D.D. is most often suspected or diagnosed after school entry, at around six or seven years of age. Children with the A.D.D. style may be fine in a play-based program, but they have trouble once they have to sit and work independently in first or second grade.
- The diagnosis of A.D.D. is not based on laboratory tests. It's based on observations made by parents, teachers, and A.D.D. professionals.
- Children usually do not grow out of A.D.D., though there is less hyperactivity after puberty. Unrecognized and unmanaged, people with A.D.D. are at risk for developing debilitating social and academic problems.
- If unrecognized and untreated, children with A.D.D. have a high (30 to 50 percent) chance of school difficulties; this may mean special-education placement, repeating a grade, dropping out, or being expelled.
- If unrecognized and unmanaged, 20 to 30 percent of these children may have problems with the law.
- Research has shown that children with A.D.D. show different brain wave patterns, which supports the view that in some children, A.D.D. has a neurobiological basis. It may, with further research, become possible to identify subtypes of A.D.D. from the EEG (brain wave) profile.
- Children diagnosed with A.D.D. should *never* be treated *with drugs only.* They require additional management techniques to improve their behavior and learning skills.
- In 1995, 1.5 million children in the United States (2.8 percent of schoolchildren) age five to eighteen years were being treated with Ritalin. From 1990 to 1995, the number of children on A.D.D. drugs tripled in the United States. In Canada between 1990 and 1995, the use of Ritalin increased three to four times according to a 1996 publication by Health Canada.
- A survey of the driving records of people with an A.D.D. diagnosis showed that they got more speeding tickets and had four times as many accidents in which someone was injured. However, when their knowledge of driving was compared to a control group, there was no difference.
- Divorce is twice as common in families where a child has A.D.D.
- In 1990, in a monthly survey of 2,400 practicing physicians, there were two million patient visits associated with the diagnosis of A.D.D. By 1994, this number had increased to 4.7 million. Approximately 90 percent of these patient visits resulted in a prescription for drug therapy.
- If recognized and managed, most children with A.D.D. can be taught to use their differences to their advantage. They show creative accomplishments and are a credit to themselves, their family, and society.

The Big Four

Selective attention
The child with A.D.D. operates at the two extremes of attention rather than in the middle like most people. There is *inattention:* "He can't stick to an assigned task. He just can't seem to pay attention when I am talking to him." There is *hyperfocus:* "His concentration is fine when he is doing his own thing, like watching TV or playing video games, or when he is in a novel situation."

Distractibility
The thoughts of a child with A.D.D. seem scattered. He has many different ideas popping into his mind at once and jumps from one to another faster than you can keep up. Often he tunes out while you are talking to him.

Impulsivity
The child with A.D.D. acts before he thinks, and this gets him into trouble at school and at home. He blurts things out or makes careless errors, like adding when the sign is for subtraction.

Hyperactivity
This trait occurs in only some children with A.D.D. When present, it can make diagnosis easier.

tion well to whatever interests him but gets restless and tunes out quickly whenever things become routine or boring. Your child's attention span may even at times be better than his friends'. Except with activities of their own choosing, children with A.D.D. need things to be presented in a stimulating way to prevent boredom. This is why they are better at hands-on learning that involves building models or playacting than they are at sitting and listening or reading a textbook. Children with selective attention *select out* what is important to them in that moment. And once they are distracted and off task, these children have more difficulty tuning back in to the task at hand.

I never yelled at Mary from across the room. If I needed to ask her something and she was occupied in a constructive way, I would consider whether what I had to say to her could wait. It is so hard for her to be interrupted. I always tried to avoid a war over nothing.

Selective attention can work to a child's advantage or disadvantage. Selective attention allows a child to get into things in a deeper and more creative way, provided he is interested. The disadvantage is that, while we all have some trouble focusing on boring things, children with A.D.D. find it virtually impossible. They just can't make themselves do things that are not of personal interest.

Homework assignments are a prime example. Sometimes, with older students, the pressure of a deadline may finally get them to settle down to work. Often the whole family suffers because of the child's procrastination. Everyone has to get in high gear the night before a project is due. But never forget that light at the end of the tunnel. It represents real future opportunity. If you can get through these early years, your child's ability to hyperfocus, to maintain deep prolonged attention, on projects that interest him in high school and college may just earn him top honors and a successful career!

Selective attention can work in sports. Selective attention is at work not just in the classroom or at home, but also in sports.

Here, too, it can be an advantage or a liability. Take hockey as an example. In the 1970s, while collecting data for her thesis on the effects of the drug Ritalin in hyperactive children, researcher (not yet Dr.) Lynda noticed that a disproportionate number of the A.D.H.D. boys who were hockey players played goalie. This is the position that makes the most of a child with A.D.D.'s inborn characteristics. The goalie receives individual instructions and therefore does not have to pay attention during strategy sessions in the dressing room. When he's on the ice, his attention can wander while the puck is at the other end of the arena without adverse effects on the score. However, when the puck crosses the blue line and is in play close to the goalie, he must become mentally locked on to it and allow virtually nothing to distract him, including screaming fans. He does not have to think about what to do, which would slow down his reactions; he just reacts. His parents may be proud of their goalie in the hockey arena, but his hyperfocus can, on the other hand, be irritating when repeated calls to come to supper are ignored because he is locked on to the TV or a video game!

How does this goalie do when baseball season comes around? If he has good skills and is placed in a position that sees lots of action, such as pitcher, catcher, or first base, he will probably use his hyperfocus and be fine. However, if he is made an outfielder, he really will be out in left field. He may be watching birds, picking the dandelions, or playing with the dirt. The coach or his parent may have to yell at him to watch the ball. It never surprises us when a parent of such a child reports that their child tried Little League, but only for one season.

Hyperfocus is a form of selective attention. This trait is quite obvious to parents of children with A.D.D., but educators and psychologists tend to look more at the child's attention deficits than at his potential strengths. It's not that these children *can't* focus, but rather that they focus *inappropriately.* (This echoes what we say about activity level: it is not so much that they are more active, but rather that they are active at inappropriate times.) They are able to click into a state of concentration that, if recognized and channeled, can work to their advantage as adults. Of course, hyperfocus can also be extremely frustrating to the parent of a child who tenaciously sticks to his own choice of activity when it's time for dinner.

Matthew, age seven, was building with his Lego. He was very creative. His mother went to the door of his room and told him that dinner was on the table. He said, "Okay, I'm coming." Ten minutes later his mother went back to his room and asked him why he hadn't come. He replied, "You never called me!"

Matthew was not lying. Matthew was not being a smart aleck. He was simply completely engrossed in his building. Matthew had heard his mother the first time, but nothing his mother had said had registered in his mind.

Many conscientious students who do not have A.D.D. have the ability to hyperfocus. To distinguish between the hardworking student who can spend three hours studying physics and the student with A.D.D. who has gone into hyperfocus, ask yourself whether the child in question would be angry if interrupted. The child with A.D.D. is likely to overreact and respond emotionally.

Charlie, an elementary school teacher, was a very bright and talented man. Pupils, particularly the hyperactive boys, loved being in his class. Even as an adult, Charlie couldn't seem to sit still or stop talking. He had his second black belt in karate and was going for his third. He was, at the same time, a serious hockey player — the team's goalie. Hyperfocus had both assisted him to obtain the grades needed for college and sustained his high level of participation in sporting activities without serious injury. Despite his ability to go into a state of extreme focus with sports, music, or a computer, he found it difficult to read a book. He would avoid reading if at all possible. If he absolutely had to read a book, it would take him ages. Charlie tried neurofeedback training. One evening he did neurofeedback for forty-five minutes immediately prior to a hockey game against what he described as a vastly superior team. Despite sixty-five shots on goal, he got a shutout! He was also beginning to find it easier to stick with reading.

The ability to hyperfocus may be used by the student and adult later in life to remain in a super-high state of creative focus and concentration while developing computer programs, writing papers, performing surgery, and so on.

Attention span is related to age. A child of two with a very short attention span is not considered to be outside the normal range. The same attention span in a four-year-old, however, might be considered a problem. Attention span, however, is not usually noted as a difficulty by parents of preschoolers in the same way that hyperactivity or impulsivity is. Attention differences usually become noticeable when the child enters grade school. Johnny could be quite attentive in the doctor's office and in other one-on-one situations. But in school and when doing tasks independently at home, he did not appear to be able to maintain his attention for very long at all. His mother had not noticed this when Johnny was a preschooler. His attention to play activities had seemed appropriate for his age. The fact that he paid less attention to her instructions than to his play had seemed similar to the behavior of her neighbor's child. Now that Johnny was in third grade, he was supposed to be able to listen for five or ten minutes and work on tasks in school without constant supervision. But Johnny required the same supervision to complete tasks that most children do when they are preschoolers.

Memory is selective too. Children who have A.D.D. differ from other children in what they recall from reading. The usual style of people with A.D.D. is to remember a few facts that caught their interest. They do not actively read; they skim over the words and may lock on, ever so briefly, to some interesting detail. If it is a page of English history they were reading, they might recall, for example, that the king was bowlegged but not remember which king it was or when he reigned. With assigned passages, they read just to get it done, not to process the information. Sometimes, after two minutes of reading during the intake process at the A.D.D. Centre, clients react to Dr. Lynda as if she is trying to trick them when she asks, "What did you learn reading that page?" Some respond, "I don't know. You asked me just to read it!" It is as if reading and remembering are two unrelated activities.

The different pattern of recall of people who have A.D.D. is not a matter of will; it is their inborn style. Teachers or relatives who say, "He's lazy. He could do it if he wanted to" just don't understand. They are not aware of the child's inborn difficulty controlling his focus and concentration. Often these children (and adults with A.D.D., too) just cannot make themselves do something, even when it is important. That is what distinguishes them from people who do not have A.D.D. Everyone has more trouble with boring things, but most people can make themselves do them as needed. The person with A.D.D. often cannot force himself to pay attention even when he would like to.

I have to be careful not to launch into a long lecture when I'm correcting Benjamin. One time I took a long time correcting him over a squabble about a toy. After a few minutes I asked if he'd been listening to what I said, and he responded, "You have little brown flecks in your eyes."

Questions You May Have About Selective Attention

Don't all children show these traits?

Yes! Most children will have some difficulty with attention. What kid hasn't done silly things without thinking about the consequences? Many children drift into daydreams when they are supposed to be listening to instructions. Whose child hasn't become a little hyper or rowdy at a party? At what point does a curious, creative, energetic child get tagged hyperactive? The difference is that children with A.D.D. demonstrate the following:

- *most* of these traits
- *most* of the time
- to an *extreme* degree

The main goal in treating A.D.D. (and the goal of this book) is not to change the inborn traits of a child but to channel the qualities to work to a child's advantage. There are two

sides to every coin: you want to get to the point where the behavior is seen as spontaneous and not impulsive, energetic rather than hyperactive, and where the person is able to juggle many tasks successfully rather than flitting from thing to thing.

How do children with A.D.D. differ from their peers?

There is a noticeable difference in behavior between these children and their same-age friends. Sometimes parents refer to their child with A.D.D. as being immature. They notice that their child shows traits of inattention, distractibility, impulsivity, and high activity on a level similar to that of a much younger child. This age-inappropriate behavior is the characteristic that separates children with A.D.D. from their peers. Sometimes the behavior that seems inappropriate would not be considered exceptional in a younger child. Parents often notice that their child with A.D.D. plays better with younger or older children than he does with his peers.

Although Andrew was eleven, he still wanted his parents to do everything for him. Rather than put up with his whining and have things take five times as long, his mother still helped him get dressed in the morning, and his father got him into his uniform and tied his skates for hockey. If they didn't do these things, he would wander around distracted by everything and never get ready.

What happens to these characteristics when children grow up?

Dr. Lynda recalls seeing a birthday card with the text "You may be getting older . . . but

Gender Differences and A.D.D.

A.D.D. is not necessarily milder in girls, but it can be different. Boys with unrecognized and untreated A.D.D., especially if they are impulsive and overactive and also have learning difficulties and family problems, tend to show antisocial behavior and are at risk for later substance abuse. Girls with untreated A.D.D. tend to show more emotional problems, such as anxiety and depression. More boys than girls are diagnosed with A.D.H.D. (A.D.D. with the hyperactive component). Some studies quote ratios as high as 6:1. A good estimate is that boys with A.D.H.D. outnumber girls 3:1. But we believe these figures are misleading. A.D.D. traits are often overlooked in many children who are not hyperactive, especially girls. Girls with A.D.D. are more eager to please and are less likely to be disruptive, so their difficulties may not be so readily noticed. Their A.D.D. problems show themselves as anxiety and learning or cognitive problems. Boys with a high level of activity may sometimes be incorrectly identified as having A.D.D. Hyperactivity tends to lessen in the teen years, so the incidence of A.D.H.D. becomes less. In an Ontario, Canada, population survey, about 9 percent of boys and 3 percent of girls aged six to eleven had A.D.H.D., but these rates dropped to about 3 percent of males and 1.5 percent of females in the teen years. The ratio of males to females characterized as A.D.D. without hyperactivity in this study was more even and stayed at about 1.4 percent for children and teens. The rate of diagnosis evens out in adulthood, when the number of males and females with A.D.D. is similar.

As is borne out in scientific studies, observant teachers and experienced parents have long known that boys and girls act and play differently. Researchers observing normal preschool children during free play sessions show that girls tend to stick with a task longer than boys do. Girls show a greater preference for social interaction, whereas boys are more interested in objects and action, such as playing with blocks and trucks. Boys pay more attention to environmental sounds, such as fire engines and loud noises in the hall; girls are more sensitive to verbal sounds of classmates and teachers. Boys are more likely to act out in school, becoming either the class discipline problem or the class clown. Girls, on the other hand, are less impulsive and more likely to be spacey and daydreamers. In general, girls adapt more easily to the traditional classroom setting. They find it easier to sit still and listen to a teacher. Boys are generally more distractible, restless, and unable to selectively filter out competing influences in the classroom. In some respects, boys enter school with a disadvantage, since the traditional classroom and mode of teaching is usually geared more toward the female gender and is usually run by female teachers. This may partially explain why children with A.D.D. do better when they get a male teacher (another reason is that male teachers usually talk less). Still, as one wise mother summed it all up, "I'm not going to let him grow up being rowdy and disruptive just because of his gender."

Besides gender differences in children with A.D.D., there are gender differences in how parents respond. Not surprisingly, fathers tend to be more tolerant of their child's hyperactive behavior. Perhaps this is because the father can see himself more easily in his child. Fathers, especially those who do not spend a lot of time with their child (and when they do, it's all fun and games), tend to overlook the annoying parts of the child's personality. Mothers, on the other hand, because they are more likely to be on the receiving end of school complaints and because they take on a greater share of house and child management, are more likely to recognize problems in their child and label them such. Mothers are more likely to seek treatment and persevere with it. Fathers are more likely to reject drug treatment and discount the value and necessity of other management techniques. In some ways the parents' different gender perspectives on A.D.D. are helpful and lead to a balance; you do not want to make the child a behavioral and educational project, but you do want to get him the help he needs. A.D.D. management is a family enterprise, and it succeeds best when mother, father, and child all work together as a team.

you don't have to grow up." She immediately bought it for a friend she regarded as having A.D.D. In many ways, including their attention span, people with A.D.D. remain immature as adults. The extremes of focus continue. Many scholars and executives who have A.D.D. note that they can lock on to documents that they are creating or plans they are developing, and virtually nothing can distract them. Many jobs, however, also involve some boring paperwork or reading. To accomplish these aspects of their jobs, they delegate whenever possible. In addition, many of these individuals develop strategies to deal with their difficulties concentrating. This, ironically, may make them better students than those who never have to work at learning how to learn! We know a brilliant physicist with A.D.D. who became an expert in test-taking strategies and wrote eighteen books on that subject. Yet he still has trouble sitting through a lecture without impulsively calling out a question or comment!

As noted at the beginning of this chapter, the life histories of many creative geniuses, from Mozart to Edison, suggest that they had A.D.D. They obviously had tremendous natural abilities, but what may have made the difference in what they achieved was the way they could harness their ability to hyperfocus and use that and their other A.D.D. traits to their advantage. These hyperactive children became hyperproductive adults.

Is attention span a problem only when the material is boring?

"It's boring" is a complaint that parents of A.D.D. children can expect to hear frequently. Although an uninteresting assignment certainly accentuates the difficulty, parents and teachers should understand that the material itself is not the only problem. Attention can wander even when something is interesting and important. The individual with A.D.D. is tuning out and then tuning back in every few seconds.

Michael, an adult professional, described his difficulties in high school. As a child, he had been anxious to achieve and was a very hard-working, sincere student. On intelligence tests he scored at the gifted level. Nevertheless, some subjects were almost impossible for him. He said, "I really wanted to be able to speak French and took it in school for eight years, lived one summer with a French family, studied hard, and still could not speak or understand the language. I find that when someone starts speaking French to me, my mind is gone within the space of one sentence. It's hard enough listening to a full sentence in English!"

The one time Michael could listen well was in debates. He was the captain of the debating team and won consistently. In a debate he could go into a state of hyperfocus. Here is how he described it: "I am totally involved in and an integral part of what I am debating. I listen intently for arguments that I can shoot down in rebuttal. I can retain my thought patterns. I am very quick with new, rather outrageous angles on any argument, and I speak forcefully and well."

What happened when he loved a subject and also did well in it? He was fascinated by physics and always got A+ on his exams. Yet he just couldn't keep his attention on what the physics teacher was saying for more than a couple of minutes. Physics was so logical he could figure it out by making up games with the basic principles from his text. He did his learning outside the classroom.

Michael developed strategies for helping himself compensate for his own difficulties with attention. Like most good students who have A.D.D., he can attest to the fact that he had to work much harder because he could not just sit and listen and pick it all up in class.

Distractibility

Children with A.D.D. get easily distracted by quite unimportant matters. They may start half a dozen things and not finish any of them.

J.J. was on his way upstairs to brush his teeth. His mother had reminded him to do this. (Even though he was twelve years old, she still had to prompt him to get on with his morning routine.) When he got to the bathroom he spotted a bug on the wall. He watched it intently to see where it was crawling. He got fascinated by the way the insect's legs moved. His insights into insect ambulation were cut short by his mother calling that the school bus was coming down the road. J.J. had totally lost track of time and the purpose of his bathroom visit.

J.J. and the bug illustrate what we mean by inappropriate distractibility. His mother might feel that stopping to watch an insect when the school bus was due in ten minutes showed an inability to set priorities and keep what was important in mind. What could possibly be the positive side of distractibility? Well, if an adult inventor got sidetracked and went off on a mental tangent while watching a bug move up the bathroom tiles, it might lead to the development of a new kind of vehicle that could navigate slippery surfaces. And probably no one would care that he forgot to brush his teeth.

I needed to take care of outside distractions before expecting Ryan to sit down and pay attention. The sensation of an empty stomach was too much stimulation for him, just as the distraction of someone speaking to him or music playing in the same room was. He couldn't get past them because he would perseverate on them, such as his wet socks, a bug in the room making noise, or a tag on his shirt collar.

Both external and internal stimuli can be distracting. Children who have A.D.D. are easily distracted by virtually any visual or auditory stimulus (except when they are in hyperfocus). In the past, some schools actually attempted to decrease distractions either by putting the child into a room by himself or by placing a screen around him so he couldn't see the other students. Predictably, these methods usually increased the difficulties the child was experiencing. Here's what Dr. Bill remembers about his own distractibility:

When I was in third grade my teacher, Sister Mary Boniface, sent me to work in a cloakroom next to the classroom. I guess she was tired of my not getting my work done and thought isolation might help. Her plan backfired. It made my behavior worse because I felt too confined and couldn't concentrate at all. My learning problem turned into a behavior problem when I spotted a basketball in the corner and started bouncing it against the adjacent classroom wall.

While a child with A.D.D. does better if placed close to the teacher, where there are minimal visual distractions, isolating him doesn't work due to internal distractions. This is also why teenagers can spend a long time in their room with their homework without accomplishing very much. Internal distractions include ideas popping into your head that are not related to what is happening around you or to what you are supposed to be doing. One of Dr. Lynda's adult clients said his mind was like an ideas salad: all the thoughts were in shredded bits tossed randomly together.

David, at age fourteen, explained that all his life his mind had seemed to be continually bombarded by one thought after another. Usually, he noted, the first thoughts were related to what was going on in the classroom or to the book he was supposed to be reading. Quickly, however, he would go off on a tangent and develop some whole new theme in his mind. David happened to be a superb talker and he could amuse adults and children alike for long periods of time with fantastic stories and ideas. At times this was received with accolades and at other times with quite the opposite. Impulsiveness and internal pressure seemed to make it almost impossible for him to identify people's reactions quickly enough and stop himself in those situations where these digressions were inappropriate. He would say, "I'm never at a loss for ideas."

As David grew older, his high IQ, creativity, endless energy, and never being at a loss for new ways of looking at and doing things earned him one leadership position after another. The downside was that others often became upset when he suddenly switched topics as if not listening to them. This was a symptom both of his internal distractibility and his impulsiveness. Once, when he was the head of a large organization, a staff member in the middle of a key meeting confronted him, saying, "You are like a knight charging along on a great white stallion, going suddenly one direction and then another.

We feel like we are trying to keep up while riding donkeys and without any sense of where you may turn next." The comment was meant both as a compliment and as a criticism. David was admired for his ideas, his energy, and his devotion to accomplishing changes that would eventually help the organization. But his style was also a problem for staff members who felt confused and left out of the decisions that were being made. His inattentiveness and his impulsiveness made it seem that he was ignoring people. He might pass them in the hall without seeing them when his mind was elsewhere. When they came up with an idea, he rapidly developed it to the point where they felt he had taken it over. David was a developer and not a maintainer. He can expect to change jobs frequently.

The "hunter mind." Another way to think about a person who is easily distracted is to say he is in scanning mode. Thom Hartmann, in his numerous books and on the "A.D.D. Forum" he runs on CompuServe, compares the person with A.D.D. to a hunter who is constantly scanning his environment for signs of prey or danger. The hunter locks on and goes into hyperfocus when he spots something worth pursuing. In the classroom, a child with a hunter mind notices someone's new shoes, hears a pencil drop, gazes out the window, checks the clock, and so on, while supposedly listening to the teacher.

In contrast to the hunter is the farmer. What kind of attention does the farmer need? He certainly cannot go off chasing a rabbit when the grain is ready for harvesting. The farmer must do things in a repetitive and a routine way. He must also plan ahead. If he were to live only from moment to moment, he might miss harvesting his crop, and his family might starve.

Made in America?

The incidence of A.D.D. is higher in North America than anywhere else in the world. Why is this? One explanation is that A.D.D. exists everywhere but is more often recognized in North America. Another explanation is the gene pool theory, the belief that people, especially men, with A.D.D. traits were more likely to become immigrants to the new land; they were restless in their homeland and had the drive, risk tolerance, and creativity to make the drastic life change of moving to America.

Or is A.D.D. made in America? Is it the product of a society that can make an industry out of anything? Sometimes a simple observation gets itself labeled as a condition. Children act differently; they get labeled A.D.D. Researchers get grants to find a neurobiological cause, which gives the label some scientific credibility, which creates a need for treatment. Eventually, you have a hyperactive treatment industry feeding hyperactive consumers. Drug companies make money and promote awareness of the condition. Support groups form, which mushroom into organizations. More drugs are discovered, A.D.D. centers open, books and magazines appear, training equipment is designed and sold, counselors and therapists have jobs, and eventually even genetic markers for the condition are found — which really lends credibility to the fact this is a genuine disorder. Somewhere along the line the basic issue gets lost. Is something really wrong with these children? Or are they just different kids who don't fit so conveniently with the rest of the bunch — are they just hunters in a farmers' world or the round pegs in square holes?

Perhaps A.D.D. is heightened by modern media, which serve up quick sound bites and visual bites. Television producers gear their programs to audiences with thirty-second attention spans. Remember the movies you grew up with, *Cinderella* and *Snow White?* They were easy on the eyes and easy on the nerves. Contrast these with the modern hyperactive animated features, such as *Who Framed Roger Rabbit* and *The Lion King*.

Video games reinforce hyperfocusing ability of children with A.D.D., who are riveted to the screen as the good guy chases the bad guys through one world after another. The child with A.D.D. is likely to excel at Nintendo. Yet, take the same child and put him in a classroom without the exciting sounds and graphics of the video screen and with no joystick, and his ability to focus is lost. Even the best teacher can't compete with the way information is presented to a child on a video screen. There has also been a reduction in exercises like memorizing poems that required one to develop concentration and memory strategies.

Finally, could A.D.D. incidence be influenced by parenting and education styles? The baby comes into the world needing certain input — to be held, fed, and nurtured by caring adults. But where does he spend the first few hours of his life outside the womb? In a plastic box or a noisy incubator in a noisy nursery. He is then fed by the clock (which makes no biological sense) with a factory-made formula (which makes no physiological sense). He then gets put in day care as early as one month of age, where he may or (more likely) may not get the experiences he needs from an ever-changing array of caregivers who are undervalued and underpaid. His parents, as nurturing and as loving as they try to be, try for quality time with their child, but it's a juggling act where balls do get dropped. This child graduates from day care into a classroom of thirty children, all with different personalities and different styles of learning, and he is required to conform. If he is a "good" child, he receives no special label but may get lost in the shuffle. If he doesn't conform, he has a "disorder" that needs fixing, because it is quicker, more convenient, and less costly to change the child than to make the system more flexible. The A.D.D. label in some cases becomes society's way of evading the blame for not having given this child the secure, responsive world he needed in the first place. This is when overdiagnosis is a real possibility, when children with poor work habits and poor listening skills, but without neurologically based attentional problems, get referred for assessments by teachers and parents who are overloaded.

The "hunter mind" concept helps to explain why children with A.D.D. so often seem more at home out in nature, where there is more stimulation to distract them. It may also explain why Dr. Bill was so uncomfortable when confined in a school cloakroom. Even today he works better in an outdoor environment, preferably around water, and gets restless and starts pacing if confined to a small room to work.

Impulsivity

Children with A.D.D. act before they think. This quality is called spontaneity when the results are positive, and impulsivity when it gets a child into trouble. This trait is noticed at an earlier age than a child's difficulties with attention and distractibility are. Impulsivity can be a problem even with toddlers.

Julie ran into the kitchen alerted by a peculiar smell. Kevin, aged three and a half, had put his favorite stuffed animal in the oven. He hadn't been left alone for more than a minute. Julie rescued the singed cat, feeling grateful that Kevin had not burned himself and that they had no live pets for his experiments.

Julie had endured every possible variation of impulsive behavior since Kevin had begun to move about the house. After three years nothing surprised her. Kevin had not meant any harm to come to his fluffy cat. It was just a sudden idea that had popped into his head. Fortunately Julie understood this and did not overreact. Some parents might feel that all Kevin needed was more discipline. But he was not a naughty or mean little boy. He just had not connected his actions to the consequences that could follow. Kevin's behavior was a problem, but he was not a child with a behavior problem. This is an extremely important distinction. As the mother of one of Dr. Bill's patients explained, "What helped me to manage my child was separating the sin from the sinner. I had to take a professional-like distance when helping him to manage his behavior, or else I would get into such an intense emotional state."

When older children with A.D.D. are asked, "Why did you do that?" they usually shrug and respond, "I don't know. I didn't really think about it." This is very different from an emotionally disturbed child who carries out a similar action while seething with anger, resentment, and other very strong negative emotions. Children with these emotions have thought about what they are doing and are quite aware of the consequences and how others are going to feel. Children who have A.D.D. truly never think the action through and may feel terrible about it afterward.

Harsh punishment by parents who do not understand their child's impulsivity is not only ineffective in reducing such behavior but also may produce resentment and a poor self-image. These can then lead to a true behavior problem. This difference in motivation has too often been overlooked by experts who lump A.D.D. symptoms together with other problems that may have an emotional basis, such as oppositional defiant disorder, conduct disorder, and substance abuse. These conditions may coexist with A.D.D. but are not necessarily directly linked to A.D.D. On the other hand, A.D.D. should not be used as an excuse for intolerable behavior.

Leaps without looking. Impulsive behavior isn't always a knee-jerk reaction to a stimulus. The core problem is failing to think through the consequences before acting. Sometimes, without any attention to the end result, there will be a great deal of planning.

Harry was a creative five-year-old. He became obsessed with the desire to parachute after looking at pictures in a comic book. He gathered together several umbrellas and a few balloons. Fortunately, and quite by chance, his mother passed by his room just as he was about to jump from the second-story window.

On another occasion, Harry decided to preserve the boutonniere that his older brother had worn to a dance. Harry carefully broke candles into a large pot and then heated the pot on the stove. The wax exploded, the kitchen ceiling caught on fire, and the fire department rushed to the scene. This disaster failed to dampen Harry's desire to invent, and the fire department became involved on yet another occasion, when he attempted to throw a glider, specially loaded with firecracker "wing cannons" and a cherry bomb in the bomb bay, out the third-story window. On this occasion he didn't factor in a poor throw and flammable curtains.

Harry was a sincere boy who never wanted to get in trouble. He was extremely polite and obedient. His hair-raising adventures were not the bad behavior of an emotionally disturbed child. This is an extremely important differentiation. Harry could very easily have been incorrectly labeled dangerous or a pyromaniac. The resulting "treatment" by well-meaning professionals could well have led to a decrease in self-esteem and a downward spiral into truly bad behavior. Fortunately he was seen briefly by a child psychiatrist who recognized both Harry's psychological normality and his A.D.D.

Is accident-prone. Acting without thinking of the consequences may get these children into dangerous situations. They have to be taught to think first. A classic worry of mothers of young children is that they will run out onto the street after a ball and be hit by a car. Paul is an example of how impulsivity and being accident-prone sometimes go together.

Paul, aged ten, was very active. Running around the back of an old apartment building with his friends, he suddenly saw a downspout that went up the side of the building. "We can get on the roof," he yelled and began to rapidly climb up the rickety pipe. It gave way, but the resulting twenty-seven stitches to his face did not appear to slow Paul down at all! Only two weeks later, he crashed his sled on a forbidden toboggan run in the local park.

Some very impulsive children with good coordination manage to grow up without injuries, but their near misses cost their parents plenty of gray hairs. One mother told us that even in the heat of summer she had her son wear long trousers because his legs were so bruised she was afraid people would think she had been beating him. One boy laughed when, in the course of taking a medical history, Dr. Lynda asked about trips to the hospital. The emergency room nurse had nicknamed him Little Frankenstein because of all the scars from stitches on his head and face.

Teenagers and adults with A.D.D. have to be particularly careful when driving a car. Internal distractions make it harder for them to focus on the road, and impulsive actions may make for sudden lane changes or decisions to run a yellow light. These factors combined with drowsiness on long drives are good reasons people with A.D.D. should take extra care when driving.

David was thinking about a great new plan that had just popped into his head while he was driving down the highway. Suddenly he saw a sign and remembered he needed gas. He slammed on his brakes and swerved from the outer to the inner lane, cutting off a truck as he headed for the exit ramp. All of these thoughts were in his head virtually at the same instant. It all happened so fast!

A study published in the medical journal *Pediatrics* in December 1996 compared the driving records of young adults with A.D.H.D. with a control group's. The two groups did not differ in their knowledge of rules of the road or in their driving experience. But when their driving abilities were checked on driving simulation tests, the A.D.H.D. group had more crashes and scrapes. The driving records showed that the A.D.H.D. group had more traffic citations for speeding, more license suspensions, and were four times more likely to be involved in injurious crashes.

Frank, who became a successful salesman and entrepreneur as an adult, laughed until he got tears in his eyes, recalling his teenage experience in the cathedral one Sunday. As an altar boy he had worn his hair slicked into a wave above his forehead more extreme than Elvis Presley's. As the solemn religious procession moved slowly up the aisle with Frank carrying the large candle, his mind was not really on his job. As he looked around and dipped his head, the grease on his pompadour ignited. Fortunately, only Frank's cool image suffered damage as the quick-thinking priest used the holy water to extinguish the blaze.

Loses things and breaks things. Many children with A.D.D. shift so quickly from one activity to another that they completely forget where they put their pens, books, notes, and other belongings, which end up being scattered everywhere. These children may act suddenly, often with good intentions, and break whatever they are holding, such as a pencil or a dish. They act in these incidents without thinking. There is usually no intention of doing wrong. One mother said, "I just buy two or three pairs of the same kind of mittens, because I know he is going to lose one here and one there. It's much easier just to recognize that this is going to occur and not make a big deal of it." This same mother reported that her son lost two backpacks in one year:

I try not to get angry with him. I know he doesn't mean to do it. When he lost the second backpack I didn't punish him, but I did send him back out in the snow to look for it, because I want him to learn to be responsible. He really didn't know where he had lost it. He just put it down when something distracted him and forgot it! His dad is the same way. He buys extra pairs of reading glasses.

Before you conclude that this mother was too lenient, you should know a couple of important facts. She has a very happy family. Her son has no behavior problems, and, though greatly challenged by A.D.D., he is a very thoughtful, well-mannered, kind, and polite boy. Her understanding approach meant that, although he lost his backpack, he didn't lose his positive self-worth. His mother applied discipline appropriate to the situation rather than meting out punishment.

Here is how another mother handled it when her son lost some expensive orthodontic equipment:

When Jason lost his dental retainer I walked him through the scene step-by-step. "Where did you last wear it? Where did you put it down?" Then we discussed future rules and consequences. If he becomes a repeat offender, he'll have to work to pay for the lost retainer.

It is not unusual for adults to forget completely where they have parked the car. Jokes about absentminded professors may have a basis in fact. More than a few scholars have A.D.D., and, while their hyperfocus contributes to their brilliant academic work, it causes them real difficulty with the activities of daily living: keeping track of their car keys, glasses, the food they were eating, their coffee cup, and even where they parked their car.

Acts impulsively in social situations.
Once children have entered school, teachers and parents may begin to notice difficulties in group situations. As with other A.D.D. traits, this difficulty is frequently observed in children with A.D.D. but is not specific to them. Any number of children may react to social situations as Kevin did.

It was supposed to be a great outing, but the Sunday school picnic turned out to be one disaster after another. In any group of children Kevin appeared to disintegrate. He would begin to jump up and down and run around yelling like a madman. The other children began to avoid him. No one would ask him to join in a game with them. Whenever his parents tried to introduce him to one of the activities, he would take over, and he seemed to be totally oblivious to the rules of the game despite his ability to rattle them off before a game started. After a while his parents were exhausted and embarrassed and just gave up. They decided not to attend events where there would be group activities with other children.

Kevin was both hyperactive and impulsive. He was quite unable to wait his turn or to ignore all the impulses that rapidly came into his mind. This meant that cooperation, sharing, taking turns, and delaying gratification were all very difficult for him. In social situa-tions, unfortunately, unpredictable behavior is not well tolerated by peers, and many children with more severe A.D.D. cannot maintain friendships. As Kevin grew older, he knew something was wrong, but he really didn't understand why other children weren't asking him to play with them. Other children found his impulsive actions, egocentricity, and his failure to pick up on nonverbal social cues irritating. Despite their reactions, time and again, he didn't learn from his peers, and he always went too far, past the limits of acceptable social behavior.

Tells lies impulsively. Some children with A.D.D. quickly say anything in order to get themselves off the hook. Impulsive lies are different from regular lies, which may require more thought and cause some guilt. Impulsive lies can be seen through easily, because they haven't been thought through. The child may be standing there covered with crumbs, saying, "No, I didn't eat the cookies for the bake sale!" The child may lie about minor things, such as saying he brushed his teeth when the toothbrush is dry. Or he may lie when asked about his homework. On his way to watch television, he may blurt out, "We don't have any tonight!" when in fact there are two assignments in his school bag. Once he has lied, it is difficult for him to back down. He may already be sensitive from other such incidents. He may stick to his story, since not losing face is important, but as he tries to explain, the lies may become more and more fanciful. Parents becoming upset can compound the problem. Maintaining his self-esteem is crucial. Try to understand the child's behavior in terms of his impulsivity and tendency to answer without thinking. Yes, he is being dishonest, but it isn't a calculated lie; it's just an attempt to obtain the immediate goal of watching television. It is better to avoid confrontational yes-no questions that back your child into a corner. Instead of asking, "Do you have homework?" ask him specifically, "What do you have for homework and how long do you think it will take?" He'll have to think for a minute to answer this.

Kids with A.D.D. fabricate fabulous stories, and parents and teachers can try to channel this into creative writing. In terms of handling the lies, try to establish a dialogue that allows for mistakes. Help the child admit that he said what he wished was true rather than what was true. Always leave a way to save face. Ask, "Do you want to think about that answer?" or "Did you make a mistake in saying . . . ?" As with so much else related to A.D.D., this is a stage that children without A.D.D. also go through. Just ask the parent of a four-year-old. The child with A.D.D., however, does not grow out of telling impulsive lies, so the parent needs to help him more.

Acts impulsively in the classroom. An impulsive style of completing school assignments is typical of the child with A.D.D. Most will rush through an assignment to reach the end. Hyperactivity contributes to this problem, but even children with A.D.D. who are not hyperactive may be careless with their schoolwork. They do not stop to reflect on what they are doing or to double-check their answers. They may not notice the sign in an arithmetic problem and may add when they should subtract. They usually give the first answer that comes to mind. Parents and teachers label their errors as careless and comment, "He needs to work harder" or "She is performing below her potential; she has to put more effort into her work." In the classroom, some of these children either cannot remember to put up their hand or simply cannot wait to answer. If something comes

into their mind, it is suddenly and loudly blurted out even if another child is answering the teacher's question. They may interrupt because they are afraid they will forget what they wanted to say if they wait. Other children with A.D.D. never spontaneously offer an answer, and they seem to be off in another world. Their classmates may nickname them space cadet. They display the inattentive rather than the impulsive type of A.D.D.

Ten-year-old Jay was given a math problem: "Mary is twice as old as Tom. Mary is six years old. How old is Tom?" Jay immediately blurted out, "Twelve!"

The impulsive child rapidly does something with the numbers: twice six is twelve. The more reflective child thinks through the relationship between the numbers given and the question being asked. Students with A.D.D. will try to guess what you are going to ask before you finish the question. Sometimes this is because they cannot inhibit a response. At other times they are embarrassed because they didn't maintain their attention and can't remember the question. If you repeat the question, they may still not get the sense of it. They may quote back the problem. They may give an answer that has little relation to the question asked. With persistence it is possible to teach these students thinking strategies that help them listen. Usually, however, it is difficult to get them to apply these strategies consistently in school. The exception is the student who is anxious. Anxious students, including those who have A.D.D., will work very hard to use learning strategies. (For techniques to help children respond accurately to questions, see chapter 7.)

Is intensely curious. In children with A.D.D., curiosity fuels their impulsivity. Their behavior often resembles Curious George's.

Impulsive or spontaneous? Impulsivity usually has a negative connotation. But, as with most A.D.D. traits, it is a double-edged sword. The actions of some impulsive individuals are sometimes viewed quite positively.

Ashton, a college student, recalled happily the years he had worked at a boys' camp. He quickly became known as the ideas man. Within a couple of summers he had risen to major leadership positions, due partly to his (almost obsessive) persistence but mostly to his innovative thinking. In this setting, whenever he got a sudden great idea and acted on it rapidly without think- *ing through all of its ramifications, it usually worked out. He and others called the behavior creative spontaneity. Whenever things didn't work out, others called his behavior impulsive.*

Hyperactivity

Increasingly, A.D.D. is being regarded as a separate syndrome from hyperactivity. Some of the most challenging children with A.D.D. do have, in addition to the main three characteristics (selective attention, distractibility, and impulsivity), an extremely high activity level. But not all children with A.D.D. are hy-

---

Personality Problem or a Neurological Problem?

Despite evidence to the contrary, in some professional circles, A.D.D. is characterized as a fringe diagnosis. Researchers on A.D.D. believe it is neurologically based, perhaps due to an imbalance or a difference in neurochemicals in a person's brain, or even to a difference in brain structure. But others dismiss these kids as simply undisciplined, unstructured, unsupervised, or just plain unlucky in what they got for an environment. Neurologists may believe the problem is in the hardware, or wiring, of the brain. Behaviorists may believe it's in the program, or the child's environment. In between are parents who have to live with and teachers who have to educate these children. Parents, especially, want more information about what's behind the problem. Some informed parents feel resentful when A.D.D. is portrayed as a temperament trait, a personality difference, or a parenting problem, believing that this minimizes the toll this difference has on the child and his or her family. They feel that this difference would be easier to deal with if they were certain that it had a physiological basis.

The answer to this dilemma may be simply that there are differences of degree in A.D.D. Some children may truly have a neurobiological difference, or "disorder," or "deficit"; others may be at the end of the wide range of temperament and personality traits that earn them a reputation for being challenging or even difficult kids. In essence, it's not important what you call this disorder or difference, or even whether it's in the genes, the brain, or the environment, or in the parents' or doctor's imagination. It's what you do about it that matters. No matter the cause of the problems, it's important to focus on evaluating these challenging children and developing a management plan that channels whatever you call it to work to the child's advantage.

peractive (see below). Until a few decades ago, the terminology used emphasized hyper-activity, such as Hyperactive Child Syndrome or Hyperkinetic Reaction of Childhood. The most current diagnostic categories, used since 1994 in the United States, are from the American Psychiatric Association's *Diagnostic and Statistical Manual of Mental Disorders,* 4th ed., commonly known as *DSM-IV.* These are the current diagnostic codes:

314.00 Attention-Deficit/Hyperactivity Disorder, Predominantly Inattentive Type

314.01 Attention-Deficit/Hyperactivity Disorder, Predominantly Hyperactive-Impulsive Type

314.01 Attention-Deficit/Hyperactivity Disorder, Combined Type

A child's hyperactivity may draw attention to the other A.D.D. traits in children who have A.D.H.D., Combined Type. Some children are very restless and active even when asleep. But the child's activity level itself is not really the major concern. In fact, in studies using pedometers and other devices to measure activity level during the day, the finding was that the actual activity level of the children labeled hyperactive was no greater than that of regular children. The problem is that these kids are *active at inappropriate times,* in ways that bother others, when they should be listening and sitting still. Hyperactivity is really an inability to regulate the activity level to meet the demands of a situation. The inappropriate moving and fidgeting shows up in such places as the classroom, the dinner table, and church. The activity level is often already noticed in infancy.

Stuart was just sixteen months of age. His mother came into the doctor's office looking exhausted. She began her story: "We've done the best we can. My husband nailed the crib to the floor so that Stuart would stop making it move across the room. It doesn't even have wheels! I put foam rubber underneath the crib and all around it because he topples out. I tried sleeping in his room so that when he climbed out of the crib he wouldn't hurt himself. But I wasn't getting any proper sleep, so I finally put a hook on the door and used a monitor so that I can hear him and go into his room the moment he gets up. He's everywhere. He flits from thing to thing faster than I can think. He started running at ten months and hasn't stopped since."

Stuart was extremely hyperactive at a very young age. Fortunately most mothers of children with A.D.D. are not faced with this extreme so soon. On the other hand, some mothers know they are in for some wild years because their child was already a tummy thumper in the womb.

In the school age years, these children find it very difficult to handle group situations and expectations.

Peter was in kindergarten. The teacher did her best to interest him in activities. She found, however, that it was simpler to give him a few basic rules and let him wander. He didn't seem able to take part in circle time, where the children were required to sit still and listen. He would be up and roaming within a minute if she got him to the circle at all. During playtime he could never settle on one activity, such as painting, but wandered instead from activity to activity. He would pull out a toy or game, but would immediately get distracted and dive into the next activity.

Fortunately, Peter's teacher understood his difficulties, took his actions with humor, and

How Are Left-Handers and People with A.D.D. Alike?
They're Both Normal!

The person who has A.D.D. is normal. The brain functioning is different, but the person is not abnormal. As we mentioned above, a comparison that helps in understanding that "different" does not mean abnormal is to think of people who are left-handed. "Lefties" are different from the majority of people who are right-handed, and that difference is inborn and brain based, just as A.D.D.'s is. But we do not consider left-handed people to be abnormal. Left-handedness is considered a normal variation. Some things in life are certainly a little more awkward for lefties because our society caters to the majority who are right-handed. Some cultures place more importance on this particular difference; for example, some discrimination against left-handed people was found in Japan but not in present-day North America. Attitudes also seem to change within cultures over time: Great Aunt Dorothy, who at 102 is the senior member of Dr. Lynda's family, relates that

she was forced to write with her right hand as a child: "Mother said it was important for me to be like others in case I became a teacher and had to teach others how to write." Research on lefties indicates that they are overrepresented in creative fields, so it would seem that there are perhaps some advantages linked to this difference, too. We think about A.D.D. in a similar fashion — it is a normal variation that quite likely has some value for our species. Of course it is a much more challenging difference than being left-handed, at least in North America. A.D.D. is a particularly vexing problem in our culture because of the value we place on school learning. The classroom is usually the place where children with A.D.D. are at the greatest disadvantage. Perhaps in the future, the A.D.D. style will be a smaller handicap as our lives become more dependent on computers and classroom teaching practices change.

helped him learn one simple rule at a time. Rather than punishing him, she set up a reward system. By doing so, she avoided compounding his difficulties. She made school an understanding and pleasant place for him and got his school career off to a positive start.

In grade school Peter was examined by a psychiatrist. He was placed on stimulant medication. The usual dosages had no effect, but higher doses seemed to calm him somewhat. The psychiatrist's report, however, noted that, even on medication, Peter

climbed over every piece of furniture in the office within the first minute or two of coming into the room. While he ran, jumped, and climbed, he talked nonstop at such a speed that even his own mother could hardly understand him. If someone tried to make him sit in a chair, he squirmed, shuffled his feet, fidgeted, played with anything he could lay his hands on, tried to tip the chair. Positive reinforcement and negative consequences were equally ineffective. The idea of training Peter in self-monitoring seemed like a fantasy for some distant year.

Fortunately Peter was able to begin neurofeedback training (see chapter 8), and he is now able to walk into the waiting room and sit down and read, even when he is not taking medication. It has taken much longer for neurofeedback training to work with Peter than with other children with A.D.D. who are not hyperactive.

Even outside the classroom, children with A.D.D. exhibit an inability to inhibit activity.

Eight-year-old Jeffrey was at hockey practice. The coach asked the team to line up on the ice in a straight line. Jeffrey really wanted to please the coach, but he just couldn't stop himself. He skated in and out between the other players.

A.D.D. Without Hyperactivity — A Distinct Syndrome

"He's as slow as molasses in January. How can he have A.D.D.?" Not all people with A.D.D. are hyperactive. Many, in fact, are lethargic and seem to spend much of their time in their own world. Sometimes they are unfairly labeled lazy. Teachers think they don't care. These children's A.D.D. traits are often missed because they are not disruptive. The child with hyperactivity is more readily diagnosed because he is disruptive, annoying, or inconvenient to a family or school system that has order as a high priority. A.D.D. without hyperactivity is recognized at a later age (if at all), when there are obvious problems with underachievement in school. Because girls are generally more eager to please and less disruptive, the diagnosis is often missed. The teenager nicknamed Spacey Gracie may really have A.D.D.

"She's lazy and unmotivated." Some children with A.D.D. may be described as bright daydreamers. They have an invisible disability. Compared to hyperactive children, they are often sensitive, rather anxious individuals who exhibit low self-esteem. These children are rarely identified as having A.D.D. until their teen years. Many of them confide their frustration that other kids who seem no brighter have an easier time learning things in class or organizing their time. These teenagers can be extraordinarily frustrating to their parents, who want to light a fire under them! They want them to show some inner motivation. These students don't complete assignments and seem not to care about the consequences. Parents often lament, "If only she would show some drive!"

Susan lounged in the chair nibbling potato chips. She was supposed to have brought home her school planning book to go over how she was going to organize her work for eleventh grade. She said, "I forgot." She had a long history of "forgetting." Her homework was never completed. She had almost no notes from class. She had a tendency to

tune out in the middle of a conversation and then have to ask what was just said. Susan's parents had all but given up. Nevertheless, Susan didn't want to fail in school. She really didn't want people to be upset with her. She was bright, but she felt that she was just hopeless at school. She was so discouraged that she thought she should quit school. With her pleasant manner, she had already been hired for several different part-time jobs, but she could never hold a position. She got along with her coworkers but she didn't complete the work. She made too many errors and didn't appear able to follow instructions no matter how much she wanted to. Because she herself had identified her inability to pay attention and her tendency to daydream, stimulant medications had been prescribed. She said she took them because everybody wanted her to, and they did stop her fidgeting, but she didn't think they had much effect on her attention span and concentration.

"He's in his own world." Other students who have A.D.D. but who are not hyperactive may show high achievement in some area such as music, dance, art, or sports. They have worked very hard at the activity they like and have used their ability to hyperfocus to excel, but with regard to their school performance, they might still look unmotivated and lazy.

Donald was a bright nineteen-year-old boy. He had quit in his final year of high school because he couldn't seem to stick with his books, and the teachers complained he was just taking up space. He wanted to complete school, but he viewed the prospect as impossible. His mother said he lived in a dream-world and never got anywhere on time. He had tried a number of jobs, but he was al-

ways late, and he made silly errors because he could not keep the instructions straight. He was a top-level cyclist. On one occasion he got to a championship race three hours early and then missed the start of the qualifying race. His mother said that she knew that there had to be something very wrong with him. Testing demonstrated a high level of alpha brain waves, which are usually associated with a resting mode or a meditative state. Indeed, he was walking around much of the time totally spaced out.

Susan and Donald are typical of children who have A.D.D. without hyperactivity. These children may be very bright, yet they underachieve. They want to do well in school but feel quite helpless to do so. Sometimes these children show the trait quite early, as shown by this quote from a first-grade report card, "Donny does love his daily dose of daydreams."

A.D.D. traits can shift during the course of a child's development. In taking histories of hundreds of people with A.D.D., Dr. Lynda has heard from a number of clients that they were hyperactive in their early years but after puberty became daydreamers, and classic examples of A.D.D. without hyperactivity.

OTHER INBORN TRAITS ASSOCIATED WITH A.D.D.

Besides the big four — selective attention, distractibility, impulsivity, and, sometimes, hyperactivity — most children with A.D.D. show other traits that can contribute to their difficulties in both academic and social situations. Once again, depending on how these traits are recognized and shaped, they can work to the child's advantage or disadvantage.

Is A.D.D. in the Genes?

"He's just like his father," comment many mothers. Though there is not always an evident hereditary link, researchers agree that A.D.D. is a neurologically based disorder that is genetically determined. Evidence for genetic factors comes from studies of twins, adopted children, and other family members. Currently there is exciting research going on that may identify more precisely the genetic mechanisms that operate in some people with A.D.D.; for example, a particular variation in the chromosome that controls certain dopamine receptor sites in the brain (dopamine is one of the neuro-transmitters) was found to occur more frequently in people with A.D.D. Parenting style is important in terms of how the inborn temperament develops, but it does not produce the basic A.D.D. symptoms. Keep in mind that the likelihood is that the father of the child with A.D.D. survived, and perhaps even thrived, without any label, diagnosis, or treatment. These parents, and it can be either mother or father who shows the traits, are often entrepreneurs or successful in sales and have used their high energy and hyperfocus to advantage.

Intensity

Being very intense may get some A.D.D. children labeled troublemakers. They may also be described as too emotional. Persons with A.D.D. may have problems separating their immediate feelings from the content of what you are trying to tell them. This emotional in-

tensity can be very annoying to others. They seem to get stuck and will be persistent about whatever they want or are interested in. Trying to get them to listen to reason will be to no avail. If they want that new item for their collection now, it does not matter that you have no time to drive them to the store until Saturday. They will keep asking for it, seemingly around the clock.

Intensity can, on the other hand, make some individuals with A.D.D. positive examples for their classmates. "Look how hard Glenn works — nothing will get in the way of his achieving his goals."

John was a very bright student who swam competitively almost at the Olympic level. Whatever John did, he did with great energy. He did very well at subjects that caught his interest at school. He was highly motivated and quite tenacious. He turned his intensity to his advantage in the classroom and in the pool. On the other hand, John couldn't keep a summer job. He had very few longtime friends. He desperately wanted to be accepted and appreciated but his intensity was overpowering. In discussions, John would move close to others, find some deficiency in what they were saying, and, with his eyes bulging (he was tested but was not hyperthyroid), blurt out absolute proofs that they were wrong. He routinely drove people away from him in a very short period of time. John knew that his intensity put people off, but he knew that his intensity also kept him focused on a single topic instead of drifting from one to another. He was placed on both antidepressant and stimulant medications. He had years of psychotherapy. Only with neurofeedback training did his A.D.D. symptoms abate, including his intensity. Now he is holding a job. He is still somewhat in-

tense, but he controls his intensity much better. This means that he is able to use it to his advantage both at work and socially. People now interpret his being intense as a sign of his genuine interest in them.

Tendency to Overreact

Parents nearly always comment on how their child with A.D.D. tends to overreact. On the positive side, parents enjoy their child's enthusiasm when the overreaction is on the joyous side. But when the child is disappointed, he can't seem to console himself, even when he may obtain his desire sometime in the future. He wants it *now,* just as a very young child would. These children react as if the whole world has collapsed. Often parents are astonished at how quickly the child gets over the eruption.

Joanne will scream and throw things, and five minutes later she will calmly come and ask me for a treat. It is as if nothing has happened, but I'm still standing in the kitchen trembling and upset by the explosion that took place just minutes ago!

The overreaction followed by a quick shift in mood can be baffling. Remember that this child may be as self-centered at nine or ten years of age as other children are when they are just three or four years old.

*Jean was ten. She was a pleasant child but was described by her mother as "having a mind of her own." She had been doing very poorly at school and had been diagnosed with A.D.D. and placed on medication. Despite the stimulants, Jean would dig in her heels over minor conflicts. She would scream at her mother, who reported that Jean had always overreacted when told to do anything. When she was asked by her fa-*ther *to read from one of her schoolbooks, she immediately stiffened, pushed the book away violently, and began a stream of angry protests.*

Jean was sensitive about her difficulties in reading. Her father was trying to be supportive and had explained carefully to her how he could help with her reading. Jean just didn't seem to be able to moderate her first reactions, either emotionally or behaviorally, even though both parents had tried to help her control and guide her own behavior.

Chris, age nine, spilled the jug of milk. His mother, Anne, firmly told him to be less careless and to think before he pulled so much stuff out of the refrigerator at once. She reminded him that he was supposed to be doing his homework and he had left it after only two minutes. He could have his snack when she came back in ten minutes. Chris screamed, "You never give me anything to eat. You put my snack behind the milk jug." Anne calmly tried to ask Chris where the homework was that the teacher had put in his school bag, but Chris continued his tirade, "Willie [the dog] ate it. I did so bring it home. I left it in the front hall while I went to the bathroom. He ate it! You always blame me!" Chris stomped out of the room. Ten minutes later he came back into the kitchen. "Mom, can I have my snack now? I need to have it quickly because Zachary is waiting for me outside."

As a young child, David had been extremely hyperactive and impulsive. Now in ninth grade, he complained that he couldn't pay attention in class and felt frustrated by his difficulties in class and in reading textbooks. He desperately wanted to do well, however, and even though he resented the long hours he had to study, for the most part he earned A's. On one occasion, David's father went into David's room when he was writing a paper and in an intensely creative mood. His father said, "The lawn isn't mowed." David responded by hurling his textbook at him, then sweeping his lamp and glasses off his desk. David was not usually an aggressive or violent boy. Despite his impulsivity and hyperactivity, he had never had a detention at school, and he abided by household rules, too. He explained that he had just gotten a great idea when his father interrupted him. David's father knew that flare-ups typically occurred only if David was disturbed while focusing intensely on a task, and he put his arm around David's shoulder. A few minutes later they both said they were sorry, and life went back to normal.

Although in David's case flare-ups were infrequent, they are a common occurrence in some persons with A.D.D. To most people, David's response to being interrupted is a major overreaction to a minor irritation. To David, however, his response seemed completely justified, providing he didn't actually hurt anyone.

When intensity causes problems in school or social situations or gets a child in trouble with the law, it warrants a closer look. Sometimes two conditions coexist, which physicians refer to as co-morbidity. A psychiatrist might be needed to distinguish between symptoms that indicate A.D.D. and those that indicate other disorders, such as Oppositional Defiant Disorder, Conduct Disorder, or Depression. On other occasions this intensity is just a symptom that may be associated with A.D.D. A careful history can help to distinguish it from other disorders.

If a child is having violent outbursts, a consultation with a child psychiatrist is a good idea. Sometimes a combination of medications can be helpful. With the technology available today, such as SPECT scans (single-photon emission computerized tomography), which capture a picture of blood flow in the brain, it is sometimes possible to show under-active or overactive areas of the brain, and this information about brain function can help the physician make a decision about which interventions, including medications, to try. At present, relatively few physicians have expertise in both brain-imaging techniques and behavior disorders, but we can expect this approach to increase in use as knowledge increases. The use of combinations of medications such as antidepressants, major tranquilizers, or anticonvulsants can be helpful with complex behavior problems, but it takes a very knowledgeable specialist to supervise the use of these drugs.

Managed by the Moment

Children with A.D.D. seem to be governed only by what is happening now. They don't learn from their past, nor do they think very far into the future. Rules appear to be forgotten, consequences of an action are simply not considered. This "managed by the moment" tendency extends to saying whatever is expedient to get out of an uncomfortable situation. Parents worry about their child not being truthful with them, but this kind of lie is the result of impulsivity, not deceit. Being managed by the moment implies a changing of focus and a flitting from activity to activity, doing each briefly but with great intensity.

In school Gary had been reprimanded again and again for getting out of his seat before he had finished his assignment. Today the teacher carefully told him exactly what to do and reminded him to stay in his

*seat until she checked his work. Two min-
utes later he thought of something he had
to tell Simon. It was extremely important
because it was about the ball game after
school. He rose from his seat and started
across the room.*

The present moment was what was in
Gary's head. Gary had no intention of being
disobedient. The teacher's instructions had
just completely left his mind. He no longer
even realized that the assignment she had
given him was literally in his left hand. Being
managed by the moment means that Gary
suddenly switches gears and completely forgets what he has been doing previously. It
also means that he may be totally involved in
whatever he is into at the moment. Living in
the present is in many ways a gift, as people
who do so may experience life more intensely.

Even the sensation of an empty stomach
can be a stimulation that needs to be dealt
with on an immediate basis. You need to
take care of such distractions before expecting your child to sit down and pay attention. Children with A.D.D. have trouble
getting past distractions and tend to perseverate, whether the distraction be a wet
sock, an irritating collar tag, or a bug on the
wall.

A Need for Frequent Rewards

Children with A.D.D. cannot be tempted by a
reward that is a whole morning or even an
hour away. This is true of nearly all
preschoolers, and almost all children of any
age with A.D.D. For reward systems to be effective, rewards need to be given very frequently. This may be every minute or two
initially, and with some young children every
few seconds in specific situations. You can

try decreasing the frequency of rewards over
time.

*Jay was seven years of age. He was a very
bright child, but it was virtually impossible
for his teacher to engage him in group academic activities, even though there were
only seven other children in his classroom.
Indeed, even in a one-on-one situation,
printing or reading for two minutes was
impossible. Medications did not work well
with Jay, so his parents and teacher began a
positive reinforcement system. In neurofeedback sessions, special techniques that recognized his need for frequent rewards were
used to help him sit still and maintain his
attention to the feedback. Jay's task was to
sit still and concentrate on the computer;
when he did this, a fish moved across the
screen, and Jay accumulated points. Tokens
were used to reward him. The trainer would
move a token toward the computer in a pretend flying saucer flyby but would stop or
reverse the token's movement every time the
fish stopped moving. At first the token
reached Jay's reward pile in front of the
computer in about eight seconds. He
couldn't sustain his attention any longer
than that. Gradually this time increased to
ten seconds, then fifteen seconds, and so on.
After a couple of months of two sessions a
week, this technique was no longer necessary, and Jay could sit and read a story or
do his homework with the trainer while receiving feedback.*

A need for frequent rewards or feedback
shows itself in older students as a relative inability to stick with a project and see it
through to the end. They require some interesting feedback along the way.

Some students with A.D.D. who exhibit
anxiety and an almost compulsive tenacity
when they go into a state of hyperfocus may

also have a need for frequent rewards. Although they don't seem to need frequent external rewards, it may be that they have learned to reward themselves for each piece of work they accomplish. Therefore they are able to wait longer for external recognition.

Poor Handwriting

Although this idea has not received much attention in the research literature, many parents, teachers, and people working in the field have noted that cursive writing is difficult for children and adults who have A.D.D. Dr. Lynda has observed that a lot of the adolescents and adults whom she sees still print and never have made the shift to cursive writing. What is puzzling for parents and teachers is that these same children may have excellent fine-motor coordination. Some of them are even superb artists. If they take the time to draw their letters, script may be beautifully done, but their regular cursive handwriting when they have to write for a couple of pages is completely illegible.

Douglas had A.D.D. and was very artistic. He was a third-year honors college student. One of his professors singled him out in front of two hundred other students and told him to come to the front of the lecture hall. There the professor handed him back his examination paper and loudly announced, "It looks like a chicken walked across your pages. I have taken twenty percent off your grade." Douglas was used to this. It had been occurring since his earliest years in school.

Poor handwriting seems to represent more than just that the child's thoughts are speedier than his motor response. The writing may actually be quite neat at the beginning, but within a very short space the letters change

in shape, size, angle, and spacing. It is very frustrating for children to have one teacher after another complain and lower their grades. By all means have your child learn to type at an early age and encourage him to complete his assignments on the computer.

Boredom

How many times have you heard your child exclaim, "It's boring!"? Of course all children say this occasionally, but children with A.D.D. seem to say it about almost everything. Boredom is an important factor to consider when designing a program for a child with A.D.D. Feeling bored has never been described as characteristic of A.D.D., but it is interesting how often parents of children with A.D.D. characterize their child as easily bored. Often the problem is that there is little tolerance for things that are slow paced. Reading, for example, does not hold their interest as well as a video can. Stories with a lot of description rather than action will have little appeal. A comic book is more attractive than a novel because it moves along quickly.

The child's boredom can be quite frustrating to others, and the child's need for constant stimulation can drain energy from harried parents. In many families where there is a child with A.D.D., there is also one parent who has A.D.D. In the adult the trait manifests itself as a constant need to fill time and keep busy.

Zach, age twelve, was always doing something with his hands. He couldn't tolerate standing around making small talk. He would start fiddling with something or flipping pages in a magazine. This made it hard to hold a conversation with him. Zach sang in a church choir and he looked angelic when dressed in his burgundy gown

Biological Differences in A.D.D. Brains

New studies using a variety of different technologies show interesting differences in the brains of people with A.D.D. Electroencephalographic (EEG) studies taking readings from the surface of the scalp reveal slower overall electrical activity. Other studies using SPECT (single-photon emission computed tomography), which can look at deeper structures, have found reduced blood flow in the brain's frontal area and limbic system, areas that are important for impulse inhibition, when the person with A.D.D. is under stress. This may explain the impulsiveness of children with A.D.D. Blood flow was also decreased in the area of the striatum, the part of the brain that processes motor inhibition. This may contribute to hyper-activity. Researchers have also used PET (positron emission tomography) scans to study the brains of adults who were diagnosed with A.D.H.D. in childhood. A PET scan measures the rate of glucose metabolism in the brain, an indirect measurement of brain activity. PET scanning showed decreased glucose metabolism (that is, less activity) in the frontal region of the brain in the A.D.H.D. group. This suggests that people with A.D.H.D. process information differently, especially in the frontal lobe. This area of the brain, called the executive area, processes incoming information and selects out which information is relevant to the person, what needs to be acted on, and what should be ignored. To a child who has A.D.D., all information may seem equally important — the noise of the car passing by and the teacher's lecture. His brain can't selectively tune in to the teacher's visual and verbal instructions while tuning out classroom and outside noises.

Because some children with A.D.D. show dramatic improvement with stimulant medications, this finding provides a clue to the mechanisms of A.D.D. Stimulant medications are thought to work by increasing neurotransmitters, chemical messengers that are responsible for information processing throughout the brain. Since stimulant medications affect these neurochemicals, A.D.D. in some children is thought to be basically an imbalance of neurotransmitters.

The studies correlating brain activity with A.D.D. are still preliminary, yet the evidence is accumulating that the brains of at least some of these children perform differently, especially the areas of the brain that process behavior and learning. Children with A.D.D. do have a biological difference that needs to be recognized, respected, and managed. These findings take the pressure off parents who may feel responsible for their child's problems. They also diffuse the unfair accusations that these children are simply kids who were never properly disciplined. Research is proving what parents and teachers long suspected: these kids behave and learn differently, so they need to be parented differently and taught differently.

and white surplice. When a photo of the boys' choir was taken, there was Zach in the front row, the only chorister playing with the hem of his surplice.

OTHER WAYS TO SPOT A.D.D.

The traits described below are not included in the standard medical or psychological profiles of A.D.D. They are, however, related to the big four — selective attention, distractibility, impulsivity, and, sometimes, hyperactivity — and are mentioned frequently by parents, so we have added them to our list of traits. They provide other clues to what is different about a child with A.D.D.

Extremes of Energy — Whirling Dervish or Couch Potato

Children with A.D.D. can be an enigma to those around them. They can go from being a whirling dervish to a couch potato, from intense concentration to a state of being completely zoned out. At one moment the student insists on doing his homework with loud rock and roll playing on the radio. The next moment he complains if someone drops a pen.

Robert recalls doing his boring textbook reading in the main room of a fraternity house or on a bench in the city's railway station, but when he needed to write a paper, he looked for a secluded, quiet spot in which to work. At these quiet times he would yell if someone opened a squeaky door; no noise whatsoever was tolerated when he was totally focused on writing. He lived in a world of extremes. When given

material that he found boring to read, learn, or memorize, he could concentrate best when surrounded by a great deal of external stimulation. If he went to a silent room to do a boring task he got virtually nothing done, because his mind would keep jumping from one thought to another.

Low Arousal Level

Although low arousal or alertness level isn't in the diagnostic lists of symptoms, it is repeatedly mentioned by adolescents and adults.

William did very well in high school in sports, clubs, and academics. Nevertheless, his friends knew he was different. They recognized his brilliance in debating and in class discussions. But they couldn't understand why, if he was so intelligent, he had to study so very many more hours than anybody else. His closest friends knew that he just couldn't stay awake during class. These friends used to tell him that he shouldn't stay up so late studying, but that was how he made up for what he missed in class.

The majority of students with A.D.D. (with or without hyperactivity) are in a state of underarousal most of the time. They report falling asleep in class or when doing homework. They talk of going into a state very similar to that which people enter just prior to falling asleep at night: drowsy, drifting off, and dreaming. This underarousal perhaps explains why stimulant medications work with them.

Students can describe this sleepy feeling afterward, and their brain waves, monitored using neurofeedback equipment, confirm their description of this state. Even throughout the day, their brain waves look like the sleepy brain waves of everyone else. The amount of sleepy brain wave activity often increases when the child with A.D.D. is given something to read. As the child reads, he drifts off. His eyes may glaze over or wander. The slower, sleepy waves begin to intensify, and the student's arousal level measured by his electrodermal response (EDR) falls drastically. When the teacher calls his attention to what he is doing and asks questions, the slow waves decrease, the fast waves increase, and the EDR rises. The student says that he begins to feel more awake.

Different Diurnal Rhythms

There is a natural body rhythm called the diurnal rhythm, and for every individual, time of day is an important factor in wakefulness or level of arousal. Levels of activity and wakefulness drop in most people sometime after lunch. This drop seems to be more extreme in children who have A.D.D. This makes their school performance even worse during the afternoon. At this time of day, there is more slow brain wave activity, which is associated with inattention. The low point in the early afternoon can be even worse if the child has stayed up late the night before. Getting a good night's sleep is very important for children who have A.D.D. Unfortunately the common stimulant medications used in children who have A.D.D. can interfere with sleep.

It was 2 P.M. and the second afternoon class had begun. Mike, who was thirteen years old, was in ninth grade. He was a bright boy who had skipped a year of school when he was younger, going from third grade to fifth. Although he got good marks, he had a terrible time staying alert or even awake in class. Teachers were too slow. He could stay alert if he kept asking questions, but he was a fairly shy boy who lacked confidence, and he didn't want to draw that much attention to himself. He kept missing every few words and just hoped the teacher would repeat what he had said. This difficulty reached its zenith each day between 2 and 4 P.M. He was a gymnast, so he would try to keep himself awake by lifting himself off the seat on his hands and then holding his legs out straight ahead of him. Other times he would draw pictures in his notebook or carve pieces of chalk into little boats or cars underneath the desk. Sometimes he would excuse himself and go to the washroom and sleep for a couple of minutes.

Because of differences in diurnal rhythms, differences between children with A.D.D. and those without are accentuated at certain times of day. A.D.D. difficulties also increase with fatigue, during intellectually demanding tasks assigned by others (though not if the child has created the task for himself), and during boring, repetitive, or lengthy assignments. Children perform better if the task is broken up into small sections, each with a specified objective and reward. Students can help increase their alertness by sitting up straight rather than giving in to fatigue and slouching. Old-fashioned teachers who stress posture are actually encouraging what is physiologically correct for remaining wide awake.

Lack of Consistency

"The only consistent thing about my kid is that he's inconsistent" is how one parent summed it up. Teachers and parents of children with A.D.D. report a high degree of variability in work performance, test results, assignment completions, and grades. "One day she gets an A, the next day a D." Expect good days and bad days. While the occasional hyperactive child is "on" all the time, giving neither parent nor teacher a moment's rest, most are up and down in both energy level and school performance. The child may be both fast and accurate on one occasion and slow and inaccurate on another.

Graham's mother said that he was so frustrating. One teacher said he did wonderful work. Another said he didn't pay any attention and never completed a single assignment. Yet another teacher said she liked Graham, but she never knew from one class to the next if he was going to be "with it or out of it." Sometimes he would complete the assignment perfectly. Then he would make a mess out of the next assignment and even leave out whole sections.

Graham was given a test used in assessing A.D.D. called the TOVA (Test of Variables of Attention; see page 61). This is called a continuous performance test, because the task requires the person to watch the computer screen continuously for twenty-two-and-a-half minutes. Graham was asked to push a button every time a certain figure appeared on the computer screen. His performance was highly variable; sometimes he would hit the button immediately when he saw the figure, and at other times after a delay. This is quite characteristic of children who have A.D.D. Sometimes when a task is carried out quickly and efficiently, the child stays interested in it. Much of the time, however, the opposite is true. The child's mind wanders, and his performance on whatever task he is involved in is quite variable.

Poor Listening Skills

"Weakness in auditory memory" is a phrase often found in psychology reports about children with A.D.D. Granny would say, "in one ear and out the other." However you describe it, it means that the child has a problem holding information in his mind while someone is talking. This could be the teacher's verbal directions in class or a parent's instructions at home. The psychologist often detects the problem on tests in which the child has to repeat digits (doing it backward is especially difficult) or do arithmetic in his head.

Forgetfulness

These children may lose their shoes (or even one shoe) or the teacher's note or forget to give it to a parent. They also forget things you have told them and cannot be relied on to take messages over the phone. Train them to write messages down, but make sure you have the pen attached to the notepad or they may walk away with the pen and lose it.

Poor Sense of Time

A child with A.D.D. follows her interests rather than watching the clock. She has little or no sense of time passing. She watches television when she should be getting dressed or talks on the phone when there is homework to be done. She would be late for school if you did not keep after her. Once at school, the teacher comments that she doesn't make good use of time, so work is unfinished. Sometimes the dawdling is so severe that the child is frequently late for school or makes a parent late for work.

Trouble with Transitions

Children with A.D.D. have trouble shifting from one activity to another. They need to be prepared for a change of routine. If you have to cancel an outing they were looking forward to, be prepared for trouble.

Egocentricity

Don't expect children with A.D.D. to easily see your point of view. They will also have difficulty seeing the teacher's point of view or that of their playmates. Frequently they will complain that someone has been unfair to them, meaning that the person did not see it their way. This egocentricity interferes with friendships. They want other kids to go along with their ideas. It is not that they are selfish; they just live more exclusively in their own world and see things from their own idiosyncratic point of view. Even as adults, they will get extremely frustrated when others don't see things their way.

THE BRIGHT SIDE OF A.D.D.

Many children with A.D.D. have enormous energy and drive. They can be funny, entertaining, and creative. For most children with A.D.D., the future is bright if their needs are recognized. It helps if parents accentuate the positive. Some of the brightest and most capable students and businesspeople take advantage of the positive traits of A.D.D. These include:

1. Spontaneity
2. Creativity
3. Fast thinking: the ability to see the big picture and to rapidly make connections

Feelings of Parents of Children with A.D.D.

Parents of children with A.D.D. often feel embarrassed, out of control, or responsible for their child's bad behavior. Especially if your social circle is full of highly controlled individuals, you are bound to be bothered by messages that suggest that your child acts the way she does because you are a bad parent. You may feel cheated: the child you expected is not the child you got. When your child is compared with others, it's usually unfavorably. You may become angry when nothing seems to be working, frustrated at your lack of success, and often feel embarrassed in public, certain that everyone else is thinking, "Why can't she control her kid?" The behavior of a child with A.D.D. is seldom his parent's fault. Parents of children with extra needs deserve medals, not criticism.

As you begin to understand more about A.D.D., you may feel guilty about all the times you yelled, grounded, and pulled out every technique in the book to punish behavior that your child couldn't control. Realize that you did the best you could with the knowledge you had at the time and concentrate on the present. You may need to explain to your child your previous misunderstandings, wipe the slate clean, and get on with the future.

4. Hyperfocus: intense concentration on something of interest
5. Tenacity, an aspect of leadership (remember Churchill)
6. High energy, hyperproductivity

It is crucial for parents to see these positive traits in their children, even though some can have their annoying side. Spontaneity can slide into impulsivity, for example. It is critical to your child's gaining self-confidence and establishing a positive self-image that you notice and build on these good qualities.

Hugh was eighteen years old. He had failed one year of high school. He was hired by one of his teachers to work at a summer camp. The teacher hired Hugh partly out of kindness but partly because, although Hugh was shy and had not been a leader at school, this teacher sensed a peculiar kind of drive in him. At the first meeting of the counselors, Hugh was assigned to be an archery instructor. Within two days the entire archery range was transformed. Hugh set up a highly imaginative system showing kids how to pretend they were native people having to survive with a bow and arrow. When the camp needed a sailing instructor, Hugh quietly volunteered. Within a week his infectious enthusiasm had staff members staying up late each night repairing the old boats. He made diagrams and models to teach racing rules. He set up racing buoys around the lake. Late into the night he was seen typing up programs for each level of sailing. He wrote a sailing manual and had the first draft completed by the time the next group of campers arrived.

Hugh demonstrated spontaneity, creativity, tenacity, and almost unbelievable energy. Hugh had strong A.D.D. traits and was quite hyperactive in his elementary school years. He had tremendous difficulty learning when he was in a classroom. His class notes were a complete disaster. Yet, when it came to hands-on learning or creating something practical, like the sailing manual, he excelled. Nonacademic settings like camp often give people with A.D.D. the freedom to use their talents.

A Positive Note

While we cannot ignore the negative aspects of A.D.D., it is important to remember that many children with A.D.D. are extraordinarily bright and talented. Remember that A.D.D. is not always a deficit, not a disorder in the usual sense, not a disease. It is a label given to a child who has a different style of thinking, learning, and behaving. As we have discussed, Attention Deficit Disorder is not the most accurate label. Yet because of its rhythmic ring, A.D.D. is probably here to stay. Attentionally Different Deportment or Attention Differently Developed would be more accurate. Regardless of how you define A.D.D., the main message of this book is that A.D.D. left unrecognized and not carefully managed can become a disability. If understood, accepted, valued, and shaped, these traits can work to the child's advantage.

Does Your Child Have A.D.D.?

HOW CAN YOU TELL if your child has A.D.D.? Perhaps you clearly recognize your child from the descriptions in chapter 1, or maybe you see only a few A.D.D. traits in your child. You may be reluctant to tag your child with the A.D.D. label. Or, you may feel that an A.D.D. diagnosis will enable you to better understand your child and begin interventions that will help him succeed in life.

Identifying A.D.D. in a child requires a partnership between parents and professionals. With few exceptions, parents are in the best position to identify A.D.D. because they are living with the problems. Professionals make a clinical diagnosis largely on the basis of what parents tell them. The expertise is in asking the right questions and coming to an understanding of the child's behavior based on experience with hundreds, or even thousands, of other children with A.D.D. and other diagnoses.

I knew I had found the right doctor when she said to me, "There is only one person in this office who can diagnose A.D.D., and that's the parent."

There is no single test for A.D.D., unlike for an illness like strep throat. A.D.D. requires a clinical diagnosis based on a doctor's or psychologist's clinical judgment. As with other clinical diagnoses, there are subtypes and different degrees of this disorder, with mild cases merging into the normal range. In these respects, diagnosing A.D.D. is similar to diagnosing depression. We all feel blue sometimes without being clinically depressed; likewise, we all are inattentive sometimes without having A.D.D. Besides history taking, observation of the child, questionnaires, and psychological testing, there are some additional assessment methods available today, such as computerized tests and quantitative EEGs, which may reveal differences in brain wave activity. These can help clarify the picture.

WHAT PARENTS CAN DO

Before seeking professional help you may want to get a clearer view of whether your child's difficulties fit the criteria for A.D.D. Your child has unique traits and unique needs, and the more you know about them, the better you will be able to use the resources available to you. We want to take you through a step-by-step approach that allows you to identify the type of difficulties your child is experiencing and to what degree. Doing this homework will help you decide whether to seek professional advice. It will also help you describe your child to the professional you consult. Remember, the actual label is not the important thing in most cases. Parents need to know what they are dealing with so they can move on to the next stage, where children learn ways of coping with their difficulties in a positive and productive fashion.

Labels

Labeling a child A.D.D. is a mixed blessing. In order to understand a child, it's necessary sometimes to make a diagnosis. Categorizing a child helps professionals choose a treatment plan. That's the way doctors think: "First, name the problem. Then match it up with a treatment." Insurance claims and school systems tend to foster the use of labels. If a child doesn't have a "diagnostic code" or "disease," your insurance won't pay for the treatment, and your school won't provide services. Calling it a learning difference won't work. If your child's management is going to be provided for under the disability laws, he's got to have a "disability." (For related discussion, see "Know What the Law Allows," page 273.)

Besides giving the management plan a starting point, labels have other worthwhile uses. They relieve the child of inaccurate tags like "bad" and "dumb." Learning their child "has something" is often a consolation for parents. It relieves them of the guilt they feel that their child acts the way he does; they feel better knowing he does so not because of something they did or didn't do. Also, getting a diagnosis raises parents' hope for a way of handling the problem.

However, labels have a downside. It's all too easy to blame everything a child does on his A.D.D. and to overlook other problems at home or at school that contribute to his behavior or difficulty in learning. Labels should not be used as an excuse for obnoxious behavior or lax discipline. Children with A.D.D. must still take responsibility for their own actions, and it requires some effort to accomplish that.

Labels are loaded. Tagging a child A.D.D., whether or not it's accurate, can become a self-fulfilling prophecy. Teachers may teach down to the child. These children may be treated differently by family, siblings, and friends, all persons who are privy to the label. The more the child is treated differently, the more likely he will be to think he is different and to act differently. To some children, being different means being less. Eventually, the child may live up to the expectation that he has a disorder.

A label at least gives parents and professionals a starting point from which to develop a plan of action. Eventually, as the management plan takes over, the label becomes less meaningful. Don't saddle your child with a psychiatric-sounding label, and if he already has that label, try to limit the length of time he has to wear it. In our society, there seem to be more labels for what's wrong with children than what's right.

Step 1: Fill Out the A.D.D.-Q Checklist

It is impossible to compose a "one size fits all" checklist for A.D.D., which may be why there are many types of questionnaires and checklists in use. What the A.D.D.-Q does best is help you organize your thinking about the problem and give the professionals whom you choose information at a glance and a summary of your own insights into your child. Keep in mind that A.D.D. traits are found in most children from time to time; this questionnaire looks at the *degree* to which these traits are present as well as at the traits themselves. Unlike most questionnaires, which confuse behavior problems with A.D.D. symptoms, this questionnaire focuses only on A.D.D. It is based on our understanding of A.D.D. gained through our clinical and personal experience.

One morning while driving her ten-year-old son, Tyler, to school, Sue tuned in to a radio talk show about children with A.D.D. In response to a caller's question, "How will I know if my child has this problem?" the expert listed features similar to those in the A.D.D.-Q. Tyler said, "Gosh, Mom, everyone acts like that sometimes."

Tyler was right. But as we discussed in chapter 1, children with A.D.D. show certain behaviors not sometimes but most of the time and in a persistent pattern. Also, the degree to which they show them is inappropriate for their age and level of development. If your child scores in the "Almost always" range for most of these questions, it does not mean your child absolutely has A.D.D., but it does mean that there may be enough concern to seek professional help, to evaluate your child's behavior relative to his age and development.

To get the most out of the questionnaire, each parent should fill it out separately so that you have more than one perspective. Also, put your first answers away and answer the questionnaire a second time a few days to a week later. If on one of those occasions you were feeling particularly frustrated with your child, the score may be a better reflection of your mood on that day than an accurate picture of your offspring.

Step 2: Assess the Severity of the Problem

In addition to describing your child by completing the checklist, you should think about how the problem behavior affects your child, you, and the rest of the family. Does it cause occasional inconvenience, or are the child and family under constant stress? Perhaps the child's differences are a minor problem that time and maturity will resolve. Or perhaps the child is an average kid, but he is in an academic setting that is a poor match for his abilities or learning style, making the difficulties really a situational problem. To help you assess whether this problem is a "biggie" or a "smallie" and to pinpoint where your child is having the most difficulty (home, school, or play), complete the A.D.D.-Q Supplement on page 44.

Step 3: Get Information from Significant Others

While parents are undoubtedly the experts on their child's behavior, they may find it hard to be objective. Love and constant proximity make parents more accepting of their child's quirks; yet the child has to function in a society that will be less tolerant. Some children function well at home but fall apart at school. Some children learn well with one

My child's teacher observes: _____

_____

_____

My child's caregiver and/or other adults observe:

_____

_____

_____

My child's friends observe:

_____

_____

_____

teacher yet clash with another. Children with A.D.D. have *cross-situational problems;* that is, the difficulties occur at home, at school, and with peers. If problems occur in only one area or situation, then it makes sense to change that situation rather than change the child. To get a broader perspective, ask for observations from your child's teachers, caregivers, and any other persons who spend time with your child and whose observations you value.

Step 4: Discover Your Child's Special Something

If you have read and enjoyed the *Calvin and Hobbes* comic strip, you'll agree that A.D.H.D. children have a certain charm, even though they are a handful. If you haven't met Calvin and his stuffed tiger, we highly recommend you purchase one of the anthologies.

In half an hour you'll learn more about the imaginative and energetic side of A.D.D., as well as the challenges at home and school, than you would in the same time spent with a specialist. And laughter is, in our view, your most valuable survival tool!

The Calvin and Hobbes *comics are my favorite. I've read them all. Their creator captures the spirit of active boys all in one character. My son is Calvin.*

Remember that A.D.D. is a description of a *difference.* A child who has this difference needs to be recognized and helped before the difference becomes a disability. There are two sides to each special trait found in children with A.D.D. Each trait can be an asset or a liability; it can work to the child's advantage or disadvantage. A child's personality is like a flower. Parents and teachers are like gardeners. They cannot change the color of the flower or when it blooms, but they can

The A.D.D.-Q

Child's name:_____ Date:_____ Grade:____ Date of birth:_____ Age:_____ (Place a check '✓' in the appropriate column for each item.)	Never or very rarely	Some-times	Often	Almost always
• **ATTENTION SPAN**				
1. When my child is deeply interested in an activity I have difficulty dragging her away.				
2. My child does pay attention to things *he* wants to do.				
3. My child has difficulty paying attention to things *I* want her to do.				
4. My child has difficulty paying attention to things *others* (e.g., teachers) want him to do, such as instructions.				
5. My child daydreams, drifts into her own world, oblivious to what's going on.				
6. My child notes unimportant details that interest him, yet misses the main idea.				
7. My child doesn't pay attention to important details and often makes careless mistakes when doing schoolwork.				
8. My child's school grades do not reflect her true ability — she underachieves.				
9. My child is inconsistent in his work and behavior. He is fine one day but not the next.				
10. It is hard for my child to follow routines, such as getting ready for school or getting ready for bed.				
11. My child gets easily sidetracked from a task someone else asks her to do, such as homework or household chores (e.g., on her way to brush her teeth, she stops to examine a bug on the wall).				
12. My child honestly forgets to bring her assignments home. (Forgetting is not done in an angry or oppositional manner most of the time.)				
13. My child needs a lot of supervision to complete assignments (schoolwork, chores) that require sustained attention.				
14. My child's attention span is getting worse relative to other children the same age.				
• **SPONTANEITY**				
15. My child fails to think through what he is about to do or say; that is, he leaps without looking.				
16. My child has difficulty waiting his turn (e.g., he interrupts others, blurts out answers before a question is completed).				
17. My child has difficulty waiting in line, sharing, and cooperating.				
18. My child often gets into potentially dangerous situations.				
19. My child has difficulty waiting for rewards or delaying gratification (e.g., she wants the toy *now!*).				

20. My child's ability to control impulses is not improving with age.				
• **ORGANIZATION**				
21. My child's schoolwork, belongings, time management, and personal functioning seem very disorganized.				
22. When my child is working on his own hobbies or creating his own projects, he is extremely organized.				
• **EMOTION**				
23. My child overreacts to minor disturbances.				
24. My child is easily bored.				
25. My child shows rapid mood swings.				
26. My child has difficulty adjusting to sudden changes in routines.				
• **ACTIVITY LEVEL**				
27. My child's activity level is inappropriate for the situation (e.g., she has difficulty sitting still in class, in church, or during meals).				
28. My child is restless, fidgets, and squirms.				
29. My child seems always on the go, as if driven by a motor.				
30. My child seems sluggish, lethargic, and unmotivated.				
Total Checks in Each Column				
SCORE (the total number of checks in each column multiplied by 0, 1, 2, and 3)	x 0 = 0	x 1 =	x 2 =	x 3 =

TOTAL = _____

Interpretation

This questionnaire is designed to help you organize your thinking about your child. You can use the total score to track your child's symptoms over time. If you have checks only in the "Often" and "Almost always" columns for positive items such as numbers 1, 2, and 22, then A.D.D. is probably not a problem. On the other hand, if you have a great many of the other items marked in the "Often" and "Almost always" columns, then it may be advisable for you to take this questionnaire and discuss your observations with a professional. (Hyperactive children will have higher scores than children who don't have hyperactivity.) Remember too that your child's age may affect the score. Younger children usually have higher scores.

Why are there more items under the first two topics?

"Attention Span" and "Spontaneity" cover the major symptoms of A.D.D. It becomes increasingly difficult to separate other behavior disorders from A.D.D. when we ask questions about organization and emotions. Activity level can be average or at either extreme, hyperactive or lethargic.

What about angry, defiant behavior?

A.D.D. is a very different problem from Conduct Disorder and Oppositional Defiant Disorder. In the A.D.D.-Q, we want to emphasize A.D.D. but also recognize that your child's scores can be higher if your child is angry and has other behavioral difficulties. Some parents will want to rate their child on the degree to which the symptoms of A.D.D. are accompanied by an angry, defiant, and oppositional attitude or behavior. That is something more complex than A.D.D. alone, and behavior management becomes extremely important. These children are the ones who are at risk for getting into trouble with the law, especially if they grow up in difficult family situations. One frustrated parent opened a counseling session with Dr. Bill, pleading, "I just want to keep him out of jail."

The A.D.D.-Q Supplement

THE *EFFECTS* OF MY CHILD'S BEHAVIOR These questions give you an opportunity to think about your child's and your family's need to have things change. How severe is the problem.	Never or very rarely	Some-times	Often	Almost always
1. My child's behavior keeps me from liking him.				
2. My child's behavior is causing family problems.				
3. My child's behavior is interfering with our marriage.				
4. My child's inattention is keeping her from learning.				
5. My child's behavior makes it hard for him to keep friends.				
6. My child seems to be bothered by her behavior.				
7. Underachievement is resulting in lower self-esteem.				
TOTAL CHECKS IN EACH COLUMN				
SCORE (the total number of checks in each column multiplied by 0, 1, 2, and 3)	x 0 = 0	x 1 =	x 2 =	x 3 =

Difficult Situations

My Child's Reactions

The most difficult situations for my child are: 1. _____ 2. _____	My child's reactions in these situations are: 1. _____ _____ 2. _____ _____
The most difficult situations for others are: 1. _____ 2. _____	My child's reactions in these situations are: 1. _____ _____ 2. _____ _____

This table will help you evaluate progress six months from now.

prune the plant so that it blossoms more beautifully.

What qualities make your child special, valuable, delightful? What *positive* things do you have to say about your child? Is she creative, enthusiastic, persistent, artistic? List the qualities in your child you don't want to change.

Recognizing the positive side of your child's personality lessens the chance of his being overtreated, inappropriately treated, or given drugs for a caregiver's or teacher's convenience rather than for his own well-being. Consider this example of a child who was medicated for A.D.D. with hyperactivity:

Billy's parents were divorced, and Billy lived with his mother during the week and with his father on weekends. During the week Billy's behavior was made tolerable by drugs. On weekends, his dad refused to give his son the prescribed medication. A social worker doing a home visit found dozens of magnificent drawings that Billy felt free to do on weekends, when not under the influence of the medications. His creativity was masked by medication. At his mother's home he behaved "better" but created less.

The fundamental question that parents, teachers, and professionals must ask, especially when considering medication, is whether the treatment is for the convenience of the caregivers or the well-being of the child. By looking at both sides of your child's

---

Framing

Your child's perception of how you view him depends upon how you frame your attitude toward him. Children with A.D.D. sometimes live in a frame of negative labels, and eventually these color the child's behavior. If your child is surrounded by negative expectations, like "bad," "lazy," or "dumb," sooner or later he's bound to live up to them. Even when it's difficult to see the bright side of your child's behavior, try to stay positive. A positive attitude is especially important in protecting your child against negative comments. If someone says, "My, he's disruptive," come back with, "Yes, sometimes he's so enthusiastic." To the person who says, "She sure is hyperactive," say, "Yes, she is interested in everything." When your critics see that you do not see anything seriously wrong with your child, they may change their attitude, too. More important, when your child sees that you are framing him in a positive way, it dilutes the negative things other people have to say about him.

One of Dr. Lynda's favorite read-aloud stories for her son with A.D.D. was about Flat Stanley, a boy whose shape was like a cardboard figure. When his mother was out with Stanley one day, the grocer remarked, "My, your son is flat!" Stanley's mother replied, "Yes, and he's smart, too. His report card has four A's." The story went on to some funny situations in which being flat was an advantage. If the storybook Stanley and his mom could find the positives in being flat, you can find the positives in having A.D.D. Use your repertoire of alternate and uplifting labels: "bright," "enthusiastic," "resourceful," "determined," "passionate," "deep-thinking," "sensitive," "expressive." Framing a positive attitude about your child helps him have a positive attitude about himself.

Qualities I <u>Don't</u> Want to Change
1.
2.
3.
4.
5.

personality, you and your child's helpers, like gardeners, are more likely to focus on providing the right soil and careful training of the vines than on using heavy artificial fertilizers.

I could better accept my son's behavior once I began looking for progress, not perfection.

Step 5: Analyze How the Problem Is Progressing

Is your child's learning or behavior problem getting better, worse, or staying the same? This is an important piece of the puzzle that only you can provide. Is your child growing out of the problem, or is your child growing into worse problems? Pick out the problems that seem to cause the most difficulty for you and your child and chart their progression.

Jason's mother pulled her three-and-a-half-year-old son out of a structured preschool environment, feeling that the school's expectations and the child's maturity level didn't match. She said, "I don't want him labeled hyperactive just because he can't sit still during circle time." She found that Jason was able to join the circle when he was enrolled in a different preschool the next year.

Doing your homework will help you discover if it might be better (and simpler) to change the circumstances than to try to change the child. However, if over a one- or two-year period, the child's behavior shows little progress in a specific area, a red flag should go up. It may be time to seek professional advice.

Problem	Getting better	Staying the same	Getting worse
1.			
2.			
3.			
4.			
5.			

Step 6: Select the Right Professional Help

Some parents may decide as they are working through the previous steps that they need assistance from an A.D.D. specialist. A professional can help in assessing your child's difficulties as well as in deciding what to do about them. A number of standardized questionnaires have been used in research studies on A.D.D., and most specialists will have their own selection of checklists or questionnaires for you to complete.

Whom should you consult? This section will acquaint you with the various kinds of professionals involved in working with children who have A.D.D. (See also pages 50–55.)

Management of a child with A.D.D. requires a *multidisciplinary approach*. Your child may visit a variety of specialists (psy-chologist, learning specialist, behavior therapist, neurologist, pediatrician, speech pathologist, audiologist, etc.) during the process of diagnosing and treating his difficulties. Yet you must have one team quarterback who looks at what's happening all over the field and decides on an overall plan of attack for your child, the teachers, and the family. One of our goals in this book is to help you become the quarterback.

First, a medical checkup. Before you see a specialist in A.D.D., your child should have a thorough checkup by the doctor who knows him best, either your family doctor or your child's pediatrician. There may be hidden medical problems that cause or contribute to your child's learning or behavior problems, such as chronic ear infections, allergies, inap-

---

Be Discerning

To bring out the best in your child with A.D.D., you will need to become your child's strongest advocate. In your search for the right doctors, the right specialists, the right equipment, the right medications, the right books, and so on, you will be faced with a long menu of "treatments." Some have stood the test of time and are validated by research; some are just plain common sense but don't lend themselves easily to being proven by placebo-controlled, double-blind studies; and others are in the category of A.D.D. fads. In evaluating your choices, ask yourself, "Does the way in which the technique is advertised to work make sense? Do the persons touting the technique have the credentials to evaluate it objectively?" Many parents who have lived and learned with their A.D.D. child eventually get a gut feeling that a particular method is or is not for their child.

When asking a consultant for an opinion about a certain technique, remember the Achilles' heel of all experts: they tend to discount what they do not understand or are not familiar with. You may be asking your consultant for an opinion on a technique that she has not personally studied or used, and the information she gives you may be based only on hearsay, prejudice, or outdated information. To make a truly discerning judgment, you have to do a lot of homework, leg work, library work, and phone work to put together the right management plan for your child.

propriate nutrition, or neurological or endocrine problems, such as a thyroid disorder. Always eliminate physical causes first. If there are no apparent physical problems, your child's doctor may be able to recommend a person who specializes in recognizing and helping children with A.D.D.

"But couldn't my child's doctor handle the problem?" you may wonder. Possibly, but not necessarily. Considering how much is known about A.D.D. and how little time today's primary-care physicians have to spend with individual patients, your child's doctor may not have the time or training to manage all aspects of the child with A.D.D. Ask the doctor what's best for your child. The type of health insurance you have may also influence your choice and your doctor's advice.

Besides the fact that most primary-care doctors have neither the time nor the training to manage a child with A.D.D., under the current medical system of managed care, doctors are not adequately paid to manage effectively a child with behavioral or learning problems, especially one with A.D.D. Ideally, parents and the doctor who knows the child best should act as general contractors, seeking consultation from subcontractors (psychologist, psychiatrist, neurologist, learning specialist, etc.), who each contribute special expertise to each problem area the child has. The first visit to your child's doctor is primarily for the purpose of evaluation: Does your child have A.D.D. or something else? Then, based upon this evaluation, your doctor will outline a plan of action either at the first visit or at a subsequent office visit. It may require at least an hour of the doctor's time to evaluate thoroughly the parent's observations, teacher's observations, and consultation from significant others, and to examine and interview the child. In choosing whether or not your doctor should be the primary person

evaluating your child for A.D.D., consider these factors:

- Does your child's doctor have special training in managing behavioral or learning problems?
- Does your child's doctor have a special interest in this field?
- Will your doctor be fairly compensated for the time spent? It is human nature that any consultant is more likely to provide better service if that person is compensated fairly. Managing any behavior or learning problem is time-consuming and costly. You can find out your doctor's form of compensation by asking your insurance company how your doctor is paid. If you have the traditional, or fee-for-service, type of insurance, your doctor's fee is commensurate with the time spent and the magnitude of the problem, which is the fairest way to pay any consultant. But if you have managed-care insurance, your doctor will be paid a flat rate or "capitation," which for the school-age child is around $10 per month, regardless of the frequency of office visits or time spent with your child. In Canada the provincially run health insurance is fee for service and there is no cost to the patient for any doctor's services.

If you believe it's in the best interest of your child to be referred directly to a specialist in A.D.D., ask your doctor to recommend a specialist. Be aware that some managed-care plans reward the primary-care doctor with an "incentive" at the end of the year, basically for limiting the number of referrals to specialists outside his or her own practice. At this writing there are bills before state legislatures to make this practice illegal. Inquire as to the legality of this practice in your state or within your insurance plan, or come right out and ask your doctor. There are also bills pending that would require the doctor to disclose to the patients, upon request, the method of payment from an individual insurance plan. These are important facts for patients to know.

Unless you do your homework in selecting the right specialist to work with you in managing your child, you are likely to wind up a ten-minute office visit with a prescription for Ritalin rather than an overall plan of management.

Beginning your search. The stakes are high. Your child has a lifelong ability or disability. How you deal with it now is important to your child's chances for long-term happiness and success. Dr. Bill notes, "One of the first pieces of advice I give parents when they come into my pediatric office is 'Observe your child's specialness.'" In order to choose the expert who is really right for your child, you must first do your homework and know your child and his difficulties very well. You must also be well informed about A.D.D. yourself. We want this book to help you attain a high level of understanding about children who act and learn differently. As you begin your search, ask others for help. Reliable referral sources may include:

- your child's doctor
- friends who have children with A.D.D.
- school personnel: teachers and school psychologists
- parent support groups (see "A.D.D. Resources," page 295)

Interviewing specialists. Before beginning the interview, put yourself behind the eyes of the specialist. He or she wants to know the extent of your child's problems and about your family. The information you have compiled in the first five steps outlined above provides the specialist with the information needed to discuss your child's needs and offer possible answers to her difficulties. Being able to present this information clearly and in an organized way starts your relationship with this specialist off on the right foot. You want to gain this professional's respect right from the start. If you haven't done your homework and just provide the specialist with a vague "I think he has A.D.D.," you may be in for some lengthy and costly appointments.

You are assessing the prospective specialist as you tell him or her about your child. Is this a person with whom you can feel comfortable over what may turn out to be a multivisit, multi-year program? Is this someone to whom your child will respond? Assess the level of expertise of this specialist. How many children in the practice, for example, are being treated for A.D.D.? It may be difficult for you to evaluate expertise, since you may have just begun your educational journey, but use your common sense. Do the specialist's answers to your questions seem reasonable and fit your child? Most important, does this person sincerely care about helping your child? Does this specialist have a passion for the profession? Professionals should like what they are doing. Parents are usually perceptive about these qualities. Trust your reactions.

Look for an approach balanced between trying proven remedies and being open to new ones. On the one hand, a professional should protect you from A.D.D. fads, unproven and questionable remedies that are offered to parents desperate to try any treatment at any cost to help their child. On the other hand, wise professionals search for ways to expand and improve their approach to managing A.D.D. rather than clinging to their own pet ways. Ultimately, when it comes to managing A.D.D. or any other chronic, life-changing problem, you must be an advocate for your child. Be appropriately skeptical, but never stop learning and searching.

WHO'S WHO IN THE A.D.D. FIELD: A GUIDE TO THE PROFESSIONALS

There are several types of medical, psychological, and educational specialists who work with children with A.D.D. Whom you consult depends on the kind of problems your child is experiencing and your feelings about what should be done. Chances are you'll encounter a number of these professionals during the assessment and treatment process.

Medical Specialists

Family Physician. This may be the doctor who not only knows your child best but also understands your family situation. General practitioners or family physicians may or may not have knowledge about A.D.D. It really depends on how often they have worked with children who have attention problems and their level of interest in the field. Family doctors and pediatricians are the professionals most people consult first. Many family doctors care for children with A.D.D., most often by prescribing medication. They can also make referrals to other specialists.

Pediatrician. A pediatrician is a physician who spent at least three years in a program specializing in the care of children after earning an M.D. Most will have a fair working knowledge of A.D.D., but their training and experience has focused on how to treat ill-

---

Start Early

Intervene before the attention difference becomes a disability. It is important for parents to recognize that their child may have A.D.D. and to seek help before he develops unhealthy patterns of behavior and a poor self-image. Those developments compound the already existing problems created by the child's inborn temperament and A.D.D. traits. Get help before a negative way of acting, thinking, and learning becomes the norm for your child. All too often we see children when they are already into the cycle: problems paying attention lead to learning problems that lead to behavioral problems that make the original problem even worse. Get help before your child gets tagged with, and believes, labels such as "bad," "dumb," and "lazy." In a kindergarten class with two Jasons (Jason B. and Jason M.), hyperactive little Jason B. knew he was "B for bad." The teacher, in a frustrated state, had actually said this one morning, and the children never forgot it.

---

nesses and not on how to manage behavioral problems. As with family physicians, expertise will vary according to the pediatrician's experience and interest. Most pediatricians prescribe medication for A.D.D. and, of course, they have more experience prescribing for children than the average family doctor does. A pediatrician is the specialist to screen for A.D.D. look-alikes, which mimic A.D.D. but are really the behavior or learning problems that result from an underlying medical condition.

Child Psychiatrist. Psychiatrists are medical doctors (M.D.'s), and as such can prescribe medication. Child psychiatry is a subspecialty of psychiatry. You can expect most child psychiatrists to be knowledgeable not only about A.D.D., but also about psychiatric disorders, like childhood depression, that may mimic or be found in conjunction with A.D.D. This makes them good at teasing out questions of co-morbidity, situations in which more than one problem is at work. Most child psychiatrists have experience with prescribing a wide range of medications to treat A.D.D. and other behavioral and learning problems.

Pediatric Neurologist. If a professional suspects that your child has a neurological disorder, you will be referred to a pediatric neurologist. These specialists may or may not have special training in A.D.D. Their main area of expertise is diagnosing and treating conditions such as seizure disorders, Tourette Syndrome (a movement or tic disorder), and brain tumors. Only a small number of children with A.D.D. need to see a neurologist, mainly to eliminate the possibility of these other problems. One tool neurologists use is the EEG (electroencephalograph; see page 61). The waves are "normal," meaning that there are no abnormally shaped waves, as there would be in an illness such as epilepsy. However, children who have been studied at research centers show that there is a different pattern in the majority of children with A.D.D. The pattern is one with a predominance of very slow waves, where "slow" means fewer waves each second. This pattern is typical of what one would see in a much younger child. Because the waves themselves are normal, the neurologist may refer to the EEG as being entirely within normal limits. In addition, even if the child's EEG

shows the pattern that is suggestive of A.D.D., this is not something that every neurologist is trained to look for.

Psychiatrist. Psychiatrists may get involved when an older adolescent or adult is suspected of having A.D.D. Psychiatrists vary in their training and orientation, so seek out one who has an interest in and experience with A.D.D. You do not want an adult with A.D.D. to spend years in psychotherapy when medication and educational strategies would quicken the relief of symptoms and neurofeedback might offer a long-term solution. Psychotherapy is not usually the way to treat this problem — most people will not improve their attention problems through fifty-minute sessions of talking. Of course, therapy can be appropriate to deal with other issues in a person's life. Secondary problems, including marital stress, may require interventions such as family therapy.

ENT Specialist. An ear, nose, and throat doctor may get involved if your child has frequent ear or throat infections, or possibly hearing problems, which may have a negative impact on the child's learning ability. Intermittent hearing losses associated with ear infections affect the development of the child's listening skills and increase the tendency to tune out.

Audiologist. Audiologists are trained in the assessment of hearing. They can also do testing for central auditory processing. A child with an auditory processing problem hears tones normally, with no hearing loss, but does not process the words in the same way most people do. You can compare it to listening to a radio signal that is garbled. Some children with A.D.D. are misdiagnosed as having hearing problems because they don't listen well, and some children with hearing and auditory processing problems are erroneously thought to have A.D.D. Both conditions create similar problems in the classroom. Testing determines for certain what you are dealing with.

Ophthalmologist. Ophthalmologists are physicians specializing in the treatment of diseases of the eye. They are not usually involved in working with children who have A.D.D., but they may be consulted to rule out vision problems. If the child cannot see the chalkboard, he will have trouble paying attention to what is on it. Remember that young children may not report difficulties with vision because they have no idea what correct vision is.

Optometrist. Optometry is not a medical specialty, so the optometrist does not prescribe medication or do eye surgery. This specialist tests vision and prescribes corrective lenses. Optometrists also test for other visual problems, such as poor scanning or poor peripheral vision. Some prescribe eye exercises to improve these problems. The optometrist can determine if the child with A.D.D. is having trouble learning to read because of problems with vision. Glasses may help.

School Personnel

Classroom Teacher. The child's teacher is often the first person to identify a child's problems because she or he can view the child's behavior in relation to that of other children the same age. Teachers' knowledge and opinions regarding A.D.D. vary greatly. Some want children medicated even for minor difficulties, and others do not believe in using drugs. Some will happily make modifi-

cations in the classroom to ensure the child's success, and others may think the child should not have any special treatment. Your being able to work well with this person is very important, so you will want to know what attitudes you are dealing with and judge how they affect the teacher's relationship with your child. Your child spends more time under this person's guidance than anywhere else. Teachers are the most important influence on the development of the child's academic self-esteem and skills.

Principal/Vice Principal. The school administrators will be involved in the decision-making process if your child requires any special services. The principal, or an assistant, may be involved also if your child has some disciplinary problems in addition to the basic A.D.D. traits.

Resource Teacher/Special-Education Teacher. If your child is struggling academically or has learning disabilities in addition to A.D.D., a special-education teacher may be consulted. This can be on an informal basis for some catch-up help, or, if your child is seriously behind (this usually means he is functioning two grade levels behind his age group), there may be some formal testing followed by the implementation of an individual education plan (IEP). The interventions can range from classroom modifications to time spent working with a special teacher in a small group to placement in a special classroom. The special-education teacher is often called on to do some testing as a first step in identifying the needs of a particular student.

Teacher's Aide. An aide may be assigned to a classroom to help particular children. This person does not usually have teaching credentials but will have training in such areas as behavior modification and other management techniques. The goal is usually twofold: to improve a particular child's learning and behavior and to prevent the child from disrupting the rest of the class.

School Psychology Services. The school district's psychology staff may act as consultants on a child's behavior, or do psycho-educational assessments when it appears that the child may need modifications to the regular school program. A school district's staff may include psychologists who have a doctoral degree (Ph.D.) and others with a master's degree (M.A. or M.Sc.). Staff titles vary from place to place. Some school boards rely on referrals to outside agencies, such as hospitals and children's mental–health care providers. A school psychologist assesses your child only with your written permission and shares the findings with you before further action is taken. The school district psychology staff is an excellent resource that is available to you at no cost. Often, however, there is a waiting list for assessments, and the school will have to agree that your child needs this service. You may not want to wait until your child's problems are severe enough in the school's view to make him a priority for assessment.

School Social Worker. The school social work staff may be called in if there are family issues that need to be addressed or if there is an attendance problem. School social workers may also work on problems between the child and her peers. As is the case for all school personnel, there are wide differences among social workers in their knowledge of A.D.D. The parent is the best judge of whether a particular social worker might give helpful support.

Speech and Language Pathologist. Language problems are more common in children who have A.D.D., so your child's assessment may include testing by a speech and language pathologist. Speech therapists do much more than work on articulation problems. They are knowledgeable about all aspects of processing and producing language, so they can help with everything from improving listening skills to developing verbal reasoning skills. Sometimes they do not work directly with the child but, after doing an assessment, provide suggestions that the classroom teacher and the parents can implement. If the school does not provide speech pathology services, look for them in hospitals or speech and hearing centers recommended by your doctor.

Community Resources

Psychologist. Psychologists in private practice, as well as those working within schools, can test a child for A.D.D. and other learning disabilities. Which tests they use will depend on the presenting problems. There are many different subspecialties within psychology, and someone who is consulted about A.D.D. will usually have a background in clinical child psychology or educational psychology. Psychologists as well as physicians can officially diagnose A.D.D. Other professionals may only give an opinion, not a diagnosis. Psychologists cannot prescribe medication (although they might consult with an M.D. about medicating a child). Psychologists manage A.D.D. using a variety of interventions: behavioral therapy, cognitive therapy, and counseling parents on how to manage the child. Most of the professionals doing neurofeedback training (see next page) have a background in psychology.

Psychometrist. A psychometrist administers psychological tests and writes assessment reports. Most have a master's level degree in psychology and work under the supervision of a registered psychologist.

Counselor/Therapist. People doing counseling have a variety of backgrounds. They might be social workers, ministers, or psychologists, for example. Counselors and therapists are not regulated the way registered psychologists and physicians are, so you should ask about training and qualifications. What is this person's experience with youngsters who have A.D.D., and what type of interventions will he or she use?

Learning Specialist. Besides the professionals at your child's school, you may want to consult other learning experts. You might consider hiring a tutor for a particular subject or enrolling your child in a learning center that provides supplemental education. Learning centers usually do academic testing to determine at what level your child is functioning. The staff then designs an individualized program for a particular area, such as reading, math, or study skills. The direct teaching of skills is very helpful for students who have to make up what they have missed in class.

Behavior Therapist. If there are particular behaviors that could be improved, and you feel you need some outside help, a behavior therapist could help set up a behavior modification program and monitor it with you. Behavior therapists usually have degrees in psychology, or they may have other training in working with children. Many are on staff at a hospital or a children's mental health clinic.

Neurofeedback Provider. Neurofeedback is the newest specialty in the A.D.D. field. It has been used in research settings for more than twenty-five years, but only in the 1990s has it become widely available due to faster computers and an increase in the number of people entering the field as research on its effectiveness grows. Neurofeedback for A.D.D. is based on research that shows that the brain wave pattern is different in individuals with A.D.D., and that people can learn to self-regulate brain waves by using computerized feedback. Neurofeedback is also called neurotherapy or EEG biofeedback. Most providers of this service have a background in psychology, but there are also many other professionals, including nurses, physicians, physiotherapists, and teachers, who are trained in doing neurofeedback. It is primarily an educational intervention: the person learns the skill of self-regulation. Certification in this field began in late 1996 through the Biofeedback Certification Institute of America. BCIA certification is not a license to practice. It just shows that a person has completed a required course of study, spent a specified number of hours doing neurofeedback under supervision, and passed an examination to test knowledge and skills. The certification process is so new that many people with a lot of experience are not yet certified. The important questions to ask are: What experience does this person have using neurofeedback? What experience does this person have with A.D.D.? How have their clients fared? For more on neurofeedback, see chapter 8.

To keep yourselves from developing an attention disorder after wading through this sea of specialists, you will find it most helpful simply to make a first appointment with your child's primary-care doctor. In collaboration with your child's doctor, get a referral to an

A.D.D. specialist who will then help you set up a team approach with the right specialists in the right sequence, the goal being to work out an overall management plan for your child and your family.

WHAT SHOULD YOU EXPECT DURING AN ASSESSMENT?

We have heard stories about assessments for A.D.D. that range from a five-minute chat with a doctor followed by the writing of a prescription to a week-long workup that involved a thorough medical examination (including tests for thyroid function and vision), audiology assessment, many psycho-educational tests, questionnaires filled out by parents and teachers, interviews with the child and parents, and even a trial of medication. There is no standard assessment procedure; rather, each professional or organization develops a unique system.

There are, however, a number of bases that should be covered during an assessment. Getting an assessment of your child's difficulties and planning a treatment program is not, by any means, one-stop shopping. (The exception might be if you live near a research institute that specializes in A.D.D. But even then, the researchers might have a particular bias toward one intervention, such as medication, cognitive therapy, behavioral management techniques, or neurofeedback.) Nearly everyone who writes about A.D.D. emphasizes a multimodal approach. This means that you as a parent can expect to tackle the problem from a number of different angles and coordinate different interventions to fit your child's needs.

A diagnosis is really just a name that makes for easy communication: we talk about a diagnosis rather than a list of all the symptoms.

Sometimes it is necessary to have a formal diagnosis in order to access services for your child or to have health insurance pay for treatment. Whether an A.D.D. or A.D.H.D. diagnosis qualifies your child to be considered for special services (see "Know What the Law Allows," page 273) depends on where you live. In the United States, for example, one of the factors governing the provision of services is the Individuals with Disabilities Education Act (IDEA). Note that the goal of an assessment is not just to come up with a diagnosis. More important than a diagnostic label is coming up with an action plan to help your child reach his potential. With the right plan, everyone will have fewer frustrations related to A.D.D. and you can feel like you are moving forward.

History

The core of any assessment is a detailed history. In order for a psychologist and other professionals to understand the person they see before them, it is necessary to hear what this person was like as an infant, a toddler, and in preschool and the elementary grades. Indeed, it is helpful to go back even further and hear about the pregnancy and birth and to gather details about parents and grandparents. Remember, A.D.D. is often familial. When there is no one else in the extended family with A.D.D. characteristics, that is also of interest, because it will affect how this youngster is viewed. One grandmother may say to her weary daughter-in-law, "His father was just like that as a boy. It's exhausting, but it gets easier." This creates a different environment from the one in which the grandmother remarks, after a scene at the dinner table, "No one in our family ever acted like that!"

The person taking the history will also ask

Definitions of A.D.D.

Researchers and professionals need to use operational definitions (definitions they can operate with) in order to be sure, for example, that all the subjects in a study meet the same criteria, or, sometimes, just to be able to talk to one another. For research purposes, "intelligence" is defined as "what an IQ test measures," and researchers can then match groups for the variable of intelligence based on IQ scores. In everyday life, intelligence is a more complicated concept; we base our judgments about how intelligent someone is on many variables, such as how the person speaks, reasons things out, and performs at school or on the job.

The operational definition that has been used for attentional problems is the symptom list for Attention-Deficit/ Hyperactivity Disorder found in the *Diagnostic and Statistical Manual* (*DSM*) of the American Psychiatric Association. The version currently in use is the *DSM-IV* (meaning it is the fourth revision, published in 1994). Family doctors, pediatricians, and psychologists, as well as psychiatrists, use the *DSM-IV* criteria when making a diagnosis. The *DSM-IV* has three subtypes under the A.D.H.D. diagnostic category. These are:

314.00 Attention-Deficit/Hyperactivity Disorder, Predominantly Inattentive Type
314.01 Attention-Deficit/Hyperactivity Disorder, Predominantly Hyperactive-Impulsive Type
314.01 Attention-Deficit/Hyperactivity Disorder, Combined Type

In practice, many people use A.D.D. to refer to the inattentive children and A.D.H.D. for hyperactive ones. Parents are confused by Attention-Deficit/Hyperactivity Disorder, Predominantly Inattentive Type. Why mention hyperactivity at all in the diagnosis if it is not among the symptoms? Also, Attention-Deficit/Hyperactivity Disorder, Predominantly Hyperactive-Impulsive Type is rarely appropriate, because it is reserved for children who are hyperactive and impulsive but not inattentive, and nearly all the A.D.H.D. kids are inattentive. (The exception is very young children who are not expected to have very long attention spans.) Most often the technically correct diagnostic label is Attention-Deficit/Hyperactivity Disorder, Combined Type, but that name does not explain to parents what is combined. Another complication is that the hyperactivity often disappears in adolescence, but the impulsivity may remain. Then what diagnostic code do we use for the person?

Our preference is to use just A.D.D. (Attention Deficit Disorder) and to qualify it, if necessary, by saying "with hyperactivity" or "without hyperactivity." These terms were used in earlier versions of the *DSM*.

Since psychiatrists specialize in mental illness, it is not surprising that the *DSM-IV* definition of A.D.D. has a decidedly negative slant. Our A.D.D.-Q includes a wider range of behavior than the *DSM-IV*, including such traits as "hyperfocus." Our questionnaire provides a way of understanding your child. It is not meant to be the basis of a formal diagnosis; by convention, the basis for that in the United States is the *DSM*. Regardless of what professionals call this "disorder" or "diagnosis," the concern of parents is not so much what to call it, but the fact that their child needs help.

about A.D.D. symptoms that are present and to what degree they exist. (This is where having done the A.D.D.-Q will come in handy for parents.) The history will also cover risk factors, such as depression or alcoholism in extended family members.

The child's medical history is important, too. More frequent in the A.D.D. population are birth difficulties (including not just prematurity but also post-maturity — infants who kept everybody waiting an extra week or two), head injuries, allergies, and frequent ear infections at an early age that required antibiotics and may have led to the insertion of tubes.

Details from school are also critical because children with A.D.D. invariably underachieve, and the report card comments are very telling: "needs to pay better attention". . . "fails to finish his work". . . "more effort needed." Extracurricular activities are also of interest: sports played and what position (remember, kids with A.D.D. make good goalies); music lessons (children who have A.D.D. would rather play by ear than read music); clubs (kids with A.D.D. may get overexcited in groups or have trouble following directions); and favorite free-time pursuits and activities they lock on to, such as TV and video games.

The professional will want to know what has already been tried and with what result. To give a longitudinal perspective, it is helpful if the parents take along copies of reports previously written about the child. Notice that we say "parents." It is always important and impressive if both parents attend the assessment interview, because it gives the interviewer an additional perspective, and it gives the child the message that both parents are behind this effort to make life a little easier. In the real world, admittedly, it is often just the mother who brings the child. This re-

flects the fact that mothers typically carry the greatest burden when it comes to raising a child with A.D.D.

Questionnaires

There are a number of ways to supplement the history. The most common is to use questionnaires, and these come in a wide variety for both parents and teachers to complete. Sometimes they are sent out as part of the pre-assessment information gathering, before the evaluator meets the child. Some professionals prefer to see a child without having any previous reports, so that initial impressions are not colored by the reports of others. In that case, questionnaires may not be completed until during or after the first meeting. Questionnaires nearly always rely on observations made by others and thus tend to focus on the symptoms that are disturbing to parents and teachers. You may want to balance the questionnaire information with some comments on your child's strengths.

Psychological Testing

In addition to questionnaires, there is psychological testing or, as it is sometimes called, a psycho-educational evaluation. This is done by a psychologist or someone supervised by a psychologist. This testing includes individual IQ testing and academic testing. Sometimes it also includes tests that identify learning disabilities. The psychological testing usually does not include personality testing or projective techniques. This is because A.D.D. is a neurological problem and not an emotional one. Certainly these children sometimes have difficult lives, but their A.D.D. is not usually the result of tough times; it is the result of how their brain functions.

IQ Tests

The most important reason for giving an intelligence test is to identify your child's strengths. On the ten to twelve subtests that are administered some scores are bound to be higher than others, and being aware of these stronger areas can help you and the teacher assist your child in finding ways to compensate for weaker areas. Test scores partly reflect how your child takes tests, and in children with A.D.D. they may underestimate what knowledge he has or how intelligent he is.

Although IQ tests have come in for a fair bit of criticism about such issues as cultural bias, they are still excellent for their intended purpose, which is to predict academic success. Scores are thus sometimes used to place children in special programs, such as smaller classes for those who learn at a slower pace or for those at the other end of the scale, who acquire academic skills more easily. But keep in mind that the score reflects only functioning on *this* particular test at *this* moment in time and is not the last word on your child's potential, either in school or in life.

The most commonly used individually administered tests for intelligence in North America are the Wechsler scales. There are versions for preschoolers through adults. For children between six and sixteen years, the version used is the Wechsler Intelligence Scale for Children, third revision (WISC-III). The WISC-III produces three separate scores: a verbal score (a child responds verbally to a question), a performance score (the child performs a task, like assembling a puzzle), and a full-scale score. The standard score is not usually given to parents, because it is not easy to interpret the number if you do not understand the statistics of normal curve distributions. As well, there is nothing magic about the number, since there is a margin of

error of about 5 points. More often, the psychologist explains the scores in terms of percentile ranks. A score at the thirty-fifth percentile rank means your child did as well as or better than 35 percent of children of the same age. These scores are not perfect predictors of school success, and they are even less accurate as predictors of success later in life. This is because an intelligence test samples just a few specific skills (verbal reasoning, vocabulary, spatial reasoning, etc.) and does not tap many other factors that can contribute to success, such as creativity and persistence.

Individually administered intelligence tests are much more accurate than group-administered ones, especially for children with attention problems. Some children with A.D.D. have been known to make a pattern on their answer sheet rather than reading and answering the questions during tests given to the entire class. You should therefore not panic if your child got abysmal scores on tests given to the whole fourth-grade class, but you might want to have some individual testing done, so the low score does not define the child in the eyes of future teachers.

Intelligence scores in children with A.D.D. may accurately reflect current functioning, but they frequently underestimate the child's potential. It has been reported in research (and Dr. Lynda sees it regularly with her clients) that people's scores on the Wechsler scales increase with neurofeedback training. This may be not because they got smarter but because they could attend better in the testing situation and, having learned to concentrate, finally started to show their potential.

Patterns found on intelligence tests in children with A.D.D. An IQ test cannot be used to diagnose A.D.D. because there is no single pattern that is unique to children with

A.D.D. But certain subtests are particularly affected by the ability to sustain attention. On the WISC-R (revised), which was used until 1991, children with attention problems were more likely to show the ACID pattern. That acronym stands for the subtests called Arithmetic, Coding, Information, and Digit Span. Children with A.D.D. tended to get lower scores in these areas. Why are these four troublesome? Arithmetic involves problem solving using one's head alone, and these children may do poorly because of their difficulty with working memory, in this case, keeping numbers in mind while they do calculations in their heads. Sometimes they just do not catch the spoken question in the first place, as their minds are elsewhere. Digit Span also involves attention and auditory memory: the child repeats strings of digits of increasing length both forward and backward. Repeating digits backward puts a strain on working memory. Coding involves copying a digit-symbol code for two minutes. It is astonishing to see some children stopping to scratch the back of their neck after forty seconds or so as if there were no time limit. You can just imagine the problems they have copying things from the board in school. The information subtest involves questions that sample knowledge of subjects such as science, geography, and history, and it is the only subtest directly related to school learning. Information scores tend to be low in children with A.D.D. because they do not pay attention well to things they find boring, and the facts drift by them without registering. In young children from families that encourage learning, the information score will often be above average, but the older the child with A.D.D. is, the more likely it is that his learning has not kept pace with his peers'.

On the WISC-III currently in use, the psychologist calculates four index scores in addition to the verbal, performance, and full-scale scores. Of particular interest is the Freedom from Distractibility index, which is calculated from the Arithmetic and Digit Span subtests. As noted above, these require good listening skills and working memory, so children with A.D.D. may find them difficult. Processing Speed index is also weak in some of these children. This index is calculated from scores on Coding and on a subtest new to the WISC-III called Symbol Search. The child must scan a line of symbols looking for a match, marking "yes" if he finds a match and "no" if he does not. Both these tasks have time limits and involve paper and pencil, so weaknesses demonstrated here often go along with the commonly found weakness in written work and copying in the classroom.

Be sure to have the person who does the testing discuss the results in detail with you. An intelligence test produces a wealth of information about how your child does certain things, compared to others of the same age. Although the above discussion centers mainly on the areas of difficulty that may show up, don't forget that the major purpose of the profile obtained on the WISC-III should be to identify your child's *strengths*.

Academic Tests

Tests of reading, math, and spelling and writing are usually done to supplement the information given by the teacher. Scores on standardized academic tests help determine whether your child is underachieving in relation to his ability as measured by the intelligence tests. Since the norms for standardized tests are based on the total population, the results may not reflect your child's standing among his classmates. If your child is at a school where class averages are high, he may be near the bottom of his class even though he ranks mid to average on the standard test.

As well, if your child is younger than most of his classmates, that will be a factor in the comparisons.

Tests for Learning Disabilities

Remember that being behind in academics is not the same thing as having a learning disability (LD). There are many reasons that a child may not be keeping up with his classmates. These include emotional problems, family difficulties, cultural differences, low IQ, and poor teaching. Many students with A.D.D. who are capable of producing good work under the right circumstances have low grades because they are just not doing the work. They also miss things because they are inattentive in class: for a hunter in scanning mode to catch everything the teacher says is well nigh impossible. Also, the child's individual learning style must be considered. If the child is a visual learner, and the teacher presents the material in an auditory mode, the student will not learn as well.

Nevertheless, children with A.D.D. frequently also have specific learning disabilities, separate from A.D.D. Depending on which study is being cited, the figure for children with A.D.D. having coexisting language disabilities is anywhere from 30 percent to 80 percent. We believe that the actual incidence is probably much lower than most research studies indicate. Research subjects are usually children with more complex problems who are referred to university clinics.

Thus, testing for learning disabilities is not usually necessary. However, here are some things to keep in mind if you and your child's teacher think that there may be an LD component in your child's problems. First, have the school psychologist do the testing. This is the least expensive alternative, and, in addition, the school psychologist will have ready access to school records and be able to do the necessary liaison work to get programs in place if there is, in fact, a need for special programming. Second, be aware that there is no specific battery of tests that everyone in the field uses. Often an LD is diagnosed on the basis of a discrepancy between the child's ability, as measured by intellectual testing, and his functioning level in a particular subject area such as reading or mathematics. The best definition we personally have heard is that the LD child is one who is very, very, very hard to teach. Usually a learning disability is associated with a processing problem — the child's brain does not process in the expected way the information it hears or sees.

There are dozens of different tests that can be used, depending on the nature of the suspected disabilities. Disabilities may, for example, involve perceptual-motor functioning (the child cannot accurately copy what he sees), or the problem may be with auditory processing of information. "Dyslexia," a rather old-fashioned term that is still in use, indicates reading problems. There are whole books about the field of learning disabilities. A good recent title on the topic is *Attention Deficit Disorder and Learning Disabilities,* by Barbara D. Ingersoll and Sam Goldstein. The effective interventions that they review for LD students include using phonics and word analysis skills in the teaching of reading, metacognitive strategies (making the child aware of how he learns and remembers things), peer tutors, and computers.

New Approaches to Assessment

A careful history remains the basis of the clinical diagnosis of A.D.D., but today there are also high-tech ways to identify A.D.D. characteristics. The most promising of these new approaches are computer-based continuous performance tests (CPTs) and the quantitative EEG (electroencephalograph), which looks at the child's brain wave pattern. Both of these approaches are still in their infancy. Both look promising and will doubtless be refined further in the very near future, as there is a great deal of work and research currently being done with them. The monitoring of brain wave patterns using EEG equipment can also be used for training to improve concentration and attention span in individuals with A.D.D.

Continuous Performance Tests (CPTs)

Computerized continuous performance tests (CPTs) were developed for use with people who have A.D.D. They grew out of laboratory tests used in the 1950s to assess sustained attention in people with brain damage. In the tests, the task is to watch a screen and hit a key or a trigger when a certain number, letter, or shape that is the target appears. CPTs are repetitive and boring. Tests currently in use include the Test of Variables of Attention (TOVA), which has separate visual and auditory versions, the Brain Train IVA (a combined Intermediate Visual Auditory test), the Gordon Diagnostic System, and the Conners' Continuous Performance Test.

The TOVA is currently the most widely used. The scoring system has norms for males and females from ages four to eighty. (Four- and five-year-olds are given a shorter version of the test. Individuals aged six through adults complete the same 22½-minute task.) Failing to hit the trigger when a target appears is an omission error and counts toward the Inattention score. Hitting the trigger when a non-target appears (quite easily done when the targets are frequent and the test subject gets trigger happy) is a commission error and counts toward the Impulsivity score. Also tracked are the subject's reaction time and variability of that reaction time; variability is measured because people with A.D.D. tend to be inconsistent in their reaction time, which is in line with the inconsistency you find in their everyday behavior. Reaction times are often slow in people with A.D.D., perhaps due to general underarousal in the brain. There is no typical scoring pattern seen in people with A.D.D. who take the TOVA. Some people have elevated scores on all four scales, and others on only one. Some individuals with A.D.D., especially the ones who are eager to please and are not hyperactive, have normal scores on the TOVA. This points up once more that people with A.D.D. are a very heterogeneous group.

Because of problems with false positives and false negatives, professionals must interpret CPT scores using their clinical judgment. A false negative means that the person has the problem but the test did not pick it up. Other criteria must also be considered. An uncooperative child who does not really try to do the test's task might produce a false positive: the child does not have the problem, even though the test score suggests he does.

Electroencephalogram (EEG)

As technology has become more sophisticated over the last twenty years, evidence has been mounting that the brains of some persons who have A.D.D. function differently from others'. This difference shows up on an EEG, or electroencephalogram, a tracing that shows electrical activity of the brain measured with simple, painless sensors on the head. (The principle is the same as that of an

EKG [electrocardiogram], which measures electrical activity of the heart using sensors on the chest.)

Neurologists and biofeedback specialists look at an EEG in different ways. Normal brain waves are "background" to the neurologist, who reads an EEG looking for pathology. Neurologists are highly skilled at detecting abnormalities that may signal that the patient has a seizure disorder or a space-occupying lesion in a specific area in the brain. A problem like petit mal epilepsy shows up as an abnormal spike-and-wave pattern. If no pathology shows up on an EEG done in a hospital and read by a neurologist, it is correctly pronounced normal. A neurologist would read the EEG of a person with A.D.D. as normal, because the difference is not a sign of pathology — that is, it is not abnormal. Biofeedback specialists, on the other hand, look only at the "background" normal brain waves. The procedure for looking for an A.D.D. pattern differs from what is done in hospitals and is called a quantitative EEG (QEEG), because the amount of electrical activity at different brain wave frequencies is quantified.

Whereas an EEG done for a neurologist typically uses nineteen leads from sensors on the head, neurofeedback practitioners use a variety of EEG equipment. Some use nineteen leads (especially at university centers where they are also doing research) and some use fewer to sample brain waves only from the sites of interest for A.D.D., which are central ones near the top of the head. There are now EEG instruments designed for research that use 256 sensors.

What is different in the EEG of persons who have A.D.D. is the relative amount of slow brain wave activity (theta and/or alpha waves) compared to faster wave activity (sensorimotor rhythm and beta waves). All these wave forms are normal, but the balance between slower and faster waves is different in people with A.D.D. Several studies have demonstrated that students who are diagnosed as having Attention Deficit Disorder exhibit more slow wave (theta) activity than students who do not have the symptoms of this disorder. This research is very promising and confirms that a QEEG is helpful in an assessment of an individual who may have A.D.D. More research needs to be done to help answer such questions as whether different EEG patterns can help identify different kinds of problems within A.D.D. If you are considering neurofeedback training to improve your child's concentration and attention span, the EEG assessment done by a neurofeedback provider will be among the first steps taken.

PUTTING IT ALL TOGETHER

The reason you have gone to all this effort to determine whether your child has Attention Deficit Disorder is to come up with a plan of action. During the assessment process, you will also have expanded your own horizons concerning A.D.D. We hope that you will have developed an awareness of the bright side of A.D.D. as well as a realistic view of the difficulties your child and your family may face. By now you will also have some ideas about what kind of intervention might be helpful, given your child's unique combination of challenges and abilities. You have also discovered that this is a book for parents who want to be actively involved in helping their child. It is not for parents who just want to be told where they can go to have their child fixed. A.D.D. is not that kind of problem. Both you and your child have to take responsibility and then take action. You didn't create the initial inborn difference, but you can modify it. You can remove obstacles from your child's path or at least help him handle them. The motto at Dr. Lynda's ADD Centre is: "You can't change the wind, but you can adjust the sails."

The one thing that you can be sure of is that your child will get older and will change, and that the joys and challenges will differ with each new stage of development. The rest of this book is dedicated to giving you information that will help you meet the challenges and increase the frequency of proud moments. We wish you fair winds and smooth sailing and offer you suggestions on how to trim your sails. It is your strength that will pull them in and let them out as necessary on your unique journey.

II

UNDERSTANDING YOUR CHILD'S UNIQUENESS

*P*arents don't cause a child to have A.D.D. Children come wired *this way. Heredity is a major influence, and this, obviously, is beyond your control. Children with A.D.D. don't need a different kind of parenting than other children; they just need more intense, more consistent parenting. You don't cause A.D.D. by your parenting style, but unresponsive or controlling parenting may contribute to the problems of living with A.D.D. You can't prevent A.D.D. by your parenting style, but you can make it more manageable. What parents do beginning at birth — even during pregnancy — can prevent the child who has A.D.D. traits from being labeled a problem or a bad kid. And, in our experience, the smarter the child, the greater the chance that child has of doing well — even with A.D.D. How you care for your baby and child can lessen the probability that differences will become disabilities. The messages you give your child, even at a young age, influence his self-image. You can start him out with the resources to have the best behavioral and educational head start.*

Smart from the Start

IN THIS CHAPTER we briefly share practical ways to get the right start with your infant and toddler. The information given here serves as an introduction to a parenting style that Dr. Bill calls attachment parenting, which he describes more thoroughly in some of his other books.*

Attachment parenting really can make a difference in how children with A.D.D. turn out. Attachment parenting is a parenting style that brings out the best in parents and their babies. It helps parents know their child well and enjoy parenting. In a nutshell, attachment parenting is about helping parents and babies fit. Understanding your attachment to your child, even if that child is twelve years old, will help you trust your own instincts and your own knowledge of your child as you deal with the problems of A.D.D. It will also help you trust your child. And if your children are still small, or if you happen to be pregnant,

use these suggestions to lessen the chances of difficulties with A.D.D. in the future.

GIVE YOUR BABY A HEALTHY WOMB ENVIRONMENT

Research suggests that children with A.D.D. have brain pathways that are wired differently from other people's. There are lifestyle decisions that mothers can make that will influence, for better or for worse, how baby's brain develops. For example, the fetal nervous system is affected by what's in mother's blood during the nine months of pregnancy and especially during the critical first three months. Inhaling or ingesting poisons can harm the baby's developing brain. Cigarette smoke, alcohol, and drugs have all been shown to affect brain development and increase the risk of a child's having learning and behavior problems.

In contrast to the "don'ts" of drugs, alcohol, and nicotine during pregnancy, there are some "dos" that affect the developing fetal brain in a healthy way. A healthy diet is a plus. While it takes very poor maternal nutrition to harm baby's developing brain, in general, the better you nourish your

---

* *In* The Baby Book *(Little, Brown, 1993), Dr. Bill and his wife, Martha, describe the overall benefits of attachment parenting and how this style of infant care brings out the best in babies and parents. In his book* SIDS: A Parent's Guide to Understanding and Preventing Sudden Infant Death Syndrome *(Little, Brown, 1995), Dr. Bill discusses the scientific basis of the healthy womb environment and how attachment parenting enhances the physiological development of the infant.*

body the better your baby's brain will grow.*

What's going on in mother's mind may also affect baby's mental development. While the science of fetal psychology is itself in its infancy, there is growing evidence that babies' brains are influenced by events outside the womb. For example, parents who sing and play Mozart to their baby in the womb increase the likelihood of their baby's liking Mozart later and being soothed by singing. There is a story that cellist Pablo Casals started to sight-read a new piece and realized he knew what was coming next in the music even before he read it. He later learned that his mother, also a cellist, had rehearsed this piece daily in the later stages of pregnancy with Pablo.

A mother whose pregnancy is filled with a consistent pattern of fear or anxiety has a greater chance of producing an anxious child. Mother and baby share hormones, and an environment full of stress hormones may affect the wiring of the developing brain. Stress is inevitable in life, especially during times of change such as pregnancy. It's what you do about it that matters. A mother who eats well, gets regular exercise, and takes time to work through her own fears and anxieties will create a better womb environment for her baby. Other family members should be aware of the need to nurture mom, so she can be mentally as calm as possible to nurture the new life growing inside her.

GIVE YOUR BABY HEALTHY FIRST IMPRESSIONS

How baby and parents get started with one another sets the tone for future relationships between parents and child and between the child and others. Unless a medical complication prevents it, a newborn should stay with mother, in her arms and at her breasts. Fortunately, many hospitals now encourage rooming-in to facilitate this. Immediately after birth, babies need to know where they belong and that the world is a warm and comfortable place to be. This should be the first message babies receive and store in the "file cabinet" of their developing brain.

The next message babies should receive is that their cries will receive a response and their needs will be met. Caregivers (primarily mother) should respond intuitively in a nurturing way to baby's cries. When parents show a healthy, positive attitude toward a baby's cries, the baby develops a positive sense of who he is. A baby's cries are a signal, a language to be listened and responded to rather than a problem to be fixed or a habit to be broken.

When parents consistently give an immediate and nurturing response to their baby's cries, baby learns to cry less and better (a nicer cry, a more pleasant language than the irritating, ear-piercing sound of an unanswered cry). Practicing this signal-response exercise hundreds of times during the early weeks helps parents learn when and how to respond. This is not the time to worry about spoiling or feeling manipulated. A healthy cry-response system can be developed only by repeated practice.

GIVE YOUR BABY A HEALTHY NUTRITIONAL START

The evidence that breastfeeding is best for babies is overwhelming, but does breastfeeding have anything to do with managing A.D.D.? It is well documented that breastfed

---

* *For more information on the relationship between mother's diet and how a preborn baby grows, consult* The Pregnancy Book: A Month-by-Month Guide, *by William Sears and Martha Sears, with Linda Hughey Holt (Little, Brown, 1997).*

babies have fewer ear infections, allergies, and gastrointestinal disorders than non-breastfed babies, and we have noticed, as have others, how frequently children with A.D.D. suffer from these medical problems. These problems often compound the behavioral ones, and health problems during a critical stage of development may have subtle effects on lifelong learning. Frequent ear infections, for example, may affect hearing and thus hamper language development. As well, frequent infections may be associated with later development of A.D.D. Breastfeeding will not, of course, eliminate A.D.D. in a child or prevent its development, but it may help a child develop better, and it certainly makes him easier to parent. Breastfeeding is just part of careful management, and it may reduce secondary problems. And there is no doubt that it promotes attachment.

As the *USA Today* (2/2/92) headline — "Mother's Milk: Food for Smarter Kids"— suggested, in addition to breastfeeding's important role in the prevention of medical problems, it may aid in the development of better brains. In a study published in the British medical journal *Lancet,* premature infants fed breast milk averaged 8.3 points higher on IQ tests at ages seven and eight than preemies who had been fed formula. The research suggested a dose-response relationship: the more mother's milk the children got, the higher they scored.

Why breast milk builds better brains is not completely understood. Besides factors yet to be discovered, it's probably due to the additive effects of the following:

• *Increased nurturing.* Studies show breast-fed babies feed more often than do formula-fed babies, who are more likely to be fed on a schedule. Also, because breast-fed babies feed more often, they tend to be touched and interacted with more.

• *Increased touch.* Breastfed babies are more likely to sleep all or part of the night in the same bed with mother, a healthy parenting practice that further increases daily touch time. Infant-development specialists believe that touch — and the lack of it — has a powerful influence on a child's physical and intellectual development. Breastfeeding mothers may also be more sensitive to their child's signals; to be successful at breastfeeding, a mother must watch her baby rather than the clock or the marks on the feeding bottle. This sensitivity carries over into other areas.

• *Increased brain-building nutrition.* Breast milk contains around four hundred nutrients that are not found in formula. For example, mother's milk contains brain-building fats that provide the components for building myelin, the insulating sheath around nerve fibers that help messages travel faster. Mother nature recognizes how vital these special fats are to baby's brain. If a mother's diet is deficient in these nutrients, her mammary glands produce these brain builders. Human milk has adapted perfectly to the changing brain development of the human species; that is, before modern science began tampering with infant feeding.

Breast milk provides a lot of cholesterol (not too much, not too little — sort of a medium cholesterol diet), and cholesterol promotes brain growth. Infant formula contains little or no cholesterol, an executive decision probably based more on marketing than on sound nutritional principles, since people automatically avoid products that contain cholesterol. Consequently, babies do without this brain builder unless mother breastfeeds. Breast milk is rich in other brain-building nutrients as well. Lactose, the main carbohydrate in breast milk, is the sugar the brain prefers. Some formulas contain no lactose. Taurine is a brain-building protein appearing in human milk. Only recently have some formula manufacturers added taurine, but they are still uncertain about how much to add.

• *Increased responsiveness.* We cannot say this too often: a parent's responsiveness to the cues of his or her child is one of the most healthy attitude builders. A breastfeeding mother is more likely to respond in a more nurturing and a more natural way to her baby's needs and cries because she has a hormonal head start. When her baby cries, the blood flow to mother's breasts increases, and she has an overwhelming biological urge to pick up and nurse her baby. The more often she nurses, the higher the levels of her maternal hormones (prolactin and oxytocin) — biochemical messengers that travel throughout her brain, affecting how she acts toward her baby. These hormones are thought to contribute to the immeasurable, but vitally important, mother's intuition.

The reason we stress the importance of building brains is that A.D.D. specialists have observed that smarter children with A.D.D. are better able to compensate for their attention or behavioral differences. High intelligence is a protective factor.

WEAR YOUR BABY

If parents carry their baby in a baby sling (another feature of attachment parenting), is he less likely to develop problems? We believe yes. A baby sling is a comforting tool to help baby feel better, a nurturing tool to help baby grow better, an interacting tool to help baby learn better. Many children with A.D.D. have problems feeling secure and problems learning. They also are disorganized. Carried babies feel more secure, learn more, and are better organized. Spending at least several hours a day in arms or in the sling helps baby feel emotionally and physically secure. Carried babies fuss less and so are more fun to be with. Mother mirrors that joy to her baby. Baby can then divert the energy she would have wasted on crying into growing and learning. Slings contain the baby physically and lessen the amount of startling and immature baby movements (flailing arms and legs are characteristic of a disorganized nervous system in the early months).

A baby learns a lot in the arms of a busy caregiver. Being in arms, near eye and voice level, baby is intimately involved in the world of the caregiver. When daddy speaks, baby hears; where mommy goes, baby goes; when babysitter takes a walk, baby senses the rhythmic movement. Being worn on an adult body exposes baby to a myriad of movements ranging from subtle to intense, all of which stimulate baby's brain and sense of balance. Carried babies also interact more with their caregivers, so they have practice attending to what those caregivers do and say.

As a young child, Laurie was insatiable as far as attention went. No matter how much time we gave her, she would be upset when it ended. For her, the term "endless attention" had real meaning.

HELP YOUR CHILD HANDLE FRUSTRATION

Because of their impulsiveness, children with A.D.D. set themselves up for frustrations. Setbacks will be a frequent part of life for these kids. Your job as a parent is not to prevent your child from facing frustrations but rather to help him learn how to manage them.

During the first six months, as baby is learning to trust the caregiving environment, parents are likely to hold frustrations to a minimum. They are mostly "yes-yes" parents. They pick up the crying baby within seconds; the beginning crawler gets stuck under a table, and they rescue her. These are natural responses necessary to help a baby who is too young to emotionally and physically handle these frustrations. But as time goes on, it's best to underreact when baby gets frustrated. You are busy on the phone and your seven-month-old sits nearby and fusses to get picked up. Instead of leaping to scoop her up, you look at her reassuringly and say, "It's okay, no need to fuss." She takes her cue from you and busies herself with her toy for another few minutes. Or, your ten-month-old explorer crawls into a corner and can't figure out how to make his way back out. He gets frustrated and fusses for help. Instead of rushing to the rescue, be on standby, offering verbal encouragement while he works himself out of the jam. The eighteen-month-old climber finds himself perched at the top of the couch and can't climb down. Instead of lifting him down you become a facilitator, showing him how to place his feet so he can get himself down. Your laid-back reaction gives your baby the message: "No problem. No need to fuss. You can handle this situation." Let your baby handle small frustrations at first, and then more significant setbacks, according to her development. You are teaching your child to manage frustration rather than preventing her from facing it. This is an especially important skill for children with A.D.D., for whom setbacks will be a frequent occurrence.

Conveying this "no problem" attitude de-pends on your getting connected and building trust with your baby. Your baby must be able to read your level of anxiety (just as you read his tolerance limits) and trust that you will intervene when he really needs it. After repeated situations such as these, the growing child files away a balanced message: "There are frustrations in life, but I can handle them; if I cannot handle something alone, I can count on others to assist me."

STUDY YOUR CHILD

One of the goals behind Dr. Bill's principle of attachment parenting is for parents to know their child. Suppose you are sitting in his office talking about your six-year-old, who has A.D.D. — or, for that matter, any potentially chronic problem that places extra demands on your parenting. The first piece of advice you will receive is, "Study your child; read your child; become an expert in your child. You must, because no one else will. Doctors may change; teachers will change; therapists will change; but you will always be your child's mother or father."

Knowing your child helps you get behind the eyes of your child; this is an especially valuable tool for living with a child with A.D.D. Learn to see the world through your child's eyes. How it looks to her is probably very different from how it looks to you. A.D.D. management is not primarily about "fixing" the child; it's about improving relationships: parent-child, teacher-child, peer-child, and counselor-child. To help your child work on this, you must see these relationships as your child sees them. This will enable you to customize your approach. Professionals will give you checklists, recipes for behavior modification, techniques for discipline, and a variety of general guidelines

The Payoff

A high-touch, high-commitment style of parenting (what Dr. Bill calls attachment parenting) reduces the chances of a child's developing problems as a result of having been born with A.D.D. traits. You invest early for later payoff. If you spend a great deal of time close to your child in their earliest years, they will be secure and independent in later years. Children who are the product of this style of parenting are likely to be:

Less impulsive. Impulsiveness gets children into all kinds of trouble. Attachment-parented children are more likely to develop a set of inner controls. They are more apt to think through what they're about to do.

Less restless. Children who spend their baby and toddler years in a parent's arms and at mother's breast have an inner peace and well-being that is reflected in their outward behavior.

More trusting. A trusting child is less likely to be an angry child and more likely to use adult resources for help.

More empathetic. When children grow up in a home where caregivers are sensitive to their needs, sensitivity becomes part of their normal behavior. Children with A.D.D. tend to be egocentric, and that, coupled with impulsiveness, tends to get them tagged as uncaring or insensitive to other people. Attachment parenting counteracts to some degree the tendency for children with A.D.D. to be egocentric. They are better able to get behind the eyes of others and imagine how their actions affect other people.

More interdependent. *Inter*dependence is a healthier trait than either dependence or independence. A developing child first goes through the stage of dependence, when everything must be done for her. Soon cries of "I do it myself" echo throughout the home. But because this child is able to trust others, she ultimately recognizes that "I can do it myself, but it's better if we do it together."

Stephen Covey, author of the best-selling *Seven Habits of Highly Effective People*, stresses that interdependence is a characteristic of the most successful people. Children with A.D.D. will need help. They will be exposed to a parade of professionals, each one providing guidance in different areas at different times in the child's life. Children who are the product of attachment parenting have learned from infancy to use adult resources to get what they need. They become resource-full. At the same time, they maintain a healthy sense of self.

More physically self-aware. Children with A.D.D. often lack physical self-awareness, a sense of where their body is in space. Children who receive attachment parenting, on the other hand, know their bodies, are more comfortable with their bodies, and do not shy away from being touched. Probably this is because they spent so much touch-time with their caregivers.

More able to delay gratification. Fathers and mothers who practice attachment parenting know how to respond appropriately to their child. They know when to say yes and when to say no. As a result, the child gets used to making appropriate judgments and eventually learns to say no to himself.

More organized. Attachment-parented infants spend more time in the state of quiet alertness, the behavior state in which children are most energy efficient and learn most effectively. Being nursed frequently and carried securely in a baby sling organizes an infant's behavior, makes it more predictable. Lack of organization (going in many directions at once) is a characteristic of many children with A.D.D., and it contributes to disruptive behavior and poor school performance.

that work for most children with A.D.D. most of the time. Yet all of them won't work all of the time for your child. Your child will be creative in outwitting you. You will need to keep one step ahead of him. As one mother of a child with A.D.D. said, "Every time I think I have the game won, she ups the ante."

Even having had previous children gave me no advantage over the first-time mother. Michael was a new game. I slowly found my way, but only by intense observation of this different child. He was a mystery I had to unravel.

The success of almost every part of your action plan for managing A.D.D. will depend upon how accurately you assess and report the actions of your child. Even your doctor's periodic adjustments in medication dosages will depend upon your reporting. Your child — and everyone else involved in his care — relies on your information. You will be your child's advocate, judge, social worker, determiner of school placement, and disciplinarian. As a parent of a child with A.D.D., your job description will constantly widen. Knowing your child well is the most essential qualification you can bring to the work; studying your child is a process that begins in babyhood and continues until he is an adult.

James is a very well adjusted twelve-year-old, because we worked so hard to be and stay connected. If I hadn't worked so hard to bond with him, I would have no way into his life. Our bond is our path to find each other when we need to.

Knowing a child through attachment parenting also makes parents more discerning. Throughout your A.D.D. journey, you will encounter many A.D.D. fads and alternative treatments in addition to traditional approaches. You will need to make judgments about the accuracy of claims and whether a particular approach fits your child at a particular stage in his life. Knowing your child well will help you develop a sixth sense about what treatment plans to try, how best to carry them out, and when it's time to change directions.

I was so frustrated going from specialist to specialist and being told that Mark just had a discipline problem. I always left feeling that I was a bad mother and he was a bad child. In my heart I knew that he would behave if only he knew how, and I could help him if only I knew how. We both needed to be taught some skills and not just a bunch of judgment labels.

DISCIPLINE YOUR CHILD

Because of their impulsivity, children with A.D.D. often get tagged as "discipline problems." Think of discipline as first developing the right relationship with your child, in addition to using the right techniques. In disciplining their children, every parent goes through the following stages; parents of children with A.D.D. just have to go through them more intensely and creatively.*

- **Stage 1: birth to one year.** This is the stage of getting to know your infant, becoming an expert in your baby, and getting connected to your child. The tools of attachment parenting we discussed above, primarily breastfeeding and babywearing, help cement this connection. This is one of the most important stages of discipline. This is when parents and baby build a foun-

---

* *Parents of children with A.D.D. will find lots of useful discipline tips in* The Discipline Book, *by William Sears and Martha Sears (Little, Brown, 1995).*

dation of mutual trust: parents learn to trust themselves, and baby learns to trust his or her environment. As one parent whose child later developed A.D.D. said, "I'm so glad we started off with the attachment style of parenting. For us, attachment parenting was like immunizing our child against behavioral problems. It empowered me with a knowledge of my child. It proved to be a valuable asset."

• **Stage 2: one to two years.** Now that you have built a trust-based relationship with your baby (which is required before you can become an effective authority figure), during the second year, discipline means setting limits and providing structure. This means you create an attitude in the child and an atmosphere in the home that makes it easier to respect limits. Setting limits refers to the house rules; the structure part refers to setting the conditions that enable a child to more easily follow these rules. For example, parents set limits about what the child may or may not touch. They provide lots of "yes touches," preapproved objects for busy minds and busy bodies to play with, and they put the breakable, but tempting, "no touches" on a high shelf out of harm's way.

• **Stage 3: two to five years (the preschool years).** During these years, as your child becomes verbal enough to understand your directions, you concentrate on shaping behavior, or conveying to the child the behavior you expect. The preschool child is looking for a norm, as if he is thinking, "How do I behave here?" The home is a mini-society, the first social group in which the child needs to behave. It's up to you to show him how. Shaping your child's behavior implies guiding your child's individual personality traits to work

to his or her advantage. Children with A.D.D. require more shaping. Try not to confuse shaping with control. Lifelong discipline does not mean controlling your children, but rather teaching them inner controls so that they can later shape themselves. Shaping your child's behavior is like being a gardener: you can't control the color of the flower or when it blooms, but you can prune the plant and feed the soil to shape the flower to bloom more beautifully. Throughout this book, especially in chapter 5, we will give you time-tested behavioral shapers to help you weed out those behaviors that work to your child's disadvantage and nurture those that help your child mature.

• **Stage 4: five to ten years.** Because children with A.D.D. are somewhat impulsive and egocentric, they often have difficulty considering the effect of their behavior on others before they act. An important goal of discipline during the school-age years is teaching children to think through what they are about to do and to make wise choices — to consider how their actions are going to affect other people before they act (see the related section "Learning Empathy," page 109). Besides empathy, sensitivity is a quality that you want your children to develop. One of the goals of discipline at this stage is to raise kids who care. Many children with A.D.D. tend to be emotionally sensitive children. You can help this quality work to the child's advantage by teaching empathy.

For parents of challenging children, "discipline" means basically doing what you need to do to like living with your child. "Discipline" also means giving your child the tools to succeed in life. Throughout this book, we will give you tools and show you how.

Understanding and Steering Development

The most important part of any task is the beginning of it, especially when we are dealing with anything young and tender. For then it can be most easily molded, and whatever impression anyone cares to stamp upon it sinks in.

— Plato, *The Republic*

The key to understanding later behavior lies in understanding early development, especially the first three years of life. The same key factors that influence the young child continue to influence the teenager and, later, the adult. As Wordsworth observed, "The child is father of the man."

In this chapter we talk first about the special relationship between the temperament of a child with A.D.D. and the messages that child receives. Then we discuss factors that influence behavior and development in all children. Parents of children with A.D.D. need to be more aware of this information than do parents of less challenging children, because children with A.D.D. are more vulnerable and are thus in need of the best parenting possible.

BUILDING A SOLID FOUNDATION FOR THE CHILD WITH A.D.D.

Children with A.D.D. are temperamentally different from other children, and their temperament influences their early social development. Their personalities help to shape the messages they receive from others, and these messages, in turn, shape children's beliefs about themselves and the world.

A.D.D. Traits as Personality Shapers

Caregivers are constantly giving children messages about how to think, feel, and behave, and about who they are. Children who are inattentive, easily distracted, extremely active, and very impulsive tend to receive quite different messages ("No! Don't touch that!") from those directed toward quiet, happy, attentive children ("What a nice smile!"). The messages your child receives mold the *assumptions* your child makes about himself and about how other people are likely to react to him.

These assumptions (e.g., "I'm a good person" or "I'm always in trouble") determine how your child perceives the world — it is either against him or for him. These perceptions determine how he will behave. His behavior results in predictable reactions from parents, teachers, and peers. These reactions almost always reaffirm or reinforce the assumptions your child has already made about himself. In fact, human beings find it so important to reaffirm their basic assumptions that they will continue to act in ways that bring about the usual reactions, even if these reactions are negative.

Clearly your early messages have a great deal to do with the fundamental assumptions your child makes about himself and the world around him and thus influence his behavior as he grows. This is why it is important for parents to act in ways that send their child positive messages, even if the child sometimes makes it difficult to do so.

Assumptions that you hold about yourself govern your behavior. To help you understand the important dynamics of how assumptions are formed and maintained, remember the word ABRACADABRA.

Your child's temperament, plus the messages he receives from important people, lead to his forming assumptions about himself and about how others will react to him. These assumptions determine the way he perceives the world and how he will behave. His behavior causes others to react to him in predictable ways, and their reactions affirm the assumptions he has about himself.

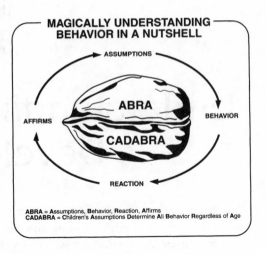

MAGICALLY UNDERSTANDING BEHAVIOR IN A NUTSHELL

ABRA = Assumptions, Behavior, Reaction, Affirms
CADABRA = Children's Assumptions Determine All Behavior Regardless of Age

Give Positive Messages in Negative Situations

The early years of development are critical ones for parents of children who have high levels of activity and impulsivity. These children can place unusually high demands upon even the most flexible of families. Promoting healthy emotional development is a challenge. You have to get on the same wavelength as your child, so that you can see situations through your child's eyes. This will help you send a positive message even when your child's behavior is not very pleasing.

Alex was a very active six-year-old. Suddenly, and quite unexpectedly, he knocked over his four-year-old brother's carefully constructed castle as he pretended his action figure was the mightiest of all. Alex didn't think about this action before doing it. He didn't contemplate the possibility that knocking down this beautiful structure would be devastating to his brother, who had been working all morning to build it. Alex had no malice aforethought, no intention to be bad or to pull down upon himself the anger of his brother and the wrath of his mother.

How should his mother respond? On the one hand, Alex must learn that his behavior was not acceptable. On the other hand, he must not be left feeling that he is a bad person. If he were to develop a self-image that he was bad, behavior problems would escalate because, as noted above, children behave according to their assumptions about themselves.

Questions to Ask Yourself Before You React

What was my child's real intention?

How is my child feeling now?

How will my child react to my reaction?

What messages do I want to send?

What messages do I want to avoid sending?

What do I want my child to believe about himself?

How can I affirm my child's independence?

How can I help my child feel connected?

How can I encourage my child to take responsibility?

Let's consider two possible but opposite reactions on the part of Alex's mother and see how they might affect Alex.

Reaction One: Mother Acts Before She Thinks

Alex's mother hears angry yelling, races to the scene, and begins to scream at Alex.

Alex is a very sensitive child. He can feel devastated by mom's criticism. He didn't mean to destroy his brother's creation, but she doesn't seem to understand this. When Alex feels hurt, he doesn't, however, look sad. He looks angry. Perhaps he learned at a very young age that a good offense is the best defense. So he responds with a full-fledged temper tantrum, defending himself against bad feelings by blaming everyone else. His temper tantrum guarantees that his mother will continue to direct her attention at him (the tantrum is making her scream all the more loudly) rather than taking care of his little brother's hurt feelings. This is all very predictable for Alex. His temperament is to be an extrovert. He reacts to situations with quite assertive action. (An introvert, by comparison, would look inside and overemphasize his own contribution to causing the upset and might become anxious or depressed.)

The message Alex receives, unfortunately, is that he is a terrible, awful person. His mother has not actually said this, and certainly doesn't mean it, but this is what Alex infers from her angry tone of voice. After many such interactions, he assumes that he is not a good person and that others will always find him at fault. It seems to him that negative behaviors get attention. This assumption is unconscious rather than conscious, but it begins to control his behavior, and he uses his bad behavior to get attention and exert control over his environment. Control reduces anxiety by making his world predictable. However, control for such a young child is scary. The young child wants to be held, loved, and cared for and to have the big people be responsible and in control. Though the child doesn't understand where his anxiety comes from, it generates more calls for attention and adult presence and, thus, more negative behavior. Alex has not learned to take responsibility for his own behavior or to initiate positive interactions with others.

Reaction Two: Mother Thinks Before She Acts

Alex's mother hears angry yelling, races to the scene, but then slows right down and appears to enter the room very casually. She immediately kneels on the floor between the two children and says, "This was a beautiful building job, Aaron. I know Alex feels sorry he knocked it down. Now let's see if we can make a really big castle that we'll leave up to show Dad tonight. Shall we each have a special room? What do you want to call your room, Aaron? What will your room be, Alex? Would you both like a hot chocolate while we build?"

Mother's questions are designed to obtain positive answers and to set the stage for a positive, constructive interaction in which both boys will feel understood, loved, and supported. She has moved swiftly so that neither boy has had time to move from his original position on the floor; the conflict will not escalate with her between them. Most important, she remains firm, but calm. "Calm" is the key word, for, above all else, children do what you do and not what you say. (If for even a moment you lose your cool, it may take many days to recover your lost ground.) Later, Alex and his mother quietly talked about how Aaron probably felt when his castle was knocked down.

What enabled Alex's mother to turn this negative situation into a positive interaction with both boys? She knew that Alex didn't really mean to do something bad. He was just impulsive, and she was careful not to mirror his impulsiveness in her reaction. Instead, she modeled thoughtfulness and, rather than dwelling on his bad behavior, moved Alex on to a good cooperative task, one in which he could feel in control and feel connected to his family.

The messages Alex receives are that he is understood, appreciated, and loved. Alex will have a positive feeling about himself. He can apply the positive lessons he has learned with his mother to working with his teacher and his friends at school.

The amount of effort Alex's mother exerted often isn't necessary when a child is born with a quiet, attentive, reflective, happy, easily adapting temperament. It is, however, very necessary for children like Alex, who are born with the challenging temperaments associated with A.D.D. and A.D.H.D. But remember the old saying, "You get out of a job what you put into it." Though they take much more effort, these children also bring great rewards.

Children's behavior is shaped, for better or for worse, by the messages they receive from those around them. From these messages, they perceive how others view them and form assumptions about themselves. It's a fact of human nature that people react to "good" babies and cooperative children with more positive messages. Children who are not so easy to be around are more likely to receive negative messages about themselves. Impulsive, inattentive children are particularly at risk for growing up with a hard disk full of negative messages about themselves: "I'm bad," "I don't stop and think," "People don't like me," "I'm a nuisance," "I'm lazy." If children sense that those around them don't like them, they eventually learn not to like themselves. What starts out as an inborn temperament trait becomes poor self-esteem and a source of lifelong troubles.

Recognize this risk. Research shows that even teachers who use positive strategies with other pupils seem to forget them and are negative with children who have A.D.D. Children with A.D.D. do not bring out the best in adults. You have to make a conscious effort to be positive. When your child is the only one in the play group who won't sit still and listen to a story, shield him from negative messages from yourself or others that something is wrong with him because he is not like the other children, who are sitting nicely. We value and praise "good" babies and "easy" children. The convenient child is likely to get more positive strokes from parents and teachers than the one who extracts every ounce of parental energy and requires creative teaching. These kids should not be made to believe they are abnormal just because they are inconvenient and don't seem to fit in.

Fill your child's developing mind with messages about what's right with him rather than reflecting to your child how displeased you are with him. (When he's old enough to understand, you can tell him that you don't like his behavior but you do like him. This distinction is lost on toddlers, and an older child who hears this phrase too often may cease to believe it.) Treat bad behavior as an exception, with the message that your child is basically good: "Danny, that's not like you to hit little Sam. You're such a good big brother. Let's play nicely together like you usually do. I'll get started on building the train track with you and Sam."

Unless Danny has really hurt Sam, it's best not to dwell on the injury. Get them back into cooperative play. If Sam were bleeding, you would handle it somewhat differently, paying attention first to him and letting Danny help find a Band-Aid to "make it better." Even then, you give the message that you are sure Danny must feel bad about hurting his brother because he is usually so good with him. If you tell him often enough what a good big brother he is and set up situations where he can be, then he will be.

An important starting point in learning to live with and manage a challenging child is to change the messages you give from negative to predominantly positive. Accept that if your child's hard drive is filled with five years of negative messages, he's not going to change overnight. You will have to work at rescripting his worldview and his view of himself.

Build Healthy Brains

Our brains contain cells called neurons, which resemble billions of tiny chemical batteries with electrical wires, many of which are unconnected. At the end of each neuron is a feeler, called an axon, which makes connections with the tiny feelers, dendrites, of other neurons. As the brain develops, connections are formed, based on the child's actions and thoughts. When the infant repeats an action or thought, he forms patterns of association. These patterns get stored as expectations of daily living, which we have called assumptions about how the rest of the world is going to interact. For example, the infant cries and she gets picked up. As this cue-response is repeated, it becomes a pattern of association: baby cries and she expects to be picked up and comforted. She learns that distress is followed by comfort, and eventually this will help her comfort herself, as well as rely on others for help.

After storing months and years of patterns, they become part of the child's nature, and the types of messages that were stored shape the developing personality. They influence what she thinks about herself, whether or not she trusts others, whether joy or sorrow is her predominant mood. Eventually the child's behavior will be a composite of her inborn temperament and the messages she has received and continues to receive about herself.

Brain research has identified which systems in the main are associated with emotion. Early experience plays a large role in how these systems in the brain develop.

Factors That Influence Behavior and Development

People interact with others in a manner that is governed by a balance of factors, as indicated in the diagram below.

1. Inborn Temperament. Your child is born with a little personality all his own. This personality is a baseline that can be modified through his experience in the world. Rate your child on the following characteristics. Ask yourself if your child has really changed very much since he was a toddler with respect to each of these traits. Most children remain true to the pattern they showed as an infant. The easy baby grows into an easy toddler, and the challenging baby continues to keep parents on their toes.

Your child's profile on these measures is unique. Remember what your child was like as an infant. Was she an easy baby and sort of quiet, relaxed, attentive, focused, happy, regular, and adaptable? Or was he more time consuming, being active, intense, easily

distracted, impulsive, and irregular? Depending on your own temperament, you might react quite differently to the first child than you would to the second.

When you think of these aspects of temperament in terms of a child with A.D.D., you see that A.D.D. is just a pattern of temperament characteristics that tend to be at the extreme, more challenging ends rather than in the middle.

2. The need for dependence. It is the nature of human beings to be social animals. We have a need to be loved and cared for. We want to be part of a group. Even if your child is really a very fast moving and independent little person, there will still be dependency needs that you must pay attention to. Feed him, nurture him, rub his back at bedtime, make him feel an important part of the family.

3. The need for independence and control. Most parents of children with A.D.D. have commented at one time or another, "My child wants what he wants when he wants it!" Sometimes this can be quite frustrating. You just have to remember that a degree of independence is essential for normal healthy growth and development. Gradually during the years from age two on, the child must learn to balance his needs with the needs of others around him. If you push too hard on this, you might have either a rebellion on your hands or, at the other extreme, a somewhat withdrawn and depressed child. With A.D.D., it is more often a rebellion. All children have a need to feel in control to make their world predictable.

4. Temperament modifying the need for dependence. A child who is anxious is usually more dependent on people, especially

FACTORS INFLUENCING BEHAVIOR

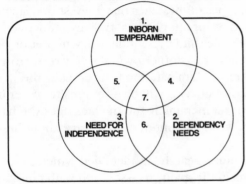

	Extreme	Moderate	Mild	In between	Mild	Moderate	Extreme	
Active								Placid
Relaxed								Intense
Attentive								Inattentive
Focused								Distractible
Reflective								Impulsive
Happy								Depressed
Secure								Anxious
Regular								Irregular
Approaches others (Extrovert)								Withdraws (Introvert)
Adapts easily								Adapts poorly to new situations
Not easily startled								Easily startled
Sensitive (to how others feel)								Relatively insensitive
Independent	Interdependent							Dependent

mother. These children seem to need others in order to feel complete and secure. If your child seems to be "tied to your apron strings," don't push him away. This kind of child is usually extremely sensitive to feeling rejected. Even though you want him to stand up for himself, you need, in the early years, to first give support. That might be a hug or might involve doing something with him rather than expecting that he do it alone.

Two neighbors came to visit Judy. Each brought her six-year-old child, and the plan was that the children could play while the moms had a visit. Judy's son Tommy, who was also six, kept clinging to mom. He wanted to be in the same room as mom and her friends. He didn't want to go off with the other children and play. Judy felt embarrassed and somewhat angry. How-

ever, she quietly counted to ten, relaxed her shoulders, and got him involved in helping her serve the guests some tea. Gradually Tommy seemed to relax. He and Judy then took some cookies and milk to the two visiting children, who were playing in another room. They greeted the goodies enthusiastically, and Tommy was the center of attention. His anxiety decreased, and mom was able to leave him playing with the others.

5. Temperament modifying the need for control. The child who is hyperactive and impulsive, on the other hand, may tend to be controlling, showing "I want what I want when I want it" behavior. This behavior is difficult for others to handle.

Jason was six years old. Jason's mother was in the same situation as Tommy's. Two friends had arrived with their children. Jason was off with the kids immediately. It seemed like only a minute had passed when a scream was heard. One of the boys came running to his mom. "Jason pushed me!" he cried.

Jason wants other children to like him and play with him, but he feels comfortable only when he is in charge. He has his own agenda. If others don't fit into it, he acts without thinking. In this case he had wanted the wagon, and when his friend ran to it first, he impulsively pushed him away.

6. Dependence and independence in balance. Your growing child will express both needs: to be dependent on you and to be quite independent. How this is expressed will vary according to your child's age and stage of development. Your toddler may demand your help and then push you away once the job is started. Do not feel hurt; he is just expressing both needs in sequence. The desire to please is developing, but there is also a desire for control and independence. It is a big job to balance the two. These needs should eventually come into balance, with your child having a strong sense of self (independence) and also a secure connection to others (dependence). This is what solid self-esteem is all about.

7. The balance between temperament, dependence, and independence. The healthy child displays a peaceful balance between competing needs for independence and dependence and his inborn temperament characteristics. The difficult child does not display this same peaceful balance. The child with A.D.D. who is hyperactive is a good example of not being in a peaceful bal-

---

The Balancing Act

To understand independence, think of Frank Sinatra singing *My Way*.

To understand dependence, think of Barbra Streisand singing *People (Who Need People)*.

While we are on the topic of famous actors and singers, did you ever notice how people accepting Academy Awards for their individual achievement begin by graciously thanking all the people on whom they were dependent? Successful people balance independence with dependence. Interdependence represents the highest level of functioning.

---

ance. Often children with A.D.D. fluctuate between being whiny and dependent one minute and wanting to do something alone and their way the next.

Messages. While temperament and the needs to be dependent and independent are considered inborn, the messages that we constantly give our children provide the surrounding environment. We give messages about how to think, feel, and behave. Later we instill values in our children — messages about what to believe in. Whatever you say or do is a message to your child. At each stage of growth, the child learns from these messages. The messages that come very, very early in an infant's and toddler's life form the framework for her self-image and perceptions of the world. Since, to the very young infant, mother really is the entire universe, then the messages mother gives are interpreted as how the universe responds. As the little infant's universe broadens over the next few months, messages begin to come from other sources, such as father, brothers, and sisters. These messages set the stage for how the child expects other people to respond to him.

Ways of interacting with others become habits or coping styles as the child grows to adulthood. Dr. Lynda went to a twenty-five-year reunion of her junior high school class. Guess what she noticed. Though people's outward appearance had changed dramatically, mannerisms and interactions were constant. The cheerful ones were still cheerful and outgoing, and the shy ones were still quiet.

Conflicting Messages. During the process of early development, messages from different important people in the child's life may conflict. She has to find some way to make sense of these conflicts. Some children become anxious and withdrawn. Hyperactive children more often go to the other extreme and try to take control. Either way there is no peace. Inside herself the child feels uncomfortable. Since there is no balance or equilibrium, the only way she can make the world predictable is by behaving in a manner that makes the people around her respond and act in a predictable fashion:

Mary was six years old. She was a very active little girl. She was living with her mother since her parents had separated. Like many little children, Mary somehow felt responsible for the family breakup. She seemed anxious that her father might not come and get her on the weekends, and she acted like an angel with him. She desperately needed her mother, but, like many children in this situation, she behaved in an extremely difficult manner. She con-

fronted her mother constantly. She loudly refused to do what her mother told her to do and had temper tantrums whenever her mother made her toe the line. She seemed to be constantly testing her mother to reassure herself that her mother wouldn't leave her (or to get it over with if she was going to leave). Her drawings and her play with her dollhouse continually repeated the theme of people leaving.

Mary got a clear message early in her life. Important people can suddenly leave you. Mary's behavior expresses her need to have her parents demonstrate to her over and over again that they are going to continue to be with her. She also fights against feelings of being powerless (a serious issue for her, as she had been powerless to stop her parents from separating). Unfortunately, Mary has learned some very hard lessons about life at a very young age. She has also created ways of interacting with very close and important people in her life, and these ways are likely to remain with her throughout her life. These ways of interacting may be counterproductive and inappropriate in later relationships and may be difficult patterns to overcome as she enters adolescence and adulthood.

Your child's behavior becomes fairly predictable very early in life, based on his temperament and his needs for dependence and independence. Your parenting behavior and the kind of messages you give your child also become very predictable within the first few months of his life. In most households, for the most part, everything is predictable, and, in a sense, the child plays a large part in making it stay that way. Sometimes the child's predictability involves being unpredictable. His parents say things like "We never know what he'll be up to next," and "We have to keep our eye on him every minute." What that child can predict is that he will often be in trouble and feeling guilty.

UNDERSTANDING SOCIAL DEVELOPMENT

Social development proceeds in a few simple stages. Just as there are stages for developing motor skills and language skills, so are there stages for developing social skills. Understanding these stages is important with regard to A.D.D., because these children so often seem immature. What this really means is that they have not mastered these social stages in the same way or at the same age as other children. Each stage has its own social task to accomplish. Each stage appears to also have certain unfortunate outcomes associated with it if the task is not successfully negotiated.

These stages are reminiscent of the dependence/independence balance discussed above. At each stage, there is a natural tendency to move either toward or away from the parents. At each stage, mom and dad can either flow with and assist the natural course of their child's development, or they can resist the natural course of development. The child is going to grow up anyway. It can be a smooth path or a bumpy road. Knowledge of the sequence of stages that you can expect will help smooth out the bumps.

During the first few years of life, the infant/toddler goes through four crucial stages of psychological and social development.

1. The infant remains very close to mother, totally dependent, almost a part of her. During this attachment stage, basic trust develops. The child trusts that his needs will be met if mother (or an-

other nurturing figure) is always available to him. The ability to tolerate frustration in later life is based on this fundamental trust.
2. The child moves away from mother to explore everything, acting as if she or he were queen or king of the world! The child develops mastery and self-confidence.
3. The child reapproaches mother some of the time but also wants to be on his own some of the time. He is indecisive, oscillating between the two desires. He comes to realize that others, including mother, have a life of their own and are not there just for him.
4. The child moves more carefully away and becomes increasingly independent. Some parents experience this as "the terrible twos." A more positive way of thinking about this stage is that your child is becoming more assertive. Your job is to help him do that appropriately.

For the rest of the child's life, he will be handling the push and pull of moving toward and away from others in an increasingly complex social world. His ability to balance his own needs for independence and dependence along with the needs of others in a healthy fashion rests to a large degree on the messages received from others during the early formative years of his life.

These four stages are about separation and individuation: the young child separates from mother and becomes an individual in his own right. Parents need to be tuned in to and support each stage.

Here is an example of a mom's intuitive handling of an incident during the second stage, when the child first exerts independence.

Elizabeth at fifteen months is an outgoing child. She is in a stage of being "queen of the world," very much into doing her own thing and being quite independent. Elizabeth has decided that she is going to eat with her hands. She likes playing with her food as much as she likes eating it. It is a mess! Mother likes things neat. Mother has a choice: she can insist that Elizabeth stop this behavior immediately, or she can join in and then redirect Elizabeth.

Elizabeth's mother puts a plastic drop cloth around the high chair and quietly reassures herself that this stage will pass without incident if she doesn't make too big a deal of it. She buys Elizabeth a cute fork and spoon with Minnie Mouse on the handle. Rather than punish or ridicule Elizabeth for using her hands, she praises her whenever she uses her new utensils. "Minnie Mouse is so happy when you use your spoon. You're eating your meat just like a big girl with your fork!"

Sometimes it takes creativity to think of a positive approach. Sometimes you have to bite your tongue not to be negative when your child creates a mess that will take extra time for you to clean up. And children always seem to do this when you are already in a hurry. It is, however, well worth the effort to take the time because, in the long run, it will save a lot of arguments and hassles. If mother yells and gets upset, tells Elizabeth she is a bad girl, or, worse yet, slaps her hand, Elizabeth will respond with a temper tantrum. In addition, in order to establish her own independence, which is terribly important for her self-esteem at this stage, Elizabeth may make mealtime a battleground with her mom. Mother could stop the "eating with hands" behavior by using punishment, but there would be a high emotional cost to pay. In the long run, the extra time mother takes to help Elizabeth and redirect her behavior will turn out to be a very small investment of time compared to the lengthy battles that will ensue if she resists the natural expression of independence at this stage of Elizabeth's development.

We chose an example involving food because many children with A.D.D. are fussy eaters. They may want their mothers to keep different foods separate on the plate. They may refuse to eat something if there is sauce on it. They may for a time eat only a few favorite foods. The wise mother will make combinations to fit her child's tastes. She won't insist that her child eat what the family is eating or eat everything that is put in front of him. Eating battles are not ones that parents win. A little child has very, very few things he has virtually total control over. These include eating, vocalizing, and eliminating. The wise parent stays well clear of making any of these areas a battle zone.

The fourth stage, when the child really wants to be independent but does not yet have the judgment and skills to manage it, can be quite challenging.

Susan was a quiet, happy two-year-old. Mom was loading the dishwasher. Susan asked for a drink. Mom said she would get it just as soon as she finished the dishes. She asked Susan if she would like to help and gave her a plastic bowl to put in. Susan pitched in, and the job was soon completed.

Jason was an impatient, impulsive, very active two-year-old. He raced into the kitchen and yelled, "Want juice!" But he wasn't able to complete his sentence. Mother began, "Jason, we'll both have a drink when I finish —" Jason interrupted, "Want juice now!"

These two children interact very differently in similar situations. The approach of each of these mothers is quite different too. The time commitment each of these mothers must make in helping the home run smoothly is also quite different. Clearly it will be easier to get Susan to be appropriate about asserting her needs than it will be with Jason.

In adolescence, these stages of separation and individuation crop up again, and you get another chance to get it right. The content is different (hairstyles, clothes, choice of friends, control of the telephone), but the issues (independence versus dependence) are the same. If you put in the required energy during the first three years of life, the teenage years should go more smoothly. If you are currently struggling with a teenager, try to understand the conflicts in terms of the emotional tasks that your child is trying to accomplish. That way you are less likely to overreact. Do not be afraid to set boundaries and limits but also try to see it from your offspring's point of view.

Your understanding of child development is a powerful part of your parenting repertoire. While keeping your child's inborn temperament in mind, you can use your knowledge of development to guide your own actions in shaping your child's behavior. You will also find that your knowledge makes you a more careful observer and interpreter of behavioral messages. The more knowledge you have, the more you will enjoy the parenting process.

III

MANAGING A.D.D.

A.D.D. is not just one problem affecting one person. It is usually many problems affecting many people. So you cannot take a "one size fits all" approach to helping a child with A.D.D. You must focus not just on the child but also on relationships: parent/child, teacher/child, relatives/child, and peers/child.

In part 3, we will introduce you to many approaches to managing A.D.D. There are more techniques for modifying behavior than you would likely ever use with one child, but we want to give you a wide range of things to try so that you can choose ones that you are comfortable with and that you think will work with your child. This is a smorgasbord of approaches for getting the best out of your child; you select the ones you want to try. Appreciate that work in all of the following areas will be necessary for most children. The areas we will cover are:

- Behavior-improving strategies. *Here are practical ways to shape your child's behavior so that he can eventually learn to manage himself.*
- Family environment: setting up for success. *You want to enjoy living with your child, and you want your child to sense that you do. Your child will copy the behavior he sees at home, so we will help you give your child healthy models to imitate.*
- Learning strategies. *These techniques will help your child learn how to learn and to take responsibility for his own achievements. We'll suggest time-management techniques to help your child organize himself at home, at school, and in social activities.*
- Training the brain. *We will show you how neurofeedback, a new and exciting approach to A.D.D., can empower your child to improve the way he concentrates and reduce his impulsiveness.*
- Medications. *We'll cover when to consider medication, what medicines to use, and how to best use them. We'll give you the tools you need to participate intelligently in this decision and make informed choices.*
- Other helpful strategies. *These include a healthy diet and sensory-motor integration techniques.*

Strategies for Improving Behavior

IMPULSIVENESS AND PROBLEMS with paying attention lead children with A.D.D. into trouble, and their behavior problems may land them in the principal's — or the doctor's — office. They often cross the fine line between being creative and being disruptive. Not all children with A.D.D. develop behavior problems, and that is a credit to the parenting they receive. Certainly they are at higher risk than the average child, and it takes more effort on the part of their parents to keep them on the straight and narrow.

Dr. Bill notes: When Bob was four, he saw a "birdhouse" up on a tall pole. It was red with a pointed roof and had a white door with a window in the center. He stood on his tricycle and opened the door, but there were no birds at home. A few minutes later, a few fire engines came along. When a firefighter asked Bob if he had pulled the alarm, he said, "No. I only opened the birdhouse door." The firefighter was very understanding and explained what had happened. Bob's father, on the other hand, was embarrassed and punished Bob severely. I tried to persuade Bob's father to see the situation from the perspective of Bob —

an innocent little boy who was curious and clever. Situations such as these are so damaging when handled badly and the child is treated like a criminal.

Behavior problems don't exist in a vacuum. They tend to create other problems. Children who are disruptive in school or unruly at home know that they are being labeled bad, dumb, or wild. The resulting poor self-image makes it harder for them to manage themselves. This makes their behavior still worse.

Besides their disruptive behavior, their inappropriate moral development gets children with A.D.D. into trouble. Their egocentricity contributes to this: they often think others

THE A.D.D. BEHAVIOR CYCLES

DISTRACTIBILITY IMPULSIVITY HYPERACTIVITY

ACCEPTABLE BEHAVIOR

POOR SELF-IMAGE POOR SCHOOL PERFORMANCE

DISRUPTIVE BEHAVIOR

GOOD SELF-IMAGE

"YOU'RE OK!" LET'S TRY IT THIS WAY

BAD CHILD DUMB CHILD LAZY CHILD

are being unfair to them yet that other person may not even know what the problem is. Most children by the age of seven develop some inner sense of right and wrong. Many children with A.D.D. do not truly understand when they are doing wrong. Parents and teachers notice how surprised children with A.D.D. look when they are confronted with criticism. They don't seem to have a clue how they got into trouble. Even when you walk them through the sequence of events leading up to their goof, they often don't understand. Their behavior was okay from their point of view, and they can't see the other person's point of view. It seems that their cognitive development of cause and effect is inappropriate for their age. As we mentioned above (see page 74), children with A.D.D. have difficulty thinking before they act, and they have a hard time predicting the effects of their actions on other people. Whereas most children naturally learn empathy and understand the consequences of their actions, children with A.D.D. often have to be taught these moral qualities, and they may not sink in the first time you tell them.

You will be amazed at how your child's A.D.D. symptoms improve when he gets his behavior under control. Notice we said, "*He gets his behavior under control.*" It's not the parents' job to control the child but rather to help the child learn to control himself. Here is a step-by-step plan to help you improve your child's problem behaviors.

STEP 1: IDENTIFY YOUR CHILD'S BEHAVIOR PROBLEMS

The first step is to decide what problems need work. Sometimes the behaviors that get on your nerves are not the most important

ones for your child to correct first in order to get along better with his teacher and his peers. Try to be as objective as possible in deciding which problems to work on first. You may have to do some research to pinpoint exactly what needs to be changed. Talk with your child's teacher, observe your child interacting with his peers, and watch his behavior at home carefully, like a scientist rather than a police officer or judge.

What are the main behavior problems? When do they occur, and why? Fill in the chart below and rate the severity of each problem.

Now that you know what you want to change and why, let's look at what to do. The best place to begin is with yourself.

STEP 2: IDENTIFY PROBLEM AREAS IN THE FAMILY ENVIRONMENT

Before you even start "fixing" your child, you need to look closely at your child's environment (home, school, social) and identify factors that hinder good behavior. The family-functioning inventory chart on page 141 may help. Think about what's going on that could trouble your child, such as problems in your marriage or a major change, like a recent move, a change in school, or a recent death or illness of a special person or pet in your child's life. Of course, no child lives in a perfect family or a problem-free world. But parents need to recognize that while some things can help your child behave better, other things can contribute to your child's acting worse. Identifying these problem areas may require some soul-searching.

Often what is needed to improve a child's behavior is for parents to work on their rela-

Problem	When It Occurs	What Triggers It	Magnitude 1 (mild) to 5 (severe)
1.			
2.			
3.			

How are these problems interfering with:

1. Your relationship with your child? _____

_____

_____

2. Your child's relationship with his friends? _____

_____

_____

3. Your child's relationships at school and his ability to learn? _____

_____

_____

tionship with their child. In our view, a parent's ability to discipline a child is grounded in the parent's relationship with that child. Tips and techniques don't work very well if your child doesn't trust you, or if you don't know your child very well. What is your relationship with your child? Are the two of you really connected? Do you know your child's strengths and weaknesses? Do you have fun together? Do you enjoy one another? Are you able to get behind the eyes of your child and understand the world from her viewpoint?

STEP 3: MODEL HEALTHY MESSAGES

In the words of many a wise grandmother, "Children do what you do, not what you say." What kind of actions are you modeling for your children? Above all, model the behavior you want in your child. If you want your child to be less aggressive, model gentleness. If you want your child to speak in a pleasant voice, let him hear your calm, pleasant voice, not your complaining or rude voice. If you want a

How to Use Behavior Strategies Effectively

1. Stay calm and quiet.
2. Listen reflectively to your child's point of view.
3. Be sure you genuinely understand your child's upset feelings.
4. Be very sure your child really understands what he or she was not supposed to say or do.
5. Keep what you say simple and short.
6. Be sure you are consistent and predictable from one time to the next. (Your actions must not vary with your mood.)
7. If you are going to take action, it's best to take it soon. (But don't take action immediately if you aren't in control of your own emotions.)
8. Keep the consequence short. (Don't take away objects or privileges for a whole week, for example.)
9. Keep the consequence small. (Don't take away the bicycle that your child uses for healthy activity with his friends if taking away the next television program will be just as effective.)
10. Avoid threatening. (If you need time to come up with a constructive solution without too much of your own out-of-control emotions mixed into it, use a phrase such as "I'll think about it and tell you later.")
11. When it's over, it's over. Give your child some positive attention with conversation and/or play.

more joyful attitude from your child, check carefully the attitude that prevails in your home. Watch especially for a critical, can't-be-pleased attitude. From morning until night, provide your child with examples of the behavior that you want him to copy, and weed out the behaviors in yourself that you don't want him to imitate. Look also at other significant models in your child's life, such as siblings and friends. Are there ways to improve these models? Sometimes getting an older sibling to model desirable behavior is very effective.

Stop Signals

It's not enough just to tell your child not to be impulsive. You've got to show him how to control his impulses. Give him some "think it through first" tools to help him recognize the impulse and consider the consequence before he acts. Plant this sequence in your child's behavior-shaping repertoire:

Before you do it:

- Say to yourself, stop!
- Count to ten.
- Imagine what will happen if you do it.

This sequence teaches a child to bide his time and to think reflectively. It slows him down. Oftentimes a few moments' thought is all that is necessary to keep the impulsive child out of trouble. These exercises will help a child in the classroom and on the playground, where their impulsive comments can get them into hot water. Later the child will appreciate the saying "You will have a lot of horse sense if you learn to bridle your tongue."

The "Joining with and Modeling" Strategy

Some compliant children will do what you ask them to do without step-by-step instructions or hands-on assistance. The child with A.D.D. needs a more active message. Model what you want your child to do. The school-age child with A.D.D. is more likely to cooperate with your request and get a job done if you join with him and do the task together. The three- or four-year-old child with A.D.D. is unlikely to complete even small tasks that you assign. Often he just can't pay attention to the matter at hand for very long. Don't be upset! This is a wonderful opportunity to remain totally in control and at the same time model "helping each other" with a task (e.g., picking up the blocks and putting them away).

James, age four, and his younger brother, Peter, were told to put away their toys. Peter immediately went about the task diligently and completed it in a very short time. James started the task without argument, but within a minute or two he had become interested in one of the toys he found on the floor. His mother, fortunately, had predicted this would occur and was there ready to help. She said, "James, that X-Wing fighter is really neat! Would you like to hang your X-Wing like it's really flying?" He readily agreed. [Note how his mother joined into James's interest area. She acknowledged he was distracted but did so in a nonthreatening way.] She continued, "James, I'll help you tidy. As we tidy your room, you could put out any model planes and star fighters that you want to hang up. We can start redecorating by putting your X-Wing up just as soon as your toys are on the shelf." When James became distracted again, she said, "Let's put that Star Wars *figure with the X-*

Wing on your desk for our redecorating. I have a really neat idea about how we can hang your X-Wing with Dad's invisible fishing line. Let's work quickly so we can finish and do it."

Count Your Messages

Remember how important it is to frame things for your child in a positive way. Here's an exercise to help you judge whether you are giving your child predominantly positive or negative messages. Choose a day when you will be spending a lot of time with your child and count the number of positive and negative messages. This can be done mentally, on paper, or by using the green counter/red counter technique. Get two golf-score counters (the kind you can wear on your wrist) in two different colors. Put one color (say, red) on the left wrist and use it to count every time you give a negative message with words, tone of voice, or your actions. Put a green counter on your right wrist and count every time you compliment or praise your child or give him any kind of positive message. You can also use this technique to check what kind of messages you and your spouse are giving each other to see what you are modeling for your child. At the end of the day, you may be shocked to see that you scored twenty to fifty red messages yet only five to ten green. Now that you're aware of this, try to change your ways. With thought and effort, you can reverse this! Your child's self-image will improve, and so will your image of him.

Oftentimes, an adult with A.D.D. is raising a child with A.D.D., as in this example:

Lynn was an adult with A.D.H.D. who was nearly as hyperactive as her eleven-year-old boy. Her husband was relatively quiet and calm, but their marriage was becoming tense, and they suspected their child was picking up on their negative behaviors. Using golf counters, Lynn discovered that she dumped more than one hundred negatives a day on her husband and child, while her green counter sometimes showed as few as ten compliments. Lynn said, "I was shocked. I knew I was being negative, but I never really realized how much so! Once I learned to reverse the counts, these silly little counters saved our marriage and improved the attitude of my son. Now he's smiling, more relaxed, and more sure of himself."

Think about all the times you've been with your child over the past week. How many of these were positive interactions, when your child got good lessons and positive messages from you, and you liked his behavior? How much of this was spent in negative interactions, nagging or correcting?

What's the predominant pattern here? Are you spending large chunks of time having fun with your child in conditions that encourage desirable behavior? Or is the reverse true? Are you spending a lot of time in conflict with each other, struggling and not enjoying one another? Perhaps you're not spending much time together at all.

Maybe you need to play more ball together, go camping, go for walks, or just put on some music and enjoy it together. Do fun things together, so your child knows how it feels to act right — and likes the way it feels. Set conditions that will make the desirable behavior easier for him. Don't take him to the art museum, where he has to be quiet and move slowly. Take him to the beach, where there's room to run. In managing the child with A.D.D., outside influences are as important as those within the child. Use the outside influences, which you can control, to direct the inner influences, which are beyond your reach.

Hidden messages. Both your behavior and your child's behavior contain hidden messages. Ask yourself, "What are we really telling each other?" Thinking about those messages may lead to changes in the way you handle a situation.

Denise noticed that whenever Emily played around when she was supposed to be getting ready, she responded by getting angry at Emily. "What is it about her dawdling that makes me so mad? And what kind of message am I giving her when I respond this way?" Denise wondered. She realized

POSITIVE INTERACTIONS	NEGATIVE INTERACTIONS

Be Specific

Many parents pride themselves on being good communicators. They work hard at it if it doesn't come naturally. They learn that children respond well to positive statements and poorly to being told no. But a mother with a child who has attention differences will experience trouble when she uses subtle directions, gentle persuasions, and reasoning techniques. Many children with A.D.D. simply do not understand communication that is not crystal clear and to the point.

Seven-year-old Jamie asks if she can take her porcelain doll on a weekend camping trip. Mother says something like, "If you do, your doll could easily get broken." What she means is, "Don't take the doll." The problem is, this subtle message flies right by Jamie. What she hears is that mother is leaving it up to her. When the doll shows up in the seat of the car next to Jamie, mother wonders why; she also realizes that now she's caught in a bind. If she insists on the doll's staying home, she faces a major temper tantrum. If she lets the issue slide, she knows she's dropping the ball in teaching Jamie how to make appropriate choices. She's also setting herself up for a crisis if the doll gets broken, so she may have to spend the weekend helping Jamie keep the doll in one piece.

Jamie's mother didn't run into such dilemmas with her older daughter, Kayla. She's learning that her younger daughter needs more direct, firmer guidance. In this example, mother could have said something like, "That doll can't go. You know the rule: she has to stay in the house. Let's go pick out two other dolls that can go outside."

that she was assuming that Emily was acting this way on purpose. Upon reflection, it occurred to her that Emily might not even be aware of the passing time, so she decided to set up a schedule for her to help her accomplish the various tasks on time. "From now on, I'll give her time checks instead of yelling at her," she resolved.

Saying "It's five minutes till breakfast — better get your clothes on" and "We're leaving in three minutes, so it's time to put your shoes and coat on" was much more constructive than saying "Why aren't you dressed? You'll make me late for work!" By giving Emily periodic time checks as she accomplished her tasks to get ready, Denise conveyed the positive message that she believed Emily could complete them.

STEP 4: STRUCTURE YOUR CHILD'S ENVIRONMENT

"Structure" doesn't mean rigid, soldierlike behavior. By "structure," we simply mean the conditions (play environment, learning environment, home routines) that set your child up for the behavior you like. Providing structure is just a commonsense survival technique.

Concentrate on not only setting limits but on setting up a structure to make these limits easier to follow. Anyone can make rules; a caring parent makes the rules work for her child.

Identify Your Child's Behavioral Triggers

Parents of a child with A.D.D. have many job titles, and one of these is "detective." Stake out your child's behavior and, based on your observations, list those situations that encourage good behavior and those that trigger bad behavior. Many children behave best in the morning. The behavior of some children deteriorates when dad goes out of town. Some children do well when playing with one or two friends but become aggressive in crowds of three or more. Construct a behavior profile to help you recognize in what situations your child behaves best and worse.

You might add a behavior profile on yourself. When are you at your best and worst? It helps to know both your child's limits and your own.

Structure the Day to Fit Your Child

From your child's behavior profile you know what situations bring out the best and worst in him. It's certainly easier to make changes in your daily schedule than it is to change the temperament of your child. If your child's behavior is at its best in the morning, plan activities such as play group, outings, shopping trips, and preschool in the morning. If your child falls apart in the supermarket at 4 P.M., don't even think about going shopping then. If your child needs time to unwind after school, save homework for after supper. Some parents find it's easier to organize their day around their child's temperament.

Structure Your Child to Fit the Day

While it's often easier to change your plans than change your child, some situations are not very flexible. If dinner at Grandma's is scheduled for 6 P.M. and that's not negotiable, plan ahead. Think about what you and your child will be doing during the visit and come up with a play-by-play plan for setting your child up for good behavior. Have your child take a late afternoon nap or rest. Talk with your child about what kind of behavior you expect and what activities are going to occur that evening. Take along quiet toys and be prepared to spend enough time interacting with your child and monitoring activity that your expectations have some hope of being realized. Plan on leaving before your child's behavior starts to deteriorate.

Occasionally, you may need to lay out your child's whole day on paper to create structure where the child sees none. Including such items as the attitude she gets out of bed with, how quickly she dresses herself, brushes teeth, eats breakfast, gets ready for the school bus, and says yes to each of your requests throughout the day, create a chart. With each step completed, she gets a star or

My child does best when . . .	My child does worst when . . .

point on the chart. The points are redeemable for rewards. Once your child realizes how much happier you both are when a day goes smoothly, she becomes self-motivating.

Structure the Classroom to Fit Your Child

If your classroom visit or your child's teacher's observations reveal distractions in the classroom (see "Interview the Teacher," page 173, and "Do a Classroom Visit," page 176), try to restructure the environment. Ask to have your child seated in a less distracting place, away from the windows or a distracting classmate and closer to the teacher. If you notice the classroom environment has a rowdy zoolike atmosphere, ask to have your child transferred to a calmer class, where the teacher has a more structured disciplinary system.

When Peter was eight, I hired a child mentor, figuring Peter was more likely to follow another child's example than an adult mentor's. I hired one of his friends to model some exemplary behavior for him, figuring that if he saw one of his friends doing something, he would be more likely to believe it was within his grasp.

Match Playmates and Personalities

Kids with A.D.D. often choose the wrong friends because they're attracted to colorful, flashy, interesting things — including people. If you notice Amy plays well with Sara but clashes with Becky, realize that Amy is not yet ready to cope with a child with Becky's personality. With time you can help your child play compatibly with a wide variety of children, but for now, limit play dates with Becky to times when you can supervise the children

closely. Remember, circumstances in life are seldom ideal, and you must give your child the tools she needs to succeed. This requires your active participation at many stages.

Match the Child and the Toys

If Brian is a thrower, structure his toy choices. He'll do best with foam blocks that can't be turned into dangerous projectiles. If he throws his wood blocks, they get "time out" on the high shelf in the closet. If you don't like noisy gun play, put the toy guns away, or reserve them for outside or the basement. If toy squabbles occur between siblings or playmates, "time out" the toy or use a timer to teach the children to take turns.

Busy the Bored Child

A bored child, especially one with A.D.D., is set up for trouble. And a bored child with a busy parent is a high-risk mismatch. Many children with A.D.D. are unfairly labeled as behavior problems when they are simply bored. Busy these bundles of energy with activities that sustain their interest before they deviate into undesirable alternatives. Recognize, too, that the announcement "I'm bored" may mean a child needs your attention, not just something to do.

STEP 5: DEVELOP WAYS TO SHAPE YOUR CHILD'S BEHAVIOR

We have used some practical tools or "behavior shapers" in our own families and with children in our medical and A.D.D. practices for many years. "Shaping behavior" simply means giving your children positive verbal and other cues that move them toward the behavior you want. If you want your child with A.D.D. to be able to play unsupervised with his sibling for ten minutes without fighting, you may have to start by leaving them for two minutes and then come back to compliment them. Then you can gradually increase the time. Shaping behavior with positive rewards is based on the same principles whether you apply them to teaching a seal a complex trick or teaching your child to behave well. With children you have a wider range of rewards, so it should be easier, but parents are not always as patient or consistent as animal trainers.

You also need to be adept at setting up situations that direct your child toward desirable behaviors and away from undesirable ones. Kids with A.D.D. have trouble reading social cues, such as body language and tone of voice. By repeated shaping, you *condition* your child so that the desirable behavior becomes part of him, his usual way of acting, his personality, his norm. The ultimate goal of behavior shaping is to instill inner controls, so that children correct themselves because they feel better when behaving well.

Consider your disciplinarian role to be like that of a gardener. Every child's personality contains flowers and weeds. You can't control the color of the flowers or when they bloom, but you can plant an arrangement that is pleasing. Then weeds pop up seemingly out of nowhere. You can pick the weeds and prune the plants to help the flower bloom more beautifully. If you pay too much attention to weeding but neglect to water the flowers, you'll get rid of the weeds but the flowers may wilt. Behavior shapers must get rid of the weeds *and* help the flowers bloom, so that people see primarily the flowers in the child and not the weeds. Here are some behavior shapers that parents and teachers can use.

When Drew made up his mind to do something that was definitely out of the question, the only way I could get him to change his mind was to give him an alternative to hang on to, such as, "We aren't going to be able to go to the movie this afternoon, but we are going to be able to spend some time at the park."

Catch Your Child in the Act of Being Good

This commonsense principle is the oldest behavior modification technique around: catch your child in the act of being good and praise him. Your grandmother probably used this technique; you may remember the warm feeling you got as a child when a parent or teacher recognized your good efforts. Yet this simple technique is often neglected. It's human nature to focus on the child's "bad" way of acting. Bad behavior draws more attention than good behavior. Parents and teachers are more likely to correct or punish misdeeds than they are to praise good ones. Studies show that parents and teachers are more likely to react negatively to children with A.D.D. than they are to children without A.D.D. To a certain degree this is defensible. Adults get worn down by the energy and persistence characteristic of these children's behavior. They jump on the negatives, while the positives, which may be infrequent, go unremarked.

Children must learn that good behavior is expected of them and that it is not always praised or rewarded. Yet they must also learn to like the way they feel when they behave well. Your praise and recognition will help them come to prefer behaving well, even when it's not easy. If bad behavior is the only kind that draws a parent's or teacher's attention, a child will have to behave badly just to get reassurance that someone notices what he does.

To use this technique, you may have to reshape your own behavior, especially if you and your child have developed a predominantly negative pattern of interactions (i.e., you're always saying no or telling him what he did "wrong"). Remarking on what your child did right may seem unnatural to you, especially if your parenting mind-set includes the fear that you will "spoil" your child if you are not always correcting him. Counting your positive and negative messages for a day can be a valuable exercise. Try the green counter/red counter technique described above (see page 93). You may be surprised by how many negative messages your child gets from you each day.

The good news is you can change these messages by practicing a few well-chosen words:

"Great job!"

"Way to go!"

"Yesss!"

"I like the way you used a lot of color in that picture."

"Thanks for helping with supper."

"That makes me happy."

Basically you are saying to the child, "I like you, I think you're great!" The child is getting a lot of positive messages from you in the form of genuine praise. And if your child feels that you like him, he will like himself.

Use Rewards That Work

Rewards capitalize on the pleasure principle: behavior that's rewarding continues; behavior that's unrewarding ceases. Pet trainers use this principle; so do dolphin trainers at Sea World. "Kid trainers" can use positive reinforcement, too. Yes, rewards are bribes. If the word "bribery" offends you, call them "incentives" or "motivators" instead. You may feel skeptical about reward systems, believing them to be external gimmicks that don't really change your child from within. To an extent this is a valid criticism, since the ultimate goal is to give the child inner motivation, and points or prizes alone will not accomplish this. But reward systems are useful as a starting point, especially when nothing else seems to be working. You can use a reward system to redirect a negative child and give him a taste of success. Eventually, the child gets used to the good feelings he gets from all those "points" or "treats." These good feelings then become the child's own *internal reward* and motivate continued good behavior. Eventually, you can reduce the

---

The Good-Behavior Candle

As a Cub Scout leader, here's a trick that Dr. Bill has used to hold the attention of a dozen rowdy nine-year-olds and keep them on task. At the beginning of the Cub Scout meeting a candle is lit, and as long as there are no disruptions the candle stays burning. As soon as someone disrupts the meeting, he must blow out the candle. Once the candle burns all the way down, the group gets a special treat. Naturally, it's in everyone's best interest to keep the candle lit, so the children help keep each other in line. You can adapt this technique to get jobs or homework completed or to improve table manners among siblings. Don't use this technique, however, if one child is going to be too frequently singled out.

external rewards and just rely on social rewards, like smiles and praise.

A child's behavior affects the parents' behavior. Undesirable behavior in children often leads to unrewarding behavior in the parents. You need to shift from that kind of negative spiral to a positive-feedback loop. Once your children see how much happier you are when they behave, your improved attitude is another social reward.

Choose the Right Reward System for Your Child

Which rewards work varies according to the personality and age of the child. Customize these suggestions to fit your family. Here are some general guidelines for working out a reward system for your child. Add your own finishing touches to these general principles.

- *Use social rewards more than material rewards.* Choose rewards that bring you and your child together to do something fun. You won't feel like you're a behavioral scientist in a laboratory dangling bits of cheese in front of little rats to guide them through the maze, and your child will see that your family values people more than things. Toy rewards are more popular with younger children. As your child gets older, either combine or replace them with social rewards. Keep the child connected to *people* (e.g., "This coupon is good for one lunch date with Mommy or Daddy" or "When you finish putting away your toys, we'll sit down and play a game together").

- *Let your child help choose the rewards.* "If you could choose some special place to go or some special thing to do, what would you choose?"

- *Choose immediate rewards.* Children with A.D.D. can't wait. Rather than promising a big treat at the end of a week of agreed-upon behavior, issue smaller rewards sooner. You are likely to get better results. The younger the child, the more frequent the payoff should be. Toddlers may need hourly, or at least daily, rewards; preschoolers, daily rewards; school-age children, weekly rewards; teenagers can hit the jackpot at the end of the month.

- *Use reward games that the child likes.* Remember, the child with A.D.D. tends to get bored with the same game. Change the game or change the way you play it, as needed.

- *Relate the reward to the behavior you want changed.* "When you show me you can keep your room tidy for a week, then we'll get the bedroom furniture for your dollhouse."

Should you take away points? When you're using positive reinforcement to shape behavior, it's important to give your child the message that nothing detracts from the good he has done. If you're making an effort to give your child positive instead of negative messages, you may not want to take points off the reward chart. For some children, the "two steps forward, one step back" nature of a give-and-take system may be too frustrating. Others respond well to give-and-take. Using give-and-take is more realistic in preparing your child for real life. Some actions produce positive effects, and others negative. Remember, sometimes there are positive lessons to learn from messing up.

Creative, Time-Tested Rewards That Work

These are systems that we have used in our own families or suggested to parents of children with A.D.D.

Tickets and tokens. Depending on the age and motivation of your child, you may have to give tokens once every few minutes, once an hour, or only at the end of the day. Tickets and tokens are particularly useful to keep the wandering little mind on task. Break up a job or a homework assignment into small parcels, and issue a "job done" ticket at the end of each step. Then present the child with a special double-value ticket once the goal is reached, when the homework or job is completed and done well.

Connect the dots. This technique provides small, frequent rewards to keep a child on task and a visual gauge of how much progress is made toward the long-term goal. After you have identified the change in behavior you want to see (e.g., "Each time you are dressed and ready for the school bus on time without my nagging"), have your child draw a picture (or draw it yourself, if your child is still a toddler) of the reward you have agreed on. It may be a bike, a toy boat, a doll, a ball, a special outing. Then use dots about an inch apart to outline the picture. With each instance of good behavior, the child connects two of the dots. When all the dots are connected, she collects the treat. You can also use this reward technique to remind children of their responsibilities. Each time they remember to put away their toys, clean up their room, or take out the trash, they can connect two dots. Focus on positive behavior (erasing lines doesn't work very well). Display the picture in a high-visibility location, such as on the refrigerator or on a kitchen cabinet, and at the child's height. This both reminds the child of the expected behavior and allows her to proudly display her progress.

Happy and sad faces. Make or buy stickers with happy and sad faces. A grumble, a "no," or any negative response to a parental request puts a sad face on the chart. Cooperation, a "yes," or another positive response merits a happy face. When happy faces outnumber the sad faces on a predetermined number of days, the child collects the prize. Do not use this approach unless you're sure the happy faces will prevail.

Happy hands. This motivator helps remind the child of responsibilities and provides rewards for jobs well done or for good behavior. Place your child's hands on a piece of paper and draw an outline, going around each finger. Above each finger write or draw a job to be done or a desirable behavior. The left hand could list morning jobs and the right hand after-school jobs. As the child does the jobs, he colors in each finger and gets a happy-face sticker above each fingertip. When both hands are filled in, your child gets a special treat for having "so many happy faces on happy fingers." You could also dub this game "Hands for remembering."

A behavior bus. Draw a big bus with square windows and write the job to be done or the behavior desired in each window. The goal is to get a happy-face sticker on each window. Once the bus is filled with happy faces, the bus drives on to get the prize.

Give-and-take systems. A reward system can be used to accomplish two goals: encourage desirable behaviors and get rid of undesirable ones. The give-and-take technique accomplishes both. Put a dime in the jar or a point on the chart for desirable behavior; take a dime out of the jar or a point off the chart for bad behavior. Or, starting the day with five dimes in the jar, you take one out for every "no" you get from your child and add one for every "yes." Just be careful you don't let your child get into a negative balance and end up owing. Generally, rewards are better than "response costs" — approaches in which negative behavior costs the child points.

Store success. Supermarket shopping and children with A.D.H.D. are not the best match. Even if you survive the trip up and down the aisles and manage to avoid the breakables and the junk food, waiting in the checkout line is bound to do you in. Appreciate a basic principle of behavior modification: if there is a major behavior you want to shape, begin with baby steps and progress gradually. Here's a sequence to set the child up for successful shopping.

• Begin with a small store and look in the window before entering to see if it's busy. If it is, come back at another time. Go into the store to purchase one item, say, a container of milk. Have the exact change ready when you enter the checkout line and have

---

Generalizing

Many children with A.D.D. have trouble transferring the rules learned in one situation to another situation; they have difficulty generalizing. Your child may know what she may not touch in your house, but don't expect her to respect the same "no touches" when she goes to Grandmother's house. She may, but don't count on it. You must make your rules exceptionally clear and simple and repeat them when changing situations. "Just like at home, we don't put our feet on the furniture at Grandmother's house."

---

your child pay the cashier. When the child leaves without whining and has behaved in the store according to the prearranged agreement, he gets a point and a reward. The next day go to the same store and get two or three items.

• Gradually increase the size of the store, the number of items, the number of points your child gets, and maybe even the size of the reward as his behavior improves.

• Finally, try the supermarket. Select the time of the day when your child is at his best, usually the morning. Tell him what you're going to be doing and the kind of behavior you expect in the store. Set up a point system on your shopping list. Write the items you need to purchase on your shopping list in one column and categories of good behavior on the other. You can assign a certain number of points for aisle behavior, checkout-counter behavior, and helping behavior. Agree on a reward before you enter the store and write it down and draw a picture of it on your shopping list. This prevents tantrums later. Let your child help pick out the items, and also let him check off each item on the list. As he does this, award points for good behavior. When you reach the checkout, your child will have earned his treat.

Jill, mother of five-year-old Andrew, came in to Dr. Bill's pediatric office for counseling and confided, "Our whole day is spent in conflict with each other. I find myself constantly saying no to him, and he's saying no to me. Andrew won't obey even when I ask him to do the simplest things. I find myself becoming a cranky mother, and I want to be a happy mother."

Dr. Bill suggested she try a reward system. "Tell Andrew exactly the behavior you want. Say to him: 'I want to be a happy Mommy, not a cranky Mommy. Let's try to have more yes days.'" Then Jill made a chart with Andrew to keep track of yeses and nos. She told him, "Every time I ask you to do something and you say, 'Yes, Mommy,' we'll put a 'yes' on the chart. At the end of the day, if there are more yeses than nos, that's a 'yes day,' and we'll do something special together." Soon Andrew realized that the happy Mommy was more fun to be with than the cranky Mommy, and they began to have "yes" days. Also, Jill found that Andrew absolutely hated to lose points, so occasionally she would add a "take-away" slant to the reward system. She began the day with a dish of ten dimes, and for each "no" she took one out. Varying the game and the approach held Andrew's interest and got more consistent results. Eventually, they were able to have "yes" days even without the chart and the reward.

Give Reminders

"She's twelve-years-old! Do I still have to remind her to brush her teeth?"

Reminders are words, pictures, checklists, or brief notes that jog children's lazy memories and keep them from forgetting rules or routines. Frequent verbal or visual cues can keep an active mind on task. You know from experience that your child is likely to get sidetracked on the way upstairs to brush her teeth, so when she reaches the landing, call out a gentle prompt, "Teeth." A certain look may remind the about-to-mess-up child that he knows better, or a short verbal cue can steer him toward the expected behavior ("Where do jackets go?"). Reminders can even be in the form of pictures. To remind him of what he has to take to school, help your child draw or paste a picture of a back-

pack on a piece of paper, and around it draw or paste pictures of items that go into the backpack each day. Tack this poster next to the door he uses in the morning.

Every child needs a few of these prompts every day. The child with A.D.D. just needs more of them. Reminders are more likely to be followed than a barrage of daily orders, because reminders don't provoke a power struggle. Your child already knows the rules. Your reminders just start the memory process going and prevent a behavior problem from occurring. As you enter the supermarket, say, for example, "Remember, we *walk* down the aisles."

"But I forgot." As lame as this excuse sounds, all children forget. Children with A.D.D. forget more often, so they need more reminders. During a particularly intense day your child may need hourly, sometimes minute-by-minute, reminders, using all the positive verbal and body language you can muster up: "I need your eyes," "You're forgetting . . . ," "You know what to do. . . ." Be sure the art of reminding doesn't deteriorate into the hassle of nagging. Keep your body language positive, your voice light and happy, and your manner more playful than authoritarian. Then your child is likely to perceive your constant prompts as help rather than nagging.

To avoid nagging, once your child can read, *write your reminders* in the form of little Post-it notes for your child. Try some humor: "Dress the bed, then dress yourself," "Your lunch is packed and in the refrigerator asking to be eaten." If you have an artistic flair, illustrate the notes.

Count Your Child

During your early disciplining, you may have frequently used countdowns, such as, "I'm going to count to three . . . ," expecting your child to behave positively by the time you hit three. Dr. Bill's four-year-old child "hops to" at just the mention of counting. She doesn't like to be "counted," preferring to behave on her own. She knows that once "three" comes, she's going to be physically assisted in cooperating, and she will do anything to avoid being picked up and carried like a baby. You can also teach your child to use counting to control his own impulsive behavior. Counting can be a cue to help him "think before he acts." Help him learn to do this by catching him in the act: "Before you throw the toy, count to five, and then imagine what might happen." The next time your child is about to act impulsively, issue a reminder, such as, "Count to five," or "Wait a minute," or "Imagine what might happen." Repeat these drills so that eventually he will be able to use this skill on his own before he acts.

Remember, one of the main challenges for children with A.D.D. is to teach them to "look before they leap." Teach your child to internalize his own counting drills and use them to control his impulsive behavior. Psychologists call this process of having an inner dialogue to guide behavior "internal verbal mediation." Teaching your child to have a dialogue with himself is a useful skill in developing self-control.

Card Your Child

This technique is a sort of warning system that gives your child time and space to change disruptive behavior before it gets worse. It also buys an angry, impulsive parent time to plan a gentler strategy. Get three cards, each a different color, and draw a face on each card — sad, sadder, and saddest. You can use these cards as they are, or you can glue a magnetic strip to the back of each one to stick them to the refrigerator. When your child begins a disruptive behavior, give him the first card or stick it on the refrigerator door. If the behavior continues, the second, sadder, card goes up. If this doesn't prompt him to change his behavior and you have not yet come up with a better strategy, the third and saddest card goes up. If your child is still misbehaving after all three warning faces are displayed, then it's time for time-out or, preferably, time-in (see below). One mother tried a very interesting variation on the three-card method. She let her son put the cards up for her, if she started yelling. She gave her son the message that we can learn from each other. Big people make mistakes, too, and they also must correct their errors.

Time-Out or Time-In?

We have noticed that for many children with A.D.D. (and other children, too), the classic "time-out" method of behavior modification doesn't work. Their anger escalates when they are sent to another room for a time-out, and they become resentful at being sent away. Time-out reinforces all the negative messages they are accustomed to receiving about themselves. This is why the time-in chair works better for many, especially for younger children. In time-in, the parent has the child sit in a chair or stand in a corner in the same room as the parent. The child must be silent for a short period of time, but is not isolated. This gives the message that although you will not tolerate the behavior, you are not rejecting your child. Children three and older can be given a count of three to sit down. If your child does not sit, state firmly the one-minute time-in is now two minutes. Repeat this procedure, raising the number of minutes until the child sits in the chair. Screaming or abusive arguing from the child while sitting adds minutes until it stops. You must decide beforehand how high you will go in time, three, five, ten, or fifteen minutes. Obviously, fifteen minutes is too long for younger children. We prefer short times, no more than five minutes. Once you reach that limit, shift to taking away something (see below). If the undesirable behavior persists after time-in, then begin over again with one minute in the chair, then two minutes, and so on until you again reach your limit, and then take away another thing.

With the time-in method, you don't have to carry, drag, or otherwise force your child upstairs or off to another room. Time-in also spares the child's room from being trashed out of anger and resentment. While the child is sitting in the time-in chair, stand next to him. This positioning makes it difficult for the child to suddenly move out of the chair. You may even stand behind your child with a hand firmly, but lovingly, on his shoulder. Or you may stand in front of him with your hand on his shoulder. (Be aware that some children with A.D.D. get upset if they are touched.) The child will find it difficult to get up out of his chair with you standing in front of him. Young children, and particularly young children with A.D.D., dislike doing nothing, even for a very short time. Time-in will get the corrective message across very quickly. One minute for each year of age is a good guideline for the length of a time-in. For more on using time-ins, see page 122.

Occasionally, parents may have to tell a child during a time-in that they are going to help him by holding him. This is truly gentle but firm holding, which reinforces closeness and caring, not anger and control. This can protect a child from throwing himself into an extreme temper tantrum in which he might hurt himself.

The teddy bear technique. With preschoolers, try the teddy bear technique.

When a child needs a time-in, have her put her teddy bear (or any other favorite doll or stuffed animal) in a chair. Then both of you can talk to the bear about behaving better. This bit of playacting uses time-in as simply a break in the action to allow her to think about her undesirable behavior and to change what she is doing. Time-in also gives parents a chance to cool off and plan a better discipline strategy.

The timer alternative. Use a kitchen timer. Tell your child he has to sit quietly for three minutes. Turn the dial on the timer to three minutes. If he fusses or doesn't sit down by the count of three, then start the timer again. Restart the three-minute time-in every time the child starts to argue. Children tend to respond to the demonstrative action of restarting the time-in period. Eventually some children, after acting out, go to their time-in seat and set the timer themselves.

Use Take-Aways

By the time your child is five years of age, you can increase time-ins to five minutes. But once you are at the five-minute mark, tell the child that you are going to take away something he likes (don't say what) if he doesn't be quiet and sit by the time you count to three. If he continues to be unruly, say, "Okay, I am now going to take away the first ten minutes of your favorite TV program, and we will start all over again." You don't tell him ahead of time what he is going to lose, because if you do, he will often just snap back that he doesn't want what you threatened to take away anyway. Think ahead to what's coming in your day and use it for ammunition. If you were planning to make Play-Doh, now that won't happen. Leave yourself with a lot of ammunition. The privilege you take away should be small. Don't take away a bicycle for a week for a relatively minor infraction.

If he tries to bargain, "Mom, I'll be quiet and do whatever you asked in the first place if you let me watch my whole TV program!" remind him, "No, we don't bargain; you know that when I say something, that's it. But if you cooperate now, you will not lose any more things that you like. I know you are really a helpful boy and that you are just mad right now."

Once your child has calmed down and is able to listen, even if only briefly, ask, "What would you like to do when we are through?" This can help change your interaction into a positive one. When he is in the middle of the storm, say nothing at all or a word or two at the most. Talking to the child at these times only adds fuel to the fire.

"I'm Going to Do It with You." Here's a technique to try that stops short of taking away privileges. If your child is not doing what you've asked, try counting to three. If this doesn't work, say to him, "Do it, or I am going to help you do it!" Use a stern voice as if your doing it with him is a very significant happening. Count to three again, and then act by taking his arm or hand and doing the task that was to be done. This method avoids the trap of repeating your request over and over again and the need to make threats about taking things away. It works, in part, because children like to do things themselves and partly because your stern tone has conveyed some urgency.

Visualizing Time and Privileges

Many young children do not yet have a good understanding of the concept of time, so they may not understand what it means to lose ten minutes of television time. Here's a

way to make this concept less abstract. Use a simple horizontal row of squares. These squares may represent periods of time. You could also use them to represent different activities or privileges, if taking away privileges is the concept you're trying to demonstrate. Draw the privilege in each square. When the child does not do what she is supposed to do, cross the squares out to show that something has been taken away.

Mary, a hyperactive four-year-old, loved to go to the park and be pushed on the swing. Her mother said, "Mary, before we go to the park, I want you to put your toys away." This was not a difficult job; Mary's shelves had pictures on them that showed where each toy belonged.

Mary's mother created a little chart to represent units of time and used a timer that would ring every five minutes. Every time it rang, Mary would lose one time square on the chart. The chart and timer gave Mary's mother a way to show Mary that when she dawdled, got distracted, or didn't put her toys away, she would not get to stay as long at the park. Mary caught on to this way of conceptualizing time quite quickly and understood that the more squares that were crossed off, the less time she would have at the park. As the diagram on the facing page illustrates, Mary lost two time frames. At this point, she became motivated to put her toys away so that she could still get to the park and play.

When Mary grew older, her mother made a big circular chart like a clock, with twelve segments representing five minutes each. This chart was another way to help Mary understand the concept of time. If Mary misbehaved, her mother would count to three and then Mary would lose five minutes of some favorite activity. [When you

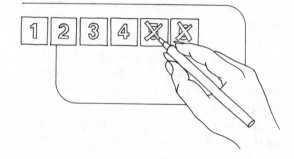

done), but she did join with Mary and help her through whatever it was that was bothering her so that no further playtime would be lost. This became a positive reinforcement for Mary's not dawdling any longer and gave Mary a positive feeling about herself for succeeding.

In setting up this system, Mary's mother was careful about making sure Mary understood how the chart and the timer worked. She stated clearly to Mary (eye to eye, firmly, in as few words as possible) what she must do. Then she asked Mary to repeat back to her what she had said. The first couple of times she used the system, she made sure she explained each step again. Mary knew exactly what would happen.

Keep these tips in mind when you try this method:

1. Make sure your child really understands what she is supposed to do.
2. Tell your child simply and exactly what will be lost if she doesn't do what she is supposed to do.
3. Give her a count of three to do what she is supposed to do (or give her a few minutes on the timer, depending on the task).
4. If she doesn't do what she is supposed to do, remove one time segment and tell her that she has another count of three (or another few minutes on the timer). If she still doesn't do what she is supposed to do, remove a second square, and so on.

You can use this simple chart to take away little things, but please be sure they are very small. Visualizing what they are losing, step by step, can be quite powerful for children. This is especially so if they have helped draw the diagram. Other activities to take away be-

take something away, appear confident that it is something meaningful to your child, no matter what your child may say about its worth.]

Mary continued to fool around and not put her toys away. Her mother said, "The timer just went off; you've lost the first part of your time on your tricycle," and she showed Mary what this looked like on the chart. After the timer went off again, Mary's mother said, "You've now lost two parts of your time on your tricycle. I think you may want to put your toys away so you can still have some time riding your tricycle before supper."

Mary said, "I don't care. I don't want to ride anyway."

Her mother responded, "I know you really do want to ride, and we still have lots of time, as you can see on the chart. Here, I'll help you a bit and we can do it together. That way, you'll still have some time on your tricycle."

In this example, Mary's mother picked up on the fact that, for whatever reason, Mary was not in a good mood, and sensed that this conflict was likely to end up a battle royal. So she made a fast decision. She didn't give back the time lost (that was already said and sides playtime include TV time, video game time, or, with older children, telephone time.

Use Consequences to Curb Impulsiveness

Choices have consequences, and children must learn this. Because of their impulsiveness, children with A.D.D. are less likely to think before acting. They act before considering the consequences. Making wise choices in life begins with learning one basic lesson: "Think through what you're about to do."

Here are some exercises to help impulsive children think before acting and imagine the consequences of what they do before they do it.

"When . . . Then . . ."

Plant the idea early that actions have consequences. By age three a child is able to remember and reflect on prior instructions.

No Excuses

A.D.D. is no excuse for not disciplining disruptive, bratty behavior. Don't blame all behavior on biology. Regardless of the label on a child, parents are still responsible for discipline and, more important, for teaching children to discipline themselves. After all, your child has to learn to live in your home and in society and to adapt to life and learning situations that may not always be so accommodating to him. The tag "A.D.D." actually increases the parents', the school's, and the child's responsibilities. There are greater challenges to meet, and there is more to learn about how to manage behavior and learning.

You may have to tell your two-year-old over and over again not to run into the street. By three the child is able to store these instructions in his memory bank and make them part of his operating code. By three a child can also understand the concept of consequences ("When I do this, that happens"). You can reinforce this way of thinking by using the "when . . . then" formula:

> "*When* your teeth are brushed, *then* we'll begin the story."

> "*When* you finish your homework, *then* you can go out to play."

"When . . . then" is especially useful for small children, since you describe the events in the order in which they will happen.

Be sure to use "when" rather than "if." "When" is more positive and tells your child the behavior you expect; "if" suggests a choice you don't really mean to offer.

Learning from Mistakes

Experience is the best teacher, and it's often the one that makes the greatest impression. Children with A.D.D. often have to learn "the hard way." If, despite your guidance, your child still chooses the wrong path, let him experience the consequences and learn from them (as long as there's no danger). For example, your child leaves his tricycle in the driveway, despite repeated admonitions to store it in the garage, and the bicycle gets backed over by a car. Let him go without a bike for a while. Or, your child is dawdling despite your frequent reminders that he is late for his baseball game. He sits on the bench for the first two innings.

Imagining the Consequences

Help your child imagine what the consequences of a particular action might be. Natural consequences that you have not arranged are happening in everyday life. You can also set up parent-made consequences, customized for a particular situation, that you hope will have lasting learning value. Here is a logical consequence that parents in Dr. Bill's pediatric practice tried.

Judy and Tom had just moved into a new house, and their four-year-old son, Aaron, had his own room. He was feeling very proud and grown-up enjoying the privacy of his new room, but door slamming was becoming a problem, especially when he got angry. His parents repeatedly told him that slamming the door was annoying and had to stop. If it didn't, he would no longer enjoy the privacy of having a door. His dad would remove it. Aaron got a "Yeah, sure, Dad's going to take the door off" look of disbelief on his face. He continued to slam the door over the next day, so when he went out to play, off came the door. A week later Tom put the door back on, and it hasn't been slammed since.

Letting children experience the natural consequences of their own mistakes often has more lasting benefits than logical consequences you manufacture, since kids may perceive parental consequences as threatening or believe you are bluffing and really won't carry through. When you do threaten consequences, you must carry through or your credibility will be lost in the future. Natural consequences are valuable to the child because they make sense. Children have a keen sense of justice and look for a logical connection between the "crime" and the "punishment." With natural consequences the punishment naturally fits the crime.

It is important to teach Tony responsibility. He loves to blame someone or something else for anything he has or hasn't done. Basically, I put on the training wheels and then take them off when I think he is strong. He falls sometimes, but I let him experience the natural consequences of not having done or remembered something. When he forgot to tell me about the pizza lunch at school and get the necessary money, he had to eat his sandwiches.

Learning Empathy

This concept is a biggie. Because of their impulsiveness, children with A.D.D. don't realize beforehand that their actions may have consequences for another person. They don't stop to think about how that other person may feel. This seeming lack of caring gets them misunderstood, mislabeled, and just plain in trouble. Some children with A.D.D. lag behind others in moral development. They do not grasp the concept of empathy at an appropriate age. They tend to be very egocentric and to see things from their own point of view. Although their own feelings may be easily hurt, they do not show a reciprocal regard for the feelings of others. They will often complain that someone was "unfair" if that person did not see things their way. They may not show the flexibility necessary to go along with other people's ideas. It is hard to get them to shift to seeing others' viewpoints, so it's best to start teaching empathy early.

You can counteract this egocentric tendency by focusing extra attention on teaching empathy to your child. The first and most important way you teach empathy is by example. When you respect and make an effort to understand your child's feelings, you are also showing him how you expect him to treat others. This is far more effective than lectures. You can model empathy in other relationships, too: "Grandma is feeling sad today. What can we do to cheer her up?" Teaching empathy also means helping your child understand that his deeds have consequences for others. Tell him about the feelings you have as a result of his actions ("That makes me feel . . ."). Be sure he makes the connection that positive behaviors from him result in positive feelings in others, and negative behaviors result in negative feelings ("I sure like it when you . . ." or "I feel angry when you . . ."). Notice we don't say, "You make me so mad." Help your child get behind the eyes of other people, especially those on the receiving end of his behavior. Give your child practice in thinking about his own and others' feelings: "Do you think she feels sad?" "How would you feel if someone hit you?" Look for the "teachable moments" that crop up nearly every day and give you an opportunity to help your child learn empathy.

One day Dr. Bill saw two eight-year-old neighbor boys perched on the hillside ready to toss water balloons onto cars passing below. Obviously, these children had not thought about the effect of their behavior on the drivers of the cars. This was a teachable moment. He sat down with them and asked them to imagine what they would feel as the driver of a car if a water balloon exploded on their window. They needed to learn to put themselves in someone else's driver's seat. An accumulation of many such lessons over time will truly "put the child in the driver's seat" in terms of being in control of their behavior. You want them to get to the point where they think through what the consequences will be for others rather than being totally focused on their own immediate fun or needs. You may hear that children with A.D.D. are at increased risk for sociopathic behavior, or just plain for winding up in jail. Statistically, this is true. Yet the main quality that separates the child who uses his traits to

society's advantage from the one who gets into big trouble is the quality of empathy — the ability to understand and sympathize with the feelings of another.

Getting a family pet proved to be a good start for teaching my kids caring behaviors.

Give Responsibilities

Giving your child responsible jobs to do is a powerful way to shape behavior. Responsibilities give children direction. When they have jobs to do, they have fewer opportunities for bad behavior. Adults often find their value in their work. They call it "being of use." Children who are given chores feel they are part of a group. They are depended upon, and they are valued by the family. The child with A.D.D., in particular, needs to feel busy and needs to be on the move. Give your child special jobs. The word "special" is a good marketing tool and is likely to promote cooperation. Try these tips:

- Give the preschool child jobs around the house: dusting, tearing lettuce for a salad, setting the table, helping with dishes.
- Give the school-age child jobs around the house: laundry, helping with the cooking, and packing lunches.
- Create job charts: some jobs might be for pay; others for the privilege of living in the family. Give genuine praise for a job well done. Working alongside children is a useful way to keep them on task.

Withdraw Privileges

Besides all the "gives" that shape behavior, taking away luxuries is another way to keep the child on track. For this technique to have the desired result, it's important that children not view it as a punishment. If done correctly, what's taken away should be a logical or natural consequence of the child's actions: "If you ride your bicycle without a helmet, you lose the use of your bicycle for two days." Remember to withdraw privileges, not the necessities of life. You don't deprive the child of a meal or a warm winter jacket, but turning off the TV has never caused lasting harm. Losing privileges teaches the child realistic lessons for later in life: privileges are based on responsibility (e.g., If you want to keep your credit card, you must pay the bills).

Withdrawing privileges works best as a behavior shaper if you have worked out with your child beforehand a mutually agreed-upon consequence: "After you finish your homework, you may watch TV." Then, if he does not finish his homework, he already knows that he will not be watching television. As your child gets older, the stakes get higher. With increasing maturity come greater responsibilities, which bring greater privileges; however, neglecting these responsibilities brings more serious consequences.

I had to see things from his perspective to truly understand Matthew's difficulties. To be fair to him, I had to have compassion, but I also had to make him accountable for what he did — every time. Otherwise, he would never learn to live in a world that wouldn't be as understanding as his parents.

Make Contracts

Children who have A.D.D. need to have their good behavior acknowledged more than other children do. You can use contracts as positive, fun, point-earning games that allow you to keep your child's behavior on track. Contracts make your expectations clear to your child and also teach your child that he will be rewarded for following through. He earns points according to a plan that is laid out in advance. Making a contract, sticking to it in order to earn points, and saving points for something worthwhile are all valuable experiences for children who are very impulsive and want what they want "right now!"

Like most older children with A.D.D., Rebecca was notorious for finding loopholes in rules, so we had a contract that stated specifically what each checklist item meant. For example, "get dressed" meant wearing clean clothes appropriate to the day of the week and weather, with a belt if she had belt loops. "Do the silverware" meant making sure it was free of food before putting it in the dishwasher. "Showering" meant washing with soap and shampooing her hair. We sat down and went over each item so that she knew exactly what was expected of her. We kept the contract handy for reference, and this avoided misunderstandings and arguments.

The two sides of a contract. Dr. Lynda has parents make charts as a way of drawing up clear contracts with school-age children. On the parent's side of the contract is the promise to give points, which will add up to a reasonable reward within a reasonable period of time. The time period could be a few days, a week, or a month, depending on the reward. On the child's side of the contract is an agreement to carry out certain chores and household and homework routines and perhaps not to do certain other things. Even young children understand that mom and dad must do certain things at work and are then paid for doing them.

Step 1: Discuss the System with Your Child

When you are making a contract with your child, sit down in a pleasant environment where there are no distractions. Make sure you do it at a time when your child isn't in a rush, wanting to go out with his friends! Tell your child clearly and directly that you are very happy with some behaviors and name these. Then tell him that you are not happy with certain behaviors and name these specifically. Make sure you emphasize the good things your child does and also firmly tell your child that you want to see an immediate change in the behaviors that you are going to put on the chart.

Ask your child what he would like to earn as a reward. Make sure that he is also included in choosing most of the behaviors for which he can earn points. Make your discussion really upbeat. The conversation might run something like Peggy's with her twelve-year-old son, Jay.

"I really like most of the things you do. I want to make a list of some of the good things and let you earn points for doing these things. You can save the points to get rewards, which you can choose. You can choose rewards from the store or you can choose to go to some special place with a friend.

"Although I'm happy about most things, I'm also unhappy about how you some-times speak to me and about a few of the things you do. [She grouped these things in a short, neat, well-organized list.] You can earn rewards for not doing these things. I'm going to make it even more fun by letting you do a series of things without my nag-ging at you. When you do the whole series you can call me to 'inspect.' You will get a point for each thing you have done, and, if

they are all done, you get two extra bonus points and you can play or watch TV. The faster you get things done, the longer you have to play!"

Step 2: Put the Desired Behaviors on the Chart

Children with A.D.D. have trouble carrying out a sequence of tasks. Therefore, your con-tract should demand that a short series of jobs or behaviors be completed without your intervening. Because Jay would dawdle and forget to do things before and after school and in the evening, Peggy made *sequences of behaviors.* She wanted her son to do a series of tasks on his own without her nagging him over each one. She wanted him to learn to be in charge of his own behaviors, to internalize controls. Besides the points he was awarded for completing tasks, once Jay finished any sequence and called for his mother to review his work, he could turn the TV on, have a snack, or play. Peggy had brought a blank chart to her meeting with her son. After they had made their list together, they entered all the behaviors on the chart. After they filled it out together, their chart looked like the one on pages 114 and 115. Customize your chart to fit your family and your goals. For ex-ample, initially you could target just one time of the day.

Step 3: Change the Reward System Frequently

From time to time Peggy and her son, Jay, changed the way the chart worked to keep it interesting. For a while they made each point worth a small amount of money. The points became extra allowance at the end of the week. At the end of the week all the points over an agreed-upon amount (e.g., 200 points) were worth a special bonus (e.g., 10 times the original point value). For example, if Jay got 210 points, the extra 10 over 200 would be worth 100 (10 × 10). If the value of each point was 2¢, then the first 200 points would have an allowance value of $4. The 10 points over the 200 mark would have a value of $2 (2 × 100), which would go into a *joint bank account* (helping Jay to learn about saving) with his mom or dad to be used later for agreed-upon constructive items. This huge bonus turned out to be a tremendous motivator. Jay got his favorite new skates that winter. Peggy also decided that "recreational electricity" (i.e., TV and video games) had to be earned. Points could be used for this rather than for extra allowance.

On another occasion, Jay and his mom decided it would be fun to have a five-day rule for each item. This meant that checking off any item for five days in a row would mean a bonus of 10 points. This rule provided a psychological boost. Any time Jay messed up for a couple of days, he could think of the next day as a fresh start on another series of five checks in a row.

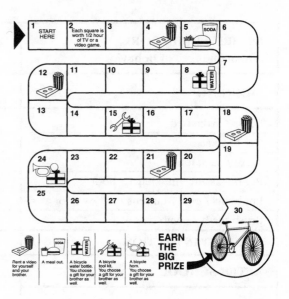

Step 4: Add a Second Chart

Children who have A.D.D. often like complicated charts. Complexity offers more action and keeps them interested. A chart can resemble a path that pictures the prize your child wants to earn. Instead of money, Jay saved points to earn something he really wanted, a new bike. Jay and his father went to the bike store and got a picture of the bike he wanted — a beautiful red mountain bike. On the picture they carefully drew a path and cut the picture into 30 pieces. They drew another path on cardboard, where the pieces could be stuck on as they were earned, one piece for every 100 points on his regular chart. It took about three months to fill in the puzzle and earn the bike. It was Jay's idea that whenever he earned anything he would also get his younger brother a small prize. This was a wonderful addition to the system, and Peggy made sure that Jay knew how much she and his dad respected him for thinking of his little brother. The numbers in

---

Benefits of Charts

1. Charts help your child build a positive self-image.
2. Your child will know that you really do notice the constructive things he does.
3. Charts motivate your child to organize and complete his assignments.
4. Charts decrease the need for reprimands, which tend to reinforce a negative self-image.
5. Charts nurture good habits, which will transfer to the school situation.
6. Charts teach your child to be responsible for himself.

DESIRED BEHAVIOR* and Sequences of Behavior	Day 1	Day 2	Day 3	Day 4	Day 5	Day 6	Day 7
MORNING							
Dress / make bed							
Get breakfast							
Make / pack lunch							
Put books, etc., into bag by door							
Put boots / coat / mittens / hat by door							
Brush teeth / comb hair							
PARENT INSPECTION							
AFTER SCHOOL							
Get home by 4:30							
Put clothes / boots away							
Show Mom or Dad homework book							
Agree on evening homework schedule							
Agree on the "hourly product" (what must be accomplished by the end of each hour of study / homework)							
PARENT INSPECTION							
AFTER DINNER							
Clear table							
Take turn doing dishes							
Finish homework							
Study / review							
Call Mom or Dad to check product after each hour of homework or study (2 extra points for each half hour if "product" completed)[†]							
Sport (1 point for each hour)							
Music (1 point for each half hour practice)							
Club (Cub Scouts; 1 point for each session)							
PARENT INSPECTION							

DESIRED BEHAVIOR* and Sequences of Behavior	Day 1	Day 2	Day 3	Day 4	Day 5	Day 6	Day 7
BEFORE BED							
Put clothes in laundry bag							
Brush teeth							
Call for story							
PARENT INSPECTION							
OTHER POINTS							
Before School: • Be cooperative and helpful							
• Listen and answer politely							
After School: • Be cooperative and helpful							
• Listen and answer politely							
Evening: • Be cooperative and helpful							
• Listen and answer politely							
All times: • Answer phone politely and write a message neatly							
TOTALS							

* *The behaviors in this list are Peggy's selections. Make your own list with your child.*

† *Some children with A.D.D. need checks every 20 minutes. Some may even require a parent to sit next to them while they do their work.*

the boxes tell the order in which the squares are to be filled in.

Step 5: Keep Your Child Motivated

To earn a big prize takes a long time. (Help your child figure out about how long it will take.) The smaller rewards take only a few days to a week to be earned.

You can change the number of points needed to fill in each square and the number of squares in the puzzle to fit your own situation. Perhaps you can find a poster rather than a magazine picture to put up for your puzzle. High-frequency reward systems are better for children who are impatient and hyperactive and who find it hard to wait for the big prize.

Step 6: Let Your Child Do the Charting

At first you may have to fill in the chart with your child. Gradually allow him to take over doing it all for himself and reward him for this. This internalizes a positive habit and gives responsibility instead of encouraging him to think, "Can I trick my parents?" This negative habit of trying to put one over on someone is what people often develop when authority and control are completely external. You want your child to develop internal controls, so you must encourage the normal, healthy process of letting him take over tasks his parents used to do for him. If your child gets bored and is not filling in the chart regularly, you can carry on the charting for an interim period of time. You take on this task in a very upbeat fashion with a statement such as, "I want you to know that your father and I see all the good things that you are doing, so I am going to continue filling in the chart for you. You may continue to earn things. When you feel that you are able to start filling it in again, like older kids do, then you will get

bonus points for each day that you take care of the charting."

Step 7: Focus on One Behavior

Often parents tell us that there is one behavior that is just so irritating that it is upsetting the whole family system. The optional "rule of the month" charting method can be used to put a huge emphasis on that one behavior. You give a lot of extra rewards for the positive behavior that will substitute for the one that is driving you crazy. For example, you may choose talking back, speaking rudely, or

Controls from Within

"Internal control" means that your child is remembering what he should do and is getting it done on his own. You don't nag. Internal control is essential by the time your child reaches adolescence or you as a parent are going to find yourself in a rather helpless position. You will still be trying to lay down rules and control your child's behavior at a time when it is really not possible for you to do this. You cannot possibly be with him all the time. You are not allowed legally to impose any physical restraint. Your "child" is far too large for you to stop him from doing whatever it is he decides to do anyway! In today's North American society, you are not going to receive coordinated community support to control an acting-out adolescent. You really must establish internal controls in your child long before the teenage years. You had best start this process in the preschool years. Charting sequences of behaviors is one good way of nurturing controls within your child.

being silly and rambunctious. With school-age children, write a short contract that you both sign. Hang this contract on the refrigerator. Sam's parents used this method to stop his whining and argumentative behavior.

Sam's mother asked him to put away his toys and wash his hands because supper was ready. Sam wanted to play longer and said, "Aw, Mom. Can't I play longer?" His mother responded that she had given him a five-minute warning and now he was to do as she said and come to supper. Sam whined, "Awww, come on, Mom. Alex never has to do this. Can't I just finish building my plane? Just a couple of minutes and I'll have this finished. You never let me play. After supper it's homework."

That night, Sam's mom and dad agreed that this kind of behavior always ended up with them nagging, Sam screaming, and everybody feeling tense and unhappy. It was just no fun! They decided that the behavior chart had worked a bit, but now they wanted to really emphasize this one behavior. They wanted Sam to respond promptly to what they requested of him. They told Sam that they wanted to make obeying a request immediately (such as coming right away when called) the most important behavior to get rewards. They told him they were going to discuss this at the next Sunday family meeting.

That Sunday they made a couple of large posters with really funny cartoons of things Sam had done, with Mom flying off the handle and Dad doing silly antics. They made obeying the rule of the month simple. First, if Mom or Dad raised their hand like a traffic officer's stop signal and looked him in the eye, Sam had to stop whining and arguing immediately. They practiced this with Sam, getting him to stop

in mid-sentence. If he did stop, he got 5 points on the chart. Second, they agreed that if Sam was called for a meal, he was to come before a one-minute timer bell went off. If he did this, he got another 3 points on his chart. They made it very worthwhile for him to obey rapidly. If he uttered only one further sentence of argument after the stop sign, then he would still get 2 points. Mom and Dad also got charts. If either of them raised their voice at another family member, then the other person could put up a hand. If the parent stopped immediately and went back to a normal tone of voice, he or she got 5 points. [What can parents spend points on? Mom got to choose the movie when she and Dad went out. Dad got to watch Monday night football.]

Note that Sam's parents didn't ask for Sam's opinion when choosing the behavior for their most important rule of the month. However, on Sunday at the family meeting, they tried to leave some other things open for him to decide, and Sam changed a couple of these things. He changed the points so that he would get 7 points if he came on the run in less than one minute and increased his reward to 5 points if he just made it under the wire in two minutes. His parents made the rule fun by putting up humorous signs with neat drawings, which they had made with Sam to remind him to run and gets lots of points. They went to a store where they could purchase timers cheaply and let him buy two of them, one to set at one minute and the other to set at two minutes.

Step 8: Set Reasonable Goals and Time Frames

Set goals that make it possible for your child to achieve at least an 80-percent success rate.

You want to keep the system rewarding and encouraging. Sam's parents soon found that one minute was a little short to get to dinner, and they agreed with Sam to extend the time limits to 2 minutes and 3 minutes.

If Sam's parents had wanted to decrease some behavior that was harder to define, such as yelling at his sister, then they would have had to find ways to define and measure "no yelling." They would have had to put precise measures in place (e.g., any argument that lasts more than a count of 3 means no reward). Then they would have had to choose small, easily defined time frames for the yelling not to occur such as the following:

- wake-up to breakfast
- breakfast to mid-morning snack
- mid-morning snack to lunch
- lunch to mid-afternoon snack
- mid-afternoon snack to dinner
- dinner to bedtime

Who judges behavior? Just like a referee in a game, the parent is the only judge of whether or not a behavior fulfills the contract. Your child may discuss issues with a parent, but he may not argue. After being silent for a defined period of time, children may then request a discussion. It is very important for you as a parent to show genuine respect toward your child and your child's opinions. Reassure your children that if they accept your decision graciously, you will sit down with them later and listen to their explanation. If your child is even partially correct and explains why in a quiet, polite manner, you should reward that behavior immediately.

Beware of undermining the system. Will grandmother's giving your child gifts interfere with the chart system? Perhaps. Overly generous grandparents and other friends and relatives can undermine the chart system. If this threatens to happen in your family, then you must take firm control. Except for Christmas and birthdays, request that all family members (extended family, too) give your child things only through the chart system. Dr. Lynda has seen children who knew they could always have anything they wanted just by asking their grandmother. The chart gave the parents of these children a way to take control of a situation that was teaching children poor attitudes and producing a great deal of family tension. Children feel proud of earning rewards. The bicycle that takes months to earn will be better cared for than the one that comes as a matter of course the first time it is asked for.

Foster cooperation, not competition. It is better to foster cooperation and "earning for each other" in these charting systems than to encourage competition in the family — there is lots of room for healthy competing in sports and games. If you are going to use charts, avoid having one child feeling singled out by making one for each child and even one for one or both parents. Make each child's chart unique both in the items listed and in the shape and gimmick of the chart (e.g., triangle ski mountain, soccer ball circle, piano keyboard, car, doll, etc.). Use your ingenuity to make sure every child feels like a winner most of the time.

COMMUNICATION STRATEGIES: TALKING WITH CHILDREN WHO HAVE DIFFICULTY LISTENING

Whether your child complies or defies often depends on how you phrase your request.

Children with A.D.D. require clear, concise instructions, presented in a way that will sink in. Here are some helpful ways to communicate with the child who has A.D.D. Actually, all children will benefit from these communication strategies; families of children with A.D.D. need to use them more consistently.

I believe in bringing up "reporters," (what some people would label "tattletales"). They know I will listen, understand, and help. This means others can't scare them into silence. My children tell me more than I would like to know sometimes, but I realize what a gift this is. It is something I have succeeded in doing right with them.

Use a nice voice. Remember when your three-year-old headed off into a whining session, and you sidetracked him by calmly saying, "Give Mommy your nice voice"? It worked! Model a nice voice. Here are some voice lessons for you to try:

- *Lower your tone.* A high-pitched voice irritates and turns off listeners.
- *Speak slowly.* Speaking too fast causes your child to tune out.
- *Be brief.* Use simple words and simple sentences; otherwise, your child may become parent-deaf.

Refuse to listen to a child who yells. Say, "When you can speak in a friendlier tone [or "nice voice"], come back and we'll try again." Respect is contagious. If you model it as something you expect, your child will learn that everyone should be respected, including himself.

Talking to Teens

Take a tip from Socrates, the Greek philosopher who asked questions rather than giving answers and advice. He believed he could draw out the answers to peoples' dilemmas from inside the persons themselves by directing their thinking with questions.

Your teenager doesn't think that wearing her bicycle helmet is cool. If you order her to wear her helmet, she'll probably ditch it after she's out of sight. Instead, start her thinking: "Why do you think there is a helmet law? What do you imagine could happen to your head if you were knocked off your bicycle?" If she doesn't know, ask your physician to tell her about some of his head-injury cases.

Try to get your daughter to decide on her own that it's sensible to wear her helmet because of her own safety, her family, society (health-care costs), and her friends, and so that she can set a safe example for her younger siblings. Children are more likely to remember what they figure out for themselves rather than what their parents tell them. However, for particularly resistant teens, when it comes to safety matters, you may have to pull rank. "These are the family rules. I expect you to obey. You've got a whole life ahead of you, and you're going to need a healthy head. It's a great head, protect it. Otherwise, the bicycle stays in the garage." If she really doesn't care what happens to her head, she may be depressed and need professional treatment.

Settle yourself first. Talk to yourself before you unload on your child. When you're angry and upset, you'll show these feelings to your child, causing him to withdraw or react to your feelings and miss what you are trying to say. Get your emotions and body language under control before saying a word. This is not an easy thing for people who are excitable, reactive types to do. Stop and think about how your child sees you when you are steaming under the collar or in various stages of actually exploding. To a child, it is an alarming sight, and it will set off in him a "fight or flight" response. Either way he won't be able to learn. Consider counseling for yourself if you are unable to switch out of this mode.

Settle your child. Your child cannot process your directives if he's upset. Calm your child until he is settled enough to be receptive to what you have to say. Show him how to take a deep breath. Let him count to ten, take a time-out to cool down, or take a walk around the block. This will be easy for him if he sees you model this coping skill when you get upset.

Looks speak louder than words. Your child is receiving messages even before you open your mouth. Your facial expressions and gestures can either open the child up to what you have to say or turn him off completely. If your body language says confrontation, don't expect cheerful compliance from your child. Use the "I mean business look" when you do. Your raised eyebrow reminds her that she's off track and is not to proceed with this behavior. But be sure to give approving messages as well: a smile, a nod, a happy face, an arm around the shoulder — all conveying praise for a job well done.

Nonverbal Versus Verbal Communication

Children pick up on nonverbal messages (tone of voice, your posture, and so on) more quickly than they process the words you speak, and they attach more importance to the nonverbal message. Young children listen with their gut feelings. They will "hear" your true message even when it is disguised in words that mean something else. Try to be aware of what you are really thinking and feeling before you use words to communicate with your child. The thoughtful communicator often teaches through questions. Questions encourage reflection, consideration, and respect. Despite knowing the answers to many of the questions being asked, the thoughtful communicator asks questions in a tone of voice that reveals an honest spirit of inquiry. The tone is honest because the true master communicator is always willing and ready to learn something new from the student (child) and is listening intently to every aspect of the child's answer.

Connect before you direct. With young children, get down to the child's eye level. Engage your child in eye-to-eye, hand-to-shoulder contact. Begin this even when talking with toddlers. "Mary, I need your eyes." "Tommy, I need your ears." With practice you will learn how to engage your child *appropriately* — not so intense a gaze that you make your child uncomfortably withdraw, yet engaging enough to hold your child's attention, show her you really care, and underline the importance of what you have to say. An observant teacher and mother of a child with A.D.D. related this connecting tip: Children can take more in when you're on their dominant side. If you don't know which it is, assume it's the right side (left for left-handers). Every little bit helps.

Dr. Bill notes: As a Little League coach, to get the attention of wandering little minds and eyes, I sit the team in the dugout and say, "I need your eyes. I need your ears."

Some teens perceive eye-to-eye contact as controlling rather than connecting, so you may find a more willing listener while you're doing dishes or driving together rather than in face-to-face conversation.

Use "I" messages. Try nonthreatening openers. Begin your request with "I" or "we" instead of "you." Instead of "You left your dirty dishes on the counter again," try "We put our dishes in the dishwasher so the counter stays neat." Or instead of "You never put your things away," try "I am so tired of tripping over this skateboard." "I" messages do not place blame, so they take pressure off the child and draw him into having empathy with another's point of view. "You" messages put the child on the defensive, so that he's likely to clam up or fight you. "I" messages give him a gentle reminder to think through how his actions affect others. "I felt great when I came into the kitchen and the counter was clear." "I like it when you take out the garbage without being asked." "I felt relieved when you left a note saying what time you would be home."

Try the sandwich technique. The first slice of bread is a compliment; then feed your child the meat of the sandwich — that is, the point you're trying to make; the second slice

of bread is another pleasant, positive statement. For example, say "The cover on your homework project looks terrific. The teacher will want you to explain more fully in words what you've drawn so beautifully. I know you have some great ideas."

Avoid negative words. Refrain from undermining your compliments. If you say, "The cover on your project looks terrific, *but* you didn't finish the writeup," the "but" statement cancels out your positive opener. Give your child time to process your compliment, then state your directive positively: "Now, let's finish the writing."

Whenever possible, I try to tell Ezra what to do instead of what not to do. Instead of saying "Don't get out of your chair until you are done," I say, "You're going to sit in your chair until we're done."

Value your child's viewpoint. Some children with A.D.D. are verbally hyperactive ("motor mouths"), and parents may tune them out. Teens especially are put off when they perceive that you don't appreciate their viewpoint. You don't have to agree — often you won't — but your child expects you at least to listen. Try restating her point of view so she knows you've listened. Children with A.D.D. need to know that their viewpoint is valued.

Legs first, mouth second. It's time for dinner and you call, "Turn off the TV and come for dinner!" Some children will immediately come, especially if they are hungry. The child with A.D.D., on the other hand, is probably in a state of hyperfocus in front of Nintendo or *Home Improvement*. Instead of hollering at him, walk into the room and watch the program with him for a few minutes. Then during a break in the action, tell him, "It's time for dinner," and have him turn off the TV. Joining with and then redirecting is a good method for helping with any shift in activity.

Give advance notice. Children with A.D.D. do not make transitions well. Because they are egocentric, they do not willingly switch from their agenda to yours. If they are in the state of hyperfocus, they have difficulty complying with your desires. If you are planning a family activity, tell your child the day before or that morning rather than suddenly springing it on him. If your child is deeply involved in his play activity, give him time to sign off: "We're leaving soon, say bye-bye to the toys, bye-bye to Jimmy, bye-bye to Susie . . ." If you are ready for him to go to bed, but he isn't, let him make the rounds of all the guests, "Say night-night to Grandmother, night-night to Grandfather, night-night to Aunt Nancy . . ." By getting behind the eyes of your child and respecting his need for gradual transitions, you avoid battles and encourage compliance. Most people readily give advance notice to toddlers, but you'll have to continue to give this kind of preparation for transitions to older children and adolescents with A.D.D.

WHAT TO DO WHEN YOUR CHILD IS DISOBEDIENT

Call for a Time-In

On pages 104 to 105 we talked about time-in and the teddy bear technique. We didn't use "time-out" because it so often refers to sending the child to another room, and this is felt as rejection by an already angry child. "Time-in" means that you tell your child to sit qui-

etly in the same room where you are for a few minutes. It works for school-age children as well as preschoolers.

How-To for a Time-In

Step 1: Ask your child to sit still for one minute. The child must sit in the place you indicate until a one-minute timer goes off. If he speaks or moves from that spot, the timer is started over.

Step 2: Remove privileges. If the child speaks or moves out of his chair five times, he is given a warning that the next time the timer has to be started over, he will also lose something (a *small* privilege, such as not being allowed to watch the first ten minutes of his favorite TV program or having to wait for fifteen minutes after he gets home from school before he can have his bicycle).

Step 3: Give bonus points if the child explains his point of view *calmly after time-in.* Tell your child that you do want to understand why he did what he did. But he must sit quietly for one minute before he may explain his reasons. If he explains his reasons calmly in a quiet voice, you are going to reward him with points. Then you may add a question, "What would you like to do when we are through?" This may get both of you headed in a more positive direction.

Ben's mother used these methods. Ben was given a time-in for yelling at his mother. At the end of his time-in the following exchange took place:

Ben: Mom, I thought you weren't being fair. You let Cam [his brother] go out with his friends after dinner and you wouldn't let me.

Mother: That was very politely said. You get two points on your chart for being polite even though you are upset. You do know why I said you couldn't go out, don't you?

Ben: Yeah, I guess so. I don't have my homework done. Cam is always the goody-goody. He always does everything right.

Mother: You get another point for not saying that in a whiny voice. Now I understand why you are upset. Why don't I help you with your homework so that you can get out, too? If you and I can get it done together in half an hour, let's agree that we both get a reward. Maybe you'd like a snack before you go out, and I'll have a cup of tea.

You want your child to trust that you will not only try to understand and respect his point of view but that you are open to admitting that he has made a legitimate point. One must be very careful here. Children are children; they do not think like adults. You can easily win a debate with a child, but as a parent you must judge your child's arguments based on his age level and his feelings. Do not put him down with counterarguments, even though you are fully capable of doing so. Your goal here is to understand your child, not triumph over him. Being able to keep quiet and listen is a sign of your own maturity.

Model Appropriate Behavior

When your child is disobedient, you must remain very, very calm. You may have to sit quietly in a chair beside him. If he is really upset, say very little, a word or two at the most! Sentences at these times are like throwing gasoline onto a fire! It is useful to have a hand signal, such as a slow downward movement of an open hand, that your child understands to mean "be quiet and calm."

HANDLING THE NONCOMPLIANT CHILD

Time and again, parents who have a child with A.D.D. complain that he or she behaves badly. In addition to not listening and acting impulsively, these children also show other problem behaviors, including dawdling, procrastinating, forgetting, or even being openly defiant. Parents report that their children do not get any assigned tasks completed unless constantly nagged. These problem behaviors, though commonly seen in children who have A.D.D., are not in themselves A.D.D. symptoms. Children who show this noncompliant behavior may be divided into two groups of underachievers, who may, or may not, have A.D.D.

1. defiant "never-get-it-done" children (They say "no" and mean it!)
2. passive "never-get-it-done" children (They say "yes" and then don't do it!)

Some children demonstrate both patterns, depending on the situation. It is not surprising that the same child can display both patterns, because a very poor self-image underlies both styles of coping.

Defiant "never-get-it-done" children. These children make their noncompliance obvious. They openly refuse to do what they're asked. They stubbornly oppose their parents and teachers, and their frustration erupts in frequent temper tantrums. Behind this child's "my way" attitude lies a poor self-image, depression, and anger.

Rules for Parents (or Teachers) When Assigning Tasks

Make sure that your child:

1. Correctly hears and remembers the task(s).
2. Has the sequence of tasks correctly in mind.
3. Has some easy trick for remembering both the tasks and the sequence of these tasks.
4. Knows the time limit for the tasks' completion.
5. Knows exactly how, where, and when to get the task checked off.

To be sure that your child understands, have your child explain to you what the job is and what he is to do when it's done. These tips are particularly important if your child has difficulty with short-term auditory memory and/or sequencing.

Make sure that you:

1. Stay calm. (Children take their cue from you.)
2. Keep smiling. (Your child needs to see your pleasant face.)
3. Be generous with attention, genuine interest, and trust.
4. Give freely of your time (quantity as well as quality).
5. Remember that medications can't substitute for your time, interest, and attention.
6. Listen, listen, listen. (Children work through their problems by talking with their parents.)
7. Join and redirect. (You join with what your child is doing in order to redirect his energies.)
8. Remember that negatives build negatives. (If your child believes his parents do not think well of him, how is he going to think of himself? How is he going to perform in life?)
9. Remember that positives create positives. (If your child believes in himself, he will believe he can succeed.)

Passive "never-get-it-done" children.
These children procrastinate, dawdle, and often forget. They are underachievers who drift through school. These children do not share their feelings easily and are somewhat anxious and passive. Sometimes their anxiety about failing and their fear of what others think is obvious. Sometimes they look sad. These children are passive in the sense that they may agree to do what you ask, but then they just don't get it done no matter how often you repeat the request.

When his mother asked what homework had been assigned today, Jason, age ten, said, "I haven't got any homework." His mother was fed up. She knew this was not true, so she picked up the phone and called the mother of a classmate. Indeed, once *again, Jason had not remembered (or perhaps he hadn't even heard the teacher assign) a book report. The book was at home, not because Jason had remembered to bring it home but because he had forgotten to take it to school that morning, even though his mother had laid it by his bag at the front door. Jason's mother gave him his book, told him what the assignment was, and said that if he didn't get it done in an hour, she was going to be quite angry. She added that when Jason had written the book report he could come down for a snack. He agreed to do his homework before he came downstairs to have a snack.*

Twenty minutes later Jason wandered into the kitchen. His mother asked him what he was doing.

"I just felt hungry. You said I could have a snack," he said.

"You are going to have to learn to listen. That is only part of what I said," Mother reminded him. "You agreed to do your homework first."

"Oh, yeah, I forgot," replied Jason.

Mother went back to his room with him and found he had written out the first sentence of what she supposed was the start of his book report. "This took twenty minutes?" she asked.

"Yeah, I couldn't think of anything else," Jason replied.

Parents find this kind of sequence almost more annoying than the directly oppositional and defiant child. It is an extraordinarily irritating and tiring pattern of behavior to live with.

In both groups of children — those with oppositional and defiant behavior and those with passively uncooperative behavior — the noncompliant behavior is *not a core* A.D.D. symptom. This behavior is caused by real frustration, not just by a brain that is easily distracted. However, the core A.D.D. symptoms of inattention, distractibility, and impulsiveness do make children who have A.D.D. *more likely to develop* noncompliant defensive behaviors. They themselves are frustrated not only with their own behaviors but also with the way they are treated.

Defensive Behavior

Noncompliant behavior can be called defensive. This is really a very logical term. No one likes to feel worthless, and a child must defend against these feelings by trying to gain some control over his world in whatever way he can. What he does is a question of what

behavior comes most easily given his temperament, and what behavior brings the reaction he is seeking.

A defensive behavior may be likened to a strong castle wall. This wall helps the child to feel that he has some control over the world. This strong wall defends him by keeping out feelings that he is not an important person. The constant criticism he receives from others when he forgets things, doesn't pay attention, and acts impulsively can make him feel worthless and unappreciated and can lead to depression. He must defend against these feelings. The child's defense may be to put up a false front or wall of agreement, when he has no intention of doing what he said he would do. The defensive child remains passively inside his castle and does what he wants.

Other children seem to believe that "the best defense is a good offense." In this case the child stands on the castle wall and defies anyone to try to enter. Your child may, so to speak, fire missiles at you — usually verbal — and make a great fuss. The child puts on a strong "I'm in charge here" front and becomes openly and directly oppositional, defiant, and confrontational. Sometimes these children are even verbally or physically aggressive.

Ian was an extremely active, impulsive, outgoing child who was always into everything. Already at age four, his A.D.H.D. influenced his behavior. His self-esteem was low, and his way of fighting off anxiety and depression was to attack. The following incident occurred after only a month in nursery school.

Ian said to James, "Give me that," and snatched away the large riding truck. James was a bigger boy than Ian and he stepped past Ian and got on the truck's seat, saying,

"I had it first!" Ian looked James square in the eye and said, "So what? I want it," and with that punched James in the nose. Blood spurted out and Ian summarily knocked James off the truck and took it for himself.

Ian had become a bully. He was expelled from nursery school. The next year he was enrolled in junior kindergarten, but with no success. He was suspended twice, and then the school requested that he be evaluated by a psychiatrist and that he not return to school until his senior kindergarten year. His mother was confused. She knew Ian was a good boy at heart. She had seen him a number of times being very careful and protective of both the neighbor's baby and of their little puppy. Later a child psychiatrist helped her see the two distinct sides to Ian's behavior.

Ian seemed to need a lot more assurance that he was loved and noticed than did other children. With Ian's extreme impulsiveness it was difficult for others to give him this assurance. Ian did not feel good about himself. It seemed that he was using assertiveness as a defense. Being in charge by being assertive meant that, for a moment at least, he didn't feel weak and inadequate.

On the other hand, Ian was able to project his own needs to be loved and cared for onto smaller, nonthreatening children and animals. He could be the big important person and take care of them. Ian did this without being at all conscious of what he was doing. He could not openly admit to himself or to others that he wanted to be taken care of; this would have left him feeling powerless.

Whether the wall is held passively or aggressively is not so much the issue. The issue is that the child is defending himself against being overwhelmed by feelings of worthlessness. Either type of behavior is a way of coping with the same basic problem.

Whether his behavior is defensive or not, your child must not be allowed to succeed in undermining whatever disciplinary system you, as a parent, have set up. You must be consistently in charge. You cannot let him get away with things one day and come down hard on him the next. That would be very confusing, and your child would raise the defensive walls even higher. Whatever behavior he was using to defend his self-image would become worse! Your child needs predictable, trustworthy parents in order to feel secure. Only then can the defensive castle wall be lowered a little. However, you must also be fair and give your child some freedom. Just like the best boss at work, the most "in charge" parents are the parents who give children permission to take responsibility for significant areas of their lives. Set them up for success by judging what they can be responsible for and what still needs support. Let them be in charge in areas where they will succeed. To be fair, you must genuinely demonstrate that you are looking at your child's complaints from his point of view, and that you are not just asserting control because you are bigger, older, and have all the power in the family. Charts, contracts, and rewards can help you put your child in charge of his own behavior and raise his self-esteem. Be sure to include your child in the chart-making process.

Turtle Behavior

Many children who seem to be independent and confrontational really have a very soft side underneath. Seeing two sides to seemingly very tough children is important for the teacher and parent who wants to work with them. To help these children, direct your interventions at the underlying problem — *the child does not feel sure of himself.* He wants to be both dependent and independent at the same time without losing face. You meet these needs with understanding. Give the child a sense of security that you as a parent are calm and in complete control. But be very careful not to let him lose face. Sidestep confrontations, so the child can still feel independent. This is crucial! Treat children the way you would like to be treated. Leave their dignity intact.

Be patient. Your child will have lapses. Noncompliant behavior doesn't disappear quickly, especially the passive variety. There is often a quick, early response, but parents and teachers must remain vigilant and reevaluate their strategies from time to time. New habits are easily broken and forgotten. If you as a parent are very consistent in your expectations and helpful at the same time, the good habits will become part of your child's personality after many months or a year or two. As a parent you must model consistency, but do not be too hard on yourself, or your child, if there are occasional lapses. The important thing is to be moving in the right direction and to let your child know that he is earning your approval because, although he is not perfect, he is working on getting better.

BEHAVIOR-IMPROVING STRATEGIES FOR ADOLESCENTS

The basic principles outlined above for improving behavior apply to teens as well as younger children. Yet adolescents, by nature, present special challenges that need more mature strategies. Having survived the adoles-

cence of children with A.D.D. in our own families and having counseled hundreds of families in both our practices, we realize that there are important differences to be addressed when treating teens with A.D.D. Adolescents are in the process of separating from their parents and trying out new, adult roles. In a way, adolescence is a replay of the "terrible-twos," when a child is separating emotionally from mother, becoming independent, and doing many things, such as feeding himself, that mother previously had done for him. The developmental tasks of adolescence are similar, only this time around, the process takes place under the influence of "raging hormones."

Adolescents want total control of their lives. They want to make all the decisions. They are continually trying out new selves or new roles. This can be quite trying for parents (as, for example, when their young person comes home with green hair and a nose ring). Whatever the new self, remember to count to ten and look for the beauty beneath the offbeat exterior. Your little child is still there and still desperately needs your love,

---

Messages to an Acting-Out Adolescent

1. You are basically a great kid, and your parents think the world of you.
2. Your parents want you to be in charge of your own behavior.
3. Your behaviors are understandable but not desirable. We all make mistakes, but try not to have these things happen again!
4. There are certain behaviors that simply must not occur. These kinds of behaviors are unacceptable for any member of the family and consequences will be applied.

support, and attention. The more extreme the behavior, the deeper the turmoil and the stronger the need for you to be there consistently as a strong home base.

Consequencing

Consequences for adolescents usually include time out from desired activities (grounding) and removal of privileges. Grounding has the danger of building resentment and anger. This is especially true if you ground a child for more than a very brief period of time. Ground him for an hour or one evening but for goodness sake, *don't* ground him for a week and absolutely never for a month. The most extreme form of grounding is seldom necessary. A few rules for consequencing are given in "Consequences for Behavior," on the facing page. Removal of privileges may mean as little as taking away half an hour of a television program; in certain situations it can mean some rather specialized techniques, which are described below.

The Green Garbage Bag Method

Keeping family areas clean and tidy means not leaving belongings or any food or drink in these areas. Untidiness, in its extreme form, can be quite an irritating habit to parents. If you have put in place a good reward system for putting things away, and your child still, for example, leaves the hall a disaster area for you to come home to after a long day at work, then the green garbage bag method is a simple solution. Inform your child that you have purchased some extra-large garbage bags and that if you come home any night this week and find more than three of his things on the floor anywhere else than in his own room, you are going to put

them into a garbage bag. Tell him that the bag will be kept in the basement or some other inconvenient spot.

If the behavior continues, just pick up all the items that are on floors or furniture outside his bedroom, put them in the bag, and put the bag in the basement. It doesn't matter at this point to whom the items belong. Be honest and fair: if some of the items are yours or your spouse's, then they also go into the bag! Retrieving things from the green garbage bag is such a nuisance that often you don't even need to say anything at all about hanging up jackets or putting shoes in the proper place. If your child wants the item, he can go get it. Usually it doesn't take very long until he starts following the guideline "a place for everything, and everything in its place."

Don't apply the green garbage bag method inside your child's bedroom. Let your child's room be private space, where the mess is his own — unless, of course, it smells or is attracting bugs and thus is becoming a family problem. Remember that adolescents like to make a display of being their own person! This is a normal stage of development, and if a teenager can do it in ways that do not interfere with the rest of the family, then shut the door and try to ignore what you can.

Although it may be challenging, it is essential that you remain perfectly composed and calm through this whole procedure. When you shut the door on his bedroom, leaving it as his private mess, it is much more difficult for your child to throw a major tantrum when the green garbage bag method is applied to the parts of the house that everybody shares. Without your even saying so (and usually it is best to say nothing), it will be absolutely clear to your child that he has invaded the whole family's space with his things and that you have been absolutely fair in leaving his private space out of it. Everyone in the family is being treated the same way and must follow the same rules. This realization will not usually be openly admitted, so don't expect it! Indeed, your child may even complain vociferously when he cannot find the baseball cap he left on the hall floor. This defensive behavior is entirely predictable. Don't react to it.

Applying consequences usually involves taking away some desired event or object.

What is removed, how much, when, and for how long all depend on the child's age and the seriousness of the behavior. After a privilege has been taken away (e.g., going to a movie, using the car), you arrange for the child to earn back the privilege. This is a step that parents often don't think of, and so the consequence loses the opportunity to give positive direction. Create a separate chart with a list of things he can do within a given time period. Tell your child how many points he must achieve in this positive system be-

---

Consequences for Behavior

What Not to Do

1. Don't take away developmentally constructive activities or events (e.g., school, gym, music, sports participation, swimming lessons, and so on). Don't take away social development opportunities, like the school dance.

2. Don't punish for an unreasonable length of time. Ground a child for the evening or several days, not for the rest of the month.

3. Don't take away a large number of favorite things all at once.

4. Don't apply any major punishment at the time of the offense. Say you're going to discuss it with his mother/father. Meet with your spouse when you are both calm. Come to a mutual decision. Let your child say what he thinks would be appropriate if you think he will be reasonable.

What to Do

1. When you use grounding or removal of privileges, withdraw the smallest thing first — the least amount of time away from activities, the least desired privilege, etc.

2. If one parent is feeling stressed and irritable on a rather chronic basis, divide the family responsibilities into clearly defined areas. Assign the calmer parent to communicate with the child about difficult areas, such as schoolwork.

3. Make family rules at levels that you all agree upon.

   Level A = rules or principles that must never be broken
   Level B = rules that are very important
   Level C = rules or chores that are routines; it is expected that they will be followed

3. At all three levels of rules, you should move immediately and consistently to apply consequences for infractions. You must remember that your true feelings are conveyed by your nonverbal communication (tone, severity, and loudness of your voice, body posture, and facial expressions). Keep yourself under control and be certain that these "messages" are appropriate for the level of rule you are dealing with.

fore the privilege will be returned. Make it really easy the first time.

Randy loved the Internet. He was a real computer whiz. His parents recognized that this had both positive and negative aspects. On the one hand, his hobby might lead him to an interesting and lucrative career. On the other hand, he was not completing his homework on time. Father made an executive decision. On the positive side, he would set up a workstation that he knew his son liked. The station would have a separate electrical outlet and a phone for the modem. The workstation, however, would not be in Randy's room but in a special area of the hall outside the bedroom. Randy was told that after his evening's homework had been inspected by his dad or mom, he could have the phone and the computer activated at his workstation. He could also use the extension cord for the phone and make private calls from his room. If the computer was needed for homework, that work could be done at the new workstation. However, the computer screen was in plain view of the downstairs living room, and from a distance his parents could be certain that the computer was being used for homework and not other activities.

In this case, the removal of a privilege was subtle. Randy no longer had the privilege of having both the computer and the phone in his room. The loss, however, was replaced immediately in a very positive manner by the new workstation. The privilege of using the computer to access the Internet then had to be earned by completion of the agreed-upon study objectives, and the parents could control this process.

After a short time it became apparent that Randy would do better with his homework if he had frequent breaks. Dad agreed with Randy that he could take short breaks. They both agreed, however, that Randy would accomplish a small objective with respect to his homework before he took a break. They set up short, simple objectives before Randy began his homework. If they asked, Randy would be ready to show his parents what he had done to earn his "Net-time" break, and he had a timer to limit the break to ten or fifteen minutes.

The trick here was working with Randy and genuinely trying to agree with his suggestions. He just couldn't handle two hours of homework without a break, and he was able to show that he was more productive with breaks. The other tricky part was making sure he reached his objectives — a study or homework "product" was to be produced in each short study period of time. It is crucial that you, as the parent, make sure the objectives that are set are realistic. When you are deciding on what is to be done in a period of time, make it a little bit less than what you think could be done. Always set up for success! If without realizing it you have set the objective too high, then *before* your child fails to complete the work, *before* he makes any excuse, you take the blame and the responsibility for expecting too much. For example, you may discover that each word problem involves a lot of thinking and calculating and decide midway through the study period that three before the break is more realistic than five.

Contracts

Most adolescents with A.D.D. do not demonstrate extreme behaviors and do not need behavior charts or consequencing techniques. Most feel secure enough within themselves and their families to "separate" and to assert their new, independent roles socially and in school through constructive achievements. If your child internalized your controls before he reached adolescence, you can probably skip this section. You won't have difficult behavior problems with this child.

Nevertheless, difficulty with attention span and acting before thinking can get some teenagers who have A.D.D. into difficulties from time to time. Here is an example of one of Dr. Lynda's patients:

Although Douglas had been a hyperactive child, in adolescence he was no longer hyperactive. He was described as being irritable (one sign of being depressed) and impulsive, and he had problems with his attention span. Unfortunately, discouragement in school, negative feedback from significant people around him, and other factors had led to Douglas's developing behavior problems in addition to his problems with A.D.D. Despite years of behavior management and psychotherapy, he was not internalizing controls very well.

When Douglas was fourteen, he was chronically late — late for school, late for classes during the school day, late coming home, late getting ready to go out with the family, and so on. He regularly forgot his school assignments. He would sit in his room for hours if forced to do so but get nothing done. His room was a disaster area, and his belongings were all over the house. However, when people sat down and talked with Douglas, they found him a charming, interesting, creative boy.

As with so many bright, capable adolescents, Douglas was frustrated in school. He was impatient and wanted to pick up the work rapidly. But he couldn't pick up what

the teacher was saying in class because, even with stimulant medication, he would keep missing key words or facts. He was too proud to keep asking about what he had missed and he just gave up.

Douglas's parents were exhausted and needed a way to help their son get his life organized. One of Dr. Lynda's suggestions was a postive-reinforcement charting system that would make clear to Douglas what was expected of him and what positive rewards could be attained by acting in a responsible manner. [This kind of chart can be created with the cooperation of the teen, and he can use it as a kind of reminder list. It differs from a list in his Daily Organizer only in that he can earn extra money by keeping it up-to-date.]

Step 1: Choose Items and Make a Behavior Chart

Some adolescents respond very well to making their own chart. Others may need more guidance from you. Many find it simplest to draw the chart on a large Dry Erase Board. Ask your teen to list the behaviors he thinks are important for achieving in school and for maintaining a peaceful, supportive family atmosphere. Give him ideas to get him started. In the chart below are a few suggestions that a number of Dr. Lynda's clients have used.

Each teen has his own list of behaviors, and the chart includes thirty-one columns for the maximum number of days of the month. The teens write the lists and record the points. The amount of study time required to get a point, the supervision of study hour product, and the rewards given for points gained by the end of the month should all be appropriate to the age of the teen. In Douglas's case, his parents added the provision that all work had to be inspected by a parent

DESIRED RESULTS	DAY OF THE MONTH															Continue ⇒⇒⇒ for 31 days
	1	2	3	4	5	6	7	8	9	10	11	12	13	14	15	
SCHOOL (1 point for each half hour)																
• 2 hours homework or project work (product must be shown to parent)																
• half-hour study / review																
• 10 bonus points for A; 5 points for B+																
EXTRACURRICULAR (1 point for each half hour over the minimum)																
• organized sports (1 hour)																
• music (one-half hour)																
• other (one-half hour)																
CHORES (1 point for each task done on time)																
• garbage out by 8 P.M.																
• dishwasher emptied and dishes away by bedtime																
• other																
THOUGHTFUL BEHAVIOR																
• parents add bonus points to this row																

immediately upon completion before Douglas could claim any privileges such as listening to music or even leaving his room.

Step 2: Decide on Appropriate Rewards

If the reward is extra allowance money, then you should design the system so that the amount the teenager receives is enough to be motivating. For example, if your child averaged 40 points in the week and each point was worth 10¢, he would receive $4. On an annual basis this is about $200. Earning bonus points can make the rewards much higher and more exciting. Douglas's parents added bonus points for finishing work within time estimates they determined together at the start of each homework task, as well as extra points for doing work well and for thoughtful behavior.

A reward is given *in addition* to a routine allowance. The reward should be given out at the same time each week, when you check the chart with him. For example, if your thirteen-year-old earned $4, he would get that amount plus his regular allowance. Teens are given allowance money regardless of behavior. Even if your son earned no points at all, he would still receive his base allowance. You might give it out as a certain amount each morning of a school day. The purpose is to ensure that your teenager always has some money in his pocket. If he doesn't, he may get it by "borrowing." This is not a good habit to encourage.

ADOLESCENTS WITH SEVERE BEHAVIOR PROBLEMS

Teenagers who have A.D.D. are more vulnerable to developing behavior difficulties. If your teenager has severe difficulties, such as trouble with school and/or legal authority, and won't cooperate with you on making a chart, try a different procedure. First, change the way you respond to different behaviors. Second, set up a firm three-stage contract so that your teenager knows exactly what is expected in order to earn privileges and positive rewards — and also knows that failure to live up to the contract will result in the loss of privileges.

Change the way you respond. First you need to make sure that you respond quite differently to behavior that is wrong or hurtful than you do to behavior that is just very irritating. You must change not only what you say but, even more important, *how* you say things. Decide on three levels of rules. Dis-

cuss these with your adolescent and then post them in the kitchen. We have given an example on the next page, but you will make up your own. Change your tone of voice, your posture, and the pitch and loudness of your responses depending on which level of rule you are having to enforce. Your commitment to your child calls for you to do your best not to overreact to violations of Level C rules or duties.

Involve your child in setting the levels of rules. Setting levels for the rules gives you an opportunity to involve your child in a meaningful discussion about the things you feel are important. It gives a strong message to your child that he and you, his parents, share many of the same values; it also makes him aware that you as parents value some behaviors more than others, just as he does. It is important, too, that your child feel that you are genuinely open and interested in his point of view. He needs to see that you respect his opinion.

The Three-Stage "Earn Your Way to Privileges" Contract

The three-stage contract system is for use with adolescents who have developed some very difficult, usually confrontational, behaviors. It is for parents who are having extreme problems with their teenager. The system gives the teen the basic essentials for life and then lets him work up from there. It is like real life in the sense that the child must earn even simple privileges. But like all of our strategies in this book, it is structured to set the teen up for success. We do not advocate an approach that is called tough love. There are reported successes with this hard-line approach, but we have also seen some unfortunate outcomes. We feel that tough love does

---

Three Levels of Rules

Level A. These rules must never be broken.

1. Be honest with your parents.
2. Never knowingly hurt another person.
3. Never act in a manner that endangers yourself or anyone else.
4. Don't take anything that isn't yours or destroy anyone else's property.

Level B. These rules are very important.

1. Always let your family know where you are. [Parents must model this, too!]
2. Do homework appropriately and on time.
3. When disagreeing with parents, do so without raising your voice or saying things in an accusing fashion. [Parents must model this *consistently* before they can expect their adolescent to do it.]
4. Do your share of the family jobs.
5. Show respect for others. Don't talk back in a rude manner.
6. Keep the house peaceful.

Level C. These rules or chores should be part of the daily routine; parents expect them to be followed.

1. Keep your desk and work materials organized and neat.
2. Follow family and personal time schedules.
3. Study every night: review the day's lectures as well as previous material. Concentrate on a different subject each night.
4. Prepare materials needed for school the next day.
5. Do family/house chores.
6. Keep family trips and car rides peaceful.
7. Don't disrupt the class.
8. Don't tease others or play roughly. [This could be a Level B rule, depending on the degree to which horseplay is a problem in your family.]

---

not meet the basic standard for healthy parenting: that parents should always look past children's overt behavior to understand their basic needs and that they should always try to meet these underlying needs. These needs include the need to be loved, cared for, appreciated, and respected while at the same time being allowed to become an independent and self-sufficient adult.

The first step in the three-stage system is to make a contract. Make it clear to your adolescent that her end of the contract is to do the things set out in the three levels of rules that you put together jointly. Your end of the contract is to ensure that these rules and expectations are met. To do this, state that you will reward her for meeting these expectations. If the rules are not met, you will withdraw things that you view as privileges and not necessities. The "earn your way to privileges" contract moves through these stages. In stage 1, the teen must earn all privileges. In stage 2, he can earn extra points to get extra allowance or special privileges. In stage 3, he fulfills his parents' stated expectations on his own without a formal system, and the family works well together. Start at the stage that you feel is best for your family situation, and you may change or combine features of different stages to meet your family's unique needs.

The objectives are to have a happy, relaxed, helpful, cooperative family and for the child and parents to feel good about themselves. The system helps the adolescent learn to behave toward others as she would want others to behave toward her. The Golden Rule (Do unto others . . .) is found in all the major religions, and your children cannot go wrong by learning and practicing it at home. If she learned it easily as a child but seems to have forgotten to behave this way as a teenager, give her a reminder. She must learn that she will usually get back in life what she has put in. (This is not always true, unfortunately, but it is still a good basis on which to build.) She must also learn to find the good in those around her. In each of these lessons the parent must act as a consistent model.

Stage 1: Earn Every Privilege

Stage 1 is for a very small number of adolescents who are in a very difficult phase. The teen starts each day with nothing other than the essentials of food, clothing, a home, and school. The teen is allowed to earn "privileges," such as time outside her room, TV, phone use, and snacks.

In Stage 1, your child must go to her room immediately after school unless she is involved in an organized activity, such as sports or music. To earn her way out she must complete something. For example, after an agreed-upon amount of time (perhaps one hour), if she has completed her homework and cleaned her room, she may leave her room for an agreed-upon length of time, perhaps until the end of supper. This length of time is increased each day.

Inappropriate behavior results in the loss of the last thing earned. For example, Jen-

nifer earned the privilege of using the phone by completing homework, but then the school called to say she cut a class. She loses the phone privilege for the next two nights. If she attends all her classes for the next two days, phone privileges are reinstated. You have to decide what is reasonable, given the child's special circumstances. In the case of cutting a class, it would depend on the reasons: spending time with a friend who was

---

How to Remove Privileges

- *Telephone.* You may take it to work or have a hidden switch put on the telephone line so that the line itself can be turned off. This will effectively cut the line when you are out.
- *Television.* Take it over to a friend's house temporarily.
- *All other electronic apparatuses.* Remove them from the house, including the stereo and video games. Or, you can remove a key part from the apparatus.
- *Extra money* (some might be needed for lunch at school or transportation). You must never leave any money out of your pocket. Your wallet goes under your mattress when you sleep.
- *Access to others' belongings.* Put locks on the doors of all family members' rooms — that is, everyone should be the same. This should help eliminate "borrowing."
- *Keys.* Gather up and take all extra keys to the office. Your car keys are never out of your pocket.

Note: Do not remove school, sports, musical instruments, and other worthwhile events or items. They are developmentally constructive.

upset and needed support would be different from cutting class to avoid a test. It would also depend on the school attendance record. Was cutting class a chronic problem or a rare occurrence? When you use this stage, you must be very careful that your child earns more than she loses and that the system never has a negative balance. This is difficult to achieve, and we recommend you find a professional whom you really like and respect to help you set up the system and monitor how it is working in your family.

Stage 1 demonstrates to a teen that most of the things with which we surround ourselves are best described as privileges and not necessities. It is simply not true that everyone else has their own phone and TV in their room, despite what your son or daughter may report. Stage 1 is the lowest and most extreme stage, where almost everything must be earned and very, very little is automatically provided by the parents. We do not believe in using more extreme measures, such as kicking the adolescent out of the house. To enforce the rules, parents can remove key pieces from the TV and other electronic devices and take all the phones to work with them. (Unfortunately, phones are so cheap this has little more than nuisance value, since a child can always get one from a friend. Do not try to enforce something if it is just going to add irritation.) To move out of this level, the teen must demonstrate basic politeness, honesty, and reasonable care, with no destructive behavior in the home. When basic politeness is achieved, even in minimal starting form, then privileges begin to be added. You can work out the details to fit your particular family.

Stage 2: Earn Extra Privileges

You enter Stage 2 when the adolescent begins to behave in ways that are helpful for himself and for the family as a whole. In Stage 2, everyone in the household contributes some time and effort to make the home a really pleasant place to live. At a regular weekly family meeting, use the "Family Contributions Chart" (see pages 150 to 151) to make two separate lists: a daily/weekly regular expectations list; and an "opportunity to earn" list, with extra jobs on it. At this stage you can begin using a system for earning points for extra allowance or other special privileges or things.

When listing expectations and rewards, it is important always to set the day and time for a task to be completed and a contingency plan if it is not possible to do the task by that deadline (e.g., "The grass must be cut before dark each Tuesday. If it is raining or if the grass is still wet from rain during the previous twenty-four hours, then it is to be cut before dark on Wednesday.")

You also should be very specific about your expectations. You might, for example, have to make contracts that define what "polite," "helpful," and "basic neatness" mean in your family. Above all, don't do as Betty's mother did in the following story:

Betty's mother had a meeting with Betty. It had been suggested to her by her doctor that she listen to what Betty thought polite behavior would be. Betty said, "Being polite means that people don't scream at each other."

Her mother responded, "Well, that's a fine idea, and just what is it you do at me all the time? I suppose you're going to tell me that your voice last night was reasonable?" And she began a list of times when they had argued over the last two days, raising her voice steadily as she went on and escalating to the point of saying, "What's the use of my trying to be reasonable with you?"

At that point Betty screamed, "That's it! You just can't listen at all, can you? What's the use of my trying anyway?" She stormed off to her room and locked the door while her mother poured out threats after her as she went.

What has Betty learned about negotiation from her mother? What has she learned about working things out with other people? Notice that her words at the end echo her mother's. There are many lessons to be gleaned from this true story. One of them is you cannot move forward in a positive direction if you keep harping on negatives from the past. Another one is listen, listen, listen. Then agree with whatever good suggestion your child makes and try it! Your child will respect this and learn by your example. If you can't do this, get professional help.

Stage 3: Work Together As Partners in the Family

Gradually you move toward Stage 3, the final stage. This is a level of functioning to which every family aspires, where family members respect one another and help one another and few parental controls are necessary because controls have been internalized by the teen, making external controls redundant and unnecessary. At this stage it may be possible for parents to say that it would be really nice to have help in certain areas and have their teen hop to it, feeling good about his contribution. This help frees up mom and dad to make other kinds of contributions to the family.

Gradually, tangible rewards become unnecessary. There may still be special rewards for undertaking large projects, such as cleaning the garage. At this final stage the adolescent may negotiate to use the phone for long-distance calls, to borrow the car, to purchase special clothing, and so on. At this stage your child is comfortable asking for things without everything having to be earned.

Stage 3 is the ideal. The parents have virtually nothing to say of a directive nature because controls have been internalized by their children. Of course there are limits set, and expectations are discussed. The children contribute as much to the family as the parents do. Yes, we do meet families who are at this level, even those in which a parent and at least one child have serious symptoms of A.D.D. When Dr. Lynda was treating problem children in mental-health clinics and then as a school psychologist, it seemed to her that most of the children with A.D.D. also had behavior difficulties. Now that she runs a center that is separate from these systems, a place where parents bring their children on their own because they want their children to make the most of their potential, she sees many families functioning at this higher level.

THE FINAL WORD

The final word on how to handle yourself in a way that provides successful structure for your child came to Dr. Lynda from an unlikely source — a local Realtor who always included an inspirational quote in his periodic mailings. At the time this chapter was being written, a piece appeared titled *If I Had My Child to Raise Over Again*. Dr. Lynda phoned the newsletter publisher to check the source of this wisdom, and she said, "I've had it in my file for years, and it just says 'author unknown.' I collected it before I had kids. Now that I have two, I read it and resolve to go home and be a little better mom. But it wears off and I find myself yelling at them. Then I have to read it again."

Dr. Lynda found it reassuring that the dispenser, if not the creator, of this inspiration so readily shared her imperfections. We know that, as parents, we won't get it right all the time. And our children won't get it right all the time. Fortunately, we don't love people because they are perfect: when we love someone, we accept that person. We accept their temperament and do what we can to shape their behavior in a positive direction.

Two weeks later one of Dr. Lynda's staff members brought her a poster that had the same poem as was in the Realtor's newsletter. When that synchronicity occurred, Dr. Lynda decided to get permission to reprint the words. Here they are, courtesy of Diane Loomans and Julia Loomans from their book *Full Esteem Ahead: One Hundred Ways to Build Self-Esteem in Children and Adults.*

If I Had My Child to Raise Over Again

If I had my child to raise over again,
I'd finger paint more, and point the finger less.
I'd do less correcting, and more connecting.

I'd take my eyes off my watch, and watch with my eyes.
I would care to know less, and know to care more.

I'd take more hikes and fly more kites.
I'd stop playing serious, and seriously play.

I'd run through more fields, and gaze at more stars.
I'd do more hugging, and less tugging.

I would be firm less often, and affirm much more.
I'd build self-esteem first, and the house later.

I'd teach less about the love of power,
And more about the power of love.

DIANE LOOMANS

6

Setting Up the Family for Success

THE WAY YOUR FAMILY functions is a *model* your children will copy — a model of how people communicate, how they organize their lives, and how they get along with one another. Psychologists say, "Children re-create their environments." What they get used to at home affects how they later behave in other situations like school or in their adult lives with children of their own.

Living with a child who has A.D.D. can bring out the best and the worst in a family. We want to help you bring out the best. This chapter will help you set up your family as a successful model for your children to imitate — a model of approval rather than shame, of open communication rather than secrecy. Home is where children learn to handle stress and live in harmony.

TAKING A FAMILY INVENTORY

Understanding your family will help you understand your child. We will take you through a step-by-step approach to analyzing your family and identifying your problem areas and your strengths.

Step 1: Identify What You Want to Change in Your Family

First, write down your family's most important objective. Then, immediately below that primary objective, list three problems, the three "biggies" that are interfering with your achieving this objective. Beside each of these three (or, you may have only one or two) write down the change that you would like

Our Family's Most Important Objective:	
The "BIGGIES": problems that interfere with our lives together	The CHANGES we wish to see
1.	
2.	
3.	

to see. You'll come back to this chart and re-
vise it in Step 3 after you take a closer look at
how your family functions.

Step 2: Take a Family-Functioning Inventory

The goal of this inventory (see pages
141 and 142) is to identify in more detail
your family's strengths as well as the things
you would like to change. If you are like most
families, you will have many things you
would like to see change. The inventory is
not for scoring, it is merely to give you further ideas. You cannot fail this inventory. Its
purpose is to give you some ways of thinking
about your family.

This is not the kind of questionnaire in
which you must choose only one answer. For
example, take the first item, "Peaceful"/
"Chaotic": yours may be a peaceful family
most of the time, but occasionally you may
be in total chaos. So you would check "most
times" on the "Peaceful" side, and "sometimes" on the "Chaotic" side.

This chart is for you to have some fun
with. Enjoy this activity, treat it as a game, an
exploration, a springboard to positive
thoughts. Keep your sense of humor, especially about negative characteristics. This is
your family, and you think about it all the
time anyway. You are rating it in order to
know more about the way family members
work together and to make changes that you
know will be of value.

There are two sides to every coin. This
questionnaire helps you look at every trait
from two points of view, two different perspectives — the positive and the negative.
Therefore, try to fill in both sides. And have
fun!

We have included many items to talk about
in the inventory. Please focus on those
items that apply especially to your family
and that will be helpful to you and ignore
the others. You will notice in the inventory
that there are "builders," things you do that
have a positive effect on your child, and
"breakers," things you might not even be
aware of that are contributing to problems
or at least not helping to solve them. Pat
yourself on the back for all the builders; it's
important to acknowledge the bright side
of your child and all the strong points in
your family that are working for you. The
rest of the material in this chapter is about
fixing the breakers so that you can give
your child a new and improved model to
imitate.

Step 3: Revise or Add to Your "Biggies" List

Families don't cause A.D.D., but they can
make the problem better or worse. A supportive family environment can make living
with A.D.D. much more manageable. Look
again at your inventory. Which of the breakers have you already identified as biggies?
The inventory may show you some areas you
wish to work on, or it may help you pinpoint
the problems at the heart of biggies already
on the list.

Fill in the biggies chart again (see page
143), this time revising or adding to what you
wrote on page 139.

Now that you have identified the major areas of concern, you may wonder what you
can do at home as a family to improve things.
It's time to come up with an action plan. If
you are like most families with a challenging
child, your most common problem is
tension — feeling stressed out and disorganized.

The Family-Functioning Inventory

BUILDERS	most times	some- times	hardly ever	hardly ever	some- times	most times	BREAKERS
Positive Actions	This section focuses on how your family acts.						**Negative actions**
1. *Peaceful* You anticipate and plan for problems.							*Chaotic* Nothing is planned — each problem is a new crisis.
2. *Organized* You have a family calendar, a method to handle messages, etc.							*Unorganized* You fly by the seat of your pants — no one is sure of anything.
3. *Responsive* You join together to find solutions to meet each other's needs long-term.							*Reactive* Your knee-jerk responses deal only with the moment.
4. *Supportive* You help everyone win, do their best.							*Competitive* You are concerned about individual winning, being best.
5. *Rewarding* Family members praise one another.							*Denigrating* Family members put each other down.
6. *Protecting* You are careful with one another's vulnerable spots.							*Attacking* You lash out at each other's vulnerable spots.
7. *Trusting* You trust each other's motives.							*Suspicious* You are suspicious of each other's motives.
8. *Open Communication* You listen and use open-ended questions to help solve problems.							*Closed Communication* You confront, judge, command, moralize, criticize, and analyze.
9. *Nurturing* You encourage the individual growth of each person.							*Constricting* You insist that others behave as you do. You discourage individualism.

Positive Communication	This section focuses on how your family communicates.						Negative Communication
1. **Clear** "That door slamming scared me!"							**Confusing** "Why are you always so wild?"
2. **Direct** "Tom, I get angry when you don't listen to me."							**Indirect** "He slammed the door. Is he mad at someone?"
3. **Immediate** "Come here and pick up the coat you just dropped, please."							**Delayed** "We can't rely on you; last week you kept us waiting."
4. **Complete** "Dad, I need the car tonight. I said I'd drive us to the movie."							**Incomplete** "I have to have the car tonight."
5. **Flexible** You are willing to discuss issues and make adjustments.							**Rigid** "If you're living under my roof, you follow my rules."
6. **Reflective** "Let's discuss consequences."							**Impulsive** "You're grounded for a month."
7. **Accepting** "I know that hurts when they won't play."							**Nonaccepting** "Don't be a cry baby."
Other Try rating other characteristics that apply to your family.							**Other**
POSITIVES Column Scores							**NEGATIVES** Column Scores
TOTAL POSITIVE SCORE							**TOTAL NEGATIVE SCORE**

You will want to fill this out again in six months to follow your progress. Expect to see a shift to the positive side.

Our Family's Most Important Objective:		
The "BIGGIES": problems that interfere with our lives together	The CHANGES we wish to see	
1.		
2.		
3.		
Additional "BIGGIES" discovered after doing the Family-Functioning Inventory	The CHANGES we wish to see	
1.		
2.		
3.		

Reducing Stress

Unless they have lived with a child with A.D.D., people don't know how much stress these children place on a family. You look forward to having a child and you expect that child will obey, learn, pay attention, and not get into trouble. With regret you realize the child you expected to have is not the one you drive to school each morning. Meanwhile, the child you have has turned your peaceful home into chaos. Your bundle of joy has made you a basket case, like the stressed-out mother who went to her pediatrician relating that her child had been expelled from three day-care situations by the time he was three years old. What follows is one mother's story of how she learned to handle the stress of full-time work and three children, one of whom has A.D.D.

Mary was a hard-working, loving mother. She was under a great deal of stress, and she realized it could be damaging to her children's emotional development, espe-cially the one with A.D.D. symptoms, who was becoming the family scapegoat. Mary went to Dr. Lynda's A.D.D. Centre for help when she was on the brink of divorce and was worried she might physically abuse Andrew, her seven-year-old middle child, who had A.D.D. with hyperactivity. She would race home after a tiring day's work, open the door, and begin her evening by screaming at her kids to stop asking questions, pick up their junk, get their homework done, and so on. Then she would turn on her husband for being a useless lump who had no control over the children. Mary was stressed-out, and the whole family was suffering.

Step 4: Get Yourself Organized

Mary's situation underscores the fact that parenting skills are of use only if parents are feeling peaceful, self-confident, satisfied with their lives, and organized. No matter what technique is used to deal with your child's undesirable behaviors, be it rewarding of good behaviors, ignoring of bad behavior, time-outs, or removal of privileges, the result will likely be a negative one if the parent is feeling tense, resentful, angry, anxious, or depressed.

When Mary took Andrew to see Dr. Lynda, looking for help for his A.D.D., Dr. Lynda suggested some charting techniques for Mary to use with her challenging son but also explained carefully that these would not work unless she first got herself feeling organized and relaxed at home. Only then would she be able to model the kind of attitude and approach to tasks she wanted to encourage in her son. Mary wanted Andrew to be more organized in his schoolwork. She wanted him not to fly off the handle when he was asked to do a chore. She wanted him to calmly organize when and how he would get things done. She wanted him to be peaceful with his little sister and to help her when she needed things. Being *peaceful* was a major objective in Mary's family — a biggie that needed work.

Mary was able to learn some self-help strategies to create a more relaxed family atmosphere. While these strategies can help any family, they are particularly useful in families that have a child with A.D.D. These strategies made it possible for her to replace a reactive approach with a responsive approach to her family. Instead of spending all her energy putting out constant brushfires, she was able to prevent many of the fires from starting.

Mary recounted an event that she said was a turning point for her in applying to her family life what she had learned in counseling. Previously, she would race home, open the front door, and get right into nagging and other negative communication with her three children and her husband. This time she described a different scene.

It was Friday night, and I was coming home from work. It had been a difficult week at the office. I felt exhausted and overwhelmed. My briefcase was full of "must be done immediately" work. Probably my husband's was too. I wondered if he would be late again. Granny was sick, and I knew I should go and visit. The school had called again yesterday — Andrew got into trouble in the schoolyard (his impulsiveness again). I was so tense I could have screamed! Andrew! Whatever are we going to do about Andrew? No, perhaps not Andrew — us! I launched into my litany of complaints. I just don't have any fun anymore. We are in constant crisis, overwhelmed, disorganized. But then I remembered — we don't have to live like this!

Mary was able to step back emotionally and think about implementing a plan. She remembered a technique that Dr. Lynda calls "Letting Your Children Feel That They Are the Most Important Thing in the World." Here is how it works:

1. Park your car somewhere before you reach your house.
2. Say to yourself, "This is an opportunity. I am going to be a positive model for my child."
3. Put a relaxing tape of your favorite music in your car stereo.
4. Take out your Day-Timer and organize the things you have to do this evening. Then move the nonessential items from tonight's list to your long-term action list.
5. Organize the list of things you want to accomplish tomorrow, so you won't be

ruminating about them all evening, when you want to be thinking about your children.

6. Lie back in your car seat and for five minutes close your eyes and focus only on deep, relaxed breathing while you listen to the music and think of a favorite peaceful scene, such as walking alone on a beach.

7. Now go home, and for the first ten minutes or more, pay full attention to your children. Sit on the floor, listen to them, look at what they're doing or at their school papers, ask what they would like for dinner, get them quick snacks — have fun. Do not answer the phone. Let the machine do it.

Mary continued her story:

I said to myself, "This is the first day of the rest of my life!" I'm going to enjoy playing with the kids tonight and then read them to sleep. Then I'm going to feel just great and I'm going to be upbeat. I'll call a babysitter so that Frank [her husband] and I can go out for a great planning session over dessert and coffee."

When I reached my driveway that night, before I got out of the car, I began my new way of living. I put my favorite piano music tape into my car stereo. Then I took several deep breaths and practiced relaxing and focusing for a minute. Then I pulled out my Day-Timer and made a plan for the evening. I got so involved I even wrote out a little plan for the weekend. I put down a list of activities the children might enjoy and resolved to ask them if they would like to try one. Then I made a tentative schedule. I decided that it would be really healthy for me to get outside for a bit, so I included times to play tennis with Jason and Andrew.

But that left out little Ashley [age five]. She would get tired of being "ball girl" pretty quickly, so I decided instead to go out with the kids and get a cheap badminton set and get the boys to help me set it up. I had to shop for shoes for Ashley, so I put in a time for that and decided to make it fun by going to a mall that had a playground. Then I remembered the time-management course I had taken at work and how the instructors had warned us to book in empty time slots for unexpected calls every four hours. So I factored in some extra time to allow for getting sidetracked or delayed. I felt really good about my planning. I entered my house for the first time in years feeling upbeat and ready to handle the whole group!

Organization and Time-Management Techniques for You

Mary's story illustrates the importance of taking some time to plan. She had taken a time-management course at work and was in the habit of using her planner for her workday at the office but not for other parts of her life. Getting more businesslike about the time and activities she shared with her family was an important shift. In fact, Mary accomplished what she set out to do that evening. Her plans worked even better than she had hoped. The weekend began in a relaxed fashion, and she built on this success. She did not let herself get too discouraged by the inevitable setbacks. Because she was more relaxed, they did not upset her. If Mary did it, you can too.

Mary was an excellent and very well organized office manager. She had always put into practice time-management techniques to make sure that she was never too hurried on important high-priority matters at work. She decided, as she later told us, "Starting now, my family is going to be a different world to

Should My Child Have a Schedule?

Early in your parenting career you may have thought schedules were too restrictive. You tried to respond to your infant's needs rather than watching the clock, but as your children get older, you need to develop a timetable for sleeping and eating. For families of children with A.D.D., schedules are necessary to survive. These children need to keep busy, one way or another. Chores can fill up only so much time. Down time is needed, of course, and it is okay for a child to be bored now and then in order to learn to turn to his inner resources for stimulation. Children need to occupy themselves and not constantly be kept busy by adults. But it is a big mistake to drop the ball and leave a child with A.D.D. on his own much of the time. Sure, he may have trouble sustaining an interest in an activity just two weeks after signing up, but that should not be an excuse for not getting him involved in activities. James, whom you met earlier in the book, thrived on a busy schedule. Here is an example of a typical day in January the year he was ten.

TASK / ACTIVITY	TIME	Comments
WAKE UP	1/2 hour	Get books to door in backpack with sports equipment.
BREAKFAST	15 minutes	Review math in car on way to school (15 minutes).
SCHOOL	6.5 hours	
AFTER-SCHOOL ACTIVITY (library, outdoor play, study, music, etc.)	school basketball team (1.5 hours)	On the weekend, basketball game (2.5 hours); ski team practice and competition Saturday and Sunday = 8 hours a day for skiing.
DINNER	1 hour	chores and meal
EVENING	swim team competition (2 hours) and study (1 hour)	Study tonight cut to 1 hour due to swimming. Review Spanish vocabulary en route with Dad.

Hyperactive James, as you probably surmised, was going to be busy all the time. The only question was what he was going to be busy with (TV, getting in trouble, bugging his siblings, hanging out at the mall, *or* hobbies, sports, and some studying). His parents chose the latter. No, they didn't spend much time relaxing themselves, nor did they get to watch much TV, but, yes, they succeeded in enjoying their time with James.

live and grow up in. If I can run a successful, efficient business, I can darn well run a family!"

Just like Mary, most parents today feel overwhelmed, especially if they have a child who takes a great deal of their time, as most children with A.D.D. do. If you do not currently use a time-management system like the one Mary learned on the job, consider trying one. Personal organizers range from little ones that fit in your pocket or purse and show a week on each page to large binders with many planning sections, project tracking systems, and electronic organizers. Some of the popular commercial ones include Franklin Planners (based on what Benjamin Franklin designed for himself), At-a-Glance Organizers, Day-Timers, Day Runners, and a very extensive one by Stephen Covey of *7 Habits of Highly Effective People* fame. If you choose one of the more involved systems, you can even take a course in how to use your planner. This is an excellent investment; the course fee will include the cost of the planner. You can spend from less than $5 for a pocket organizer to hundreds of dollars on a time-management course, so analyze your needs before you buy. In the pages ahead, we will describe a system for the whole family to use together, the Pentagon Planning Center (see pages 154 to 155). Whatever system you decide to use, the bottom line is that you should have some type of daily planner for your personal use. Not only will this help you get organized, but it will also model for your children the importance of using planners. (Student planners are discussed in chapter 7, on page 179.)

How to make your chart. Managing your time starts with making lists of important things to do. Mary spent some time later that first evening making a chart with two lists:

(1) her weekly task list, and (2) her long-term task list (things that should get done before the end of the year). She then transferred some of the first list to the second because she knew that her first list must have only things on it that she could easily get done in a week. If she made the list too long, she would increase her stress and tension. If she completed the items on her weekly list, she planned to reward herself with an extra activity with the kids. And only then would she do one item from the long-term list. Items on both lists were categorized into priorities just like her lists at the office.

To make your own chart, sit down with paper and a pencil or at your computer and make your wish list of things to accomplish. Think about the different categories, such as family, studies, work, church, fitness, and volunteer work that apply to your situation. Use these categories as headings when you develop your list. When you think your list is complete, decide for each item whether it belongs on the short-term or long-term list, and then assign priorities. You could place a star by the most important things, or, if you have many items, rate them as A, B, C for "essential," "important," and "nice if there's time." Things that are routine, such as housework or religious services need not go on your list. But if there's a special committee meeting or a bake sale coming up, you need to put it on the list so you can budget time for it.

Mary's list is on the next page. Yours might have different headings and different priorities.

Most of the tasks on Mary's list required the cooperation of her husband and family. She knew she would have to involve them, so that together they could plan how and when these tasks would be completed. She would keep this personal reminder list with her, and she would find other ways to organize her family.

Important Things Chart		
KEY AREAS	SHORT-TERM (this week)	LONG-TERM (this year)

FAMILY
Have some fun with Frank
 	
Activities with children
  • Schoolwork &
    study
  • Music
  • Sports
  • Hobbies
	Family: Get tickets for ice show.
	Frank: Dinner on Friday. Find babysitter.
	Jason: Register for Little League. Needs white shirt for band.
	Andrew: Call teacher. Take to library for Cub Scout project.
	Ashley: Bring snack to kindergarten Tuesday.
		Discuss summer camp.
		
		Summer school?
		
		Look for new dance class.

FRIENDS	Write Carrie. Take Joan to lunch.	Plan surprise party for Bob and Carol.
WORK	Update resume.	
STUDIES	Finish paper for sociology class.	
FITNESS	Sign up for tai chi.	

Where to keep your chart. Mary decided she would keep her "important things" chart in her purse, so that adding or deleting items would be a simple matter. She would keep a pad and pencil by her bed at night. Why? Writing things down would become a way to reduce unproductive ruminations — thinking about things over and over and over again. If she wrote these thoughts down, she could set aside a time each day to review them over coffee and add them to her chart. She could forget about them when she was trying to fall asleep. Establishing a "worry time" would help her not worry at other times. Mary also planned to take her chart to weekly dinners out with Frank. She would insist they get away from the telephone and the children so they could talk with each other in a relaxed atmosphere. Her chart would help the two of them to make up a family activities list and a family jobs list. She decided that she would also start weekly family meetings. In this family meeting she was going to have the kids help to create a list of the little things everyone, even the youngest, could do to make a contribution to the family.

Tools such as weekly assignment sheets (see page 153) and family meetings will help reduce the stress level in your home, freeing up energy to work on other family objectives. Looking at the things Mary did to help herself and her family get organized should provide you with some ideas about positive steps to take with your own family.

Step 5: Establish Good Organization in the Family

The next step is to get your organization techniques to filter down to your whole family. Model your methods of time management by getting everyone involved in understanding the value of time and how to use it. As a family, assess the amounts of time contributed by individuals to keep the family running smoothly using the "Family Contributions Chart" on pages 150 to 151. You do this to let everyone see that their contributions are recognized and appreciated and to make sure no one person is overloaded. Change the categories as necessary to make this work for your family.

Sometimes people resist doing this kind of planning work. They find a dozen other things that absolutely have to be done instead. Note that this is exactly the same kind of resistance some children with A.D.D. demonstrate when it comes to handling responsibilities. For this reason we highly recommend you leave the house to do the job. Go out to a restaurant, or go to a park, take some snacks with you, and throw a ball around when you need a break. Whatever you do, make it fun and build in some rewards. Occasionally a family will find that it is just too difficult to get this process started on their own. Ask a good friend or relative to be chairperson of the first meeting when parents and children discuss the Family Contributions Chart. Before the meeting, make sure all your older children have seen the outline for the Family Contributions Chart, so that they can have time to think about the hours they spend in various activities. Parents should work on the chart together before presenting it to the children.

Step 6: Construct a Weekly Assignment Sheet

The next task is to create assignment sheets for each week's tasks. This is a tool that will be referred to daily and updated weekly. Assignment sheets decrease nagging, tension, and frustration in the family and increase thoughtful problem solving. They make communication about tasks clear, direct, and complete, and ensure that everyone's schedule is known and respected.

The weekly assignment sheet delegates to each family member the tasks for the upcoming week. You will notice immediately that there isn't enough time to do everything. Take some of the items and place them on a second sheet — a long-term planning sheet.

No Cinderella Children, Please!

Some parents get so enamored of family organization and job assignments that they turn life into drudgery for their children, leaving them little or no free time to "just be a kid." If you tend to be a perfectionist, you could get carried away with the prospect of harnessing everyone in the household, inflicting your need for perfection and control on your defenseless offspring. If this happens, your children will wind up missing out on their childhood, and when they do get some free time they won't know how to use it wisely. So be fair and reasonable. Truly listen to complaints.

Family Contributions Chart

KINDS OF TASKS	MOTHER Hours/week	FATHER Hours/week	CHILD Hours/week	CHILD Hours/week
INCOME: Enter the amount of time, including travel time, each person requires for his or her job.				
EDUCATION: Enter the amount of time, including travel time, each person requires for:				
School				
Homework				
Projects (long-term)				
Study (review for future tests)				
*HOBBIES: Include hours spent on a weekly basis for all extracurricular activities other than sports, such as music, Scouts, crafts, art, collecting, etc.				
*SPORTS: Include hours spent on practices, games, working out. Include travel time.				
FREE TIME: Children learn through play; adolescents learn through socializing; adults relax. Estimate hours spent.				
CHILD-PARENT TIME: Include hours spent doing things with the children (other than chauffeuring and sharing family meals).				
HOUSE: Include regular household chores.				
Inside:				
Maintenance				
Kitchen chores				
Tidy own room				
Tidy living room				
Tidy family room				
Clean bathrooms				
Neaten halls				
Clean basement				
Dust				
Vacuum				

KINDS OF TASKS	MOTHER Hours/week	FATHER Hours/week	CHILD Hours/week	CHILD Hours/week
Plant care				
Pet care				
Reorganization:				
Room #1				
Room #2				
Outside:				
Gardening				
Snow shoveling				
Clean up				
Repairs				
Car care				
FOOD RELATED:				
Plan meals				
Grocery shopping				
Put away food				
Cook				
Set table				
Clear table				
Wash dishes				
Put away dishes				
Put out garbage				
Clean kitchen				
FINANCIAL:				
Budgeting				
Paying bills				
Taxes				
Mail and correspondence				
CLOTHING:				
Laundry/Dry Cleaning				
Repair				
Purchase				
MEDICAL and OTHER APPOINTMENTS:				
VOLUNTEER: Include time spent in volunteer work.				
OTHER				

Note: At mental-health clinics we rarely see children who are involved in sports and hobbies. This is due to a number of factors, a major one being that extracurricular activities increase the child's self-confidence and self-esteem and reduce the likelihood of emotional problems.

Weekly Assignment Sheet Rules

1. If it isn't written, the assignment or message doesn't exist.
2. Everyone checks the assignment sheet on a daily basis, preferably at an agreed-upon time each day.

Rule 1 helps avoid arguments that start with "But you never said . . . !" If something is important, like the time for going to visit grandma, then it *must* be written on the planning sheet and in each individual's planner. Written reminders are good for all and essential for the child with A.D.D.

Rule 2 means that no one can say, "Oh, I didn't see/read that!" Members of some families make it a habit to read the list *before eating any food* when they come home from school or work. Others check it while they have a snack. (*Hint:* Always attach any new habit you want to form to an old habit that is a pleasant one.)

Step 7: Make an Agenda for the Family Planning Meeting

You will need an agenda to be used at your weekly family meetings. All family members can put down ahead of time what they want to discuss during the meeting.

The family meeting agenda helps communication change from confrontation to cooperation. It focuses on problem solving. It helps the impatient, egocentric child ("I want what I want when I want it") to consider the perspective of other family members. At the same time, it reduces frustration and tension by assuring everyone that their concerns will be heard and not overlooked or forgotten.

The family meeting agenda contains two types of topics: plans and problems. Plans include such things as what will be done during winter break or what to buy Grandma for her birthday. Changes in routines should also be discussed at the family meeting before they are implemented. The proposed change should be posted ahead of time on the family meeting agenda. Problems can be discussed as the "three M's" (for Makes Me Mad). Family

The Family Meeting Agenda			
DATE	PERSON	LET'S DISCUSS	POSSIBLE SOLUTIONS
Mon.	DAD	10 pairs of shoes for me to trip over in the front hall	I'll build a shoe rack on the weekend — then you guys keep shoes on that.
Wed.	SUSIE	TV remote control was found buried in the couch cushions	Dad should put it on the table after the evening news.
Wed.	JOHNNY	Susie "borrowing" my toys without asking	She won't take mine without asking, and I agree not to take hers.
Fri.	MOM	Dishes left on the counter	Put dirty dishes in the dishwasher.
"	"	Family holiday: suggestions for where to go this year	
"	"	Ball game or hiking on Saturday?	

Weekly Assignment Sheet

Person	Nonroutine Tasks Only (Do not include such things as setting the table, making beds, regular lessons, sports or hobbies, etc.)	Day	Time
MOM	*Weigh and measure Johnny and fill out form for hockey sign-up.*		
	Register Susie for gymnastics — buy leotard.		
	Label Johnny's things for Scout sleepover camp.	*before Thurs.*	
	Bake with Susie for her kindergarten party.		
DAD	*Take Johnny to hockey sign-up.*	*Wed.*	*7 P.M.*
	Go to skate exchange with Johnny and Susie.	*Tues.*	
	Clear garage to make room for one car.	*Sun.*	*A.M.*
JOHNNY	*Go with Dad to hockey sign-up.*	*Wed.*	*7 P.M.*
	Write thank-you to Grandma.		
	Help Dad clear garage.	*Sun.*	*A.M.*
	Show Mom my school planner / agenda, and plan homework / study time.	*every day*	*right after school*
	Pack for overnight camping with Scouts.	*Thurs.*	
SUSIE	*Shop with Mom for gymnastics leotard.*		
	Do picture for Grandma.		
	Feed dog while Johnny is away camping.	*Fri.–Sat.*	

Long-Term Goals and Tasks

Person	Goals and Tasks	Day	Time
MOM	*Send out invitations for Susie's birthday party.*	*by Oct. 1*	
DAD	*Take Johnny for extra skating—1x/week.*	*after Oct. 15*	*when rink opens*
SUSIE	*Decide who to invite to birthday party (limit of 8).*		
JOHNNY	*Decide what activities to do next summer.*		

members should be asked to word their complaints in an understanding way and to offer constructive solutions. Older children may write problems and complaints on the agenda sheet themselves. A parent may have to calmly help them add a constructive suggestion once they have cooled off a little. In most families with younger children, mother is the keeper of the agenda, and she holds responsibility for putting items on it for the next meeting.

Step 8: Construct a Family Communications Center

Pick an area with a phone, where you can keep the items needed at the family communications center. Put each of the charts and calendars on the table as in the illustration below. In addition to the assignment sheet for weekly goals and tasks described above, you need a Month-At-a-Glance calendar. The Month-At-a-Glance calendar is used for posting events, such as children's sports, music lessons, family outings, school concerts, parents' evenings out, and so on. A system for messages should also be by the phone. With the telephone next to the weekly assignment sheet, the message system, and calendar, messages involving changes in schedules can be entered on the appropriate sheet or calendar

without delay. Entering changes immediately is essential, especially with persons in the family who have A.D.D.; otherwise they will be forgotten. Messages that are forgotten are a frequent cause of upset in many families, and that frustration is preventable. Your message system can be as simple as a different colored pad for each family member (Mom gets her messages on blue, Dad on yellow, and so on), or as permanent as a day planner, perhaps with different colored pens with which to leave messages for each family member. Have the pen or pens attached to the phone or to the day planner (you don't want any pens to go walking). The old "there wasn't any pen" excuse will become unnecessary.

In all, there are five items in the family planning center, so we call it the Pentagon Planning Center. We particularly like this name because the U.S. Department of Defense is housed in the Pentagon, and a lot of strategic planning goes on in that building. Your Pentagon Planning Center arms your family with tools for success. Each of the five items performs a unique role, but they must interrelate, just like the five sides of a pentagon, in order to maintain stability. For what to put in your strategic planning headquarters, see the facing page.

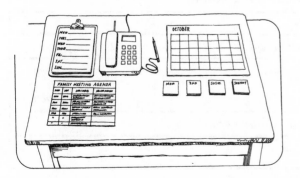

Step 9: Hold Weekly Family Meetings

The family meeting is a time to pull all this together, and it is a way of inviting children's contributions to making the home run more smoothly. Children are likely to agree to changes in household management if they have a voice in the decisions. Children will be much more accepting and eager to earn points on behavior charts if they see that their parents also use charts to stay orga-

The Pentagon Planning Center

Planning and Organizing for the Family Is Like Planning for the Whole Darn Army

1. **Month-At-a-Glance Calendar.** For recording all family activities — sports, music lessons, meetings, and social outings. (Family members over the age of nine should also have a personal **Daily Planner,** containing their agenda for each day. Personal planners travel to school or work with individuals and are not one of the items at the Pentagon Planning Center.)
2. **Day Planner or Colored Pads for Messages.** Some families prefer small message pads, a different color for each person. Other families prefer a day planner, because it allows for messages from outside and between family members to be clearly recorded under the date they were written. The day planner or message pads remain at the phone to prevent any argument about a message not having been written down. **This is crucial for families in which both a parent and a child have A.D.D.!** (You can tell people with A.D.D. about times or events or chores and they will sometimes answer you without anything registering in their minds. Later they will insist that you never told them!) This is why we have the same rule for messages as for assignments: if it isn't written down, it doesn't exist.
3. **Weekly Assignment Sheet** (on a clipboard).
4. **Family Meeting Agenda.** This allows everyone to see ahead of time what any family member feels should be discussed. It allows for written complaints (and a little time to cool off).
5. **Telephone.**

Note: The Family Contributions Chart is not included in the Pentagon because it is an assessment tool rather than an ongoing organization tool.

nized. Everyone will feel good about making meaningful contributions to the family.

Try these tips for holding a family meeting:

- Use the Cub Scout motto "KISMIF: Keep it simple, make it fun."

- Meet in a pleasant place with as few interruptions as possible. (If you are at home, turn on the answering machine and turn off the TV or radio. Some quiet classical music as background music would be all right, or, in fact, any music that everyone agrees upon.)

- You are the parent. You are the final authority, but parents should respect the opinions of the group. Initially, spouses can alternate being the chairperson. Eventually you can get to the point where the children, too, can learn how to chair a meeting. This will help them feel that they are important to the decision-making process. Develop a "share and care" atmosphere.

- This is not a place for nagging or embarrassing others or for lectures. It certainly is not a place for anger. It is the responsibility of the parent (or chairperson) to make sure this does not occur and that everyone shows respect for everyone else's ideas.

- Use the meeting to update the monthly calendar for the Pentagon Planning Center, to plan or modify the week's assignments, and to find solutions for the problems that have been listed on the agenda.

Some parents choose to meet first for a "pre-meeting," especially if there are going to be contentious issues at the family meeting. This is more likely when there are older children. Do this in peace and quiet, away from the phone and the children for just a few minutes. You should be positive, constructive, and in agreement when you have the family meeting with the children. While you as parents have already decided what will be acceptable as an outcome, the meeting must still genuinely allow everyone to be heard.

In any busy family, tensions will arise. There is more tension if one child in the family is very active, doesn't seem to hear what he is told to do, or is very impulsive. Families that do not have a child who has A.D.D. may get along just fine without having elaborate methods for organizing their lives, but it is essential that families of people with A.D.D. recognize the need for superior organization and take action on it. The reasons are very simple. If everything is organized and shared, there is less chance for disagreement. There is less room for stress. You plan and discuss events in advance (avoiding surprises), but you leave room for discussion (avoiding oppression). Family meetings serve to give children a regular lesson in how to plan together with others. They also provide everyone with a sense of being appreciated for taking on particular tasks.

PARENTING STYLES

Your child learns about how to interact with others from your parenting style. Children treat others as they are treated. Children with A.D.D. test their parents' patience all the time. While you may often be provoked to anger (and sometimes you will lose your cool), your child needs a calm, caring, level-headed authority figure who respects and takes time to understand her. Here are stories about three children with A.D.D. and the families they live in. Read and compare, and decide which parenting style works the best.

Parenting Style #1: James

Nine-year-old James, a child with A.D.D., was playing soccer with his younger brother, Peter. They knew they shouldn't play indoors, but it was just in the front hall, not the living room. Besides, it was a final challenge after the game in the front yard. Peter rebounded the ball off a wall past James. James raced after it and tried to hook it with a final kick. His intent was to send the ball back to the front hall, but the result was an unfortunate deflection near the entrance to the living room. The ball careened at great speed through the living room and hit the antique Chinese vase, sending it crashing to the floor. James looked at Peter; they both stood in shocked silence. Then James said, "We have to tell Mom. It's my fault." Peter, age eight, said, "No, James, it's both our faults. We'll go to Mom together."

Yes, this really is the way these brothers did act! Their mother, Shirley, had few rules, but they were very, very firm. Two Level A rules (see page 134) in this family were:

1. **No fighting.** Never fight with or intentionally hurt anyone, especially your brother. Play fighting only — wrestling without hitting, kicking, or hurting — is allowed. (Shirley had many times *every day*, since the birth of Peter, reminded James how lucky Peter was to have him as a big brother. They wrestled like little bear cubs, and she complimented him constantly on how he judged his strength so that he never hurt his brother. She also reminded James that Peter would probably be bigger than him one day [he had bigger feet at age two and was taller at that age, too]. She encouraged the same caring interactions between the boys and their baby

sister. The result was a virtual zero on any real fights between siblings. They were then and remain best friends.)

2. **Never lie.** Never under any circumstances tell a lie. (Shirley told them that if she heard the truth from them first, they would never have to be worried about her or their father's reaction.)

James and Peter found their mother and warned her that something terrible had happened. Then they took her to the living room.

"I'm sorry, Mom," said James. "It's my fault. I didn't mean to, but I was the one that kicked the ball." Peter immediately chimed in, "No, Mom, I was playing with him. It's just as much my fault." Shirley couldn't even speak initially. She knew her husband would be devastated; the vase had been in his family for generations. But she also saw that they understood this was a serious accident and they were very frightened and felt terrible.

These children did know what they had done. If Shirley had responded with admonitions, would it have added anything to their feeling of repentance? Actually, it could be argued that yelling at them would have made it easier for the boys. They could then have defended themselves ("It was an accident") or turned on each other ("He kicked it"). However, that was not how Shirley responded. She looked at the damage and took a moment to think. This was a challenge to her "find something positive, no matter what" approach to discipline.

"You boys are so good — you stuck together and came to tell me right away. You're just the best brothers. What do you think we should do?" She wiped away some tears,

saw the boys looking at her, and responded to their unspoken question. "Yes, I'm sad. It was a very beautiful vase. But what's done is done. We all make mistakes. I know you are very sad, too." Then she asked a question: "Is a vase really the most important thing in our lives together?" After a short silence she added, "You children are the most important thing in your father's and my life." This was a very deep message for young children, and she did not expect any response to it. The children needed closure on the accident, so she immediately returned the discussion to the broken vase. Peter suggested that they try Magic Glue. Mother responded, "That is a great idea. What do you think, James?" James suggested he get a bag for the pieces. Shirley said, "Yes, that's exactly what we will do. We will get a plastic bag and we are going to carefully pick up all of the pieces, even the tiniest ones. I know a man who repairs pieces for the museum and we are going to see if he can do something with this."

When they had cleaned up and Shirley was feeling calmer, she phoned the museum, checked the number for the person who did repairs on valuable porcelain, and then called him. She also called the boys' father so that he would have time to cool off before he came home.

By the time Dad got home, he was resigned to the facts. His boys greeted him at the door and apologized. (Their mother had discussed this with them.) He hugged them, and they all went together to the repairman to leave the pieces with him. Yes, it would be expensive, but by this time both parents had agreed that it was a learning experience. There was no question that the boys would remember this and be more careful.

Parenting Style #2: Sammy

Sammy was ten years of age. His mother was consistent, but consistent in quite a different way from James's mother. Here's how Sammy and his mother reacted in a similar situation:

Sammy broke his mother's lamp. He hid the pieces in the garbage. When his mother noticed the lamp was missing, Sammy responded that he didn't remember seeing it yesterday. But then his mother found a piece under the couch. She confronted Sammy and accused him of breaking it. He told her he didn't do it, his sister did. His sister screamed "Liar" at him, and a physical fight broke out. Their mother screamed at both of them, spanked both of them, sent them to their rooms, and told them that they would stay there for the rest of the day and their father would deal with them when he got home. She told them they had better be prepared for a licking because this lamp was valuable and their father would be furious when he found out.

Parenting Style #3: Betty

Betty was nine years old. Betty's mother was different from either James's or Sammy's mother. Betty never knew how her mother was going to react. James's mother was consistent in looking for the bright side, and Sammy's was consistent in being punitive and negative. Let's look at how Betty's mother reacted in a similar situation.

Betty broke the little mirror in her mother's bathroom. When her mother found some pieces of it, Betty heard the door slam. She heard loud cursing followed by her mother screaming over the phone at somebody. When Betty's mother finally confronted her, *she screamed back, "It's your fault, you left it right on the edge of the counter."*

Communication Style

Both James's and Sammy's mothers were predictable and very consistent. Both children knew exactly what the sequence of events would be once their mother found out what had happened. James knew that somehow, no matter how awful it was, his mother would respond in a positive, loving fashion. Sammy's mother was just as predictable, but, unfortunately, his mother would always be negative. James and his brother, terrible as they felt, still went straight to their mother and told her what had occurred. Sammy predictably tried to hide what had occurred: if you cannot avoid trouble, you may as well try to delay it. Betty did not know how her mother would respond. Betty's mother's responses were completely unpredictable. Betty could control her environment only by going on the offensive.

James's family is reasonably well organized about things that matter. Despite James's very high activity level, his mother manages to remain calm and reflective even under trying circumstances. She was certainly proactive in her response to the broken vase. She called her husband so that he would have time to cool off before he got home, and she quickly arranged a way to have the vase repaired. Sammy's family may be well organized, but his mother still is not able to feel relaxed or able to reflect before acting. You might correctly guess that Betty's family is in total chaos. Note that "organized" doesn't mean having the rooms all neat and tidy. Betty's house was compulsively immaculate. "Organized" means that the things that matter most are planned and given priority. "Organized" means that priorities are in order, with people, not things, at the top of the list.

James's mother understood immediately that her sons were devastated. They knew without being told that they could have broken any other object in the house and it would not have been nearly so significant. So she supported them emotionally and did not put them down in their moment of crisis. Even in this situation she rewarded them for something — standing by and supporting each other — and encouraged their problem-solving ideas. She protected them from the devastating guilt they would have had to endure if their father had been confronted with the news when he arrived home and they had been there to witness his initial emotional reaction. She left them with their basic trust in their parents strengthened, not weakened.

To whom do Sammy and Betty have to turn for support? Where is there to go? Even as adults, we count on our spouse and our friends to be supportive and protective when we are in trouble. Children, and adults, need to have someone they can always trust to love and support them, regardless of their situation.

James's mother was open to listening in a reflective manner. She did her best to understand her sons' point of view and their feelings before responding. Then she asked her sons to come up with constructive suggestions, a way of helping them take responsibility for their actions. She was also aware that by choosing to have the vase on display she was risking having it broken. Sammy's mother and Betty's mother were absolutely *closed off* from their children's feelings. They were confrontational and judgmental. They commanded (a superior stance). They were moralistic (a know-it-all stance) and critical (a put-down stance). They acted as if they knew it all and were not a part of the difficulty (an uninvolved stance).

James's mother allowed her sons to feel that they were genuinely helping to solve the problem. Even in a crisis, she found a way to help them grow toward healthy independence. Sammy's and Betty's mothers looked only for submissive behavior, and what they got instead was defensive denial of responsibility. That is not to say that Betty and Sammy won't develop independence in adolescence. They will (they will have to), but at a cost. Often the cost is rebellion. Teens reject those institutions that parents value (schools, jobs, sports, and other healthy activities) and may even leave home for a period of time and submerge themselves in rebellious groups and activities. This is a way of "finding one's self" but not the one we usually associate with healthy growth and development. Actually, this is exactly what has happened with both Betty and Sammy, while James, whose A.D.D. traits were more severe, is an honors student and has earned certification as an instructor and coach in both skiing and sailing. He holds responsible summer and winter jobs coaching these sports; his pattern of keeping busy has continued, except now he is paid to do it rather than his parents having to pay. Eventually there is a financial payoff to handling A.D.D. well, but it is not nearly as important as the emotional payoff. James is confident and doing well. Betty and Sammy are still struggling.

Life Lessons

The communications that took place in each of these scenarios provide good examples of how families can succeed or fail in helping their children learn valuable lessons for life. Both James and Sammy knew what was being communicated and why. In Betty's case it was confusing at first. Initially, Betty wasn't even sure her mother had found the broken mirror.

James knew that his mother was trying to work out a solution with him. Sammy knew he was being chastised and put down and he felt at that moment that he was a worthless human being. Betty really didn't know what the problem was or at whom her mother's anger was being directed until well into her mother's tantrum.

James knew how his mother felt — she was very, very sad. He and Peter also knew she understood that they were sad, too, and that somehow they really wished they could make it better. Sammy and Betty both knew only that their mothers were very, very angry and perceived that they were bad and the cause of it all. James and Peter clearly felt they could say, ask, or suggest things. Sammy knew he'd better shut up and disappear quickly. Betty knew not to ask for explanations (except maybe as a way to stall for time). She would take the offensive — just like her mother did.

James's mother, even in crisis, thought carefully about how the boys were feeling before she responded. Sammy's and Betty's mothers were completely absorbed in their own feelings, with little ability to reflect before they spoke or acted. "To reflect" can mean to bounce off, as light does off a mirror. This is a way to understand mental reflection. James's mother was thinking about what had occurred and bouncing it off other thoughts and values in her own mind. Her words and actions then reflected these values back to her sons in a manner that furthered their growth and maturity. When she asked, "Is a vase really the most important thing in our lives together?," perhaps they were too young to reflect on this question themselves, but perhaps not. They might remember those words for a long time and make them a part of their own values as they mature. No mat-

ter what the vase's cost in dollars, the lessons these children learned were far more valuable. James's mother clearly demonstrated genuine understanding of her children's needs and feelings. Her understanding helped them to understand themselves better and to learn important life lessons. Sammy's and Betty's mothers, by not reflecting on their children's feelings, missed out on important opportunities to grow with their children.

Who was in full authority, in charge of the whole situation? Although Sammy's and Betty's mothers acted in a domineering fashion, only James's mother was in charge totally and completely. Sammy's and Betty's mothers were out of control and acted like children themselves. To grow up with a strong, well-anchored sense of themselves, children need that example in the adults closest to them. A child also needs to feel very secure. Security exists in an environment where the mother and father are solidly in authority. But this authority is a benevolent dictatorship in which the enlightened dictator wants to leave the country in strong, competent hands and thus concentrates on developing the independence of the next generation.

Which child felt true guilt and responsibility? James actually said to his mother at one point, "It would be easier if you gave us a spanking." A spanking might relieve the immediate feelings of guilt, replacing them with anger about the spanking. Instead, James and Peter were helped to truly accept full responsibility for their actions, and both have grown up applying this attitude toward everything in life. Sammy and Betty, however, were quick to project the blame and responsibility elsewhere. In their teenage and early adult years, this has become a well-ingrained characteristic in each of them. This doesn't mean that

Sammy and Betty don't feel guilt; it just means that they don't truly accept it and the responsibility that goes with it.

We have spent considerable time analyzing these mother-child interactions. Try to do the same with some interaction that you have had with your child recently. Think about the messages you gave and the long-term effects of these messages on your child's development. If the first situation that springs to mind is one in which your response was less than ideal, be sure you also think of a positive interaction, so that you can compliment yourself. Build on your own positive parenting skills, just as you teach your child to build on his or her positive traits.

Every child needs love and attention. As parents we pour in love and attention like we are filling up a bucket. But some children require more attention, more of the time. The child with A.D.D. can seem like a bucket with a large hole in it. It takes forever to fill,

and if you stop pouring, the level drops rapidly. Then problems begin to emerge. Parents have told us, "He gets more attention than all his siblings put together but complains that he gets less!" The fact is, you cannot let up on giving love and attention to a child with A.D.D. This child needs constant positive messages. So if you think your child with A.D.D. takes more emotional energy than the average child, you are absolutely right. Don't be discouraged. Once you truly accept that this child will be an ongoing "drain," it somehow becomes a little easier. Rest assured; your love contains a sealant! If you pour in enough attention in the early years, the hole in the bucket will gradually seal itself over by the time your child reaches adulthood.

Now, let's hear from James's father:

My wife believed in being there for our sons virtually one hundred percent of the time. We therefore did without some luxuries so she could stay home with the two children. She was literally doing things with our eldest, James, an active boy, all his waking hours. I don't think this is for everybody. Most of us would become tired and irritated by the constant activity and demands. She never complained. Somehow she turned whatever he did into a learning experience. I know I have trouble doing that.

My role was different. I have always enjoyed activities. At one time I was a camp counselor, and I also played piano quite seriously and took part in drama and student government. So I was keen on having my children do lots of things. With James I always insisted that "we" must complete the extracurricular activity (usually one or two months) that "we" had chosen, unless it was poorly taught or coached. I would present

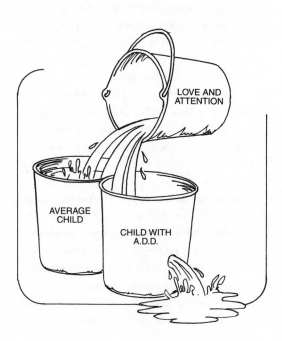

LOVE AND ATTENTION

AVERAGE CHILD

CHILD WITH A.D.D.

Choosing Sports for Children with A.D.D.

Sports can be a positive or a negative experience for A.D.D. children. Playing a sport helps them burn off excess energy and anxiety, but some team sports can be frustrating because these children have difficulty listening and following the rules. After-school sports are especially valuable to allow a child to discharge pent-up anxiety at the end of a stressful academic day and to tire him out a bit so he is more mellow and easier to live with during family time in the late afternoon and evening. Here are some tips for matching child and sport:

- *Start early.* A younger child develops a positive attitude about sports because the rules for young children are simpler, and the games are less competitive.
- *Match the child's temperament to the sport.* Set your child up for success. If your child cannot handle group situations in swimming class, for example, get semiprivate or private lessons first, until the child feels confident. Confidence goes a long way toward helping the child with A.D.D. settle down long enough to cooperate in group instruction. If your child likes to move around, she will be better off playing soccer than baseball.
- *Match the child with the right position on the team.* As a Little League coach, Dr. Bill places the children with A.D.D. on the infield rather than the outfield. When they play outfield, they literally act as if they are out in left field. They watch birds, pick dandelions, and pay attention to anything but the batter. On the infield, they have to pay attention because there is more action. On the other hand, he sometimes worries that the particularly spacey infielders might get hit with the ball.
- *Be patient.* Don't be too disappointed if the child's interest peters out once he discovers he has to work at his skills. Many kids respond like this, but it is more extreme with children who have A.D.D. Not only is their attention more difficult to hold, but they lack the patience for gradual improvement. They want to play at the professional level instantly.
- *Don't invest too much in equipment* until you know that your child will stick with the sport.
- *Practice with your child.* Your child will maintain her interest if she has more skills before she joins a team. Practice a lot in the two or three weeks before official practice starts. Children who feel confident and succeed are much more likely to stick with a sport.
- *Remember that hyperfocus can give an athlete with A.D.D. an edge* (see pages 8 and 9 to 10 and the related section "The Carryover Principle," page 202). In team sports, the child with A.D.D. will usually prefer a position that allows him to lock on and be totally at the center of the action (e.g., a goalie or center in hockey, or a pitcher, catcher, or first base in baseball).
- *Consider martial arts,* such as tae kwan do or karate. These sports can be therapeutic for the child with A.D.H.D. because they allow the child to be aggressive but in a controlled way. The child must stand in a certain spot and listen to instructions. He is more attentive because the instructions make sense and have immediate relevance to him.

my son with two or three possibilities, and together we would choose one. With music we did not offer a choice: it was a given that James would take piano lessons. Later he chose violin himself. Over the years he tried skiing, swimming, gymnastics, soccer, baseball, tennis, canoeing, sailing, summer camp, music camp, water polo, piano lessons, and violin in addition to participating in sports and music programs at school. We tried to balance individual and team sports. He was such an active boy that I unilaterally made the decision he would be in something every day after school and even on the weekends. Except for skiing, which James liked anyway, these activities usually involved only an hour or so of practice each day, so the total time away from friends in the neighborhood wasn't much. To make it more fun, we would often take a friend whose parents appreciated sharing the driving. The boys looked forward to being together and didn't look upon the activity as something that took them away from their friends! This was important. James would complain when he was younger, but I told him there was no question about whether he would go; however, he could discuss with me rewards for participating and where he would like to go for a snack after the practice. This usually worked.

As James became proficient at a few of the activities, the arguments ceased completely. Now he would ask me to be ready on time! I think any of us who have worked with children know that often they can be very enthusiastic about a new activity, then quite suddenly lose all interest. This may be related to finding out they can't do something perfectly after one or two tries. No matter how much you discuss this ahead of time, it always seems to come as a shock that they can't play

basketball like the player on TV the first time on the court. As long as you realize you are going to go through this "downer" time, you can just be calm and firm. I gave James lots of rewards but absolutely never let him miss a practice. It must become routine. Kids will pull every trick in the book to see if you will give in. As long as you never do, they learn very quickly and forget about trying to get out of it. I am sure it was actually easier doing things seven days of the week than it would have been doing them three or four days. Going to practice was a well-established part of every day.

Despite James's being bright, school was very difficult for him. He really did not learn very much from classes. He was good at sports and they kept his self-esteem high, and this carried him through a few difficult pupil-teacher personality clashes. [For a child with other interests, parents can offer choices, such as art, music (playing by ear is usually preferred to reading the music), drama, woodworking, or building models and entering competitions with them. The opportunities in most communities are almost endless, and it is well worth evaluating them with your child's natural talents and interests in mind.]

And then there was schoolwork. Perhaps the hardest lesson I learned was to bite my tongue and follow my wife's example. He would forget his books, his assignments, his pens, his whole bag. I thought he might come home some winter day without his coat on and tell me calmly that he just forgot. My wife never batted an eye. I had to give myself time out with a book until I cooled down. It didn't always work, but fortunately she covered up for my impulsive outbursts. Thank goodness only one of us has A.D.D. (I do, she doesn't). No matter *what he forgot, she just calmly got him a nice snack and involved him in an interesting way in doing some schoolwork. She might find out what the project was by calling the teacher or a friend who had a child in the same class. He would come home with C's and D's and the occasional A. What often determined the difference was his liking or not liking the teacher. It was always one extreme or the other. By eleventh grade, even he had figured out that skipping college wasn't cool, because he realized that to make his own choices (and he was very much a leader!) he needed to have good grades and a degree. He changed schools. He figured he would have to work harder to make it in the group he wanted to hang out with. These guys were good in sports, played in a band, and made the honor roll. He settled down, followed his tutor's learning strategies, borrowed his friend's notes (because he still couldn't learn anything in class due to his A.D.D.), got his very bright girlfriend to help him, and made the honor roll. It wasn't easy. But he learned to use all his positive A.D.D. attributes — spontaneity, creativity, hyperfocus, determination, and tenacity — to best advantage.*

I've rambled on a little, but I think the point I'm making is important. Time spent with one's child in positive activities that promote self-confidence and self-esteem is more important than anything else I can think of. It's the foundation.

IMPROVING PARENT-CHILD COMMUNICATION

How you talk to your child affects how your child talks to you and how your child behaves. Working on how you communicate is an important way to improve your relation-

---

"Rules of the Road" for Separated Parents

Children with A.D.D. need predictable structure, and this is harder to achieve when children spend time in two different homes. Make sure you and your ex-partner make a standard schedule for children that is entirely predictable and consistent. This is one of the most important factors in establishing a sense of security through a major upheaval in your child's life. (The marriage was very important to your child, but children are rarely consulted about separation or about Mom or Dad's new partner. Moreover, they must live important, formative years with the whole situation.) The reaction of a child with A.D.D. to change will be difficult, and it will be hard on parents. Look through your child's eyes and do your best to make her world predictable and secure.

---

ship with your child. Good communication is at the heart of solving A.D.D.-related problems and the whole process of helping children mature into healthy, responsible adults.

Communication begins before you even open your mouth. In a tense situation, try a technique psychologists call "internal mediation." This means talk to yourself before you act. Ask yourself if you are very upset, angry, or defensive in your thoughts and feelings. Are there feelings showing through your posture, tone of voice, actions, or words? Will this have any constructive effect? Sometimes letting your emotions show may reinforce your message ("I get scared when you run into the street"), but most often your negative emotions will undermine what you are saying and will be the opposite of what you really want to see happen. When you sense a surge of emotion in yourself, you may find it useful to say to yourself, "Stop!" before you respond to a child or spouse. On these occasions, ask yourself the simple question, "What is really going on here?"

Sometimes the words and facts present one message, but nonverbal communication states something else that is even more important. Consider the speaker's gestures: posture, facial expression, tone or pitch of the voice, the rate of speech, and the choice of expressions. Your child slams the phone down and wails, "Nobody likes me, not even you!" The real message is often to be found in the nonverbal area. Pay attention to the speaker's emotions before you attend to the stated facts. If you stop and talk to yourself, you can take both your own emotions and the nonverbal communication of the other person (your child or spouse) into account. Reflecting back your understanding of both dimensions of the message in a brief way lets the sender know that he/she has been heard ("I can see that you are mad that Danny has to go to practice and can't play"). You can then talk about the crisis and solve the problem ("I bet Danny was disappointed, too. Let's call Jeff instead").

Even the sound of your voice makes a difference in getting a good response from your family. Lower your tone; a high-pitched voice is irritating and turns off listeners. Slow down when speaking to children with A.D.D., and be sure they are looking at you as you speak ("I need your eyes"). Use as few words as possible — one or two simple sentences. Children hear the beginning and maybe the end of a speech. The long middle part gets lost, so don't even bother with it.

Try Alternatives to "No"

There are many difficult situations and many opportunities to say (or scream) no. This is exactly why a wise parent will actively try to avoid the use of that word with the child who has A.D.D. Many of the children with A.D.D. we see have to be told no over and over again before they obey the command. "No" has become by far the most common word spoken to them. It doesn't have to be this way.

There are many alternatives to no, although using them requires you to stop and think for a moment. Try stating an alternative ("Use your crayons on paper, please"), or provide information ("The chair might break if you stand on it that way"). Give encouragement ("You're getting closer to the correct answer"). Or, simply say "Stop!," a word that has more instructive value than all too common no. Anticipate your child's actions as much as possible and intervene before no is necessary ("That tree is tempting, but we can't climb trees at the Botanic Gardens"). Or, distract the child, and when you can, avoid environments that are full of nos, like the supermarket just before dinnertime, or Great Aunt Bertha's house full of eighteenth-century antiques.

Many parents do manage to limit the use of the word "no" with excellent results. This can, however, lead to some challenging dilemmas:

Charlie was four and a half years of age. He was an extremely active and adventurous child. Instead of using no, his mother would distract him from negative behaviors and redirect him to positive ones. When the parents were at work, a nanny cared for Charlie, and she had been carefully chosen for her positive frame of mind and experience with children. She appeared imper-

turbable. One day Charlie unwittingly tested the nanny's resolve not to say no.

   Charlie had just received a new pair of skis and a helmet, but there was not yet any snow. As the nanny came around the corner at the foot of the single long staircase that led straight up from the living room to the second floor, she spied Charlie at the top, wearing his new helmet and skis. In this situation, a loud "No!" would have been quite appropriate. However, before she could think of what to say, he pushed off, sped down the carpeted stairs, across the living room, and into the fireplace! Fortunately, Charlie was not hurt; but the nanny did talk to him carefully about how dangerous his trick was, and he never tried it again.

Fortunately, the nanny was not under stress. Had this event occurred with a baby crying in the crib and two other children fighting in the next room while the pot boiled over on the stove, the entire situation might have turned out differently. The talk that followed the stunt would almost certainly have been emotional. Charlie grew up very rarely hearing the word "no," so when it was used, he knew the command was of extreme importance and he unquestioningly obeyed without his mother's having to say it a second time. (Of course his mother would not have blamed the nanny for yelling "No!" when Charlie was at the top of the stairs.)

Communicate Instead of Blaming

When you want your message to have a positive effect on the listener, pay attention to the feelings your statements are likely to evoke in your listener. Blaming allows you to unload anger or resentment, but it is unlikely to get the offender to change his ways. Blaming messages often begin with "you" and contain words like "always," "never," or "every." "You" messages demonstrate an autocratic authority, an unwillingness to listen, a lack of respect for the other person, be it your spouse or your child. For example, "You drive me crazy letting the door slam every time you come in," or "You never listen to me." The object of the blame must immediately go on the defensive ("Well, you're always yelling"), and communication rapidly disintegrates. Try using "I" messages instead. "I" messages convey how the behavior makes you feel. "I" messages are clear and direct and not overstated. "I" messages convey a nonjudgmental attitude (of interest and curiosity) and avoid labeling and pressuring. "I" messages show confidence in your child. Try, for example, "I feel irritated when I hear the door bang. It makes me grumpy," or "I often feel that I'm not getting through to you." These statements point the conversation in a positive direction, and some genuine problem solving can follow. This is not hard to do if you stop and ask yourself how you'd like someone to speak to you.

Hint: Put a jar in the kitchen. Every time a parent makes a "you" statement (other than a polite request for someone to do something, of course), he or she must put a dollar (or whatever seems to be best for your family) in the jar. This is the FFM (Family Fun Money) jar: It is to be used for a fun activity decided upon at the family meetings. This is a way to boost your awareness and to twist a negative example into positive opportunities for fun together.

Be a Good Listener

Listening to a child conveys respect and trust. How you listen is more crucial to good communication than what you say or how you say it. Here are some listening tips:

- Try to find the good, the constructive, the positive somewhere in what the other person is thinking and saying. At the very least, attempt to "walk a mile in their moccasins" and understand your child's point of view (or your spouse's).

- When responding, try to use "I" or "we" statements to convey your point of view. Watch out for "I" statements that are really "you" statements in disguise ("I think that you are making too much of this").

- Reflect back to your child what she is trying to say to you ("You think the teacher explained this math assignment too quickly" or "You're confused by Dad's reaction"). Then let the child correct you if you've missed her message. Often it helps to write it down clearly with the child. Don't try to counter each point, just demonstrate that you have really heard and are trying to understand.

- Use the "sandwich technique." Package your own opinion between compliments that build the listener's confidence. For example, "I think, you're on to something here. But you need a more detailed plan for your science project, like the time you planned that Cub Scout activity."

Solve Problems Together

Respectful two-way communication with your children makes it possible to solve problems together. A.D.D. management is more effective when parents work with a child to improve a situation rather than imposing a parent-generated solution. Your ultimate goal is for your child to be responsible for shaping his own behavior. Including kids in family problem-solving sessions gives them a chance to learn and practice skills they will need as adults.

The first step to solving problems with your children is to listen, listen, listen. Use all of your listening and reflecting skills to help you see the problem through your child's eyes. Pay attention to nonverbal signals, as well as to your child's words. Be careful to describe your own position with "I" statements, in order to avoid blaming and emotional confrontation. Then join with your child to solve the problem. "Joining with and then redirecting" is a concept that comes from aikido, a Japanese art of self-defense. In aikido, you do not confront or attack an opponent, unlike in karate. Instead, the various moves and holds redirect the opponent's energy and momentum so that they work for you.

Your next task in leading a problem-solving session with your child is to harness his energy and get it moving in the direction of a solution acceptable to both of you. Be open to lots of ideas at this point. Once the child and you have laid out all your points about the problem, ask permission to start looking at all the alternatives, factors, data, and information that will influence the solution ("everything 'we' can think of together"). Children normally will agree to do this. As you consider ways to solve the problem, you can carefully ask questions that encourage the child to broaden his viewpoint and get him to think about factors you know should influence a solution. When this process seems exhausted, you could also ask to add a couple of points of your own, telling your child that you realize he may not agree with you but you feel these things should be written down to make the picture complete. As you lead this discussion, don't allow any one factor to dominate the picture.

Now it's time to work out an action plan. Explore all the alternatives. A closed response to a suggestion imposes your decision on the child. An open response allows the child to continue to think about and work on the problem. It acknowledges the child's right to feelings. Leaving things open for further discussion shows respect for the other person's ability to find solutions to problems. Don't leave open, however, alternatives that you will not accept. A parent can have veto power. Make it clear when and why a suggestion is unacceptable. You give security through authority, but you allow growth by letting children decide between acceptable alternatives.

By this time, some workable, mutually agreeable solutions should begin to emerge. Let your child choose what you will do, then work out the fine points together. You might also want to decide how and when you will evaluate whether the plan is working. Solving problems together is especially important when there are adolescents in the family. "Telling" a teenager something is like throwing water on an oil fire. You'll get a big flare-up, and it won't be effective. It's better to ask reflective, leading, Socratic questions. Socrates, the ancient Greek philosopher, believed that it was the task of the teacher to help students find answers to questions within themselves. Doing this takes understanding, knowledge, and skill. You'll make far fewer suggestions than you would with a younger child. Instead, through questions, you lead teens to discover answers for themselves and to be thoughtful, reflective, and creative in the process. Adolescents remember not what you teach them but, rather, what they figure out for themselves.

Private Areas

Most successful directors of boarding schools or summer camps define stealing as "borrowing without permission." Some families may have a problem with "borrowing." Even in a family where sharing is emphasized or where children share a bedroom, each child should still have some area that is private. It could be a box at the end of the bed, and this box could even have a lock on it. Would it be preferable not to have a lock and be more trusting? It is far better to set up for success than to leave open the possibility that one child could "borrow" a sibling's favorite baseball cards, or, worse, read a brother or sister's diary. Some families might even have a special box in the kitchen, where each person keeps his or her own treats. Some of us hoard food, and others eat it immediately; if a box reduces conflict, try it. It might even be necessary for a time to insist, as one would in a school or at a summer camp, that family members keep their money on their person or in their locked box at all times.

POINTERS FOR PARENTS

Your children will learn far more from what you are than from what you say. Believe in them, and if your belief is genuine, your children will believe in themselves. Listen, be in control (this provides security), be consistent and predictable, encourage, allow experimentation, respect one another, communicate love, avoid confrontation and lead them in new directions, and above all enjoy your time with your children. Don't focus on the destination; enjoy the journey. You and your children will grow old quickly, so take time every day to admire and enjoy what will never pass this way again. This is the only chance you'll get.

In child rearing, if one parent is the strict one and the other is lenient, you probably tend to overcompensate for each other. It works like a seesaw. Every time one becomes stricter, the other, in order to remain in balance, becomes more lenient, and both partners keep edging further and further away from each other. This is very confusing to children, and eventually both parents are going to fall off the seesaw!

Evaluating Your Behavior

At times it's good to stop and evaluate how you are doing as a parent. You and your spouse might like to ask yourselves and each of your children what a stranger who watched your family would say about it. How would this observer answer such questions as, "Who's the boss?," "How are problems solved?," "Do family members understand what others are feeling?," "How do they respond to those feelings?," "Is this an authoritarian family or one that is open, relaxed, and interested in others?" Make up some more questions for yourselves in a family meeting and have prizes for good ones. (*Note:* Do not have a prize for the best one. Setting up for success means that contests should be supportive of everyone, not competitive. Children have lots and lots of opportunities for competition every day outside the home. You don't need to add more competitive occasions.)

Now, you and your spouse might ask yourselves about how you interact with each other. Do your children see you complimenting each other, supporting each other, being interested in what the other is doing, asking how each can help out with the other's activities? As you evaluate your interactions, ask yourselves if some of your child's less desirable behaviors may have been learned from you, as in the following examples.

Example #1: If your child tends to demand what he wants when he wants it, is it possible that you do the same thing, under the guise, of course, of having to carry out the duties of your position of authority?

Example #2: Have you and others found that your child is impulsive and flies off the handle easily? Could it be that this isn't all due to his temperament? Could this behavior be similar to yours? Maybe you justify your outbursts by saying you are reacting to your child's disruptive behavior, but perhaps you need to model a better way of handling aggravation, both for your child's sake and to calm yourself down.

Example #3: Have you called your child messy and disorganized? Have you described her room as filthy? Is it possible that your family life is chaotic, not in terms of housekeeping but in other ways? Maybe the disorder in your child's room is a reaction to emotional chaos in the family.

Example #4: Are your children constantly fighting with one another? Must your children compete for your attention? Is it possible that you and your spouse model confrontation, competition, and arguing?

Example #5: Do your children go after their siblings' vulnerable spots and put one another down? Is it possible that you tend to aim for your spouse's Achilles' heel? Everyone has his or her own special soft spots. It might be weight, poor school performance, or something else. Identify these special spots and respect them. Do not use your knowledge to attack them. These people, after all, are your family! Home should be a safe harbor. Model caring and concern, not viciousness.

Changing Your Behavior

You can learn a lot about yourself by watching your children and recognizing habits and behaviors they have learned from you. You'll find that making changes in yourself produces remarkably quick changes in your children.

Don't spend too much energy trying to change something that you should just accept. Change what changes easily but avoid, if possible, trying to change that which doesn't. If your spouse had a firmly ingrained characteristic when you married, don't expect to change it. Rather, find something positive in it. When you can't beat 'em, join 'em. For example, if your spouse is an orderly perfectionist and you're not, instead of letting it drive you crazy, look upon it as a wonderful advantage. Think about how relaxing it is to know where everything can be found quickly and easily.

But when there are things that can and must change, tackle them one at a time. Set your family up for success (that's SURFS = Set Up Regularly For Success, versus TURF = Trip Up Routinely for Frustration). Succeeding at one change will make the next one easier.

Remember to compliment yourself and your family on things you are currently doing well. Acknowledge your successes and keep setting new goals for a more positive life together as a family as goals are met. Be aware, however, as you make changes, that especially in a family with a child with A.D.D., there may be a tendency to resist change and to want things to revert back to the way they were. As a child's behavior improves, sometimes other family members will try to push the child back into his old ways as a problem child. This is because a child who misbehaves takes the heat off others. As you make changes, you will see some subtle relationship shifts, and you may need the help of a counselor to sort them out.

Act now! Reading about what to do is not enough. Your family will not gain from these pointers unless you take action on some of them.

CREATING A SENSE OF FAMILY WORKING TOGETHER

You can give yourself a wonderful sense of building something together as a family by working on hobbies and activities together. These can be as inexpensive as using old scraps of wood to build a dollhouse with your little girl or a boat for your son, or they can be as expensive as building a real cottage, letting all your children help design and build aspects of it. The first alternative is every bit as good as, if not better than, the second.

Revisit Your "Biggies" List

Now that you have gone through the steps recommended for analyzing your family and identifying your problem areas and strengths, revisit your biggies list one more time. This time, instead of listing actions you wish to see, list those actions you are taking or determined to take.

Our Family's Most Important Objective:		
The "BIGGIES": problems that interfere with our lives together	The CHANGES we wish to see	The ACTIONS we are taking / going to take to change
1.		
2.		
3.		
Additional "BIGGIES" discovered after doing the Family Inventory	The CHANGES we wish to see	The ACTIONS we are taking / going to take to change
1.		
2.		
3.		

7

Setting Up for School Success

SCHOOL PROBLEMS ARE usually the reason a child's A.D.D. traits are recognized. Children with A.D.D. aren't usually diagnosed until after school entry. At home, parents are typically more accepting of a wide range of learning styles and behavior. They think of their child as being "all boy" or "a bit spacey" at times. The parents have had time to adapt to their child's personality and have learned strategies to direct their child's energy and cope with the quirks.

With the start of elementary school, the child is required to conform to certain norms for learning and behavior. Alone at home, or in a small preschool play group, this child did not stand out as disruptive, but in the classroom there are many more distractions that compete for his attention. He is required to sit still for long periods in a confined space. The child must conform to the teacher's schedule of activities and cannot follow his own interests to the same degree as he could at home or in preschool. More important, his performance is no longer judged just in relation to himself but rather in comparison to his classmates. He does not measure up to what's expected in school, so teacher and parents begin to suspect that the child has an

attention or behavior problem that interferes with learning.

I enrolled Tori in a Montessori school because they use a lot of manipulatives and I felt it was ideal for children with different learning styles. Also, the school was willing to let her move when she needed to. We also used sandpaper lowercase letters, since the majority of what a child reads is printed with lowercase letters. I believed in the Montessori teaching motto: "I hear and I forget, I see and I remember, I do and I understand." I found Maria Montessori's teachings helped me understand children in general, and our child with A.D.D. in particular. Montessori believed that once a child experiences success, that's how he always wants to feel. If children experience only failure, they think that this is a normal way to feel.

Children with A.D.D. behave differently and learn differently. They don't enter school with a disability. They just do not learn the same way most children do. It is important for parents and teachers to recognize these differences and to develop strategies to help these children adjust to and learn in the classroom setting. You want to intervene before these differences become disabling. Here's how.

IDENTIFY THE PROBLEM

Is the problem in the child or in the school? Is there a mismatch between the child and class or between child and teacher? Is the child just not ready for the work in this grade? To answer these questions and others that will help you identify the problem, you need to do some research. Start by talking to your child, the teacher, and other parents. You need to know details about the situation that your child is dealing with on a daily basis. Arrange for a classroom visit and observe your child in action. Here are the steps to help you identify the problem.

Gary's teacher wanted him tested for A.D.D. I was afraid that if we didn't do it or put him on medication, we'd be regarded as not interested in his academic achievement.

Interview the Teacher

Set up an appointment to talk with the teacher. Do this as soon as you realize that your child is having problems. Allow enough time for the two of you to have a detailed discussion. Let the teacher know that you want to help your child to be successful in school and that you want him to have a good year in which he acquires skills and knowledge and also develops a healthy attitude toward learning and about himself as a learner. Acknowledge that this is her goal, too, and thank her for caring.

When people, such as teachers, complain to me about Terry, I ask them to tell me specifically what he did, and I try to interpret his actions for them. Doing this raises the level of the dialogue. People feel that I see my child in a realistic way. It is easy for teachers or other parents to write you off as in denial of your child's behavior if you don't acknowledge what they are saying. But if you say, "Yes, he does do that, but this is the reason," you become part of a team who understands the child, and in the future people will look to you as the expert who can explain mystifying behavior for them. If people are frustrated or at a loss when dealing with your child, it is essential that you support them, just as you would your child, and help them develop the skills they need to interact in a positive way with your child and others like him.

I needed to be compassionate toward people who were unfair to my child, but I always insisted that they deal with her fairly. I was not always a graceful parent in dealing with Susan's teachers, but I wanted them to feel safe confiding in me. I was careful not to commiserate with them when they complained about her, because that would only reinforce their negativity. Whenever Susan's teacher called and said that she needed me to "rejuvenate" Susan, I reminded her why Susan exhibited certain behaviors and helped her separate the sin from the sinner. We developed an honest relationship, in which she felt I knew my child and could hear her criticism about her with an objective ear.

Ask about the classroom environment. This includes such details as how many children are in the class, the mix of boys and girls, the predominant personality types, and what special needs exist in this group of children. Ask also about her teaching styles: Do children work alone or in groups? How much time must they spend sitting and listening? Do they do lots of paperwork? What kinds of hands-on learning experiences do they have? How does the teacher help the children with

Children with A.D.D. in the Classroom: Round Pegs in Square Holes

Educational specialists have set up a school system in which the majority of children are expected to perform at a certain level at a certain age, and in which school entry is based upon chronological age rather than mental maturity. Classroom organization and curricula are based upon how the "average" child learns. The child who learns within the system has "learning abilities," and those who do not learn within the system have "learning disabilities." Parents need some perspective to figure out where the problem lies.

Consider the life of the preschool child. Prior to school entry the child learns by playing. He naturally seeks out activities that meet his needs and exercise his talents. He has a wide freedom of choice from morning until night and can flit from one activity to another at his own pace without being required to conform to a schedule or pay attention to a subject. Parents and other caregivers naturally structure the environment to complement the child's personality and style of learning, which can be done even in day care with a high care giver–to–children ratio. Parents have a high tolerance of their child's behavior and learn to adjust their interactions to complement their child's style. They are free to adjust the home environment to best fit their child's needs.

Then the child enters school. The child has to adjust to a system with a schedule he must fit into, that tells him what activities he must participate in at what time, even what sports he must play and how he must play them. He can no longer choose to participate in one subject and not another. From preschool to first grade, the child goes from having freedom of choice to being in a structured environment six or more hours a day, five days a week. Most children make this adjustment easily; some children are, understandably, not so adaptable.

The child who can't adapt squirms at his desk or stares out the window instead of focusing on the chalkboard. Even when his hands are tensely folded on top of his desk, his legs are running underneath. This child's well-being is threatened by the school environment. Children who can fit in are considered "normal," but others are "misfits" and, therefore, get negative labels. Put bright, creative children into a classroom where they are bored, understimulated, and just don't fit, and you can expect them to "misbehave" as a survival tool.

Then there is the phenomenon of cooped-up kids. Every schoolchild needs

learning and using their time well? Then ask about how your child is functioning in this environment.

Be observant. Does this teacher truly understand your child? Teachers vary greatly in their knowledge of Attention Deficit Disorder and in their beliefs about what to do about it. How does this teacher perceive your child? Are your child's positive qualities, such as energy and imagination, appreciated? Is your child getting mainly positive or negative messages from this teacher? (You will also need some personal space. Children with A.D.D. need a lot more. Putting thirty six-year-olds in a small, boring, low-ceiling classroom and requiring them to sit still while looking in the same direction at the same chalkboard may be asking too much, especially for children with A.D.D.

So is the disorder in the child or in the system? Do we drug the child to fit the system, or do we change the system to fit the child? It is less costly to label and drug the child to conform to the system, but is this in the child's best interest? Might it be better to develop a specific teaching style to fit the learning style of the child?

For parents and teachers, this means discovering the child's personal learning style — the way in which the child learns best. This may not be the predominant style of teaching in that particular classroom. Parents need to communicate with the teacher so that their child's individual learning style will be respected, and teachers need to be conscientious about discovering children's individual learning styles and creative about teaching to a child's strengths. For example, some children do not learn well from lectures, workbook exercises, or copying information off the chalkboard. They are more likely to learn from field trips, from playacting, from techniques in which they get their hands on material and see it, feel

it, and experience it. Requiring a child to learn in a way that is different from the way he is wired to learn sets him up to misbehave and to be misunderstood, mislabeled, and mistreated.

Just because your child does not learn in the traditional ways does not mean that he has learning disabilities. He has "disabilities" only relative to the system in which he is required to learn. He may actually have a very creative learning style that needs to be recognized and nurtured.

Parents, be your child's advocate. Be sure he is placed in the right classroom, with the right teacher, with the right style of learning. Keep informed about what goes on in the classroom. Be a volunteer or assistant at school so you can understand firsthand how your child functions in this environment. Intervene before your child's learning difference becomes a disability.

If you aren't brave parents, you can't raise brave kids. By repeatedly being Laurel's advocate, I seem to have passed on to her a bit of my spunk. One day her fourth-grade teacher was telling what Laurel felt was a scary and insensitive story. She politely raised her hand and suggested to the teacher that this story was inappropriate for the class. I was so proud of her.

your child's view on this.) It may help the teacher if you point out some of your child's strengths that she has overlooked. Share your child's special interests. If he loves baseball, maybe she can encourage him to write stories or read books about that topic.

Do the personalities of your child and the teacher clash or mesh? Does this seem to be a classroom in which your child will thrive? In many cases a child's school performance varies from year to year depending on how he gets along with the teacher. A.D.D. children are very sensitive to teaching style. For example, one year your child may have a nurturing, accepting teacher who provides just the right amount of structure and recognizes your child's talents. Another year he may have a rigid teacher who is nitpicky about neatness, insists that he stay in his seat, and gives him predominantly negative messages.

Finish the interview by establishing a method for ongoing communication. In future meetings you can fine-tune a plan for action. After your interview, write down your impressions:

A teacher notes: I had a student once who was interested only in baseball. After getting nowhere in trying different materials to try to hook him, I finally met him where he was. I bought baseball cards and used them for all his language and math lessons. He became a different child. He came alive. I was able to introduce other materials from the curriculum over time. We had a great year, and his parents were very thankful.

A mother notes: Be brave. It is very hard work being your child's advocate, but if you aren't willing to confront someone who's acting in a destructive way with your child, you are abandoning your child and the adult who cares for your child, such as a teacher. With your help, the teacher will grow in her knowledge of how to manage children with A.D.D. And who knows how many other children will benefit from your actions? If you want to raise brave children, you need to be a brave parent. Remember, you aren't to blame that your child is different. Don't be intimidated. You and your child should be treated with respect.

Do a Classroom Visit

With permission from your child's teacher, observe your child's classroom or be a parent helper for a day. Some mothers may be in a position to volunteer on a regular basis, such as one morning a week. Observe and evaluate your child in the classroom environment. This way you can draw your own conclusions rather than relying on your child's impressions, the teacher's reporting, or gossip among parents. See if you can identify which situations trigger negative behavior and which trigger positive experiences. Be on the lookout for practical things that could be done to improve the situation. Perhaps a change in seating would make sense: put the child closer to the teacher, away from the window distractions, and near calmer students. Is the teacher flexible? Are the teacher's expectations realistic? Perhaps you will notice weak areas that you could work on at home, such as handwriting or learning math facts. If your child seems to be yawning a lot or putting his head on his desk, he may need more sleep. At the end of the visit, reflect on the dominant messages that your child received that day. As you have done previously in other situations, run these observations through your intuitive feelings, as only a mother can do. Is this a place where you want your child to spend the day? List your conclusions.

Heather was having great difficulty at school and her teacher was at a loss. I observed some classes to see what the problem was. She was having trouble integrating two pieces of information that were input from two different sources. She couldn't match the symbol for the letter to the sound the letter made. So I told her teacher that she should try treating Heather one day as if she were deaf and make the lesson completely visual (show her an apple and then show her the symbol for a small "a"). The next day she should treat her as if she were blind and make the lesson completely audi-tory (say the word "apple" and then say only the sound "a"). Soon Heather had all her sounds. I also played games, such as giving her stickers with letters on them to match what was in her lunch (e.g., "S" for sand-wich).

Interview Your Child

Interviewing your child about school has to be done indirectly. Direct questions such as, "What did you do at school today?" seldom work. First pick up on nonverbal cues. Does your child look happy when he comes in at the end of his school day? Is he happy to go to school in the morning? Does he talk spon-taneously about the things he does and the friends he plays with? Does he proudly show off his creations from school? Or do you get the impression that he is struggling?

When talking to your child about school, try giving openers rather than asking direct questions. Remarks like "You look tired [or happy, or whatever applies]; they must have kept you busy at school today" give your child a chance to open up and talk about his day without feeling that you are interrogating him. After your chat, write down your impressions.

DRAW YOUR CONCLUSIONS

After you have done the information gather-ing, summarize your observations. This exer-cise will not only help you focus on the problems, but it is a good starting point for explaining your situation to your child's doc-tor or other professional.

Dr. Lynda notes: *When parents come to our center for an A.D.D. evaluation, it saves them time if they have already done some*

Using Puppets to Teach

Children often clam up when you press them directly with questions like, "How do you feel?" They often are not reflective enough to really notice how they feel. They just experience it. But they may readily disclose their feelings to an intermediary, such as a favorite toy or puppet. This is less threatening, since the puppets rather than the real people are talking. Puppets are pretend and not likely to pass judgment or punish. Hold a puppet in each hand and talk in a different voice with different expressions for each puppet. Each puppet takes a side. For example,

Charlie puppet: I really want that cookie so much. It is just sitting there on the counter and I don't think any-one will notice.

Suzy puppet: But maybe we shouldn't take that cookie. It's so close to dinner-time. Mom always says to have dinner first. I bet if we told Mom we wanted that cookie but we left it alone she would give us two cookies later.

Besides using puppets to talk directly to your child, use toys or puppets to talk to your child's doll or teddy bear, or encourage your child to talk to these go-betweens.

---

interviewing, so that the problem is defined and we can get right down to the business of what to do about it.

Summarize what you have learned from the teacher, your classroom visit, and your child. Jot down some conclusions.

What are the major areas of concern? _____

_____

_____

How are they affecting your child's learning?
His behavior? His self-image? _____

_____

_____

_____

What do you believe can be done about it?

_____

_____

_____

LEARNING STRATEGIES THAT WORK

Just as in other areas, to set up your child for
school success, you must customize, customize, customize. No one strategy fits every
family, or every child in every classroom in
every grade. We have chosen those strategies
that in our experience work for most children in most situations most of the time.
They will probably work for your child at
home and at school. Yet you and your child's
teacher must fine-tune each one of these
strategies to fit your unique family and school
situation. Most children will profit from these
learning tips, whether or not they have a
problem with attention. But for children with
A.D.D., these strategies are essential.

Improve Your Child's Organization

The only time you can expect naturally good
organization from people with A.D.D. is
when they are working on their own pet
projects. Your son may line up his miniature
trucks in a complicated pattern or organize
his baseball cards precisely (and woe befall
anyone who touches them!). He will not,
however, be able to find the hamper for his
dirty clothes or used towel, and all his other
toys will be scattered and uncared for. Study
notes, when they exist at all, will be
everywhere but under the correct subject
heading in the binder. Children with A.D.D.
need your help to get organized for school.
Here are some techniques:

Start early. "Young and impressionable" may
be a cliché, but it is so true. So build habits
early by organizing your child's room during
the preschool years. Try the old adage "A
place for everything and everything in its
place." Dresser drawers are organized according to type of clothing in each, the toy
shelves and bookshelves have designated
spots for favorite friends. There can be bins
and boxes for Barbie accessories or collec-
tions of action figures. You need not be a
neat freak but try to be orderly. Our philoso-
phy is that a home is for living and need not
look like a picture out of an interior decorat-
ing magazine. When Dr. Lynda's boys were
young, their toy shelves were hinged and on
wheels, so that they could be closed to make
the room instantly look tidier. There are now
whole stores and catalogs, such as *Everything's Organized* and *Hold Everything,* de-
voted to selling things to help you manage
your space and time. People with A.D.D.
keep them in business.

Children have a sense of order naturally.

As they organize their external world, they are really organizing their internal world too. The external world only represents internal. How your child with A.D.D. looks on the outside (how his clothes, room, desk, etc., are kept) gives you a glimpse of how he feels on the inside. As children become more organized internally, this is reflected in their habits externally, and vice versa. Children need to work through becoming organized concretely before they can internalize it.

Whenever Ben was doing homework I would see his engine seize up and his eyes fill with terror. The thought of having to do something they don't understand can paralyze children who have A.D.D. I had to teach Ben skills for how to approach homework. I would walk him through each step: "What is the assignment?" "What does that mean?" "What does the teacher want?" "What should you do first?" Parents can't just assume that children with A.D.D. learn like other children do. They have to realize that their child does not pick up knowledge in the same way other children do, and they have to change the way they see them.

Set a good example. Remember that children are copycats. You want them to copy how to keep track of things on an everyday basis. Do you have a running shopping list on which you can jot down grocery items as they are used up? Small magnetic pads that go on the refrigerator door are handy for this if you are short of counter space. A calendar for the month with large squares is indispensable. On it goes everything from parents' night at the symphony to your children's Little League and ballet times. You may also need a bulletin board with other information posted and easily at hand: team lists with phone numbers for carpooling, a school calendar of dates and events, phone numbers for the babysitter.

Get your child a daily planner. Another example you can set is using a daily planner. When your child starts using a homework book, you can congratulate him on starting a lifelong habit. A child with A.D.D. needs to develop the habit of writing things down early, so if the school does not issue a planner, go to an office supply store with your child and choose a daily agenda book. Even in a school where every child is issued a planner, the likelihood of a student with A.D.D.'s using it properly, if at all, is quite slim without some coaching. Enlist the teacher's help in seeing that it is filled out correctly every day. You will want to keep up the supervision at your end to guard against backsliding. Some supervision of the use of the planner may be necessary even through high school. (For more on the use of daily planners, see page 147.)

Instead of using a daily planner, children in the primary grades can carry a daily communication log back and forth between teacher and parents. (This is good practice for the use of a planner in years to come.) If a lot of things seem to be slipping through the cracks, you should discuss this possibility with the teacher. A daily communication book is labor intensive on both sides and a test of adult consistency, but it can greatly improve the relationship between home and school. One mother we know bought her son a backpack that had an extra outside zipper, and that was where the communication book went each day. It gave it a special status and prevented it from getting lost — at least most of the time.

Get the homework home. Sometimes it takes a lot of home-school communication to ensure that work gets home. In one extreme case, the teacher and the child's mother met each Friday for a preview of the next week's homework. (This was a teacher who planned ahead and knew from her daybook exactly what she would cover.) The child was then rewarded with points on a chart when each item arrived home the next week. If he forgot an assignment, his mother had the backup copy she had received from the teacher the previous Friday. At the next Friday meeting, the mother checked with the teacher that all the assignments done at home that week reached school, and the child was again rewarded with points. There was no gain in forgetting, but no great loss either. The child got a reward for remembering, so he gradually got more responsible. Most children will not require this much supervision, and not every teacher will go to this much effort for a single child in the class, but this routine certainly set this child up for success and, in the long run, probably saved everyone both time and frustration.

I taught him to use highlighters on his homework paper to keep track of key points. I knew he would have trouble going from the concrete to the abstract, and the highlighters would help him eventually learn to highlight ideas in his head.

Set up a study hall. Private boarding schools have supervised study halls after supper. You can have the same thing at your house without spending $25,000 a year. Study hall is not always a set place, but it is a set time. During that time students do homework, and, if that does not fill the time, they are expected to review their notes and study or read. Set the time with your child and decide what is reasonable for his age and stage. Study time need not be continuous; it could

be two or three shorter periods to accommodate your child's need for breaks. Of course, children can always study longer if they get interested in something. Those private school study hours are usually two hours per night for high school, so you may want to work gradually toward that goal.

During study hall you should minimize distractions. Ask friends to call at other times. If the phone rings, either let the answering machine get it or teach your child to explain politely that she is busy and will call back later.

You can start study hall as early as kindergarten or first grade, making it just a short time of study with a parent involved. Catch children while they are still young enough to enjoy playing school. When starting a study hour with an older child, find a way to make it special. Make it pay off for the child, either with an immediate award (e.g., a story, a snack, a game) or points on a chart that count toward a future reward. There are lots of workbooks available for every level at bookshops and stores that sell educational materials, from readiness skills on through the upper grades. You may want to use these to supplement assignments from your child's teacher and what you yourself create in the way of projects. Remember the Cub Scout motto: "KISMIF: Keep it simple, make it fun." Keep the KISMIF rule in mind.

Study co-op. If you are lucky enough to have a neighbor willing to try this experiment, set up a study hall co-op. Sometimes your child studies at your house and sometimes at the neighbor's. Often children behave better for others than they do for their own parents. (Perhaps this is why in medieval times a nobleman would send his adolescent son to another nobleman's household to be a page and learn deportment there.)

When your child and the neighbor child study together, they learn how to work with someone else in the same room without being distracted. The children do not have to be doing the same assignments, though sometimes co-operative study can be good for tasks like learning vocabulary.

Monitor your child's notebooks. Try to do this in a way that shows interest rather than like a sergeant doing an inspection. This can be tricky, because the children who need help organizing their books tend to be defensive and won't want to show their work. If the notes are incomplete, discuss ways to fill in the gaps. Try to direct your child's thinking so that he comes up with answers (see page 190). Perhaps good notes can be borrowed from a classmate over the weekend and copied. Maybe the student should contact the teacher. Just getting all the loose bits of paper out of the schoolbag and into the proper binder is probably a good place to start. The goal is a neat and complete set of notes. If it's neat in the binder, it's neat in the child's mind.

Organize a study area. Together with your child, decide on what is needed in the study area. An organized desk reflects an organized mind. Compare the study area to an executive's desk and office because you want to develop the attitude that school is your child's job and he should be professional about it. Keep the desk or table uncluttered except for things that are actually needed, such as paper, pens, and a dictionary. These days, a computer and printer might be included among study area necessities, especially for older students.

Start the School Day Right

Mornings can be a nightmare for the family that has a child with A.D.D. These children need reminders, organization, and a large dose of advance planning and patience. It is 8 A.M. and family rush hour in the Smith household has begun. Mom and Dad are trying to get themselves ready for work and are hoping and praying that when the school bus comes, Billy will not have his shirt on inside out and be missing one shoe. They have been through this scenario many times. Dad reminds Billy that it is time to get dressed. Ten minutes later Mom finds him still in his pajamas doing headstands on his bed. The school bus arrives and Billy is only half dressed and half fed, and no one knows where his backpack is. Parents are half dressed, half fed, and totally frazzled. By the time Billy gets to school and parents get to work, they all feel they have been through a major ordeal.

Does this sound familiar? Are you tired of reminding your twelve-year-old to brush his teeth after breakfast when this has been part of the routine since he was four? How can you avoid this morning stress?

Plan ahead. The night before, together with your children, pack the lunches, lay out their clothes, find their shoes, put all the homework papers in their backpacks, and put their backpacks near the door. Get to sleep early so you and your children feel well rested. Get up early so you and your children do not feel so rushed. Get yourself dressed and ready before you wake up your child.

Stay calm. Tension is contagious. Do not expect your child to understand how important your 9 A.M. presentation is. He has other things on his mind (many other things in the case of a child with A.D.D.). You do not want to send children off to school and yourself off to work feeling upset. Children are often frightened when a parent is tense and may react with attention-seeking behavior. Often these dawdling and procrastinating behaviors push a parent over the top.

Every morning as my child was getting ready for school, my anxiety about how his day would go would churn inside me and I would spill it out, so that my child was leaving for school as anxious as I was. Once I learned to control my own anxiety about his performance, he became less anxious himself.

Wake them gently. The transition from asleep to awake can be particularly hard for youngsters with A.D.D. With the exception of the early birds who jump out of bed at the crack of dawn and are on the run until they drop at night, children with A.D.D. have trouble shaking sleep and will fall back asleep very, very easily. Respect their need to make the transition more slowly and do not expect them to get out of bed the moment they awaken. Give your child a pleasant first call to awaken and then a second call a few minutes later to get up. Instead of a verbal reminder, try a touch, such as rubbing your child's back. Alarms with a snooze button are another good idea for older youngsters who can use them responsibly (i.e., not just turning the alarm off completely). Some children who get up to an alarm clock need to put it across the room so that they have to get up to turn it off.

Construct a reminder chart. Together with your child make a chart that lists all the things that must be done each morning and the order in which they should be done. This can be in words or pictures, depending on the age of your child. (For guidelines on how to construct this chart, see page 112.) Starting the day off with structure settles the mind and spares the nerves. Here are sample items for the chart:

• Get up at second call.
• Get washed/shower.
• Get dressed.
• Make bed.
• Eat breakfast.
• Brush teeth.
• Pack backpack. Remember lunch bag.

You might want to turn this into a morning schedule, with times attached to each task, to keep your child moving. Here's an example of a schedule that works for one family:

7:00 Get up and make bed.

7:15 Eat breakfast.

7:30 Get dressed, brush teeth, and comb hair.

7:50 Put coat on and check backpack.

8:00 Out the door.

You may need to allow more time, although too much time can backfire when it encourages getting sidetracked from the actual goal of "out the door."

Make sure your child eats a nutritious morning meal. If your child has food sensitivities that affect his concentration and behavior (see pages 269 to 271 for how to tell and what to do), be sure you avoid these foods for breakfast. The best meals for starting the day contain nutrient-dense foods, including some protein, and complex carbohydrates — foods that release a steady amount of energy all morning long, avoiding the blood sugar ups and downs that can affect mood and concentration. (See "Best Breakfasts," page 263.)

Pack a snack. In children with A.D.D., behavior and concentration often deteriorate in the late morning. Possibly this is because their blood sugar is dropping. A nutritious mid-morning snack can avoid this dip in concentration. A snack for afternoon recess can help avoid the end-of-the-day doldrums.

Ensure a peaceful trip to school. If your child walks to school and dawdles, arriving late even though you send him out the door on time, pay an older schoolmate to walk with him. If he is in a car pool that is filled with rambunctious kids, calm the passengers or change car pools. If the school bus is like a traveling zoo, try to get your child to sit near the driver. Sometimes you have to change your own schedule so that you can drive your child to school.

Joseph was so easily distracted when walking to and from school that he had twice lost his school bag when he put it down to throw a snowball and forgot to pick it up again. His mother felt frustrated but knew he had not done it on purpose. She got him a backpack so that he did not have anything to put down and leave behind.

Improve Your Child's Attention Skills

As the name "Attention Deficit Disorder" implies, attention problems are what bring most of these kids to the doctor or learning specialist. As we discussed in chapter 1, these children are not always inattentive, they are *inappropriately attentive.* They focus on the

---

The Problem with Tests

In teaching medical interns, Dr. Bill used to advise them, "The problem with administering tests is that you are forced to do something with the results." In many cases, tests reveal mainly how the child takes tests, not necessarily what knowledge he has or how intelligent he is. This is especially true in standardized tests, which are designed to tell about how an individual ranks compared with a group of the same age. And there are circumstances that influence test taking and the results. The child may not have been completely well that day or may have gotten a poor night's sleep or missed breakfast. He may be preoccupied with problems at home or still be wound up from an argument with an older child on the school bus. Maybe he's just plain having a bad day. Some children, regardless of their temperament or intelligence, just don't do well on tests. Parents and teachers should bear in mind that children with A.D.D. are often poor test takers. They are more prone to giving impulsive answers. They often give very brief responses or a shrug because they do not keep focused enough to reflect and give a complete response. They may rush and make careless errors. In general, a test result when the child has A.D.D. tells you how he is functioning but gives you little insight into what his potential might be.

---

wrong things at the wrong time or may even go into hyperfocus. When in hyperfocus the child has blinders on and sees only his own goal.

Teaching attention skills means helping your child's mind to focus more appropriately on tasks and making the tasks easier to focus on. As you will see, the phrase, "bring it to his attention" has particular meaning for the child with A.D.D.

Catch the child's attention. Making eye contact is a good way to start any communication with your child. Teach this to your child as a listening skill. Tell him he must practice watching the teacher when she is speaking. If a child is fiddling with something in his desk as the teacher explains an assignment, there is no hope that he will understand what to do. (For more on connecting before you direct, see page 120.)

Hold the child's attention. Swim to success using the FIN principle:

- Frequency. Children with A.D.D. need a high frequency of exposure to anything you want them to learn. Do not expect them to pick something up the first time around.
- Immediate feedback. Acknowledge each step of their accomplishment as they finish it. Children with A.D.D. do not like to wait for their rewards. The phrase "I can't wait!" is not just a figure of speech for these children.
- Novelty. Especially for something boring that has to be learned by rote, such as times tables, you had best make it catchy. Make up a story to go with a fact. "The 49ers are a lucky football team, and 7 is a lucky number, so 7×7 is 49."

Buy a computer. A computer gives frequent, immediate feedback in a novel way. It is no wonder that it holds the attention of individuals with A.D.D. The current generation of children with A.D.D. is the luckiest that has ever lived, because they have access to computers. They can learn keyboarding and get around the poor handwriting problem. They can edit what they write in a less tedious way without recopying. They can turn in a finished product complete with neat graphics and different kinds of typefaces using the publishing software that is available. Computers give children an easy way to use their creativity. In college, it is expected that essays will be typed, so you can prepare your child by starting this habit early. Computers can also be used for drill and practice of things like number facts; some programs do this with a lot of action and fun. There are countless games that encourage reading and teach subjects such as Geography while the child just enjoys the challenge.

Dr. Lynda recalls: When my ten-year-old saw me reading a biography entitled Raffles, *she asked, "Why are you reading about a hotel in Singapore?" This was some incidental learning she had picked up from playing the computer version of* Where in the World Is Carmen Sandiego? *It was also an opener to teach a little British history and explain that the hotel was named for a man.*

Check out educational software at a store that allows you to see it up and running, and take your child along to try it out. There is so much available that you might first want to go to the library and check out magazine reviews on educational software. The librarian can tell you what magazines or journals in the library's collection have this information. If you are computer literate yourself, you can doubtless find out more about software on the Internet.

Keep directions simple. Teaching the child with A.D.D. means doing a lot of creative packaging. How you present an instruction determines whether or not a child will pay attention to it. Keep instructions short, like a budget telegram. Give instructions just one step at a time. Instead of "Get your reading book, find the story, and read the first page," give the instructions one piece at a time. This also meets your child's need for a lot of attention, since you will compliment her as each part of the job is done. Work up to multiple directions gradually.

When Tom was four years old we were forever starting his school day with a fight about his getting dressed. I was using a timer with him and he still wasn't getting dressed on time for school. So I asked his teacher if she cared how he came dressed to school. She said no, so I sat him down and said, "This isn't working, so from now on, the new rule is that if you don't get dressed before the timer goes off, I'm going to pick up your clothes and put them in your backpack and you can get dressed at school. We aren't going to be late anymore and no one is going to start the day with my yelling." He understood and agreed to this. The next day he still spaced out and fooled around and didn't get dressed, so I grabbed his clothes and put them into his backpack. He dragged on my ankle to the car and cried loudly most of the way to school. He begged not to be left off, but I left him off at his classroom in his red, fuzzy pajamas. Tom never had a problem getting dressed again. Kids with A.D.D. seem to learn best from their experiences, by being able to see the results of their actions.

Divide and conquer. Especially when homework is involved, help your child divide her work into small chunks. She may find a whole page of math problems daunting, but if you have her do a line at a time, with you then checking and giving praise, she will manage better. The same principle applies to cleaning her room or other tasks. This may remind you of feeding your toddler. Presenting a heaping plateful invites resistance and possibly a mess. Small frequent feedings get more food into the child with fewer hassles, although this requires more attention from parents.

Keep study sessions brief. Give frequent breaks so that your child can get up and move about. Three twenty-minute sessions will be more productive than an hour straight. With a young child you might be looking at three five-minute stints.

Keep the work interesting. Most children show an attention deficit when presented with boring subjects. While regular students either tune out the boring material or maintain some attention in a semiconscious state, children with A.D.D. can't handle the boredom. It goes against their sense of well-being, so they develop survival strategies to self-stimulate, such as fidgeting, or other disruptive behavior. If they find a subject boring, they develop their own more interesting internal subject matter by daydreaming. An alternative to drugging the child is to soup up the way the material is presented. For example, when studying animals, it's more interesting to go on a field trip to a zoo. Or, rather than just rote teaching a History lesson, such as a famous battle, the teacher might fabricate a play, giving each of the students, especially the ones with A.D.D., an interesting part. Now that bit of history has relevance to the child and is likely to get his attention. It's an unfortunate fact, however, that schools do not always opt for the more imaginative approach. As Dr. Thomas Armstrong, author of *The Myth of the A.D.D. Child,* so aptly said, "It is easier for the school system to try to change the child, usually by drugs, than to change the way they teach."

Set a scene that is conducive to learning. You know your child best, so you can help her decide on the best study area in your home. For some children it will be the kitchen table, so that a parent is close by to monitor their work and be available for questions. For others it will be their bedroom study desk. Different tasks may call for different study venues. If there are a lot of vocabulary words to learn, it could be done outdoors. An essay might be written in the den with the door closed. You can drill math facts on the living room couch. In school the child should be seated in the area with the fewest distractions. The back of the classroom encourages children to be in their own world rather than following what the teacher is saying. Sitting next to the window tempts children to look out. But keep in mind the problems of inner distractions with A.D.D. Do not go to the extreme of putting a child in a study carrel or isolating the child in a way that may be perceived as punitive.

Vary your tone of voice. Monotones are guaranteed to induce sleep in already wandering little minds. Use frequent surprise words: "Ready?" "Look!" E-X-A-G-G-E-R-A-T-E the syllables the way you naturally did when trying to catch and hold the attention of your infant: "Goooood job."

Teach your child to sit still. Children with A.D.D. need to develop a sense of their personal space, and this begins at home. When your child is going to do something like watch TV, have him define his space and make a deal with him that he should stay in-side it until the program is over. To make it a game, let him use masking tape to mark out an area of the floor around himself, or try a blanket or sleeping bag. If he can stay within his special space he gets a reward, such as a snack. To make it more fun, let him mark out a space for you, too. (Just make sure you have chosen a program that you can both en-joy or that you have some knitting or paper-work to do.) Also encourage good posture, which will keep the child more alert. One good position is sitting cross-legged on the floor with hands out to the side as props. If your little squirmer needs help staying planted, reinforce this behavior by rubbing her back or massaging her shoulders as long as she sits still.

Adolescents may learn some subjects more easily if they keep moving. One college stu-dent reported, "I walk up and down my room loudly lecturing at the walls, debating each point, and proving how each section of work links logically to other sections. Sometimes this is the only way I can stay alert and on task." And the wife of a lawyer with A.D.D. laughed as she reported that the carpet in his office had to be replaced because he had to pace while talking on the phone.

Be realistic. Some children need to move, and it is best to arrange the situation so that they have some latitude. A teacher who lets a child run errands or erase the chalkboard un-derstands this need to move.

Rid your child's mind of ruminations.
Anyone can be distracted, but some children with A.D.D. have particular trouble shifting back and forth mentally. When they are wor-ried about something, they get fixated on whatever is bothering them. With young chil-dren, you can try verbal redirection: "I know you're worried about what to wear for Hal-loween. Let's talk about it at supper. Dad might have good ideas, too. Supper time would be great for coming up with a plan. Let's just put that little worry in a box and open the box at dinner. Right now my job is to finish dinner, and your job is to finish that math sheet. Tell me when you get the first row done." You ac-knowledge that the worry is valid, but you try to help your child get on with life.

With adolescents and adults, use a SMIRB (*S*top *M*y *I*rritating *R*uminations *B*ook). Use

SMIRB	
Important Areas of My Life and My Worries	**Other Ways of Thinking About Each Problem or Actions I Can Take**

• School subjects:
  • Topic for history paper?
  •
 	
  •
 	
• Family:
• Friends:
• Activities (Sports / Music / etc.):
• Part-time job:
• Other:
	I'll ask the teacher for ideas.

a notebook or a section in a daily planner and divide the pages into two columns. Write down the thing you are ruminating about on the left and put ideas for handling the problem on the right. Don't go looking for things to worry about, but as worries come up, you can group them by subject matter: school, family, friends, sports, part-time job, and so on. If you cannot take direct action on the worry, see if you can reframe it. Reframing involves getting a different perspective: the same picture will look different if you change its frame. It involves seeing the glass as half full instead of half empty. For example, teenagers waiting to hear about making the varsity team cannot take action, but they can reframe their worry: "If I don't make the team, I can still play intramurals. That will have less pressure and I'll know all my teammates, so it will be fun. Missing varsity won't be the end of the earth."

Once a worry is written down, you tell yourself you can't do anything about it this instant, so you will not think about it until a specific time. "Time to worry" can then be put in a daily planner, or individual worries can be assigned to study time, family meeting time, and so forth. So, when the high school student starts thinking in the middle of Algebra class about whether his girlfriend likes somebody else, he should note it quickly in his SMIRB and get on with his learning. He will feel good about taking control and can even say to himself, "I won't let that worry interfere with my success right now in this class." This skill of being able to compartmentalize concerns and reframe worries is an ability that successful adults must have. Ask a surgeon or a top executive and they will tell you they have no trouble blocking extraneous worries while working. Children who learn to do it now will have an edge. Practice it yourself before suggesting it to your child.

As the parent of a child with A.D.D., you will surely have a few worries to list.

Attention skills, parenting skills, and behavior management are interrelated. Look in chapters 5 and 6 for other strategies to hold wandering eyes and wandering minds.

Improve Your Child's Learning Skills

Children with A.D.D. need to learn how to learn. If left to themselves, their minds wander, and little, if anything, sinks in. Use these tricks and techniques to help your child learn to focus his mind on the learning tasks at hand.

Having fun with learning activities at home is a good way to encourage active learning in younger children. When your child asks questions, help him find the answers in books, on video, or with the computer. If your child has a special interest, for example, cars or horses, encourage her to learn more by providing her with books, toys, models, or posters, or by visiting museums or other special places. Look for opportunities at home to reinforce concepts taught in school. Children study math while cooking, science by helping out with home repairs, and social studies on family trips. Learning is much more than what happens at school.

See and touch. If a concept is not sinking in with your child, try planting it differently. Some children are strong auditory learners (they listen and learn well from hearing words); others are primarily visual learners and need to see something to grasp it. Still others are tactile and like to feel or learn hands-on. Children with A.D.D. often need a multisensory approach, in which all three avenues are used. Little children may learn their alphabet by singing it, feeling sandpaper letters (you can make your own), looking at construction paper letters pinned to a bulletin board, or by placing magnetic letters on the refrigerator at home.

Play games. Playing games teaches children to focus and concentrate and to work constructively in teams with others. In card games and games with dice like Chutes and Ladders, children get comfortable with numbers. Card games also are opportunities to practice remembering things. Checkers and chess call for strategic thinking. Scrabble teaches spelling and vocabulary. Playing games with your children is a fun way to work on thinking skills. The old standby Simon Says is an example of the thinking required for following both verbal and nonverbal instructions. Here are some games you can play in the car (or anywhere) to improve thinking and memory skills, and to just have fun.

1. **The Suitcase Game.** The first person says, "I got my bag and in it I packed my toothbrush." The second person repeats what the first person said and adds another item: "I got my bag and in it I packed my toothbrush and sweater." Player number three adds something else: "I got my bag and in it I packed my toothbrush, a sweater, and my puppy dog." The game continues with each person adding something else on every turn. In order to stay in the game, each person must correctly state all the previous items in the correct order.

The things added often become sillier and sillier, but remembering becomes very difficult. This game holds most children's attention and lets them use their imagination. Suggest the children form mental pictures of the objects to help them remember not only the items but also the sequence. For exam-

ple, they might imagine the dog wearing a sweater using a toothbrush.

During the game, you may have to help the child with A.D.D. occasionally; if one child has a hard time with the game, change the rules so you are playing teams and you are on that child's team. Verbalize techniques for remembering.

2. **The Alphabet Game.** In this game the first player begins with the letter "A" and fills in categories predetermined with words that begin with "A." For example, "My name is Alfred. My wife's name is Andrea. We live in Africa. We sell apples. We drive an Alfa Romeo." (Use this category only if your children are interested and knowledgeable.)

Then the next person uses the letter "B" ("My name is Becky. My husband's name is Bert," etc.), and the next person uses the letter "C," and so on. Again, you may have to form teams to help out your child with A.D.D. or your youngest child. This not only helps with alphabet order, but improves word retrieval and categorization skills.

3. **A Math Game.** With children who are learning to add, you can make a fun game out of adding the numbers on the license plates of cars in front of you. With older children try multiplication with those license numbers. You need to have a rule to keep the older child from winning all the time. You could give the older one a handicap, such as having to count to five before giving an answer, or let the older one be the one to say if the answer is correct and, if not, what it should be.

Another way to have fun with math is to make up word problems about interesting topics. Boys often like platoons of soldiers with rockets, but most parents prefer more whimsical images, such as a circus. Make up problems about how many elephants are in the ring or how many clowns in the car. With

Organized Thinking:
Executive Strategies for Learning

Learning how to learn puts your child in control of the process. Psychologists call plans for learning "metacognitive strategies," because they go beyond regular thinking and involve knowing about how you know things. Strategies for learning build awareness of the processes involved in learning and remembering things.

Teach your child to use the three steps to success listed below instead of just jumping in. Having the internal dialogue of these questions will make him stop and reflect on what he is doing. The few seconds or minutes that it takes to plan and scrutinize will pay off in huge gains in productivity. These are the three crucial steps (the executive's three questions) that must become automatic whenever your child settles down to a task.

1. What's the job here? (What am I supposed to do?)
2. How should I do this job? (What strategies will I use?)
3. How did I do? (What did I learn? How good was the result?)

Obviously, in between steps 2 and 3, the child must do the job, but this happens only after developing a plan of attack. This series of three questions works for tasks from small to large. The following is a sample of how this strategy would work for a first grader doing some basic math, subtracting 4 from 7. Here's the inner dialogue:

1. "What's the job here? What does the sign say, plus or minus? Minus. Okay, I'm going to subtract."
2. "How should I do this job? To subtract I find a difference, so for 7 minus 4, I'm going to think of how many go with 4 to make 7. That's 3, I think. I'll check with my fingers." He counts on from 4, saying, "5, 6, 7," putting down a finger as he says each number. He counts the fingers: "1, 2, 3. Yup, I got it." (Other children, less advanced in their number concepts, might think of other strategies, like using counters, putting out seven and taking away four of them. Or they might use a number line.)
3. "How did I do? That one went easily. I'm getting good at subtraction since I learned I can get the answer by counting. Soon I won't need my fingers, but I feel safer using them for now."

One of the advantages of using the three-question technique is that it makes children aware of when they do not have any strategies for doing something and need to ask for help. When you teach your child this technique, be explicit and tell him to ask for help if he cannot answer question 2. Do not assume that children will automatically ask for help. Typical students do this, but not students with A.D.D. These children need to *overlearn* because they miss so much due to inattention. What a typical child can absorb and remember in a couple of exposures, the child with A.D.D. will have to experience many more times.

older girls and boys, try using the opening ceremonies before a large competition takes place. For example, "If all the hockey players in the tournament were to skate out onto the ice, how many players would there be if there were ten teams with eleven players on each team?" Then vary the problem: "Whoops! There's an elephant! It's galumphing onto the ice at the far end of the rink. What's that? Another team. It's just dumped another team off its back onto the ice. How many men are on the ice now [11 × 11]?" That element of silliness and surprise will help keep the child with A.D.D. interested and alert.

You can make these games as simple or as complex as you like. When you're in the car, don't forget the old standby of singing together. It beats just popping in a tape (though that's fine on occasion, too), because your child is more actively involved in learning and remembering lyrics when he sings.

Teach Your Child to Be an *Active* Learner

Getting someone involved in something is the best way to engage attention. Many mothers intuitively do this from the very beginning when they talk to their babies using questions. Babies find the rising inflection at the end of each question fascinating. This is a good way to read a book to a toddler ("What's the kitty doing?") and to read stories to a preschooler ("What do you think is going to happen on the next page?"). Then, as a child enters the elementary grades, he is prepared to read any material presented to him with an inquiring, active mind-set.

If students who have A.D.D. do not actively participate in learning, they will

quickly become bored. They must make things interesting for themselves. It helps a great deal if the teacher is dynamic and instills enthusiasm in everyone. A parent can also show interest and try to liven up a topic. But ultimately it is the student's responsibility to get interested by finding a way to become involved in the material. Learning to predict what will happen as a key element of learning can make material more interesting. Active learners tend to make great leaders because they need to take control to stay engaged in a project.

How does a student learn actively? Active learners seek out information. They are constantly generating questions and looking for the answers. Instead of just reading to get to the end of the page, the active reader carries on a running dialogue with herself about what will happen next (in stories) or how the facts will be made to fit together (in textbooks). Active readers make little summaries for themselves as they go along that help them make predictions. It's no mystery why mystery stories are so popular: their plots force the reader to ask questions ("Whodunit?"), formulate theories ("The butler did it"), and then turn the pages to learn the answers.

A method of learning that has been successful in the middle grades as a regular assignment with any subject that requires a lot of reading is a prediction quiz. Students not only are assigned a chapter to read but must turn in questions that they predict could show up on a test. This helps them figure out which are the important points worth remembering. This technique helps the students make the transition to the next level of active reading for high school and college-age students. (See "Steps for Active Reading," on the next page.)

Steps for Active Reading

Key Time Frames	Key Questions	What to Do
1. BEFORE: What do I do *before I open* the book (or start listening to a lecture)?	1. **Why** am I reading this? For what purpose? **What** headings would I use, if I were the author?	1. Organize my thinking. Decide on my own personal reason for bothering with this: What will I know at the end that I don't know now? Pretend that I am the author. Organize headings and subheadings. Make predictions about the content.
2. AT START: What do I do *when I first open* the book?	2. **What** headings did the author use? **How** does his organization compare to what I would do? **What** will I learn in this chapter? Generate some specific questions related to the topic.	2. Compare the content with my predictions. Check the author's headings in the table of contents then skim through the chapter. — Read the first paragraph. — Check pictures and diagrams. — Read the conclusion. — Read any questions at the end of the chapter.
3. DURING: What should I do *while I'm reading* in order to make it easier to recall material later?	3. **How** do I learn? How do I keep my mind working so that I can stay alert and recall material later?	3. Find the facts. Answer the reporter's questions: who, what, where, when, why, and how. Keep generating new questions as the old ones are answered. Pick out the main idea in each paragraph **(key words).** Play some games with the information: join these key words/facts together into a picture, or into a sentence, rhyme, silly statement, or acronym.
4. AFTER: What do I do *after I complete* each page and then when I complete the chapter?	4. **What** have I learned? What use can I make of it?	4. Review. Review. Review. a. at the end of each paragraph b. at the end of each page c. at the end of the chapter d. a few hours later e. a few days later, etc.
SUMMING UP	Steps 1, 2, 3, and 4 all involve one simple secret process: Continuous Mental Work on the subject to be learned! Get emotional about it!	Steps 1 and 2 = Organize myself to learn. Steps 3 and 4 = Get actively involved in the material and learn using memory tricks!

Teach Your Child to Organize Information

Children with A.D.D. usually do not think about organizing their thinking. To convince them of the need to do so, get them to compare finding things in a garbage bag versus in a filing cabinet. Try these questions:

- Is it easier to find your socks in a huge bag or in well-labeled drawers?
- Is it easier to find a book in a garage piled high with books and files or in the library?
- When you go to a class and listen, is your mind like a garbage bag or a filing cabinet?

Once they are convinced that organized is better, teach them about grids so they will know one powerful way to achieve organized thinking. A grid organization will help them understand and remember academic material for presentations, written projects, and tests.

A grid is a basic and simple strategy for organizing information. Putting topics across the top and down one side of a page, you create a table for the information you need to learn. It forces you to consider all possible areas. Once areas are outlined, then you can decide which areas your essay (or presentation or study notes) will concentrate on. The reporter's questions (who, when, where, what, why, and how) are a good place to start for many subjects. In History, you might want to have different wars or battles across the top of the columns, and the reporter's questions for the rows. Think of how you could organize facts about the Great Depression, Prohibition, World War II, and so on. If you were studying animals of Australia, you could have column headings like "Appearance," "Habitat," "Food," and the different animals would be listed down the page for the rows. In Geogra-

phy, you might have countries for the columns and row headings like "Population," "Physical Features," "Language," and so on.

John was an eighth-grade student who had a great deal of difficulty recalling material after he read a textbook. To encourage him to use active reading strategies for his History text, his tutor asked John to show him what he thought the author should tell him about a war in the 1790s. He told him to try using questions like *Who* was fighting?, *When* did the war take place?, *Why* were they fighting?, and so on. When John faltered, the tutor helped by asking questions or modeling how to generate questions by thinking out loud. John and his tutor produced the grid on page 194. John generated the first column of questions before rereading and then filled in his grid as he read the chapter. This follows the active reading strategy of generating questions and predicting answers.

The tutor made it a game and modeled reading aloud to demonstrate how to reread the headings and then the passage, picking out key words and chunking words together into catchy phrases. They then paused on some difficult sets of facts and tried to figure out innovative ways of remembering them. They used:

- **Chunking** words and phrases together
- **A map** — a sketch of Great Britain and Europe and the Mediterranean. They drew ships surrounding Europe, and money signs in each of the countries surrounding France to symbolize paying allies to fight for England. This picture emphasized the British strategy.
- **An amusing picture** to help recall facts: John and the tutor made a picture of Horatio Nelson standing on deck looking at a book (for *Aboukir* Bay) with a sphinx in the background (for Egypt). Santa Claus is

The French Revolutionary Wars — Battle at Aboukir Bay		
QUESTIONS	ENGLAND	FRANCE
I. *SETTING*		
WHO — leaders (military and political)	Admiral Horatio Nelson Prime Minister William Pitt	Napoleon Bonaparte
— size of armies — size of navy		
WHY (causes)	self-defense	expansion of empire
WHAT — strategies — weapons	surround, blockade, pay allies . . .	attack empire, e.g., India
BACKGROUND SITUATION (political, economic, social)		
II. *BATTLE*		
WHERE		
WHEN		
WINNER		
HOW — weapons, ships, strategies . . .		
WHAT EFFECT — immediate		
WHAT EFFECT — later history		

on a cruise ship beside Nelson's one empty sleeve, to represent Nelson's losing an arm at *Santa* Cruz. An apple core is on Nelson's eye patch because he lost an eye at *Corsica*. Napoleon Bonaparte is depicted as rowing away in a small rowboat with his ships being "blown-a-part" in the background. Notice how a visual cue triggers an auditory association.

John was quite surprised when he was able to answer correctly the question of what he had learned. He was even more surprised at how little time it had really taken and how

much fun it had been to create the pictures. Like most people with A.D.D., John was creative and imaginative, but he had not previously brought those skills to bear on the reading-and-remembering process. John applied this process of generating questions and predicting answers throughout the scanning, reading, and reviewing stages as he continued in this chapter.

Organizing the Mind

When John finished the chapter, the tutor reviewed with him the techniques he had

used. Learning the strategies was even more important than learning the facts. He had:

1. organized his ideas about what he might learn before he started reading and checked these headings against the main headings the author used (the garbage bag mind versus the filing cabinet mind)
2. used the grid technique
3. used mental pictures to help himself recall key facts.
4. made word associations to remember names of people and places.
5. reviewed key facts when he finished each paragraph.

He now understood that his recall was dependent on actively organizing and reorganizing the information he was reading.

Organizing Written Work

Written work is nearly always the greatest challenge for people with A.D.D. They have rich imaginations, but the task of getting those ideas down on paper is daunting. They may write the minimum or tend to ramble without really making their point. Editing and proofreading are so tedious it seems like torture to them. Often the biggest problem is just getting started. Here is a way to help them organize their thoughts so they can overcome their resistance and write a paragraph with punch.

Explain that the structure of a paragraph is like a hamburger. Just as you have to hold the contents between the top and bottom buns so that you can eat it, your great ideas have to be contained between an introduction and a conclusion. Just like both pieces of the hamburger bun, the introduction and conclusion are made of the same material. You must mention the same kind of things in each. In the middle you want to have not just a plain burger patty but some lettuce and tomatoes, maybe cheese, mustard, and relish, too. Similarly, your paragraph between the introduction and the conclusion has to have more than one idea. Three sentences, making three different points, is a good guideline. You want your hamburger paragraph to be easy to digest, so make it easy to follow the ideas by having a beginning, middle, and end.

The same structure applies to an essay or a lecture. The only difference is that it gets expanded into several paragraphs. Instead of an introductory sentence, you will have an introductory paragraph. This introductory paragraph will have three parts: (1) a catchy "Hi" statement to attract the audience's attention,

(2) a statement of the problem, which is the "Why," or purpose, of your essay, and (3) an overview of "What" you are going to say.

The opening sentence must immediately catch the reader's interest. It whets the appetite, rather like the sesame seeds sprinkled on top of the burger's bun. Maybe use a quote or an interesting statistic related to the topic. The next sentence, the "Why," is your thesis statement (what you are out to prove in the essay). That thesis statement must be supported by at least three arguments. These three arguments, the "What" portion of the introductory paragraph, are just briefly introduced to act as signposts for what is coming in the rest of the essay.

The main body of the essay — the meat of it — expands on those three supporting arguments with at least one paragraph about each. If you have more than three good ideas to support your thesis, then go ahead and write more paragraphs. That is like adding extra condiments on the burger.

You finish your essay with a concluding paragraph, which is like the bottom bun of the hamburger. Its structure is the reverse of the three parts of the introductory paragraph. It (1) begins by briefly reiterating the three points or arguments that you made or areas that you covered, (2) restates your thesis and how you proved it, and (3) says good-bye and contains something generally related to your thesis statement. This ties things up and leaves the reader thoughtful.

The beginning and ending of the essay must be similar (you do not introduce new elements in the conclusion), just like the top and bottom of the burger bun are made of the same dough. The top and bottom are not, of course, identical. You can tell them apart by their shapes. They complete each other, just like the order of ideas in an essay's introduction and conclusion.

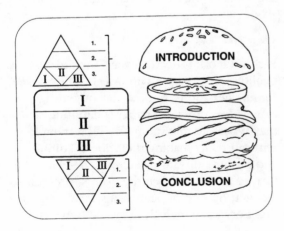

When you take the hamburger approach to writing, it makes giving your child feedback about his work more fun. Instead of telling him it's too short, you can say it seems like a plain hamburger, and you know he could create a delicious cheeseburger. If it is sloppy and needs editing, tell him it looks like the tomato is ready to slip off and the mustard is dripping. Of course children should plan before they write, and they can sketch a burger and write beside it the points they plan to make in each part — it makes a nice variation on introduction, main body, and conclusion. Most children with A.D.D. respond well to ideas that are presented visually, and the hamburger helps them get the picture about writing and having fun with it.

Organizing Textual Material — A Boxing Strategy

This strategy works well for reading new material in a science or mathematics textbook. Look through the chapter before reading it in detail. Think about how each section links to the section before it and the section that follows it. Draw a box around each new concept as it is introduced. For example, if a math textbook is going to teach about how bank interest is calculated, it must first derive the formula for simple interest. Then it will use that concept and formula to go on to the next box, where it develops the formula for compound interest. You will learn and remember if you really understand the logical connections between each of the boxes or sections of the text (assuming the author has placed them in a logical progression). A box must contain the data necessary to derive the equation or the principle being taught and to understand it. Before beginning each new box, do a quick review of the boxes previously covered.

Teach Your Child to Study *Actively*

The skill of being mentally active while reading and listening applies equally to studying for tests. It is just not sufficient to read over notes. When first reading the material, students should make notes in the margin in pencil or use a highlighter if it is their own book. The top students make summaries as well, both when reading and listening. (See page 198 for the "three facts per class" technique.) When it comes to study time, they get *active* and make new study notes that summarize their early summaries of key facts. This does not have to be done as a boring list. People with A.D.D. are creative and often draw elaborate diagrams that show the key areas and how they link up, or they draw trees with the main ideas branching off from the trunk and the details on twigs. Help your child actually have some fun as she masters a topic. This, of course, is easier if studying is not left to the last minute. With a study-hall routine and efficient use of a student planner (both discussed above), last-minute cramming should be infrequent.

Emphasize the process, not the product. Once the process is mastered, the product becomes the focus. If you focus on the product first, the child becomes discouraged. The product will automatically come once the child is comfortable with the process. Children with A.D.D. are masters at wasting time due to their inner distractions. Sure, they may spend an hour in their room with a textbook open, but very little transfer of knowledge may occur. That is why every home study period should produce a product. Call them widgets, if you like, and let your child be manager of the widget factory. Widgets can be simply a chunk of work finished: a group of math questions, a page of reading notes summarized, and so on. If a child needs more concrete rewards, let him keep track of the number of widgets produced on a chart with stars or in a jar with tokens (poker chips work well). Set up a system for exchanging the stars or tokens for prizes, privileges, or special activities. Seeing the chart or the jar fill up can make the child feel proud of the work completed. This process also teaches children how to self-reinforce, that is, reward themselves for finishing something. They learn to follow three steps to make the abstract tasks of learning more tangible:

1. Decide what they are going to produce.
2. Do it.
3. Reward themselves for what they've done, learned, or produced.

(See "Organized Thinking: Executive Strategies for Learning," page 190.)

Get your child to play teacher. To study efficiently when there are large amounts of material, a student must anticipate (make predictions about) what questions the teacher (and, later, the professor) is going to ask on an exam. This is not cutting corners; this is showing a grasp of what is important. A parent can help younger students in this process, and as the children move on to high school and college, they will start to do it for themselves automatically. This approach holds their attention because students must be active to put themselves in the teacher's shoes.

A college student who got an A+ on a midterm exam in History of Science noted, "I did not know all of the material, but the two-thirds that I studied was what I deemed to be the important stuff, and that I knew very well. There is so much information out there that one of the most significant skills I am learning is how to be discriminating about what is really important."

Use the "three facts per class" technique. Teachers have important things to say when they get up in front of the class. It is up to the student in high school or college to figure out what those important things are. In the "three facts per class" technique, the rule is to come up with three important facts from each class period and to *write them down*. Just a key word or equation need be noted for each fact; the one word stands for the whole idea. Teachers almost always give away what is important enough to be on the next exam by their tone of voice, posture, gestures, or comments. Using this technique improves attentiveness, since the student has to watch and listen in order to decide what's important. In reality, there will sometimes be fewer or more than three main points made during a class period, but three makes a good target.

The facts can go in the daily planner if there is room. Since memory can be short, those three key words or equations need to be reviewed within a few hours of first writing them down. The first homework task each evening is therefore to transfer the key words to a special crib sheet for each subject. These sheets can be the last page of a notebook or the last page in a three-ring binder. The crib sheet becomes an overview of what is important in a course and can be used to guide studying. Students who have tried this "three facts" technique tell us it makes a tremendous difference in their ability to recall material covered in the classroom.

Improve Your Child's Memory Skills

How many times have you heard, "I just forgot"? Memory and attention depend on one another. What looks like poor memory is usually a twofold problem: first, in the ability to read or listen without losing focus and, second, in recalling what was read or heard.

TIPS

Here are four tips that should help improve memory skills. You can remember them easily because the first letters spell TIPS.

Tricks of memory. Use rhyming rules very early on, like, "If you hit, you must sit," and "Girls and boys, pick up toys." Try "When you shout, Mom goes out" to teach the consequence of forgetting the quiet voice rule. These are fun to make up, and even young children can memorize them. Then rhyming tools in grade school will be welcomed as a familiar way to have facts presented. For example, perhaps you learned about the discovery of America with the rhyme "In fourteen hundred and ninety-two, Columbus sailed the ocean blue." Another one you may recall from first grade is "Stop, look, and listen before you cross the street. Use your eyes, use your ears before you use your feet."

Learning how to make up acronyms and mnemonics (memory aids) will help a child from elementary school through college. Acronyms are letters that stand for the names of companies, associations, or organizations, like IBM. Many people learned the spaces on the treble clef by remembering the word "face," and the lines with "Every good boy does fine." The names of the five Great Lakes are recalled by their first letters, spelling "homes."

One kind of mnemonic is to create a sentence in which the first letters of all the words correspond to the first letters of what you are trying to remember. Make up a sentence to remember the countries in South America; you should even be able to get them in clockwise order. A skater who started her sentence with, "At chilly practices . . ." had no trouble recalling Argentina, Chile, Peru . . . and the other nine countries. Another trick is to sing your list of things to a simple, well-known tune.

Instant replay. Today's children understand terms like "rewind" and "replay." They mean go back and do it again (the right way, of course). To help impulsive children remember rules or tasks, play the rewind game. For example, your child runs into the street after a ball without looking for cars. You then play the rewind game. Reenact the scene up to the point of danger: run toward the street, then stop at the curb, and say, "Look this way, no car. Look that way, no car." Then you move into the street. Replay this scene a sufficient number of times to ensure that it will be remembered. To help forgetful children replay the scene in which something was forgotten, such as to turn off a light, instead of saying the obvious, throw out a challenging "Replay," which invites the forgetter to backtrack, identify the forgotten action, and rectify the situation. Physically doing something with a child, if necessary, has more impact than telling him not to run out into the street or not to leave lights on. Replay games plant in your child's mind a plan to follow in future situations.

"Replay" is also a way to jog a child's memory to encourage cooperation and politeness. If your son starts to grumble when you ask him to help with the dishes, you can take a step back and say, "Replay." If your child comes in the back door and drops her coat on the floor along with her hat, gloves, and school bag, "Replay" will get her back on the "everything in its place" track.

Paint a picture. Teach children to make pictures in their mind of things they have to remember. Try creating a *remember room* when there are lists to learn or things to remember. Practice doing this in a funny and exaggerated way. Perhaps your son needs to bring his gym uniform (shorts, socks, and T-shirt) home for washing and also a library book that he keeps leaving in his locker. Have him picture a gigantic pair of gym shorts (instead of curtains) hanging over the window in his remember room, with enormous socks hanging on either side like swags. The T-shirt can be framed on the wall next to the window, and the book, giant-size, sits on the table. Now when he is standing at his locker, he just needs to recall the vivid image of his remember room to get the right things in his backpack. (This works for adults, too. Imagine a room with an overcoat and a suit draped on the chandelier and slices of bread used for a tablecloth; you'll stop at the dry cleaners and the grocery store on the way home.)

Say it again. Mental rehearsal is one of the most basic ways to get things set in memory. You just keep repeating it. Say it again, and again, and again. This is what most of us did to learn our multiplication tables. Sometimes saying something with a particular rhythm so that it sounds like rap music helps. But you can set things to other kinds of music, too, depending on your child's taste and repertoire.

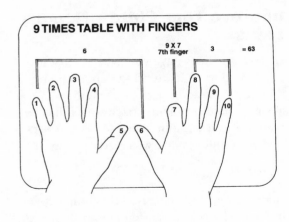

Some Favorite Tips for Times Tables

When Dr. Lynda teaches multiplication tables, she uses tricks. For example, if you can count, you can easily remember that 56 is 7 × 8, since the numbers are in sequence. To learn 8 × 8, children can think of the number of squares on a checkers or chessboard. There are lots of tricks for remembering the nine times table. For example, the first digit is one less than the number you are multiplying by, and the second digit is what goes with the first number to make nine (9 × 4 = 36, be-

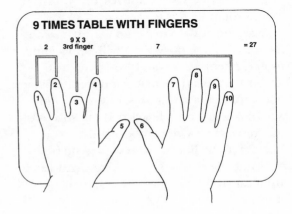

cause 3 is one less than 4, and 3 plus 6 equals 9). This sounds complicated but is easily learned using some finger math. As shown in the illustrations on the facing page, spread the fingers and thumbs of both hands and number them from one to ten, left to right. To multiply 9 × 4, tuck under finger 4 (the fourth finger from the left) and you are left with 3 fingers to the left and 6 fingers to the right of the missing one, to make the answer, 36.

Steps for Word Problems

Children with A.D.D. tend to rush to answer when given a word problem. When they rush through the problem, they often miss points or misinterpret them. They will do something with the numbers but not necessarily the right thing. They may completely miss important facts within the question or have trouble figuring out how the information connects.

Steve was in eleventh grade. He had failed math quite miserably. He had become discouraged and given up trying. His worst difficulties in math were with word problems. Steve was given a problem that most eleventh graders could handle:

"A piece of string is cut into two pieces. The second piece is 5 cm more than twice the length of the first piece. If the original string is 245 cm long, how long is the longer piece when cut?"

Steve sat and looked at the question for fifteen minutes. He scribbled on a page a few times. When asked what he was trying to do, he replied, "I'm trying to figure it out. But I can't do it." Asked what he was feeling, he responded, "I'm nervous and my shoulders and neck feel really tense."

Steve really wanted to do the question, but he was going nowhere. When asked

what was going on in his mind, he said he was skipping around the question picking out a fact here and a fact there. Then his mind would wander off the problem altogether for a few seconds. Just reading the question was a difficult task for Steve.

While it is true that all students would do well to have a logical approach to handling word problems, most students who have A.D.D. really cannot function without such a strategy. They require a rigid, stepwise, logical approach to help them stay on track and not miss crucial statements, connections, and facts. Most high school problems can be thought through logically. With the student who has A.D.D., one can use *math problems to reinforce a nonimpulsive, thoughtful, reflective approach.* The problem above may be solved by a formula or by using shortcuts, but many students do not know that. To them, some of these challenges may at first appear insurmountable. But they can do these problems using a four-step approach.

Steve was encouraged to think about this problem like a detective story. What is the first thing a detective does? He gets the facts! So that is the first step in all written problems. Once he has the facts, he sketches them. Then he needs to solve the mystery and find the truth. In math, the truth gets expressed as an equation.

Step 1: Get the facts and make sure you understand the exact question.
a) What are the facts? List them!
   Fact #1: A piece of string is cut into two pieces.
   Fact #2: The second piece is 5 cm more than twice the length of the first piece.
   Fact #3: The original string is 245 cm long.
b) What is the question being asked?
   How long is the longer piece when cut?

Step 2: Draw and label.

a) Sketch the facts

I<——————————245 cm.——————————>I

I<——?——>II<——(y = twice *?* + 5)——>I

? is a mystery number. We call it *x*.

Step 3: Find the truth.

Put the facts into truth statements (i.e., equations). Translate words into mathematical signs. Ask, "What truth(s) does the question give me that relate some or all of the facts to each other?" How do the facts relate to what we want to know?

    Two pieces add up to the whole.

      $x + (2x + 5) = 245$ cm.

Step 4: Solve the equation and check your answer.

a) Add up the *x*'s on each side of the equation.

    $3x + 5 = 245$ cm

b) To figure out how much $3x$ equals, remove the 5, remembering to do the same thing to both sides of the equation:

    $3x + 5 - 5 = 245 - 5$

    $3x = 240$ cm

c) Divide by 3 to figure out how much $1x$ equals:

    $3x \div 3 = 240 \div 3$

    $x = 80$

d) Go back to the equation and substitute 80 for each *x*:

    $80 + (2 \times 80) + 5 = 245$ cm

    $80 + (160 + 5) = 245$ cm

    $80 + 165 = 245$ cm

e) The longer piece is 165 cm.

    Using steps such as these, word problems no longer seem insurmountable. The student knows where to begin.

The Carryover Principle

Discover your child's special something. It is vitally important for your child to experience success in some activity, whether music, sports, drama, or in social or academic achievements. If she succeeds in one task, her self-esteem will be boosted, and this feeling will carry over into other fields of learning and behaving. Identify what your child is interested in and good at. Create an environment that allows her interests and talents to flourish, and this carryover may have a snowball effect in other areas of her social and academic performance.

Improve Your Child's Motivation

Your child may seem driven like a motor yet show little drive for learning. Parents frequently lament, "We just wish we could get him motivated!" This complaint is particularly true of the group of bright daydreamers with A.D.D. They seem to be drifting through life without a plan, and they do not even seem worried that they do not have a plan. The hyperactive, restless ones typically would rather be anywhere but in a classroom or study environment. When you ask them what their favorite thing at school is, they say, "Recess!" — and they mean it. Here are some ways to turn your turned-off child back on to learning.

Let your child feel a sense of accomplishment. "Nothing succeeds like success!" The more little success stories you build into your child's academic history, the more likely is future academic success. Part of success stems from the confidence your child feels in tackling new learning if past learning has gone well. Expectations are everything. Henry Ford reportedly quipped that if a man thinks he can do something or thinks he cannot, he's right. Your belief system becomes your reality. You may have to look hard to find things to praise about your child's schoolwork each day while the deficiencies glare at you, but you must accentuate the positive. A strong academic self-image depends on it.

Work on your child's skills. If your child's skills are not up to grade level, work with him at home and, if necessary, get some tutoring or other form of supplemental education. You do not want him to feel discomfort every day. It is one thing to be challenged and another to feel chronically behind. A student cannot feel enthusiastic if the work is too hard. Check with the school personnel to see what they can do to improve your child's academic skills. You may need to have some testing done to determine where the gaps are before you can come up with a plan for academic catch-up. Use private tutoring, if necessary. It is a good investment. With improved skills, your child will feel more confident. Instead of struggling in school, experiencing a negative-feedback loop that repeatedly reinforces failure, your child will see his performance improve, which will lead to a positive-feedback loop that will lead to even greater success.

Let your child in on the ending. The Inuit of the Canadian Arctic know how to give their children a sense of accomplishment while learning important tasks. As the Inuit hunter is teaching his son how to make a harpoon, the child watches until the final step and then lends a hand to complete the proj-

ect. Everyone celebrates. As the child grows, he gradually does more of the task, moving back from the end point until he can do it independently from start to finish. You can do the same thing in your kitchen. If you are making a cake, let your child help pour the batter into the baking pans. When you frost the cake, let him frost the top. If you are painting a room, let your child help with the last few brush strokes.

When you're learning some tasks, it makes sense to start at the end. Sometimes it works to do the hardest problems first. When memorizing a list or learning music, learn the ending first, then back up and learn some more. As the child plays through to the end, she'll become more confident when she reaches the material she already knows well.

Notice what is going right. No matter how poor your child's current learning and study habits are, she must be doing a few things right. Do not take these for granted. Give her some praise for the little things. Is there only a blank space where today's journal entry should be? Try saying, "You got the date down correctly. That was a good start." She will be quite aware that other students were filling half a page with writing while she got only the date down. If she didn't even get the date down, you can compliment her on having the journal with her. She does not need to be hit over the head with her deficiencies any more than a wife needs to be chided by her husband for not making gravy. Wouldn't a woman who had spent an hour in the kitchen rather hear "This pork is delicious, and we can have some applesauce with it" than "You forgot the gravy!"

Find the silver lining. Along with commenting on the positive aspects of a child's work, help frame things in a positive way.

When kids are managed by the moment, they tend to see just the bad side. They need to be trained to take a balanced view, accepting negatives and trying to improve on them but also getting some joy from life. If your child is devastated by a poor report card, he does not need a lecture from you to add to his woes, even if he is maintaining a veneer of not caring. (Inside he does care, deeply.) It might be best to put an arm around the child's shoulder and say something like, "We'll certainly have to work to bring these grades up. Luckily no one is going to ask you in high school or college about your marks in the second semester of sixth grade." Then you put the report card away and start working on doing better.

I was very careful not to let the other children in the class speak to Paul in a negative way, so that they wouldn't believe that he was bad and make him the scapegoat just because he was tagged with A.D.D. I was very careful to make the distinction between the person and the behavior. "Yes, Paul, you make me crazy when you do such-and-such, but it's not who you are. It is only your behavior, not you, that I don't like."

Learn from experience. Whenever a child brought home a really bad test grade in Dr. Lynda's house, her stock comment was, "Now you're in a position to get the "Most Improved" award on the next test." This was truly meant. The low mark could be used as a learning experience so that things would be done differently next time. Analyze the reasons for the failure. No notes to study from? Forgot the test because it wasn't written down in the student planner? Didn't study until the last minute? Went out the night before and stayed up late? Wasted time learning the wrong things? It takes away the emotional sting when something good comes out of a negative experience — that is, when students learn from it and change their behavior. Children with A.D.D. seem more resistant to learning from experience, so you should walk them through the process. You might call it a debriefing session, as is done in the military after an assignment. Don't forget to learn from positive experiences as well. When a child gets a good grade, help her link that to the way she prepared for the test.

LIFE IS LEARNING

In the final analysis, everything in life is a learning experience. In the life of your "spacey" child, you do not want experiences to just drift by unnoticed. Though they seem in their own world much of the time, children with A.D.D. have a gift for living intensely in the moment when they are turned on to something. Help them build awareness so they can access that gift more readily and in a wider range of situations. Applying the suggestions in this chapter should help children get a little more control over their attention processes, provide them with active learning strategies, give them more confidence in their memory skills, and encourage inner motivation. Add to this your positive attitude. Your approval is like having the sun shine on all your child's activities. And when there is rain, as there must be, you look for a rainbow together when the showers are over. As Helen Keller wrote, "The world is full of people doing hard jobs in difficult places. Whether they are happy or miserable depends very much on their point of view."

Neurofeedback

AMONG THE NEWER approaches to managing A.D.D., the most exciting is a learning process called neurofeedback. It empowers a person to shift the way he pays attention. After more than twenty-five years of research in university labs, neurofeedback has become more widely available. This is a pleasing development, because neurofeedback has no negative side effects. Instead of using chemicals to alter brain activity, neurofeedback training uses the latest computer technology to teach people with A.D.D. to maintain focus and concentration in situations in which they used to drift off.

The overall goal of neurofeedback is to improve mental flexibility so that a person can produce a mental state appropriate to the situational requirements. This is just what people with A.D.D. do poorly; they lack the ability to get their mind in gear and make themselves do something that seems uninteresting.

HOW DOES NEUROFEEDBACK WORK?

The brain is full of millions of neurons, special cells that are like tiny batteries in that they discharge electricity whenever activated. Sensors on the head can pick up this electrical activity. The electrical patterns produced by neurons are called brain waves. A fast computer translates this information into a video display on the computer monitor. So far, this is much like an electroencephalogram (EEG), the brain wave tracings used by neurologists and brain researchers. In neurofeedback training, however, one does not just look at the EEG signal. The EEG gets translated into information that the subject can learn from. He looks at the video display and hears auditory feedback as well. The feedback alerts him to what his brain is doing — concentrating or drifting off — and he can then use this information to change his brain activity as necessary. The computer display provides rewards for making these changes. Controlling the computer display teaches the subject how to produce the brain waves that are associated with being attentive and still. With enough practice, the subject can do this on his own, without the computer feedback.

The exact mechanisms by which brain activity becomes enhanced have not yet been established. Researchers like Dr. Barry Sterman at the University of California at Los Angeles and Dr. Joel Lubar at the University of

Tennessee have written on the neurophysiology and neuroanatomy of the brain with respect to possible mechanisms by which brain waves are modified. It is generally known that exercising nerve pathways facilitates their growth and development. Neurofeedback for A.D.D. is just a method for repeatedly exercising the pathways related to attention and impulse control to facilitate their growth and development. Neurofeedback may also be affecting the neurotransmitters in the brain. Whatever the mechanism, the net result is that the subject becomes more focused and is able to learn more efficiently.

WHAT IS NEUROFEEDBACK TRAINING?

Think of neurofeedback as weight training for the brain. If you want to build up your muscles, you go to a gym and start an exercise routine. With neurofeedback, you go to a training center and exercise the neural pathways to build up your brain so that you can concentrate better. For a child, it's like going to gymnastics or piano lessons.

The procedure is simple. Sensors are placed on the scalp, held in place with a special gel. Fine wires from these sensors conduct electricity from the child's head to a recording instrument that registers the different frequencies and amplitudes of the electricity produced in the area of the brain being monitored. Changes in the brain wave patterns show whether the person is paying attention and whether he is sitting still (or, more accurately, suppressing the impulse to move). In an EEG, the brain wave tracing is shown as a wavy line. In neurofeedback training, the computer converts the brain waves into gamelike displays (e.g., a fish moving through a maze, puzzle pieces fitting together) or colorful images, like a rising sun. The colorful displays are paired with sounds to give auditory feedback as well. The child's attentiveness controls what happens on the screen. Children can play the game only by controlling their level of concentration.

If the child's mind wanders, as it does when he spaces out in class, the colors on the monitor change or the action stops. The better he sustains his attention, the faster the activity on the screen changes. With most neurofeedback systems, the child also wins points, which can be converted into rewards.

The games can be adjusted so that children can be successful, no matter what level of concentration they begin with. They have fun. They may be doing things such as playing basketball on the screen (the opponent scores if the child's attention wanders) or moving a fish through a maze. The child feels successful, and, at the same time, he is altering his brain physiology. Just as an athlete uses weight training to build up the muscles needed for his sport, the child is exercising and producing beneficial changes in his brain (settling down, attending, concentrating), which will help him pay attention in school and elsewhere.

A Workout for the Wandering Mind

With neurofeedback, the child is exercising the pathways in the brain that control attention and mental processing. As these neural pathways are exercised, children develop a sense of what concentration feels like, and they also realize what it feels like when they drift off. After they practice these exercises over a period of time, the pathways involved in attention and learning seem to work more efficiently. This enhanced brain activity becomes a natural part of the child's functioning. It makes possible things that were very, very difficult before training.

One teenage girl did intensive training during the summer before going to Switzerland for her final year of high school. She e-mailed her mother in October, "I never knew I could sit in class and pay attention so well!" Another successful girl said after six months of neurofeedback training, "Now I know what it feels like to concentrate!" And a boy who had taken Ritalin for seven years and became able to attend high school without medication reported, "For the first time in my life I feel in control."

Twelve-year-old Christopher had been diagnosed at an early age as having A.D.D. He had taken Ritalin since the third grade, but, after an initial good response, the effectiveness seemed to wane, and he really balked at taking it as he approached adolescence. He had been through behavior modification programs designed to reward him for completing his work in class and finishing homework. His family had received counseling. His parents had put him in a private school with smaller classes and more individual attention. Despite all these efforts, this bright boy was in danger of failing seventh grade. After the Christmas report card, his parents decided to try neurofeedback.

He had been going to Dr. Lynda's ADD Centre twice a week for hour-long neurofeedback training sessions and, after five months, had completed almost forty sessions. He was well on his way to learning how to shift his brain wave pattern to regulate his own attention skills. He agreed to let a visitor to the center observe his session. Here is her description:

Christopher was sitting intently watching a computer screen. He wasn't using a mouse or a keyboard. He was just sitting calmly and watching the monitor. Looking closely, I could see three tiny circular cups, smaller than my little fingernail, sitting on dots of gel: two on top of his head, and one just behind his ear. From each of these sensors a thin wire led to a small box about the size of a cassette player that sat on the table beside him. A cable led from this small box, an EEG instrument that monitored Christopher's brain waves, to the computer. In the middle of the screen a fish moved forward through a maze. Each time it moved, it made a gurgling sound, like blowing bubbles underwater.

"What are you doing?" I asked.

"I'm concentrating," he replied.

"How do you know this?" I asked.

"The screen tells me about my brain waves. When I'm staying focused and concentrating, the fish will move through the maze, but the moment my mind wanders, it stops."

Noticing the open workbook Christopher had on the table in front of him, I asked, "Has learning how to concentrate helped your schoolwork?"

Christopher took his eyes off the screen, and a broad smile spread across his face. "Does it help? I got into the groove last week at school, and I got A+ on a Geography test! It was the highest grade in the class. The teacher was so impressed. He was so happy. Then I had a Language exam today, and I had to write a short essay. I did two pages, and the teacher was really, really pleased with me. Most kids couldn't think up more than a page. Before, I hated writing and never gave complete answers. So that's a real change."

Christopher's parents described how Christopher had gone from the three "D's" (discouraged, depressed, and feeling dumb) to believing in himself as a bright and capable boy. Five months after starting training, he was off stimulant medication and doing better than ever in school, because, as they put it, he was finally maturing and starting to use his potential. When he was a pre-schooler, they had thought he was smart, but he had never before shown it in school. Now, both in class and at home, he was acting upbeat and confident.

A year later and with no additional training, Christopher was doing fine in eighth grade. His first-semester report card was excellent, with all grades as high as or higher than they had been in seventh grade. There were no longer any failing grades, and he was also doing better than ever in his sports and other extracurricular activities. His parents remarked, too, on how much he seemed to have grown up in terms of taking responsibility.

Practice Makes Perfect

Neurofeedback allows the person with A.D.D. to learn what concentration feels like, much like feedback from the brain's balance systems allows the child learning to ride a bicycle to discover how to keep his balance. Learning to ride a bicycle usually takes several practice sessions spread over a few days. Learning to concentrate takes many training sessions, often spread over a period of months, depending on a number of factors, such as other neurological problems, severity of the A.D.D. problems, family support, and intelligence. One does not learn brain wave self-regulation as quickly as bicycle riding, perhaps because losing one's concentration is not as traumatic as falling off a bicycle. Also, the computer feedback, though fast, is not as quick and accurate as the information one receives from the inner ear about balance. Yet it is much faster than any kind of verbal feedback. If you sit with a child as she does her homework, notice that faraway look in her eyes, and tell her she is daydreaming, the whole process takes a few seconds. The response time for neurofeedback from the computer is measured in thousandths of a second.

How exactly do neurofeedback clients learn to control their brain waves? What does it feel like? Most people cannot say what they do, but they seem eventually to be able to recognize the state of concentration and also to recognize when they drift off. Much of the learning in neurofeedback seems to happen at an unconscious level, which explains how young children can set their brain wave pattern without much conscious awareness of what they are supposed to do. Andy gave this answer to the question of how he learned to control his brain waves:

By watching the screen, I have learned sort of what it feels like to produce mostly fast waves. I can't really tell you in words, but it's different. I find that if I constantly chal-

lenge myself by asking myself questions, then I keep thinking and figuring things out. If I do that, I don't get sleepy. Once I get sleepy, it's just too difficult to pull myself out of it. I can't let that happen, and challenging myself seems to keep me in this active state.

Some teenagers are afraid at first that neurofeedback will take away their ability to choose for themselves. In fact, the opposite is true. In explaining to teenagers how neurofeedback works, we often choose as an illustration some activity or sport that they are interested in.

Jason was a particularly difficult teenager, age eighteen, but a superb tennis player. The trainer said to him, "Jason, before you learned how to hit a forehand tennis shot, you may often have missed the ball, sliced it over the fence, or hit the net. After you learned and practiced how to hit a powerful forehand, you had a choice! You could still choose to miss the ball or hit it over the fence. Or, you could choose to hit it perfectly and win the point! Because you have practiced, when you choose to play hard and win, the shots become almost automatic. Similarly, before neurofeedback training, you have little choice. Your mind wanders, you are not getting the grades you want to get. After you train here, you will have a choice. You can still choose not to listen or study, but you can also choose to keep focused and learn efficiently and effectively. You will be in control!"

Neurofeedback empowers people with A.D.D. to get into the concentration zone just as well as people without A.D.D. It may take more conscious effort, but they will be able to focus and sustain their focus once they have learned self-regulation through neurofeedback. One nineteen-year-old remarked,

I didn't believe this could help. But gradually it came together. I found I was able to concentrate without being distracted by things around me. It has made school so much easier.

If learning to regulate brain waves to produce desired mental states sounds a little way out to you, remember that people have been doing this in lots of different ways for centuries. When you take a deep breath and count to ten before saying something, you are practicing mental control. When people learn prayer or meditation, they, too, are learning to control their mental state. Higher levels of martial arts training also call for learning mental control.

You cannot tell a person with A.D.D. how to concentrate. And trying too hard produces tension that actually interferes with concentration. Yet one can "get a feel for it." Learning self-regulation can empower your child by improving certain skills and reducing bothersome symptoms. Neurofeedback is by no means a cure-all. It is a technique that, in combination with other approaches (parenting and educational strategies and, possibly, medical intervention) can give the child with A.D.D. a way to manage his difficulties and make everyone's life a little easier.

BRAIN WAVES AND THEIR CONNECTION TO BEHAVIOR

What Is a Brain Wave?

Everyone's brain produces electricity. When we put a sensor on the scalp, we can record this electrical activity on an electroencephalogram (EEG). The electrical pattern is called a brain wave. Recorded on paper or displayed on a monitor, it looks something like waves on a lake. Just like on a lake, there

The Discovery of Neurofeedback for Epilepsy and A.D.D.

The history of neurofeedback is a wonderful example of scientific serendipity — discovering something special accidentally while looking for something else. It may have struck you that the SMR frequency band does not have a Greek letter name like the theta, alpha, and beta brain wave bands. That is because it used to be considered part of the beta range but was renamed after Dr. Barry Sterman identified some unique properties of brain waves at 12 to 15 cps. Back in the late 1960s, as part of the research being done in Sterman's labs, cats were taught to increase SMR. He labeled this wave form "sensorimotor rhythm," or SMR, because it was most easily measured across the sensorimotor strip of the brain, which runs across the head from ear to ear, and because these waves seemed to reflect both sensory and motor activity.

Sterman was asked to investigate how hydrazine — a fuel used in rockets, including rockets for the first manned space flights — might produce seizures, and he was experimenting with hydrazine's effects on cats. He observed that one group of cats seemed resistant to seizures. Those were the cats who had been trained during earlier research to increase the SMR brain waves. Further investigation demonstrated that what was true for cats also applied to people. When humans who had seizure disorders were trained to increase this wave form, their seizures decreased. During these experiments in the early 1970s, the observation was made that many of the subjects who displayed hyperactivity and restlessness in addition to having seizure disorders showed a decrease in these symptoms when they were trained to increase SMR. So the next question was, If hyperactive people with seizure disorders decrease their hyperactivity when they increase SMR, what happens with hyperactive children who do not have seizures? Dr. Joel Lubar had also been researching brainwaves since the early 1970s and took a special interest in children with A.D.D. Sure enough, with training to increase SMR, their hyperactivity was reduced. Since the publication of those first results in 1976, researchers have continued to study ways in which neurofeedback can improve the lives of children with A.D.D.

will be some larger waves, and on top of these there may be smaller ripples or little waves. The large waves are referred to as slow waves, and the little, irregular ones are referred to as fast waves. The large waves pass by at the rate of only two or three per second — a slow frequency. The small ripples have a higher frequency. The height of the wave is called amplitude. The greater the amplitude, the more power there is. The relationship between amplitude and power is obvious if you think of waves breaking on a beach: taller waves have more power.

How are brain waves described? Brain waves can be described by their frequency and amplitude. Frequencies are measured in cycles per second (cps) or hertz units. A hertz (Hz) is equal to one cycle per second. The height or amplitude of the brain wave is expressed in terms of power (picawatts) or electric potential (microvolts).

The brain waves that are of interest in neurofeedback are the ones with frequencies between 4 and 20 cps. The slow brain waves are called theta (4 to 7 cps) and alpha (8 to 11 cps) waves. The fast brain waves are called sensorimotor rhythm (SMR, 12 to 15 cps) and beta (16 to 20 cps) waves. The definitions for theta, alpha, SMR, and beta are not precise; different researchers separate frequency bands at slightly different places. There may also be subtle differences between high- and low-frequency waves within each group; for example, 8- and 9-Hz activity is perhaps associated with a slightly different state than 10- and 11-Hz activity, even though they are all alpha waves.

How are brain waves measured? The EEG machine measures brain waves at each frequency. To do this, a sensor that is smaller than a little fingernail sits on a little gel on the subject's head. The gel acts as a conductor between the scalp and the sensor. The number of sensors that are used varies from three in most neurofeedback training programs to as many as 256 in some research labs. The sensor conducts some of the electricity produced by the subject's brain along a wire to an EEG instrument that has filters to check how much of each frequency is being produced. The information then gets sent to a computer that produces a picture of the brain waves. The picture always shows a mixture of waves at all the different frequencies, just like the different kinds of waves on the lake. The computer is able to determine how much power there is at each frequency and if there is more slow wave activity than fast wave activity. Typically, in individuals of any age with A.D.D., you see more slow wave activity.

A moment-to-moment guide to the brain. Research shows that brain wave patterns are a reasonable reflection of what the area of the brain beneath the sensor is doing. If you were to watch the brain waves as your child falls asleep, for example, you would see the dominant brain wave frequency change to slower waves. Just before he falls asleep, you would see a lot of slow theta waves (4 to 7 cps). When he is asleep, you would see even slower activity, at 2 or 3 cps (the delta range). When children daydream in school, they also show a lot of theta wave activity, between 4 and 7 cps. If the brain is just resting for a moment and the child is reflecting on what the teacher just said, the slow wave activity might be in the alpha range (8 to 11 cps). If the child is working on a problem or actively reading or listening, you would see quite a bit of faster wave activity, in the 12- to 20-cps range.

Here is a quote from psychologist Dr. Barry Sterman about how behavior is linked to brain waves:

As one who has studied EEG patterns in normal people, I can almost read them from facial expressions and body language. I am reminded of the difficult task of lecturing to students or others shortly after the lunch or dinner hour. Some people are just unable to pay attention. This leads to glazed eyes or drooping eyelids. I can just see the alpha rhythm spreading across their cortex. Even more dramatic, however, are the slumping heads, sudden twitches, or even occasional snorts expressed by those who are falling asleep. Theta has taken over. In this context I have always appreciated the few wide-eyed listeners (usually at the front of the room) who are sitting up straight and clinging to every word. They are probably generating lots of SMR and faster frequencies.

Brain waves thus reflect what a person's brain is doing from moment to moment. With modern equipment, neurofeedback trainers can use this information to let children know the instant they stop listening, reading, or problem solving and begin to daydream. The sensor is placed over the area of the brain expected to be active when the child is sitting fairly still and reading, listening, or figuring out things. The feedback is very fast. It can be seen on the screen 39 to 150 milliseconds after it happens in the brain, depending on the equipment. Thus, with this tool, a neurofeedback trainer can see immediately when the child tunes out and when he tunes back in. Bursts of slow activity correspond to flickering attention and show clearly how a person can be really trying to pay attention but still miss part of what is said (e.g., one number in a sequence or part of the instructions).

Slow waves predominate in very young children. As children grow older, this pattern changes until the balance between slow wave and fast wave activity evens out in adults over the age of eighteen. Regular adult EEG patterns are low voltage and fairly level.

Specific Brain Waves for Specific Tasks

The human brain likes to do one thing at a time. When one part is active and producing fast waves, other parts take a rest and produce slow waves. For example, if you are driving a car, you are being vigilant, processing all the information your eyes are taking in. But if you reach toward the dashboard

A Simplified Description of Brain Waves		
Mental State	**Frequency of Waves**	**We are Going to Call These Waves**
• Sleep	• delta: 0.5–3 cycles per second (cps)	• The sleep waves
• Inner reflection without much attention focused on the outside world (being tuned out); drowsy	• theta: 4–7 cps	• The tuned-out waves
• Resting in a meditative and perhaps creative state (a second type of tuning out or daydreaming); inattentive	• alpha: 8–11 cps	• The resting, daydream waves
• Calm, not fidgeting, not impulsive not thinking about bodily sensations, often externally oriented and aware; quietly alert	• SMR: 12–15 cps	• The calm waves
• Focused, analytic, often externally oriented, intense thinking	• beta: 16–20 cps	• The thinker waves
The *slow* waves are the tuned-out waves and the daydream waves. The *fast* waves are the calm waves and the thinker waves.		

and turn your radio dial, for an instant you turn off all those vigilant areas that are processing information about the highway and turn on the small area of your brain that controls your hand. Someone watching your car might notice that it strays slightly from the straight course you were driving. Similarly, your child isn't in high gear, working on school problems all the time. She is turning on and off and on again — working, then resting, then working again. Indeed, very bright people often turn on the thinker waves (16 to 20 cps) for very short periods of time and then revert to the resting waves (8 to 11 cps). You will see more fast wave activity when a person is learning a new task than when the task has been practiced and is easier. This is because once the task is familiar, it takes less mental effort.

John, age twelve, was doing a math word problem as part of a neurofeedback training session. He skipped words as he read it, and a number of key facts did not register in his mind. His EEG showed the electrical energy concentrated in slow waves between 4 and 7 cps. Watching John's brain waves on the screen, his trainer saw tuned-out waves with high amplitude, but then John would focus for a moment, and the slow wave amplitude would drop precipitously. His reading would become more superficial, and the slow wave amplitude would instantly rise again. These bursts of tuned-out wave activity happened several times within just a few seconds! A minute or two later, there was a shift in John's concentration. The trainer noticed that the sound from the speakers was absolutely steady, indicating that John's attention was no longer flickering. He was sustaining the fast wave activity, the thinker waves (16 to 20 cps), indicating extremely focused concentration.

When the trainer looked away from the screen, he found John staring out the window watching a little mourning dove that had hatched a few days earlier on the window ledge. The trainer told him to stay focused on the baby bird and notice if he felt different. John replied later, "Yes, I could feel the difference. But it's hard to concentrate like that when I'm reading."

It is quite likely that John will remember the image of the nestling bird for years to come because he was so intently focused on it. But when John tuned out, he produced a lot of slow theta waves. With further neurofeedback training, he learned to remain for longer periods of time in the mental state of producing faster waves. The result was that he stopped missing things as he was reading or listening. He was able to advance in school.

There is nothing wrong with any particular pattern of brain waves. We need all of them for different jobs. The goal of neurofeedback is to give someone the flexibility to be able to access the appropriate state to get a particular job done. Most people naturally stay alert and focused when a teacher or someone else is giving instructions. People with A.D.D. have to learn how to do this. Teaching them to recognize and use their calm waves (SMR) and thinker waves (beta) helps them pay attention when they must.

Alpha waves. Some people purposefully spend a great deal of time learning to produce an alpha wave state. Some practice alpha states to try to access their creativity. Others are learning how to relax and meditate. Meditation can be a very relaxing and useful skill. However, meditating in the classroom or, for an adult, in a boardroom meeting, is usually frowned upon. Small bursts of alpha are normal and indicate resting and reflecting for a moment. But too much alpha means the person is tuning out the external world. This isn't what we want for classroom performance or even for good social interaction.

Theta waves. It is quite pleasant to drift slowly off to sleep. Theta waves usually predominate at these times. Production of theta waves is actually encouraged by some psychotherapists if they find that the client is able to recall memories from the past and access feelings more readily when in this state. In psychoanalysis, lying on the couch and being told to just let thoughts flow freely (free-associate) may actually encourage a patient to go into a theta state. However, once again, this is not the state of mind your child's teacher hopes to see in the classroom.

Brain Wave Patterns and A.D.D.

The brain wave pattern of individuals with A.D.D. looks immature because there are more slow waves. This pattern is independent of the person's intelligence level. It is important to note that the EEG is not abnormal in persons who have A.D.D.; there is just a different balance between slow and fast waves.

There is more than one pattern possible in individuals with A.D.D., but they all have in common excess slow wave activity. In the future, it may be possible to classify types of A.D.D. according to brain wave patterns. For example, one pattern is an immature pattern, with more slow waves (theta) throughout the brain. In another pattern, it is mainly the frontal portions of the brain, the seat of the executive functions (including directed attention, critical thinking, and impulse control), that show excessive slow waves.

The difference in brain wave patterns between a child who has A.D.D. and a child who does not have A.D.D. is more pronounced when they are doing school-like tasks, such as reading. Children who do not have A.D.D. produce more fast waves when they focus in on a reading task. Children with A.D.D. usually produce more slow waves. This means the brain is still in resting mode.

Bright daydreamers. Most individuals with A.D.D. tune out in theta waves. Some people show a different kind of slow wave activity (8 to 11 cps) when they tune out. We call this the resting/daydream wave. Traditionally, it has been called alpha. Dr. Lynda has given these alpha producers the nickname "bright

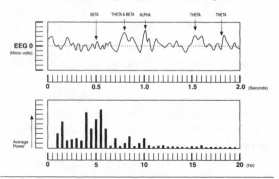

TUNING OUT BRAIN WAVES Pattern typical of person with A.D.D. while doing schoolwork

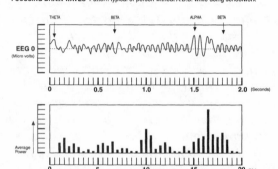

FOCUSING BRAIN WAVES Pattern typical of person without A.D.D. while doing schoolwork

daydreamers." They are often highly creative people. Brian was an example of this pattern:

Brian, age eighteen, had dropped out of his final year of high school. He had tried working but did not last at the jobs he tried. He explained, "I just can't keep my mind on what I'm being told. If I try to read the instruction manual it takes ages. I have to keep going back over and over each paragraph. I guess I'm just not smart enough."

Brian's intelligence was assessed using the Wechsler Adult Intelligence Scale. It was in the superior range. On the EEG his problem was immediately apparent. After only a short time reading, he suddenly produced a very high-amplitude alpha rhythm. He just tuned out, as if meditating or in a daydream. This pattern also appears in people who have smoked marijuana recently, which Brian had not. He was just a natural alpha producer. If he was reminded of the task, he would focus on it again for a short time, but then the resting/daydream state would reappear and he would tune out.

Using the computer monitor and watching his own brain waves, Brian rapidly trained himself to stay out of that alpha pattern when listening and reading. When he managed this and was working on some academic subject, the predominant wave pattern became his faster "thinker waves" (beta; 16 to 20 cps). He returned to high school in September and also got a part-time job, which he held on to. Later that year he was awarded a prize for his excellent results in Physics. His was a remarkable turnaround.

Hyperactive children. Neurofeedback helps the hyperactive child by teaching him to become calm and able to suppress the urge to move. Certain brain waves (calm waves, or sensorimotor rhythm) are seen when a person inhibits the urge to move around. Hyperactive, impulsive children can be taught to produce these waves. In our experience, the hyperactive child often takes longer to benefit from neurofeedback training than the child with the inattentive type of A.D.D.

Sometimes the child is not physically "bouncing off the walls" but is just verbally impulsive, as in blurting things out. This type of child may have never had a behavior problem at all. Cathy, age nine, was a good example of this. She was a very active and impulsive girl. She would constantly do things without reflecting first. When asked, "Why did you do that?", her shrug and "I dunno" were completely honest. There was no thought-out reason behind her behavior. She just acted without thinking. Cathy's mother gave this description of her daughter prior to neurofeedback training:

We're so discouraged. Cathy has been put on Ritalin on the recommendation of her teacher. It has helped slow her down and keep her at her desk, but she is still going to be placed in special education for the fourth grade. She thinks of this as being demoted. Even though we couldn't really afford it, we put her into a good private school, but that didn't solve the problem. She is at the bottom of her third-grade class. Cathy has been tested on the Wechsler Intelligence Scale for Children, and the psychologist said she was bright. She has also had special tutoring. We know she's smart, but she just cannot sit without fidgeting. She is so impulsive! We are proud that she answers questions in class, but she does it before the teacher even finishes the question.

She never thinks about what she is going to say. She seems to just blurt out whatever thought has come into her mind. Being bright, she sometimes will happen to give the right answer, but more often than not she is wrong. This behavior irritates not only the teachers but her classmates as well. She can read beautifully if you make her sit and do it. But she keeps skipping things, and if you aren't right beside her, she will say she is finished but will have missed the main points and just have remembered all the funny little things that don't matter. We just don't know what to do.

Cathy underwent the same kind of training as Christopher (see page 207), except she was trained to increase the production of brain waves referred to as SMR, or sensorimotor rhythm (12 to 15 cps). Research studies have shown that these brain waves are at work when the motor system is less active and the impulse to move is suppressed. Facilitating this state in children who do not naturally produce much SMR is helpful. Cathy learned how to voluntarily produce more sensorimotor rhythm waves. To do this she had to sit still and not even think about moving. The trainer said, "Cathy, pretend that your brain moves into your fingers every time you move those fingers. Where do you want your brain to be when you are thinking about a problem?" Cathy said, with a laugh, that it should be in her head and not in her hands.

Three months after beginning training, Cathy was off Ritalin, ranking in the top half of her class and no longer on the list for special education for fourth grade. When we followed up three years later, she was an A student in seventh grade who was well liked by both her teachers and her peers. The only modification to her school program at present is enrichment classes in math.

Impulsive children. For some children with A.D.D., impulsivity is the most critical problem. Impulsivity is a difficulty that is seen in children with A.D.D. with or without hyperactivity. "Impulsivity" does not mean that the person demonstrates a behavior problem. It refers to acting without thinking (reflecting) first.

Children with this problem appear to have too little of the faster SMR calm waves. These brain wave frequencies are associated with inhibitory functions in the brain. Donald is another example of this kind of problem:

Donald was thirteen years old. His mother, a school teacher, noted, "Donald is a good boy. He has never been a behavior problem. But I get so, so frustrated with him. I end up screaming at him. He is so bright (IQ above 130), but he just doesn't read the problem. It doesn't matter what subject it is, he just doesn't do what the question is asking him to do. He jumps to conclusions! If he is given a math problem, he blurts out an answer. He is very bright, so often it is the correct answer. However, if it is a word problem and he has to listen or read for a minute, then he will miss something and the answer will be the wrong one. If I force him to slow down and read carefully, he will get it right. It's very frustrating. He is so bright, but he constantly makes careless little errors."

Donald also had difficulty concentrating. His EEG pattern, as expected from mother's description of his style, showed a lot of slow wave activity. In addition, he demonstrated a dip in brain wave activity in the calm wave (SMR) range. Neurofeedback training for Donald emphasized decreasing the tuned-out slow wave activity and increasing the faster calm wave (SMR) activity. When he learned to do this, he also demonstrated a marked increase in his ability to read questions carefully, note the facts, and then answer the question that was being asked. He became calmer and didn't rush into things or blurt things out.

Children with social problems. Donald was also a rather difficult child socially. Other children shunned him. He did not appear able to maintain friendships.

Donald's constant questions were quite assertive and inappropriate. He said whatever came into his mind. He found it difficult to maintain friendships, and adults found him irritating, even rude. He never meant to say anything wrong. He behaved with the best of intentions. Donald really wanted to do the right thing and be liked and appreciated. But his behavior was, in a word, obnoxious. His parents tried medications. They tried behavior modification. They spoke with him about how he seemed to turn people off. Nothing seemed to have any significant effect on their young motor mouth.

When Donald increased his calm waves, it changed not only his approach to schoolwork but also his social interactions. He became considerate and polite and started making friends and maintaining friendships. This was a happy carryover effect of the training. Perhaps paying more attention to the external world caused him to notice people's reactions more, so that he modified his own behavior accordingly.

Anxious and inattentive children. Matt's story provides an example of how a child with A.D.D. and anxiety was helped with neurofeedback. Regular biofeedback to teach him how to regulate his finger temperature

(an indicator of relaxation) was also part of his program:

Matt, a bright fifteen-year-old, was in neurofeedback training primarily to learn how to control his impulsive style of doing problems in school and to learn to remain focused when studying. At the same time, he was also attempting to pass a difficult figure skating exam that would put him at the national level for competition. He had failed twice. His third and final try for some time was coming up in just a few weeks. In practice, the double jumps and other required maneuvers were easily accomplished. In competition, he missed. In the initial evaluation, Matt's mother had mentioned, "Apart from not being able to focus in class, my son does figure skating, and he doesn't seem to do what the coach has just explained to him. Also, he gets very anxious before competitions."

Matt learned quite rapidly to increase his focus by watching the computer monitor and listening to the audio feedback while doing academic tasks. However, Matt was a very tense and anxious boy. A sensor on his little finger registered a skin temperature of only 73 degrees instead of a normal 94 to 96 degrees. This was a physiologic sign of inner tension. Some days when he came into training, his finger temperature would be as high as 89 degrees, but the moment anyone mentioned skating or a school problem, it would drop precipitously to the 70s. As he relaxed, his finger temperature would rise, and this feedback was displayed on the computer monitor. Gradually he began to be able to keep his finger temperature in the 90s even when presented with an academic task. When the time for the skating competition came, he passed. His mother reported back, "He finally remem-

bered what he was supposed to be doing — for example, holding his hands correctly. He seemed to be totally into his skating and not attending to the audience and the judges. It was really different. He actually looked relaxed!"

Matt produced another interesting result after neurofeedback training. At the end of the training sessions, he was retested on the Wechsler Intelligence Scale for Children. He scored 22 points higher than he had before training. Intelligence as measured on standardized tests is not expected to shift like that. Wechsler results are supposed to be largely independent of teaching and learning. Research on IQ changes with neurofeedback indicate average gains of around 10 points, so Matt's gains were unusually good. Perhaps his initial scores were lower due to the combination of A.D.D. and anxiety and they shot up when both these conditions improved. We do not think that neurofeedback training makes people smarter, but they do seem better able to utilize their potential. This shows up in the classroom and also on standardized tests, including intelligence tests. Matt was certainly a much more confident student when he completed training than he had been when he started. Additionally, his mother reported that he talked to her more, shared his feelings more, and generally seemed more cheerful. "I actually like having him around now," she reported with a laugh.

One could argue in each of the above cases that it was not the neurofeedback training that made the difference but other things the trainer was also working on, such as coaching in learning strategies. This is a possibility. However, these children had previously had extensive tutoring. Two of the mothers were teachers. All of the parents worked with their

children and modeled logical approaches to schoolwork. The children had been taught similar strategies again and again, but nothing had sunk in. With neurofeedback they were in a different state of mind while thinking about using the strategies, and finally things clicked. The most pleasing thing about the neurofeedback approach is that the changes seen in training sessions do translate to the real world. Parents tell us that for the first time, their children settle down to do homework without being nagged. The students tell us they can listen and learn more easily in class.

Adolescents who fall asleep in class. The brain waves produced just before a person falls asleep are slow waves. These are exactly the wave patterns that are often seen when the student who has A.D.D. tries to listen to a teacher or when the student tries to study. Students with A.D.D., if they get to college, may find it difficult to remain awake during lectures. In the classroom, the production of slower waves means they are becoming less and less attentive to the external auditory and visual stimuli of teacher, chalkboard, and textbook. The student who is actively engaged in listening to the teacher, by contrast, is inhibiting slow wave activity and may be increasing fast, thinker-wave activity.

There is another observation that is important here. Children and adults with A.D.D. demonstrate a very low, a very high, or a labile electrodermal response (EDR). EDR can be measured with two tiny sensors placed on the palm or on two fingers of one hand. EDR is a measure of skin conduction, which changes when the hand perspires. If a student is drifting off and becoming sleepy, the EDR will be low. It will shift in a dramatic fashion if the student is suddenly startled by a noise or someone entering the room. Sitting up straight also produces an increase in EDR. Students quickly understand how well this simple measurement can reflect their alertness level. With biofeedback training using the EDR feedback, they become more aware of when their alertness drops and learn how to increase it. This EDR training can be done at the same time as neurofeedback.

Andy was a pleasant and polite seventeen-year-old boy. He was getting failing grades in his final year of high school. His parents said, "He just doesn't care." Andy had been diagnosed with A.D.D. when he was younger. He complained that he was constantly falling asleep during classes and when doing homework. Beneath his unmotivated, lazy exterior, Andy really did want to do well, but he was discouraged. In training when he was given a textbook to read, he kept drifting off. If he was left alone for even a short time, the alpha and then theta wave activity would increase markedly. His EDR was very low. Occasionally Andy would actually fall asleep in the chair.

Andy trained himself to increase his EDR in order to stay awake and alert. Being able to do that encouraged him to believe that he could also improve the balance between his slow and fast brain waves. Gradually, over the course of forty sessions, he began to remain alert, focused, and actively learning for longer and longer periods of time. As he did this, his calm waves and thinker waves increased. When he was being creative, he produced more of the slower, more synchronous alpha (creative daydreaming) waves. When he was actively listening or organizing, writing, reading, or expressing his ideas, he demonstrated more of the faster, less synchronous (thinker wave) beta activity.

As he proceeded with training, Andy raised his grade in English from a D to a B.

He said, "I'm just turning on my concentration when I'm in class and studying." Andy had been hanging out with a difficult group of kids who were on drugs. He decided to stop meeting with them. It wasn't easy to stay at home rather than going out with the group, and his parents worried for a few weeks that Andy was depressed. Eventually he found a new group of friends. He said, "The A.D.D. training gave me hope."

QUESTIONS YOU MAY HAVE ABOUT NEUROFEEDBACK

Is my child a candidate for neurofeedback?

Not everyone with A.D.D. is automatically a candidate for neurofeedback training. The first visit to a neurofeedback provider will determine whether neurofeedback training is appropriate for your child. While nearly all people with neurologically based attention problems could benefit from this technique, the training must be customized according to the individual's profile. This means that the person who provides neurofeedback training will first want to assess your child's brain wave pattern as well as his history. For example, experience has shown that children whose primary problem is paying attention (the bright daydreamers) respond most quickly to neurofeedback. The neurofeedback training is directed specifically at suppressing those brain waves that reflect inattention and encouraging the type that reflect paying attention. When both learning disabilities and attention problems exist in a child, that child is a good candidate for neurofeedback. As the attention span increases, it becomes easier to remediate the learning problems. If a child's A.D.D. symptoms are accompanied by hyperactivity, learning disabilities, or behavior problems, the training takes longer. As with other kinds of learning, brighter children learn self-regulation faster.

Who is not a candidate for neurofeedback?

Some children show signs of inattention and learning difficulties plus other kinds of learning problems that cause their schoolwork to go right over their heads. Their pattern of EEG activity will not be like one associated with A.D.D. These children need tutoring or special education, not neurofeedback.

One problem that can mimic inattention is anxiety. The child may indeed have trouble concentrating, but it is worry causing the difficulty, not A.D.D. Again, neurofeedback is not the answer. Instead, treatment must investigate the source of the worries, and then appropriate interventions should be applied. This may involve a change of schools, family or individual therapy, or medication or treatment for a medical disorder. Some children with A.D.D. also have symptoms of anxiety. When the two problems coexist, then neurofeedback may be appropriate and might be combined with other interventions. If there are significant problems in the family, these should be sorted out before trying neurofeedback, or the family may be wasting time and money. The beneficial effects could be negated by the continuing family stress and conflict.

Certain medical conditions can also mimic A.D.D. For example, if the child has a sleep disorder, he will be sleepy during the day and inattentive. Absence seizures, involving brief lapses in attention, will also interfere with learning. These disorders should be treated by other professionals who specialize in these conditions. If the child has A.D.D. in addition to such medical conditions, he can benefit from training, but the medical conditions must, of course, be treated by a physician.

Another limitation is age. Little research has been done with children who are younger than seven. Also, a lot of neurological maturation takes place naturally during kindergarten and first grade, so if a child's A.D.D. symptoms are not interfering too much with learning in school, it may be wise to wait and see if the situation improves after that developmental spurt has taken place. For neurofeedback to work, the child must at least be old enough to follow instructions and watch the screen. This is usually around age five or six. Dr. Lynda's youngest client for neurofeedback training was four, and her oldest sixty-three. Some centers doing neurofeedback research require a minimum age of seven and intellectual functioning that is at least low-average (i.e., IQ above 80).

When should we try neurofeedback?

We believe that it's a good idea to have an evaluation for the appropriateness of neurofeedback training as soon as you recognize that your child may have A.D.D. You can make better decisions if you know what you are dealing with right from the start and know what your options are. Investing in the training right away makes sense if the A.D.D. symptoms are interfering to a significant degree with your child's school progress and general happiness. In other situations, where the child is bright and the symptoms are not too severe, excellent parenting practices and a positive school environment may be the only interventions needed. Neurofeedback might become necessary later on as the child's academic environment becomes more demanding.

The best argument for trying neurofeedback first is that it has no negative side effects. And because you are training the brain pathways involved in concentration and learning, you can expect the positive effects to last. Stimulant medication, in contrast, is effective only for the short-term management of behavior.

Many people try neurofeedback as a last resort. Often parents do not understand what neurofeedback is, or they may confuse neurofeedback with biofeedback for relaxation. Some may have been told that this approach is expensive yet unproven, a caution that was common a few years ago when there was less research. Often, they have simply not heard about neurofeedback. Most parents take their child to a physician when they suspect A.D.D., and while most physicians are knowledgeable about drugs for A.D.D., few are aware of neurofeedback as an alternative.

Considerations of time and money will also play a role in decisions about neurofeedback training (see page 224). Neurofeedback has a relatively high short-term cost, as do most individual therapies. Medications cost less in the short term, but the costs add up if your child is taking them for many years, and years of medication is a real possibility.

Should we try neurofeedback instead of or in combination with drugs for our child?

Neurofeedback can be used as an alternative to medication or in addition to medication. Your A.D.D. specialist can help you decide what is most likely to work well for your child. In general, stimulant medications help most other management techniques work better, especially in children with significant hyperactivity. Stimulant drugs do not appear to have much effect on the EEG, but they

---

Physician or Neurofeedback Specialist? Whom Should You See First?

Taking your child to a medical specialist first is a good idea, since the physician can rule out other medical conditions, like thyroid dysfunction, which can produce symptoms similar to A.D.D. The psychologist or other professional who does neurofeedback and the physician have different but complementary roles. Disorders that should be treated medically include:

- petit mal seizures (absence seizures, causing lapses in attention)
- clinical depression
- severe anxiety
- sleep disorders (e.g., sleep apnea)
- thyroid dysfunction

In other disorders, medical treatment may be required first, but neurofeedback might be considered as an adjunct to medical treatment to target specific symptoms such as poor attention span and acting before thinking. These conditions include Tourette Syndrome and Asperger Syndrome.

---

may help the child sit still, so that he can do the neurofeedback training more easily. In reality, since most training is done in the evenings and/or on weekends so as not to interfere with the child's school routine and the parents' work schedule, medication taken in the morning on school days has worn off. In our experience, many children can be weaned off their medication entirely or the dosage can be lowered partway into neurofeedback training. The neurofeedback approach is particularly attractive when medications do not seem to be helping a child or when they have undesirable side effects.

What about side effects? How safe is neurofeedback?

Neurofeedback is not a drug. It is as safe as playing a computer game. There are no negative physical side effects. A research team headed by Dr. George Fitzsimmons at the University of Alberta noted that, as the child improves, the family has to make some adjustments because they no longer have a problem child. Brothers and sisters who are used to being the "good" children in the family may feel displaced. All changes, including positive ones, require readjustments in the family dynamics, so this could be considered a side effect.

Dr. Lynda has observed that neurofeedback may have beneficial side effects, which she calls carryover effects. In some children social skills improve. This has been particularly noted in children who, prior to training, were not able to initiate or maintain friendships. Handwriting has been documented to improve. The small number of children who have bed-wetting problems "grow out of" that difficulty. The few children who have associated speech difficulties, particularly with respect to articulation, improved rather dramatically. All academic areas, especially reading, show remarkable improvements. Children who previously seemed completely egocentric (centered on themselves) begin to consider other people's points of view. Perhaps each of these carryover effects has a neurological basis that further research will be able to explain. For now we'll just call them a happy carryover and propose a simple hypothesis as an explanation. Keeping in mind that the slow brain wave activity characteristic of older children who have A.D.D. is also seen in all young children, it may be that what we are observing is an acceleration of maturation as a result of neurofeedback training. All these happy carryover effects seem related to increased maturity and thus may be a natural result of practicing more mature brain wave patterns. Practicing to produce more mature brain waves may help a person mature out of difficulties in paying attention. It will be fascinating to see if this "giving maturation a nudge" hypothesis is borne out by research in the next few years.

Do results obtained through neurofeedback last?

Unlike drugs, which are short acting, neurofeedback appears to produce permanent shifts in learning and behavior. More research will establish if the benefits always last, or if some clients may need refresher sessions.

Why haven't I heard of neurofeedback before?

Neurofeedback training is based on more than twenty-five years of research. Dr. Barry Sterman, a professor at the University of California, Los Angeles, first published articles on using neurofeedback with human subjects in 1972. After collaborating with Dr. Sterman, Dr. Joel Lubar, a professor at the University of Tennessee, focused his research on using neurofeedback for children with A.D.D. This A.D.D. work was first published in 1976. Since then, considerable research has been done in this field, but because the research was concentrated at a small number of universities and published in highly specialized journals, health care professionals, and even educational or behavioral specialists, were not aware of the possibilities. Now, however, advances in computer technology have taken neurofeedback out of the lab and transformed it into a useful clinical tool that can be used in psychologists' offices and schools. As EEG equipment has become smaller and personal computers more powerful, there has been rapid growth in the field of neurofeedback, especially as it applies to attention problems.

I've heard that neurofeedback is controversial. Why is that?

Any technique that is new becomes the subject of some controversy. Professionals, like most people, tend to discount what they don't understand or have no experience with. Most pediatricians know nothing about neurofeedback because it was not mentioned in medical school. Professionals in the field of A.D.D. have traditionally relied on drugs and behavior modification. They are comfortable with these approaches, even as they realize their limitations. As research and experience accumulates, however, neurofeedback is becoming more widely accepted.

Some people take the position that the benefits of neurofeedback training have not been scientifically demonstrated. What they usually mean is that double-blind controlled studies (such as exist for medication) have not been done. In double-blind studies, both the research subject and the experimenter are "blind" as to whether the subject is getting the real treatment or a placebo. One group gets a real pill and the other group (the control group) a look-alike pill with no active ingredient. The researcher then evaluates the subject's behavior. After the behavior ratings have been collected, the researcher breaks the code to see which subjects had the real drug and to determine if there was

significant improvement in this group compared to the group that got the phony pill. (There may have been improvement in the control group as well due to the placebo effect — improvement that occurs because of the expectation that it will occur; see page 240.) Double-blind controlled studies can determine quite readily if a drug is effective. Using this medical model to do research, it has been established that stimulants such as Ritalin and Dexedrine produce some improvement in about 70 percent of children with A.D.H.D. symptoms. The positive response rate is higher in younger children (ages six to eleven) and lower in adolescents and adults. About 35 percent of children improve on a placebo alone.

It is not, however, an easy matter to come up with a control group for neurofeedback studies, and this makes it difficult and costly to do double-blind controlled studies of this technique. Whereas research on medications may be funded by the drug companies, who reap profits from the findings, funding for neurofeedback studies is harder to come by.

There are, however, valid methods of research that do not use placebo-control designs. Neurofeedback research often uses series of clinical cases or comparison groups. For example, a study by Rossiter and La Vaque published in the *Journal of Neurotherapy* in 1995 compared a group of children receiving medication with a group doing neurofeedback training. It showed that twenty sessions of neurofeedback (usually forty to sixty sessions are recommended) got results equal to treatment with Ritalin. Improvement was measured using behavior rating scales similar to our A.D.D.-Q on pages 42 to 43 and a computerized test called the TOVA (Test of Variables of Attention), described on page 61.

Practical, clinical experience with neurofeedback is currently running ahead of the research. Anecdotal results (i.e., reports of individual cases) are impressive, and it will take some time for research, which is slow and expensive, to catch up. There are large studies now planned in both the United States and Canada. The time line for these studies, from start to finish, is estimated at a minimum of three years. In the meantime, success stories spread by word of mouth and via the Internet. The days of neurofeedback's being controversial are quickly passing. There is enough positive evidence to recommend neurofeedback as a valuable tool in tackling the difficulties associated with A.D.D.

How does neurofeedback differ from biofeedback?

Neurofeedback can also be described as EEG biofeedback. It is a special kind of biofeedback. "Feedback" simply refers to feeding information about a person's behavior back to him or her. Biofeedback involves measuring some biological function in the body and feeding that information back to the person. With this information, the person can become more conscious of body functions, such as temperature, respiration, blood pressure, or heart rate and also learn, to some extent, to control them. For instance, biofeedback can help someone learn to stay relaxed. Neurofeedback can show if the person is staying focused and concentrating. For certain clients neurofeedback sometimes is combined with regular biofeedback, because relaxed concentration is an optimal state for learning. (For an example of this technique, see the story of Matt, page 217.)

What does neurofeedback cost?

Neurofeedback involves an initial evaluation and at least forty sessions of training. Cost de-pends on what your local neurofeedback practitioner charges per hour. This is often in line with the hourly rate charged by other mental health professionals in your area. Evaluation usually ranges from $300 to $700 and sessions cost between $60 and $120. Think of it as the cost of professional tutoring. Many parents compare their investment in neurofeedback with the cost of orthodontics. Like orthodontics, it takes time and it is expensive, but the results last. Neurofeedback is an investment in improving your child's quality of life. Dr. Lynda recalls one grandparent who said this when paying for a grandchild's training: "I had put money aside for college, but we all realized that if he didn't learn how to pay attention in class and finish his work, he'd never get to college."

Some people have extended health insurance benefits that cover neurofeedback. Because it is a relatively new intervention, some companies may not have a code for neurofeedback but might group it under biofeedback. Many plans cover psychological services and, in those cases, parents can get reimbursement up to the limit of their plan if the practitioner is a psychologist. In Canada, the provincial health plans do not cover neurofeedback because it is not considered a medical procedure.

What is the success rate with neurofeedback?

Nothing works 100 percent of the time, but neurofeedback is usually successful in appropriate candidates. The research literature reports success rates for neurofeedback training of around 85 percent. Dr. Lynda finds a somewhat higher success rate in her practice, probably because she is using more sessions when needed and is combining neurofeedback training with learning strategies. Further research is needed to identify which clients can be helped by which combinations of techniques.

Every approach to managing A.D.D. has its good points, and all of them should be considered carefully with your child's particular situation in mind. The combination of neurofeedback, biofeedback, and training in cognitive strategies is extraordinarily powerful. For a few children with extreme hyperactivity, these can be combined very well with medication. In Dr. Lynda's experience, the majority of children who are on stimulant medications when they begin training slowly come off medication as neurofeedback takes effect. A few children who were extremely hyperactive still benefit from some medication after training, particularly in group situations. Usually a lower dose of medication can be used when neurofeedback is added. Some children with A.D.D. may also benefit from short-term use of the positive reinforcement strategies outlined in earlier chapters along with neurofeedback training. Parents may also appreciate short-term support and ideas generated by a parent's group. Always consider using a multimodal approach — that is, combine all the interventions likely to benefit your child. Do not forget the basics: a healthy diet, exercise, and enough sleep. "A sound mind in a sound body" is a good motto for everyone in the family.

Parents must always be realistic. There are no panaceas. There is no absolute guarantee of improvement with any method or combination of methods used with children who have A.D.D. Nevertheless, the results with neurofeedback are very promising.

There are some situations in which neurofeedback is less successful or takes many more sessions to produce the desired results. These include children who have very extreme hyperactivity, learning disabilities, or severe behavioral or family problems.

Extreme hyperactivity in young children. At Dr. Lynda's center, out of several hundred clients with A.D.D., a few children did not make all the desired gains. Some improvements, especially in academic performance, were seen in all the children, but there was a small group of about six extremely hyperactive children who continued to need stimulant medication, though at lower doses than previously. These were children who initially climbed on the furniture during the first few minutes of an interview, despite being on high doses of stimulant medication. Some talked at a speed that made it difficult even for their own mothers to understand. When these children began neurofeedback, Dr. Lynda had thought that it would take about forty sessions. We now recognize that young children who have extreme hyperactivity may take considerably longer to improve — perhaps sixty to ninety sessions. Eventually, they do slow down and may get off medication, at least in some situations, while still requiring it in low doses for group events and for school. Other aspects of the A.D.D. problem, such as attention span and academic achievement, improve for extremely hyperactive children in a much shorter time than changes in their activity level do.

Learning disabilities. Children with a combination of impulsiveness, hyperactivity, and severe learning disabilities take longer both to begin demonstrating changes (forty to fifty-five neurofeedback sessions instead of about twenty) and to complete training (occasionally more than seventy-five sessions). This group, however, may eventually make the most dramatic changes. Emerson was one of Dr. Lynda's favorite clients at the ADD Centre.

When Emerson began training, he was four years behind his sixth-grade peers in terms of academics. His parents were teachers and had exhausted all the traditional routes for helping him. He was described as the most severely learning-disabled child seen at the local children's hospital. Emerson had been given special-education support since the primary grades as well as lots of help at home, but he still struggled with second-grade reading material at eleven years of age. With neurofeedback training combined with coaching in learning strategies, he eventually began working at the appropriate grade level. His reading, for example, went from a second-grade level to a fifth-grade level between August, when he started training, and November, when his first progress testing was done. Within a year of beginning training, his essay "On the Effects of Budget Cuts in Education" was among those published in the local newspaper. He began his essay, "As an average seventh-grade student, I believe . . ." His parents sent us a copy of the newspaper and shared their joy that their learning-disabled son now considered himself an average student. His writing was still messy, but he finished seventh grade with straight A's!

Adolescents with severe family problems. In Dr. Lynda's experience, it is quite difficult to predict which adolescents who have family problems are going to do well in a neurofeedback program and which ones are likely to leave after only a few sessions. Most of the adolescents with behavior problems get quite interested in learning self-regulation and in changing their brain waves. They appropriately feel that they are under-

taking this program for themselves and for their own benefit. The teenager who is used to being nagged likes the idea of getting his parents off his back. Most of them do well, and parents and schools report major positive behavioral changes. On the other hand, it sometimes happens that improvements in brain wave self-regulation and on standardized tests of academic and intellectual functioning do not immediately translate into improved school performance. Sometimes difficult teenagers from difficult family situations drop out before giving the program a chance to have a positive effect. Sometimes they are very passive-aggressive and assert control over the situation by refusing to do their work or by doing it at the very last minute. Dr. Lynda prepares parents at the outset that this might happen.

One eighteen-year-old told us that the training had worked. She could now get A's if she wanted to and had proved it for herself at school. It was certainly easier to listen and learn in class. She still was not doing much homework. She said it was impossible to please her father, a professional man who was a perfectionist. If she managed C's, he would want B's. Producing B's would elicit demands for A's. She felt she couldn't win, so why even try? She stopped coming to the program. We met with the parents and recommended family therapy. The effects in terms of improved attention were being sabotaged by the difficult family dynamics.

Training to decrease slow brain wave activity and increase fast brain wave activity can produce a lasting change in learning efficiency in children with A.D.D. Ideally, the graduates of a neurofeedback training program should be able, at will, to put themselves into a mental state that is relaxed, alert, and focused. In this state, they can demonstrate concentration, engage in organized problem solving, and efficiently and effectively accomplish tasks. The addition of some training in learning strategies improves their ability to listen, learn, organize, and remember material. This clear thinking can be applied equally well in academic, social, athletic, and on-the-job situations.

Dr. Lynda notes: *Without neurofeedback training, it takes incredible energy and ongoing supervision from parents and teachers to keep children with A.D.D. on track. It is wonderful to see children learning to do this for themselves as they learn to regulate their brain waves using neurofeedback.*

This is the most exciting thing I have done in my career as a psychologist. Neurofeedback empowers people to make changes and achieve things that were just not possible for them before.

Medications to Help A.D.D.

I worry about my child's taking drugs at such a young age," said a mother whose seven-year-old was given a prescription for Ritalin following the diagnosis of A.D.D. This mother was right to be concerned. While some parents praise these "miracle drugs" as saving their child's social and academic life, other parents are reluctant to use drugs to manage their child's behavior or learning. Every drug carries risks along with the benefits. You can read about the risks in the package insert provided by the manufacturer. Yet even if you make it through the fine print, you still may not know very much about the drug and what its effects will be on your child. Before agreeing to try medication to manage a child's A.D.D. symptoms, parents must ask lots of questions of their child's physician and the other professionals involved in this child's care: Is my child a good candidate for drug therapy? What results can be expected from the medication, and how will this benefit my child? Are there safer alternatives that should be tried before or in addition to drug therapy? Which drug should be tried first and why? What is the dosage? How often is it given? How can I tell if it's working? What are the possible side effects and how can I minimize

them? How long should my child take the medication? Parents should expect to participate in the decision-making process and in the evaluation of how the drug is working.

We want to help you know what questions to ask, so that you can make informed choices about medication. We hear people say, "I don't believe in drugs for children with A.D.D." This is as uninformed an opinion as suggesting that all children with A.D.D. should be drugged. Medications can do certain things for certain children. They have benefits and limitations. Drugs for A.D.D. should not be given with the attitude that they will control the child, but rather that the drug will help the child control himself.

> *A note to parents and professionals: Consider medication* in addition to *but* not instead of *other treatments, such as behavior and learning strategies.*

Since 1990 the number of American children being treated with Ritalin has increased nearly fourfold. The December 1996 issue of the medical journal *Pediatrics* reported that in 1995 1.5 million U.S. schoolchildren (2.8 percent) were taking Ritalin. The picture north of the border is similar. A letter to the editor of a Canadian daily newspaper said eloquently what many people are concerned about:

Ritalin is fast becoming the Valium of the 1990s. But instead of adults taking it to calm their own nerves, it is given to the children so they won't get on the adults' nerves in the first place.

Why is the Ritalin line at the school nurse's office so long? And why are so many children diagnosed with A.D.D.? Is this disorder that suddenly affects so many kids a side effect of our hyperactive society and its crowded day-care centers, crowded classrooms, hundred-channel cable-TV systems, and relentlessly thrilling video games? Are these children who behave and learn differently simply misfits in a one-size-fits-all educational system? Must they be drugged to make them conform to the conventions of the classroom or to make them fit into a family too busy to cope with inconvenient kids? These are all questions worth asking in relation to children with A.D.D., but the simplest explanation behind the medication epidemic is that Ritalin works.* Even more significant, it works quickly. A child who is a behavioral problem at home and failing in school can leave the doctor's office with a prescription on Friday afternoon and appear better be-

haved and more attentive in the classroom on Monday morning. In a society obsessed with quick fixes, Ritalin provides a rapid and cost-effective treatment, one that satisfies both an economic system that requires doctors to see more patients in less time and frustrated parents who love their child but "no longer like him." About two-thirds of children with A.D.D. symptoms respond favorably to Ritalin. Ritalin, therefore, seems to be the solution for the family and social problems created by children with A.D.D. But is it? While a short course of the right medicine helps to get a child back on track, we believe it is wrong to drug children without also working on the problems in their home and school environment.

Dr. Bill notes: My first thought as I'm writing a prescription for a stimulant is how quickly we can get the child off it. This means two things: working on alternative ways to manage the problem and getting an objective assessment as to when the child can manage his problem without medication.

This chapter contains information parents and teachers should consider when making decisions about using medications to help a child with A.D.D.

HOW DRUGS FOR A.D.D. WORK

The medications used to control A.D.D. are actually stimulants. This may seem puzzling: Why stimulate a child who is already hyperactive? To understand this treatment paradox, it helps to know something about neurobiology. Every time you think or act, messages travel from one nerve to another,

---

* *Throughout this discussion we refer primarily to Ritalin (methylphenidate), but there are several other medications that act in a similar fashion, and other classes of drugs, such as tricyclic, antidepressants, and SSRIs, that are also used for A.D.D.-related problems. At this writing, 86 percent of prescriptions for stimulants for children are for Ritalin.*

telling the brain what to do. The messages are carried by neurotransmitters, chemicals such as norepinephrine, dopamine, and seratonin, which are secreted at the junction between brain cells to facilitate transmission of messages. Stimulant drugs are thought to increase or stimulate the secretion of neurotransmitters. Dr. Russell Barkley, in his book *Taking Charge of A.D.H.D.: The Complete Authoritative Guide for Parents,* writes, "By increasing how much of these chemicals is available in the brain, the stimulant increases the action of these brain cells, which seem to be those most responsible for inhibiting behavior and helping us stick to something we are doing."

Here's one theory that explains why stimulants help the child with A.D.D.: in children with A.D.D., the brain centers that influence attention (learning) and impulse control (behavior) are underaroused, and all the wiggling and counterproductive behavior these children engage in is actually an attempt to arouse these laid-back parts of the brain. By increasing the levels of neurotransmitters in the brain, stimulant medications arouse these learning and behavior control centers so that the child can pay appropriate attention and control inappropriate behavior. Stimulants work on centers of the brain whose function is to inhibit impulsive behavior. This explains the paradox of giving a stimulant to calm the child down. The drug acts like a disciplinarian reinforcing "you may not do that" messages. Stimulant medications are often described as "putting brakes on the brain," but in fact, what they really do is make the brain work better, so the child doesn't have to daydream or bounce around in his seat to keep his brain waves working. Stimulants provide sort of a zoom lens that helps the child narrow his focus from general arousal to the task at hand.

THE BENEFICIAL EFFECTS OF MEDICATIONS

The effect of stimulant drugs on behavior and learning has been extensively studied. There are more than three thousand scientific articles on the subject of stimulant medication and A.D.D., and the studies show that 60 to 70 percent of children with A.D.D. show improvement in behavior, attention, and/or learning when taking stimulant medications, although the proven effects are short-lived (i.e., they do not persist when the medication is stopped).

Stimulants affect mainly the common symptom triad found in A.D.H.D.: impulsivity, inappropriate attention, and hyperactivity. Research has also shown that performance and learning tests improve when compared with the test results before the children were taking the stimulants. Work production increases, and writing is neater. There are improved peer interactions and more compliance at school. Eventually your child should feel better about himself. Most important, stimulants may help to change the parent-child behavior cycle from negative to positive. If your child is on medication after school at home, then, as his behavior improves, you will like your child more, and your child will feel more loved and accepted and therefore will continue to behave better. The whole family system will function at a higher level.

I've always loved our child. Now I like him.

Within a few days after taking Ritalin, Matthew was easier to discipline. Before, I was more tolerant of his disruptive behavior because I felt he really couldn't control himself. After being on the medication for a couple of days, he seemed less impulsive, as if he took a few seconds before he acted. My attitude toward him changed, in that I held him more responsible for his behavior because I felt the medication helped him be more responsible for his choice.

Medications have been shown to be effective for short-term but not for long-term improvement of symptoms. In an extensive review of the long-term effects of stimulant medication on A.D.D. children, Dr. James Swanson's team at the University of California, Irvine, reported that stimulant medications show "a short-term benefit for the management of behavioral symptoms of inattention, impulsivity, and hyperactivity; and a lack of demonstrated long-term effects on learning, achievement, or social adjustment."

SAFETY AND COMMON SIDE EFFECTS

Safety

Stimulants are generally regarded as safe drugs. They were first used for hyperactive children by Barkley in the 1930s, so they have been in use now for more than sixty years. Yet, like all medicines, they are not a problem-free pill. Dr. Bill first began prescribing Ritalin for A.D.D. in 1972. Twenty-five years and hundreds of prescriptions later, he is impressed by how few undesirable side effects have occurred. When side effects do occur, they may be minor and wear off quickly when the drug is stopped. Other physicians have different experiences, and some have

---

Important Ethical Questions

"The International Narcotics Control Board reports that in 1995, 250 million doses of Ritalin (methylphenidate) were prescribed in the United States . . . and warns . . . all governments to exercise the utmost vigilance in order to prevent . . . medically unjustified treatment with methylphenidate." The U.S. Drug Enforcement Administration says that "abuse of methylphenidate can lead to tolerance and severe psychological dependence."

Physicians and parents must ask themselves:

1. Am I absolutely sure that the appropriate symptoms of A.D.H.D. are present and that no other reasonable method for assisting my patient/child will suffice?

2. Can I give a child drugs that affect behavior and still convincingly tell my patient/child to say no to drugs that are mood enhancers?

3. Will medications increase a sense of having an external locus of control when what I want for my patient/child is to increase awareness of being responsible for and capable of controlling his or her own behavior?

4. Whom am I truly trying to help when I give this medication: myself as an exhausted parent, my family in crisis, the harried and perhaps upset teacher, or my child? (All are important, but the child's needs should be foremost.)

If you are satisfied on all four accounts, then short-term use of stimulant medication may be very helpful, provided you take the proper precautions to monitor both the effects of the medication and any side effects.

observed complications severe enough that they have virtually stopped prescribing these medications. Prescribing and administering Ritalin is a decision parents, teachers, and health professionals must take seriously. The U.S. Drug Enforcement Administration (DEA) certainly does.

Because of the low incidence of side effects, it is tempting to regard using Ritalin as no big deal. It is even jokingly referred to as Vitamin R, a sort of "it can't do any harm, and it might help" classification. But the DEA lists Ritalin as a Schedule II drug, which means that prescriptions for it are carefully regulated. Along with other drugs in this category, such as morphine and barbiturates, it is considered at high risk for abuse. (The street drug culture would classify Ritalin as speed.) Doctors who prescribe it are required to obtain an expensive narcotic license, renew it every two years, and write the prescription (with annoying perfection) on special triplicate prescription pads provided by the DEA. The doctor retains a copy, the pharmacy retains a copy, and the DEA retains a copy. To further avoid "prescribing abuse," the doctor is limited by law to prescribing a one-month supply, and the child must be reevaluated each month. A prescription for Ritalin cannot be called into the pharmacy over the phone; instead, the completed official prescription form must be mailed or handed directly to the patient. If the doctor forgets to cross a *t* or dot an *i,* the pharmacist must send it back, for fear that someone may have tampered with the prescription. The point is, everyone involved with prescribing Ritalin takes it seriously, especially the doctor, the pharmacist, and the DEA. So must everyone else.

It would be great if these medications worked selectively, that is, only on the brain functions concerned with attention or focusing ability (A.D.D.) or on the areas that control movement and impulsiveness (A.D.H.D.). But they don't. Ritalin and other stimulants have a wider action in the brain, which is clear from four of the side effects that have been identified by placebo-controlled research: decreased appetite, insomnia, headaches, and stomachaches. Stimulants affect the whole brain, causing both desirable and undesirable neurological effects. From 2 to 4 percent of children cannot tolerate stimulant medication because of severe side effects. In addition to what is known, or at least theorized, about how stimulants work, there is a great deal that science does not know. Stimulant drugs change the neurochemistry of the brain, but the long-term effects are unknown. When the action of neurotransmitters is artificially stimulated for a long time, might the brain eventually slow down its own production of these chemicals? By giving a child stimulant medication, you are "fooling" the brain into thinking it makes more neurotransmitters than it really does. Might this interfere with the neurological system's ability to regulate itself?

Normally, neurological systems work on a supply/demand or dose/response biological principle. The brain processes just enough neurotransmitters for the job at hand, making a thought or performing an activity. There is an internal self-regulating system. The problem with pills is they are not self-regulating.

Even though the party line among A.D.D. professionals is that stimulant medications are nonaddictive, the attitudes about drugs we are giving our children may have long-term undesirable effects. Also, even though some stimulant medications are listed in the "controlled substances" category, in reality, the control walks out the door when the parent leaves the pharmacy. "Control" simply means controlling the doctor and the pharmacy. There is no way to control what the parent does with the drug, what the child does with the drug, or whether children share their drugs with their friends.

Contraindications

There are a few, rare contraindications to giving stimulant medications. If your child fits any of these categories, make your physician aware of them before he or she prescribes stimulant medication. The contraindications are:

- any significant cardiac (heart) problem
- hypertension (high blood pressure)
- any family history of tics or Tourette Syndrome
- any history of psychosis
- significant symptoms of anxiety
- significant symptoms of depression
- any history of substance abuse
- a seizure disorder
- also taking the drug Clonidine (Catapres)

Common Side Effects

What follows are the most common side effects (meaning undesired or undesirable effects of the drug) and what parents, child, and doctor can do to lessen them. Most side effects can be avoided or reduced by lowering the dosage, changing the timing of when the drug is given, or changing the type of stimulant. To help monitor the side effects of your child's medication, complete the chart on page 234.

Insomnia. Sleep in adequate quality and quantity is important for anyone's well-being. Double that for children who have A.D.D. Individuals with A.D.D. have a low arousal and alertness level when they are involved in boring, repetitive activities, which accounts for

why many adolescents and adults have a great deal of trouble staying awake during lectures. This problem is worse for individuals who did not sleep well the previous night. Difficulties with going to sleep and staying asleep can be minimized by giving the last dose of Ritalin no later than 1 P.M. Doing so allows the peak effect to occur during the afternoon school hours yet wear off by bedtime.

Diminished appetite. This is a common side effect of all stimulants. In fact, the stimulant Dexedrine was once used as a popular appetite suppressant or diet pill. Diminished appetite can become a battle zone for parent-child conflicts. Parents feel responsible for getting a child to eat, but they soon realize you can lead a horse to water, but you can't make him drink. Constant attempts to get just one more spoonful in the tummy may be interpreted by a child as nagging.

One mother reports, "I just feel helpless. The more I try to get him to eat, the less he listens to me. I've tried everything. I nag. I won't let him leave the table until he finishes three spoonfuls. He sits there for an hour staring at this tiny bit of food on the plate. I try rewarding him for each small mouthful that he eats. I try punishing him. I say he cannot watch any television until the small amount I've pushed over to the side of his plate is eaten. Nothing works. He just isn't hungry."

This child is not being stubborn or reluctant to eat. He truly is not hungry. This is not a psychological anorexia problem. Stimulant medications truly have a physiological effect on the appetite. The good news is, like most of these minor side effects of stimulant medications, appetite suppression can be minimized.

THE A.D.D.-Q/S (Side Effects)

Instructions:

1. Teacher and parent should both fill in this questionnaire, according to who is with the child. Some questions, such as those concerning sleep, only the parent will be able to answer.
2. Do this for 2 days *before* starting medication and each day during the drug trial.

Name: _____ Age: _____

Medication: _____ Dose: _____ Time medication given:_____

Date:_____ Time chart was filled out:_____

SIDE EFFECTS These are unwanted effects apparently related to taking the medication.	No problem	Mild	Moderate	Severe	COMMENTS
1. Decreased appetite					
2. Problem getting to sleep					
3. Problem staying asleep					
4. Anxious or fearful					
5. Irritable					
6. Looks like a zombie (staring)					
7. Decreased spontaneity					
8. Depressed (even crying)					
9. Headache					
10. Stomachache					
11. Tics (e.g., twitches, jerks, blinks, squints)					
12. Vocal tics (e.g., throat clearing, sniffing, grunting)					
13. Skin rash					
14. Embarrassment because taking medication					
15. Psychosis (irrational thinking, hallucinations, *extreme* anxiety or inappropriateness)					
Rebound effect as drug wears off: increased symptoms, hyperactivity and/or depression					**Description**

- *Feed the child before giving the pill.* Give your child a "lumberjack breakfast" before the pill begins to take effect. This means start your child off with a breakfast high in protein, calories, and complex carbohydrates that get into his stomach before the medication reaches his brain. Your doctor or the package insert may recommend giving Ritalin on an empty stomach or a half hour before a meal because the drug may be better absorbed this way in some children. However, if the drug reaches the brain before the food reaches the stomach, the child may neither start nor finish his breakfast. So, in the case of a child in whom appetite suppression is a problem, forget the empty-stomach rule. Discuss this with your doctor.

- *Encourage nutrient-dense foods.* These are foods that pack a lot of nutrition into a small volume. Examples of good nutrient-dense foods are avocado, yogurt (regular rather than nonfat), fish (salmon, tuna, cod), granola cereal, cottage cheese, kidney beans, cheese, eggs, nut butter, whole-grain pasta, brown rice, tofu, and turkey.

- *Encourage grazing.* Children under the influence of appetite suppressants may be uninterested in big meals and big platefuls. Be more flexible about your child's mealtimes. Allow him to eat when he is hungry. Some children will be hungry at bedtime when the drug has finally worn off. Small, frequent feedings or grazing on nutritious snacks all day long is actually more biologically correct for the human body anyway. Besides, as we discuss in chapter 10, grazing is friendly to the food-mood connection characteristic of some of these children, as it prevents blood sugar swings and the moody behavior that goes with them.

- *Drink the meals.* High-protein shakes, yogurt shakes, smoothies, or whatever nutritious blend your child likes is a fun way to get a lot of nutrition into your child.

- *Reward the eating.* While using food for a reward is generally neither good eating or good parenting practice, rewards for eating may get needed nutrition into a child whose appetite is suppressed despite juggling the timing and the dosage of the stimulant medication. It may help to set up a reward system, whereby the child gets a certain number of tokens after eating a certain amount of food. For the young child, you will have to take baby steps in doling out tokens. Give a token for each tiny step, one for taking a small spoonful into his mouth and a second for swallowing it. Provide cheers and encouragement as well.

Growth delay. Is the worry that stimulants stunt growth warranted? (Weren't you always told that coffee would stunt your growth?) It is generally accepted that in most children stimulants have only a small effect on growth in height and weight. However, children differ, and some children may be affected more than others. Your child's physicians should keep a careful record of height and weight if stimulant medications have been prescribed. Most children who may temporarily have a slowdown in growth catch up when the medication is stopped, such as over the summer months. Nevertheless, parents worry. If stimulants diminish appetite, causing the child to get insufficient nutrition, naturally growth will suffer. But there is also some evidence that stimulants directly affect growth by upsetting the balance of growth hormones. High doses given uninterrupted over several years are more likely to suppress growth than lower doses, especially if the child is given drug holidays during school and summer vacations (see page 251).

The truth is, the stimulant-growth connection is hard to study, and statistical studies are not applicable to individual children. What would the child's height have been a year later had he not been taking medications? This is an unanswerable question. We are left to use our common sense. Any drug that has a possibility of affecting growth hormones has the risk of affecting growth, especially during critical childhood years. Parents can minimize this risk by ensuring their child has adequate nutrition, giving drug holidays as often as possible, and monitoring dosage closely to arrive at a dose high enough to achieve the desired effects but not so high as to produce the undesired effects.

The roller-coaster effect. What happens when the effects of the drug wear off? Parents sometimes report, "He's like two differ-

---

Medication-Giving Tips

Using medications to improve behavior and enhance learning is both an art and a science, and it requires close communication among everyone who works with the child. The dosage, frequency, and schedule for giving stimulant medications vary greatly from child to child. Here are some general guidelines:

- Working out the right dose requires establishing whether the drug works, what is the right dose, and what, if any, are the side effects. The usual dosage range is from .3 to .8 milligrams per kilogram (mg/kg) of body weight. Your doctor will probably start off at a dosage of .3 mg/kg (or 5- to 10-mg pill in the morning) and, based upon your charting and reporting and that of the teacher, increase or decrease the morning dose, add a second late morning or early afternoon dose, or decide that your child either doesn't need or doesn't respond to that particular medication. Your doctor may increase the medication by 5 mg weekly until either the desired beneficial effect or undesirable side effects occur. If one stimulant medication does not work or is not tolerated by your child, your doctor may try another. This trial phase may take as long as six weeks. The second phase is monitoring the long-term dosing schedule, which may include increased doses during stressful situations and drug holidays when there is no school.

- Some A.D.D. specialists feel that some children — and their parents — are "placebo responders," which means they respond to the power of suggestion and get better with just about any therapy or with a placebo (pretend) pill. For these children, a placebo trial may be useful. Some A.D.D. specialists recommend this approach first. Your pharmacist may be able to make a look-alike placebo pill.

- Don't start the medication simultaneously with a major change, such as a move, a family upset, or a change of school. To gauge whether or not the drug is necessary, first give your child a chance to adjust to the new environment. On the other hand, if you know from past experience that your child falls apart during major changes, beginning the medication just before the event may help. It will, however, be more difficult to evaluate the results.

ent persons. In the morning I like him; in the evening I don't." The ups and downs of this roller-coaster effect can be quite obvious. Sometimes a stimulant-medicated child can be managed by teachers but becomes unmanageable at home when the afternoon dose wears off. Yet a late afternoon or evening dose of medication to make the child easier to live with may interfere with the child's sleep. Children sometimes report they don't like the different feelings of being on and off medication. It's like they themselves realize they have a sort of double personality.

Teachers also dread the roller-coaster effect. They recognize how different the child acts and learns when the medication begins to wear off during the last hour of morning classes.

At least it's possible to teach Jason for a little while when the medication is working. His activity level and ability to stay in his

---

- Give the first dose of medication on a Saturday morning or at the beginning of a school vacation, so you have an opportunity to observe the effects firsthand before the next school day.
- To minimize the appetite-decreasing effects of stimulants, try giving the morning dose after breakfast or just before the child leaves for school, so it is likely to take effect by the time the first class begins. A few children may absorb Ritalin better on an empty stomach. This may, however, diminish their appetite.
- The most noticeable effects occur around one to two hours after the medication is given. If your child is required to be at his best behavior or peak performance at a certain time, you can time the giving of the dose accordingly.
- For medications administered at school, give the child a reminder, such as a watch with an alarm that beeps at the dosage time.
- Consult your doctor about drug holidays — weekends, school holidays, or school vacations, when you can skip the medication or at least use a lower dose.
- To avoid sleep disturbances, give the late afternoon dose earlier, lower the dose, or omit that dose entirely.
- Some children do better if the second pill is given after the morning recess; otherwise, the last class of the morning is an academic disaster. If safety is a factor in the hyperactive, impulsive child who walks (or, rather, runs) home from school, a third pill may be given after the afternoon recess.
- If your child experiences a rebound effect when the medication wears off (see page 238), try "piggy-backing." Give the next dose before the previous dose has worn off, usually three hours after the previous dose instead of four.
- Resist the temptation to increase or decrease the dose if your child is having a particularly bad day. First explore other causes unrelated to the effects of the drug that may have triggered a sudden change of behavior.
- If your child's appetite is diminished as a result of the medication, encourage her to eat large meals at the times of the day when the effects of the medication are wearing off. Offer your child nutritious foods frequently throughout the day.

seat are constantly changing during the morning and the afternoon classes. The dose was increased, and for a while he became quieter, but this fluctuating behavior wasn't altered by the dose increase. He is totally impossible to deal with during the last half hour of classes, and he has to be removed from the lunchroom every day.

As you can well imagine, Jason's mother was extremely concerned. She was barraged with calls to the point that she almost had an anxiety attack every time the phone rang.

To smooth out the roller-coaster effect, try what we call the "small, frequent feedings" method of administering the medication. Three to four smaller, more frequent doses may have less of an up-and-down effect than two larger doses at greater intervals. Instead of giving the first dose before school and the second dose after lunch (the standard schedule), give the first dose about one hour before school starts, a second dose at the end of morning recess (around 11 A.M.), and a third dose at the afternoon recess (around 2 P.M.). Sometimes a small fourth dose may be given around 5:30 P.M. if it does not interfere with the child's bedtime and quality of sleep. There is also a slow-release version of Ritalin available, but in Dr. Bill's experience, the regular short-acting Ritalin given in smaller, more frequent dosages is more effective in smoothing out the roller-coaster effect. However, if a child shows a good response to the slow-release form of Ritalin, it does get around the problem of having to take a pill at school, something many children dislike.

Ritalin rebound. When medication blood levels come down, children's behavior changes. Some children become even more hyperactive than they were originally once

the medication wears off; others, instead of getting "high," seem to experience a "down" effect at the end of the day or evening, and a few may become downright depressed.

I don't like the rebound effect that happens when Ryan's medication wears off in the evening. He gets moody and irritable, and his behavior is worse than before he started taking the drug. His behavior has been good at school, but he's a terror at home at night.

While extreme hyperactivity, depression, and fearfulness are rare and extreme side effects of stimulant medications, any strong reaction to the medication wearing off is a good reason for lowering the dosage, changing the timing of dosages, or discontinuing the medication and finding alternative ways to help your child.

The effects of stimulant medication will be most noticeable as it enters the body (usually one half to one hour after giving the medication) and as the medication is leaving the body (usually around three and one-half to four and one-half hours after the preceding dose). If the rebound effect of the medication leaving the body produces behavior worse than what you started with, lower the initial dose and add a small second dose. If a child's after-school at-home behavior is unbearable, ask your doctor about giving the second dose later in the afternoon or adding a small third dose in the late afternoon if that doesn't interfere with sleep.

Stomachaches and headaches. Next to insomnia and diminished appetite, headaches and stomachaches are the most common side effects found with stimulant medications. Headaches are usually transient and lessen or stop after a few weeks on the medication.

Taking the medication with a snack may help avoid associated stomachaches. These annoying symptoms occur in a small minority of patients and subside when medication is stopped or the dosage reduced. It's safe for a child to take acetaminophen for headache relief while also taking stimulants.

Tics. An unusual (around 1-percent incidence) but annoying side effect of stimulants are tics — muscle twitches, such as blinking, facial twitches, head shaking, shoulder shrugging, and nose wrinkling. These nuisances, besides being disruptive in school, are embarrassing to the child and to the parents, who had been looking forward to taking a break from explaining their child's behavior. These tics usually subside when the medication is stopped or the dosage lowered.

Rarely, stimulant medications can unmask an underlying severe tic disorder called Tourette Syndrome. This is not really considered a side effect of the medication, since the disorder is genetic, but it is brought out by the medication. People with Tourette Syndrome have a combination of motor and vocal tics. At first a parent may notice only repetitive sniffing, throat clearing, or coughing. This is followed in more severe cases by vocalizations, including guttural sounds, high-pitched noises, and barking. Some may blurt out a stream of obscenities. This disorder is thought to be the result of hypersensitivity to the neurotransmitter dopamine in the basal ganglia area of the brain. Stimulant medications do not cause Tourette. If a child develops tics while on the medication, it's important to stop the medication to diagnose whether or not the tics are a side effect of the medication or the result of underlying Tourette Syndrome, which usually will not go away when the stimulant medication is stopped.

Tics are most commonly observed for the first time in children between seven and ten years of age, and they may even occur years after the child has been found to have A.D.D. If there is a family history of tic disorders, be sure to inform your child's doctor before medication is prescribed. The doctor is likely to prescribe stimulant medication more cautiously if there is a family history of tic disorders.

Other undesirable effects. Other undesirable side effects that have been noticed in children who are on stimulant medications include irritability, depression, diminished spontaneity, anxiety, increased heart rate, and a proneness to crying. Some parents report, "Our child just doesn't seem like himself," and their children agree with this assessment. Some parents do notice a definite personality change while their child is on the medication, and they are not always certain whether it is for the better.

The undesirable side effects of stimulant medication occur in a small minority of children. When children are properly evaluated and medication is used in the proper dosage and timing and along with other strategies, stimulants are generally a safe and useful tool in the overall management package for the child with A.D.D.

Occasionally, taking medication for A.D.D. may actually be an important safety factor for a child.

Bobby was a four-year-old who had A.D.D. with extreme hyperactivity and impulsivity. Bobby's parents were advised to put safety hooks and locks on every bathroom cupboard and on all doors to the outside. Bobby's older brother, age eleven, also had A.D.D. and was quite irresponsible. Bobby's family lived at the junction of two major thoroughfares. Bobby's parents worked very hard to make sure Bobby was safe, but there was no way they could guarantee that his brother would remember to latch the front door. On the contrary, they knew that despite all their efforts, he frequently forgot. This was a life-threatening situation. Both boys were placed on medication. This slowed down Bobby's brother, and he did think about the door a little more often. Medication also helped Bobby, even at his young age, to think before he ran out in *traffic. It was a temporary, but perhaps life-saving, measure!*

HOW TO DECIDE IF YOUR CHILD NEEDS MEDICATION

The decision to give your child medication for A.D.D. requires a careful assessment of the situation. Even more important than identifying your child's A.D.D. symptoms is assessing how much the A.D.D. is interfering with his learning, development, self-image, and

---

The Placebo Effect

Here's an interesting fact: research shows that more than one-third of children diagnosed with A.D.D. improve with a placebo, a look-alike pill that has no active ingredient. This is about half as many as improve with the real medication (the effectiveness of which is reported to be 60 to 70 percent). This finding raises the question, If A.D.D. has a neurobiological basis, such as a difference in the production of neurotransmitters in the brain, as is currently suspected, how can one-third of these kids improve with a phony pill?

Here is one explanation. The child has problems with attention and/or hyperactivity, and the doctor prescribes a pill. Along with the pill comes a bit of marketing. The doctor may mention that studies have shown the "focus pill" (as Dr. Bill calls it) to be 60 to 70 percent effective. The parents and child leave the doctor's office with high expectations of a cure, or at least some help, for their child;

they have paid money for this solution, so it better work. The parent, the child, and the doctor are all programmed to believe the pill will perform. Putting the child on medication may prompt related actions: the parents may join an A.D.D. support group, subscribe to an A.D.D. newsletter, read an A.D.D. book, demand special attention for the child at school, at home, and in sports, and give the child special food with special preparation. This may be the first time in the child's life that he has received so much special attention. And the parents now have a better understanding of how to relate to their child. All of these factors can contribute to improved behavior, even if the pill turns out to be a placebo.

The placebo effect is one reason it is so difficult to evaluate the actual neuro-biological effects of any management techniques offered to A.D.D. parents and their children. It also shows the self-healing power of positive expectations.

overall sense of well-being. Parents, teachers, and significant others should all contribute their insights. When your child's problems *significantly* interfere with self-image, learning, and relationships with peers and teachers, then medication may be considered a useful tool — along with many of the other management strategies described in this book.

When Nelson's doctor suggested we give him Ritalin, I was horrified. I cried and felt guilty for not being able to cope with the way my child was. But we saw an immediate and positive change in Nelson. The medication seemed to give him what he was lacking — that pause of a few seconds in order to make a wise choice. It also helped me with discipline; now if he was naughty, I felt it was his choice. The medication seemed to lessen what was bad with him and reveal what was wonderful about him. As time went on, we realized we still had a lot of fine-tuning to do with medication dosages, schedules, behavior modification, and school. I felt that a lot of TV programs and magazine articles have given medication a bad name and have led parents to think that their children will be zombies or, worse, psychopathic killers if they take medication. This simply isn't true.

As a simple guideline, consider using medications if your child has two or all three of the key symptoms of A.D.D. (impulsivity, hyperactivity, and inappropriate attention), *and* two or more of the following apply:

- He regularly receives negative comments from his teacher or from other children, and these comments are hurting his self-image.
- He acts impulsively and has begun to identify himself as the troublemaker.

- He is beginning to hang out with a group of children who are always getting in trouble.
- He fidgets and wanders to the extent that it is preventing him from advancing academically.
- He exhibits behavior that is distracting to other students, to the extent that the school is refusing to allow him to remain in the regular classroom. (This behavior is not able to be controlled by behavior modification.)
- He is developing a negative self-image as a direct result of his A.D.D. symptoms.

In these situations, medications are usually the fastest way to make some behavioral changes, which will result in decreased negative feedback from teachers and peers.

Your observations of the medication's effects are very important to on-going decisions about how best to use the medication. Be objective. Nearly every treatment for every problem has a placebo effect, meaning the problem improves with treatment simply because you expect it to, not directly because of the treatment. Behavioral problems, especially A.D.H.D., are especially subject to the placebo effect because both parents and teachers desperately want quick results and, for the sake of the child and their own well-being, want the medicine to work. (In some studies comparing individuals on stimulant medication and placebos, more than 35 percent of those taking a placebo showed a positive response.) Managing medication requires a team approach from parents, doctors, A.D.D. specialists, teacher, and child. Everyone's observations are important, before and after medication is begun. The six points that need to be addressed while managing A.D.H.D. with medications are:

- choosing the right drug
- adjusting the drug to the right dosage
- giving the drug at the right times during the day
- deciding how long to give the drug
- deciding on the benefits or risks of drug holidays
- objectively reporting the effectiveness and side effects of a particular drug

Information from parents and teachers will affect all these decisions.

HOW TO CHOOSE THE RIGHT MEDICATION

Here is a step-by-step approach to help parents make informed decisions about giving their child medication for A.D.D.

Step 1: Make a Doctor Appointment

Before making a doctor appointment for the purpose of discussing A.D.H.D., collect all the pertinent material about your child's learning and behavior problems. Use the A.D.D.-Q to get this information down on paper. Include your observations, the teacher's observations, information from A.D.D. specialists you may have previously consulted, and whatever other information will help your doctor make a recommendation about whether or not your child could be helped by a trial of medication. List in the order of priority the problems that are the target of treatment. Focus on the ones that are interfering most with the child's social and academic growth, not just the ones that are most annoying or inconvenient. For example, hyperactivity alone, unless it is causing a child to be an academic failure or social outcast, is seldom a reason

for drug treatment. As we have previously stated, your doctor is primarily interested in two things:

1. the major problems your child has at school and at home (these are called target problems)
2. how much these problems are interfering with your child's overall growth, development, and well-being

The more accurate you are in conveying this information to your doctor, the more reliable the diagnosis and treatment you are likely to get. Remember that you are consulting an M.D. — a medical doctor, one who treats with medicine. This visit will usually be mainly about medications, not about alternative strategies.

Step 2: Understand the Medication

If you and your doctor decide it's in the best interests of your child to prescribe a trial of medication, be sure you ask your doctor the following questions:

- What is the medication, and how is it supposed to work?
- What are the possible side effects, and which ones should be reported immediately to the doctor?
- How is the medication used? (i.e., when to begin, what time of the day to give it, how often)
- How will the dosage and the timing of doses be adjusted based on the child's response?
- What should the school and other caregivers be told?
- How often will the doctor reevaluate the child?

Danger: Don't Overlook Possible Organic Factors

Douglas was a fifteen-year-old child who had behavior problems. His behavior problem was partly psychological, a result of early difficulties in his family. His A.D.D. also contributed to the development of his behavior problem. In addition, Douglas was mildly depressed. Was this possibly an inborn problem as well? Douglas sometimes flew into a rage and threw things around the room. Was this a sign of an organic (i.e., physiological) explosive disorder or just a manifestation of A.D.D. and frustration? With his friends he could be so hyperactive he seemed almost manic. Was this part of his A.D.H.D. or something else? Were his irritability and outbursts of rage side effects of stimulant medications? Were they influenced by his allergies? Were a number of different factors contributing to his difficulties?

Sometimes it is very difficult to figure out what is caused by what. Sometimes you need a neurological evaluation to rule out such things as seizures or space-occupying lesions (such as aneurysms or tumors), which can produce behavior changes. A careful history taken by a professional with a broad range of experience is still the best method for coming to a reasonable working hypothesis in complicated cases. A working hypothesis is really just a best guess based on all the information available. It is important to remember that many different things may contribute to the problems your child is experiencing. Usually A.D.D. with hyperactivity is noted very early in a child's life. A.D.D. without hyperactivity may be noticed only in adolescence or adulthood or may be missed altogether. When an adolescent comes into the physician's or psychologist's office with behavior difficulties, the professional must consider a number of contributing factors. A few common problems are listed below. This list is not exhaustive and it is meant only to give a few examples.

Douglas's physician decided that Douglas's main difficulty was his A.D.D., which was then treated with neurofeedback, medication, and behavioral strategies at home. But you can easily see that Douglas could have been diagnosed as having a number of other disorders, such as depression, which call for medications with potentially serious side effects. Another child could have exactly the same symptoms, representing a true organically based mental-health problem, and not be placed on appropriate medications — with serious results. Untreated depression, for example, can end in suicide. You go to a professional for help because you want to have someone with a broad base of experience work conservatively with you. You want the least invasive intervention first (unless there is a life-threatening emergency). But you don't want to ignore the possibility that there may be other factors involved. A guiding principle is "Medication when necessary, but not necessarily medication."

Problem	Possible Intervention
1. Attention-Deficit/Hyperactivity Disorder	neurofeedback/medications
2. Attention Deficit Without Hyperactivity (often lethargic)	neurofeedback training
3. learning difficulties (frustration, giving up, anger)	supplemental education/ learning strategies
4. depression	antidepressants
5. bipolar disorder	medications (e.g., Lithium/Tegretol)
6. explosive disorder	medications (e.g., Propranolol)
7. any combination of the above	

Step 3: Make a Medication Effectiveness Chart

Medicating a child for A.D.D. is not as simple as treating a sore throat with penicillin. There is a variety of medications from which to choose and a variety of dosage schedules, and children vary greatly in their responses.

A chart can help you keep track of your observations (see facing page). You should begin recording information about your child's behavior two days before beginning the medication, so that you have a way to evaluate changes made by the medication. You will get the most objective results by doing each day's charting on a separate piece of paper, so that your previous chart does not influence you to simply continue reporting the same positive (decrease in symptoms) or negative (increase in symptoms) observations, an observation bias called the halo effect. Your chart should list the following:

- the target problems for which the child was medicated
- the dosage and time of the medication
- positive effects and when you notice them
- negative effects and when you notice them

Provide your child's teacher with several copies of your chart.

Step 4: Evaluate Whether or Not the Medicine Is Working

After a time agreed upon by you and your doctor, and with the help of your medication effectiveness chart, note your observations: Is the medication helping, hindering, or having no effect? Don't be surprised if the teacher's assessment on the effectiveness chart is different from yours. Remember, the teacher is observing your child's behavior and learning when the medication's influence is at its peak, while you see your child mostly when the effects of the drug are wearing off. Your observations of the medication's positive effects are more accurate on weekends and holidays. According to the doctor's instructions, report your findings either by phone or in a follow-up office visit. Remember that the primary goal of drug or any therapy is not to eliminate the problems but to make them more manageable. Be sure the medication is actually improving your child's behavior and/or learning, not just making him more convenient to have around.

Most often the effects of medication are dramatic, and there will be no doubt about its effectiveness. Oftentimes, you can make that decision within a matter of days, and then fine-tune the dose or dosage schedule. Treating a child with A.D.D.-management medication in some ways resembles treating a new diabetic with insulin; it requires frequent consultation with the doctor to arrive at the right drug, the right dose, and the right schedule. Sometimes parents wonder whether the medication is working or if the behavior changes they are observing are really the result of the medication. If the doctor is also uncertain whether to continue or change the medication, he or she may advise a blind trial, meaning that parent, teacher, and child do not know how much medication, if any, is being given. If placebo pills (pills that look identical but have no active ingredient) are available, they can be used. If not, the blind trial can be conducted by giving the child a snack prepared by one parent or another family member or a trusted friend; this person grinds the pill to a powder and mixes it with applesauce, juice, yogurt, or a milkshake. The child doesn't know, the parent who is doing the charting doesn't know, and the child's teacher doesn't know if the child

The A.D.D.-Q/MM (To Monitor Medication Effectiveness)

Instructions: 1. Teacher or parent fills in this questionnaire according to who is with the child.
2. Complete questionnaire 2 hours after every drug dose (usually at 10 A.M., 2 P.M., and 6 P.M.)
3. Do this for 2 days before starting medication and each day during the drug trial.

Name:_____ Age:____ Date:_____ Medication:_____ Dose:____ Time:_____ Time chart was filled out: _____ QUESTIONS: (check '✓' appropriate column if *any* example is true)	Never or very rarely	Some-times	Often	Almost always
• **ATTENTION SPAN**				
1. The child has difficulty paying attention to things other people want him to do.				
2. The child seems to be daydreaming, almost "spaced out," drifting into her own little world, oblivious to what's going on and not paying attention to instructions.				
3. The child doesn't pay attention to details and often makes careless mistakes in schoolwork.				
4. The child has difficulty following routines, such as getting ready for school, bringing homework home, getting ready for bed.				
5. The child needs a lot of supervision to complete assignments (schoolwork, chores) that require sustained attention.				
• **IMPULSIVITY**				
6. The child fails to think before acting, does not think through what he is about to do or say, leaps without looking.				
7. The child has difficulty waiting for a turn (e.g., interrupts others, blurts out answers before a question is completed).				
8. The child has difficulty waiting in line, sharing, cooperating.				
9. The child has difficulty waiting for rewards, delaying gratification. (She wants the toy, to go biking, and so on, *NOW!*)				
• **ORGANIZATION**				
10. The child's schoolwork, keeping things together, time management, and personal functioning seem very disorganized.				
• **EMOTIONS**				
11. The child overreacts to seemingly little things.				
12. The child has difficulty adjusting to sudden changes in routines.				
• **ACTIVITY LEVEL**				
13. The child's activity level is inappropriate for the situation (e.g., he has difficulty sitting still in class, church, during meals).				
14. The child shows motor restlessness, fidgeting, squirming.				
15. The child seems always on the go as if driven by a motor.				
16. The child seems sluggish, lethargic, and unmotivated.				
TOTAL SCORE IN EACH COLUMN				
SCORE (the total number of checks in each column multiplied by 0, 1, 2, and 3)	x 0 = 0	x 1 =	x 2 =	x 3 =

TOTAL = _____

is receiving medication on any particular day. The person handling the medication must keep track of when medication was given and at what dose. In a blind trial, you might give the real pill one week and a dummy snack the next. The parent and teacher complete the medication effectiveness checklist several times a day during both weeks. After a few weeks, the person who administered the pills reveals which days the child got the medication and which days he didn't. The charts are then evaluated to see if the medication made a difference.

A MULTIMODAL APPROACH TO TREATING A.D.D.

The American Academy of Pediatrics, in its position statement on the use of medication for A.D.H.D., emphasizes that drugs should not be the only way a child's A.D.H.D. is treated. The Committee on Drugs of the American Academy of Pediatrics developed the following position statement: "Medication for children with A.D.D. should never be used as an isolated treatment. Proper classroom placement, physical education pro-

---

When to Stop the Drug

Just as it took a team approach to decide to give the child a medication, it is wise to follow a team approach in deciding when to stop it. Ideally, this decision should involve parents, child, and professional. In practice, parents often decide to stop giving the drug before the professional does, or the child just refuses to continue taking it. Other parents and teachers are so delighted with the effects of medication on their child's behavior and learning that they don't want to risk a relapse by stopping it. Some children like feeling successful and don't want to stop. Over time, many parents feel increasingly uneasy about drugging their children, and children often do not like the way they feel while under the influence of the drug. Dr. Bill is struck by how differently parents, teachers, and children regard the medication: often teachers swear by it, parents have mixed feelings, and children are less than enthusiastic about it. If these children truly felt they did better on the medication, they

would probably be more enthusiastic about continuing it. Here are some guidelines on when to put away the pills:

- You discover the alternative learning and behavior-improving strategies are working consistently.
- You gradually increase the frequency and length of drug holidays without your child's relapsing into his previous behavior or learning problems.
- You notice, by careful charting, that your child's behavior or learning shows no difference if he's on or off the medication. This means he has built up a tolerance to the drug.
- The undesirable side effects or rebound effects are less tolerable than the original problem.

In consultation, you, your child, and your A.D.D. specialist agree that it's time to stop the drug.

grams, behavior modification, counseling, and provision of structure should be used before a trial of pharmaco-therapy is attempted." Even the manufacturer of Ritalin has stressed this point.

Management of A.D.D. must always use a *multimodal approach,* which means that a variety of the management techniques discussed in this book should be tried either before or in addition to medication. However, most of the alternatives to drugs take weeks, months, or even years to show results. With medication, some results can be seen in a matter of days or weeks, depending on which drug is used. Time is important to a developing child, who cannot afford to spend years waiting for behavior modification and learning strategies to gradually have their effect. For this reason, most professionals feel that children whose A.D.H.D. is interfering with learning and development should be given medication along with other management techniques (but never instead of other tools). Once the child's behavior and attention are improving and the nonmedication strategies seem to be working, the goal can be to lower the dosage of the medication, stop it altogether, or use the medication only in as-needed situations. Having a lot of behavior and learning strategies piled on the child (and parents) is a heavy cross to bear over a long time. For some families, a short-term course of medication can lighten the load.

The best behavior modification and learning strategies in the world won't work if the child can't concentrate. In our experience, medications may allow the behavioral and learning strategies to work sooner and better. They provide a window of opportunity for making noticeable progress. Once your child sees success in one area of his behavior or learning, this is likely to carry over into his other problem areas. The goal is to reduce

the medication dosage and discontinue it as soon as possible, but only after it has helped other strategies work better.

Parents sometimes worry that taking behavior-altering drugs at such a young age will predispose the child to drug addictions later on. Long-term research suggests that this does not happen. It is true that stimulants are used as street drugs and that when abused, they are dangerous and addictive. Nevertheless, when stimulants are carefully prescribed and monitored, it is generally agreed that addiction has not proven to be a problem. These medications do not create in children with A.D.D. the same high that addictive drugs would. In fact, oftentimes, the long-term behavioral and developmental consequences of not providing a child with all the tools to manage A.D.D. early on may set him up for unhealthy behaviors later on. Children whose A.D.H.D. is recognized and managed early on are less likely to deviate into substance abuse as teens or adults.

While research has demonstrated that stimulant drugs do not appear to be addictive when properly used in appropriate cases, common sense tells us we still need to be prudent about medicating children. We could be giving schoolchildren mixed messages. While they are on their way to the school nurse to get their Ritalin dose, they walk past posters that proclaim, "Say no to drugs."

We are concerned about the effect that taking stimulant drugs has on the attitudes of adolescents. We worry about the casualness with which many teens talk about their stimulants. One day Dr. Bill was talking to some teens about their attitudes toward Ritalin. One teen shared his story:

It was one of those busy weeks at school, and I was feeling a bit hyper about all the stuff I had to get done. A friend of mine reached in his pocket and said, "Here, try one of my pills to calm you down." It was Ritalin. I took the pill, and the rest of the day I didn't feel like doing anything. In my wrestling practice after school, I felt heavy. I just lay there and didn't feel like really getting into the sport. The rest of the guys pinned me on the mat very easily.

Words of caution: Medication is never the only answer in treating A.D.H.D., nor is it a cure. If there are family or school problems that are affecting the child's behavior and learning, it's important to address these problems rather than to mask them with medication. Here's a word of advice Dr. Bill always gives parents when handing them a prescription for Ritalin: "Pills do not substitute for skills. You must teach your child self-management skills and teach yourself skills to manage your child."

QUESTIONS YOU MAY HAVE ABOUT MEDICATIONS FOR A.D.D.

EFFECT OF DRUGS ON LEARNING

Our eight-year-old daughter acts ditzy at school and can't pay attention. She's not really hyperactive, but she just can't concentrate on her schoolwork or simple jobs I give her at home. Would Ritalin help?

As we mentioned on page 230, the beneficial effects of stimulant medications are most noticeable in children with A.D.D. and hyperactivity. The fact that the incidence of benefit in children without hyperactivity approaches the incidence of the placebo effect has per-suaded some physicians to use stimulant medication only in children with A.D.D. and hyperactivity. Because stimulant medications seem to be less impressive in the child without hyperactivity, and in some doctors' experience the side effects occur more frequently in these children, it would certainly be prudent to try alternative management strategies before medication or at least to try the child on a much lower dose than if she were hyperactive. This lower rate may be influenced by the fact that the effects of the medications are less immediately noticeable than they are in children with hyperactivity, whose parents may report noticing an effect within hours to days.

In some children, stimulant medications may help them perform academic tasks that are boring and repetitive, yet researchers who have studied the long-term effects of stimulant medications generally conclude that there are no proven beneficial effects on long-term academic achievement. Long-term studies comparing medicated children with those taking a placebo showed no difference in academic achievement between the two groups. In some children, stimulant medications actually impair cognitive skills. This is especially true of the child who is drugged to control behavior. The higher dosage of stimulant medications often needed to mellow behavior may actually impair thinking. With these concerns in mind, it is wisest for parents and professionals to try alternative management methods in children with primarily attention and learning problems before resorting to medication.

PROBLEMS WITH GETTING THE RIGHT DOSE

My child's behavior at school is out of control when he's off the medication, yet if he gets enough of the drug to make him sit still, he's a zombie. How can we use medication to help him sit still and behave without impairing his learning?

This is a good news/bad news scenario. The dosage of stimulants required to improve attention is lower than the dose required to control impulsive, hyper behavior. (This is a general observation only, since the effects of different drugs in different dosages vary widely from child to child.) In some children with A.D.H.D., a dose high enough to calm their behavior can have a detrimental effect on their thinking and learning. It is difficult sometimes to juggle the dose to get the right effect: enough to improve behavior, not enough to impair learning. In some studies, children who received low doses of stimulants showed improved academic performance but got low marks from the teacher for behavior. With higher dosages, the teachers gave the children higher marks for behavior but lower marks for their academic performance, a situation called cognitive toxicity.

There is a tendency for teachers to assume that the more quietly children sit, the better they learn, and children under the influence of stimulant drugs are likely to sit more quietly. Yet sitting still does not necessarily imply that learning is going on. As a pharmacologist presenting a lecture on stimulant medication at a professional meeting said, "The child on stimulant medication is staring like a deer caught in the headlights of a car . . . and the teachers call it concentration."

The lecturer went on to say that many children are prescribed stimulants in dosages that are probably higher than needed, because, sadly, the main goal is to improve the child's behavior or to get him to sit still, even at the expense of the child's ability to learn.

We have observed schoolchildren on medication and watched their faces, in particular their eyes. Although they may be sitting still (which is different from paying attention), sometimes the children's eyes seem to glaze over or keep moving from one thing to another. The child is still out of touch, at least briefly, with what he is supposed to be attending to. Stimulant medication will help a child work on lessons longer, but he may still jump over words and even skip lines. He may scan superficially and not take everything in and therefore still have to keep rereading material.

Many of our adolescent clients have told us for years that the effect of stimulants on their ability to stay focused in class is not all that great. When children and teenagers are asked what the effect of their stimulant medication is, they often answer with a shrug of the shoulders or say they don't notice much. They may sit nicely and not blurt things out, but their concentration isn't much better.

In the words of one teen, "I don't pay attention any better, but at least I don't get yelled at anymore!" Parents add that others around the child do notice a difference, even if the child doesn't. Perhaps everybody is right: the child doesn't notice a change in attention, but people notice he sits still and sticks with things longer. Here is a typical conversation between a doctor and a sixteen-year-old patient:

Doctor: *Matthew, what effect do you feel your medication is having?*

Matthew: *Well, I don't seem to be in trouble as much, so I suppose it's a good thing.*

Doctor: *What about your ability to focus on your schoolwork?*

Matthew: *Do you really want to*
know?
Doctor: *Yes. I think your opinion*
is very important.
Matthew: *Well, maybe it helps a little*
bit. I don't fidget as much.
I don't know, not much, I
guess.

After taking Ritalin for several years, Matthew tried neurofeedback. He reported a positive effect on his attention span in the first month of training. He remained on medication, however, to control his impulsive behavior for another two months and then gradually the medication was reduced. Once off stimulants, he remarked, "I used to need to take the pills to keep out of trouble, so that was good, but this is the first time I feel in control."

The beneficial effects of stimulant medications last as long as the medication is at the blood level that is sufficient to produce the desired behavior changes in a child. Blood levels do not reach a simple, steady state. They are always a bit of a roller coaster. And all that medications can do is decrease some of the symptoms for a few hours. You, as the parent giving the medication, are attempting to choose the hours for which it is most important to have the medication at an effective dosage level. In a child with extreme behavior problems, you might have to keep increasing the dose until either side effects appear or academic performance suffers and then cut it back.

For some children, stimulant medications have turned a disastrous situation into a productive school and home experience. But every child is different. You as the parent are the final judge in determining whether your child benefits from the use of medications to control symptoms of A.D.D.

Drugs and recall. Another concern about learning under the influence of medication is an effect called state-dependent learning, which means that material learned under the influence of a drug is less likely to be recalled when the student is off the drug; conversely, material learned when the student is off the drug may not be recalled when the student is on the drug. A common example is a sober person who may have difficulty recalling what happened the night before while he was under the influence of alcohol. This effect has not been consistently demonstrated in scientific studies. Some studies do show state-dependent learning with stimulant medications; others do not. The concept of state-dependent learning would help explain why the material a child studied the evening before a test (off medication) is not well recalled the next morning when he takes the test under the influence of medication.

Adolescent alertness? As truck drivers and college students who use stimulants to stay awake have long known, stimulants have the same stimulating effect whether or not a person has A.D.D. Many people who have A.D.D. have a low alertness level in situations that they find monotonous or boring. We have found this to be a significant problem in older adolescents and college students. They may be wide awake and the life of the group just before class and then have to fight to remain awake only ten minutes into the lecture. Stimulants are not the only way to address this problem. Alertness can be monitored using electrodermal response (EDR), which is measured using sensors on the fingertips (see page 218). The following is an example of how low alertness may affect a student who has A.D.D.

After a session when he was required to read a short story and answer questions on it, Kevin said, "I noticed I was a bit groggy about halfway through the story [Kevin's EDR was at 3 at that point]. When you made that loud noise, dropping the book on the desk, I woke up and started to notice what I was reading again [and his EDR went up to 8]."

Kevin had a lot of difficulty staying awake in school and when studying. Ritalin helped him with this. Training with neurofeedback eventually replaced his need for the stimulant medication. The simplest way to get your EDR to rise is to change your posture. Sitting up straight produces increased alertness — those old-fashioned schoolteachers had it right when they had everyone sitting ramrod straight!

WHEN MEDICATIONS DON'T WORK

We have tried changing medications, juggling doses, juggling timing, and our son is still impossible to manage at home and school. Are there some children for whom stimulants just don't work? Should we just keep increasing the dose?

Studies show that stimulant medications "work" in 60 to 70 percent of children with A.D.H.D., but in some children there is either no observed effect or behavior worsens, despite changes in medications, dosages, and timing. In this situation, be sure your child is being managed by someone with special knowledge of A.D.D, preferably an M.D. who is also knowledgeable about the effects of different medications and different ways of using them. Some children will respond to one

medication and not to another. Others will not respond to a lower dose but will respond to a higher dose. Some children are nonresponders in the preschool years yet respond wonderfully to stimulant medication when they are six or seven. Be sure your child or teen is not overdosing on other nonprescription stimulants (e.g., caffeine), which can affect the response to the prescription medications.

Be sure not to increase the dosage above the schedule recommended by your physician. With Ritalin, it is rare to need to go above 40 milligrams a day. A child who needs a dose above 60 milligrams a day should stimulate you and your physician to get a second opinion and review other options. The fact that your child does not respond to stimulant medication does not prove or disprove the diagnosis of A.D.H.D. Some children are nonresponders because they have other neurological, psychological, or environmental problems that need to be addressed, because there is a mismatch of school and child, or simply because they are in the category of children who would do better with a nondrug method of management.

DRUG HOLIDAYS

I don't want my child getting into the habit of being on drugs, and I'm not sure he needs them all the time. Should I not give him the medication on weekends, holidays, and during the summer?

Although most doctors feel that there is no reason to worry about stimulant medications being addictive, there is a theoretical concern that taking medications to stimulate the production of neurotransmitters in the brain might interfere with the brain's ability to make its own. Also, it's difficult to know when a child is ready to try a lower dosage or even go off the medication unless you periodically experiment with drug-free days. For these reasons, most professionals encourage parents to give their children lower doses or no medication at all on days when there is no school, including weekends, holidays, and summer vacations. Obviously, drug holidays are only an option for drugs like Ritalin that are short acting. You cannot do this with drugs that take days to build up to an effective level.

Periodically completing the medication effectiveness chart on days when your child is off medication will help you decide if he continues to need it or if the dosage could be lowered. You may find that the management techniques you are trying are beginning to work. Drug holidays also lessen the risk of stimulants' limiting your child's growth. Periodically coming off the drug also lessens the chance of building up a tolerance to the drug and thus allows it to continue working well.

It makes sense to use behavior-controlling and learning-enhancing drugs when they are most needed. Certainly, this approach is wise if the child was put on medication primarily to improve school performance. Yet the trade-off has a roller-coaster effect on behavior. If one of the main reasons for medicating the child was to improve behavior at home, then drug holidays may not be advisable. Some parents and children do not like it when the child has two different personalities, one for school days, one for weekends. They do not enjoy the up-and-down effect of the "on-drug" and "off-drug" days. Children who are not good candidates for drug holidays are those for whom one of the purposes of the medication is to improve relationships with friends and family. Based on these considerations, discuss with your doctor whether or not you should try drug holidays for your child.

An eight-year-old notes: I like not taking my focus pill during the summer. Kids need some time to just hang loose.

BACK TO SCHOOL

My son has been off stimulant medication for the summer. Should I let him begin this next school year off the medication to see how he does?

This decision depends in part upon how well your child has done off medication during the summer. If you have seen an improvement in behavior and learning using other strategies during the summer, it may be worthwhile letting your child begin school without the influence of drugs. If, on the other hand, your child's learning showed dramatic improvement during the previous year while on medication, you may not want to risk sending him back to school without it. Getting off to a good start at the beginning of the school year is important, and the transition to a new teacher with new expectations is often difficult. It might be better to let him start the year on his usual medication and attempt a trial off medication after the first six to eight weeks of school are completed.

SITUATIONAL DOSING

Our seven-year-old doesn't need Ritalin all the time. We give it to him only during stressful times. Could this be harmful to him?

Some children need to be medicated for home, some for school, some even for the playground, and some for all of the above. Some children need one pill a day, some two, and the occasional child will need three. Some children need a morning pill, some need a noon pill, some need a late afternoon pill, and some need all three. Juggling the dosage of stimulants is both a science and an art. Parents who have to juggle stimulant dosages over a long period of time become as adept as diabetics juggling their insulin for different requirements and situations. Some parents will give the child a pill a couple of hours before a situation is going to occur that past history has shown to be disastrous, such as being required to sit still for Christmas dinner at grandmother's house. Some children have no problem paying attention in sports, which contributes to their positive self-image, but their performance is even better when they take medication in the mid-afternoon to help them concentrate on the ball-game. Taking medication on an "as-needed" basis is sound medical treatment and is not harmful to the child. Your physician should educate you about the medication so this can be done in an informed way.

THERAPEUTIC TRIALS

My child's teacher and doctor are not certain that she has A.D.D., and I'm not certain either. Should we try her on medication to see if she has A.D.D.?

Getting results from stimulant medication does not prove or disprove whether a child has A.D.D. So-called therapeutic trials cannot make a diagnosis of A.D.D. or A.D.H.D. Even so-called normal children can often show increased concentration on stimulant medication. In most individuals, whether or not they have A.D.D., stimulant medications produce improvements in impulse-control, vigilance, reaction time, and ability to stick with repetitive tasks.

CHILD EMBARRASSED

My child doesn't want to take his medication. He's embarrassed to stand in the pill line at the nurse's office.

You have to do some marketing to get your child to take medication willingly once or twice a day. Your doctor should have laid the groundwork by explaining to the child why these pills will help him. When explaining these medications to a child, Dr. Bill calls them focus pills. He uses a drawing to explain that these little pills will help the child's brain and muscles listen to and talk to each other so that he can think through his actions, pay attention, get better grades, obey mom, dad, and his teacher better, and eventually learn to focus and behave better without the pills. Be sure your child understands that the "focus pills" are not "dumb pills" (an idea your child may pick up at school). Explain to your child that many children need things to help them learn better. Some children need glasses to help them see better. Some use hearing aids. Some have sessions with the speech therapist. Some children need focus pills to help them learn better.

If standing in the line at the nurse's office is a major issue and your child wants some privacy about his pills, ask the doctor about trying a long-acting form (see "Stimulant Medication Facts," pages 254 to 255) that could be given once a day before school in the morning. Or work out with the teacher and school nurse a method of giving the child the medication that is private and does not embarrass the child. One of the reasons for giving the medication in the first place is to improve a child's self-image, so if standing in the pill line is embarrassing for him, then the medication is defeating its purpose. The reluctance to take the medication, and the associated

Stimulant Medication Facts

Ritalin (methylphenidate)

- It is approved for six years of age and over.
- The usual dosage is one 10-mg tablet twice or three times a day. Begin with 5 mg once a day and adjust the dosage according to response. It is usually given at breakfast and lunchtime, but we have observed that some children do better if their second and third doses are given in the morning and afternoon recesses. There is a wide range of effective dosages, depending on the child's individual response.
- Each dose may last approximately two to four hours, and its action usually begins about half an hour after administration. Times may vary according to a person's metabolism.
- In some children, Ritalin needs to be given about half an hour before a meal. This is best for absorption, but it may suppress a child's appetite, in which case the medication should be given with the meal.
- There is a longer-acting form of Ritalin called Ritalin SR, for slow release (the usual dose is 20 mg), which begins acting about one hour or more after administration and acts for about six to seven hours. Half its active ingredients are supposed to be released when it is first taken, and the other half after about four hours in the body's system. The advantage of the long-acting Ritalin is that the child can be given one dose at home before school, thus increasing the compliance, and he does not have the inconvenience and embarrassment of having to take the pill at school. Our experience with the longer-acting preparation has been disappointing. We find a lot of variabil-ity from child to child as to when it has its peak effect and how long the effect lasts. Also, after a few months it seems not to be as effective as regular Ritalin. With the slow-acting preparation, we find it's harder to make judgments about how well it works and what the side effects are. We always begin treating the child with the regular, short-acting Ritalin. If compliance is a problem, we try the longer-acting preparation once we have worked out whether or not the child responds to Ritalin and what the best dose is for this particular child.
- The effectiveness of Ritalin in controlling targeted symptoms in A.D.H.D., such as high activity level, ranges from about 30 to 50 percent in three- to five-year-olds and adults, and close to 70 to 80 percent in six- to twelve-year-olds. Effectiveness appears to drop to around 60 percent in adolescents. All figures are only approximations. This must always be compared to a placebo response. A placebo will give a favorable response in the 20 to 39 percent range.
- For patients who have A.D.D. without hyperactivity, the response rate is lower.
- It probably acts by influencing dopamine, norepinephrine, and serotonin neurotransmitters.
- Use among adults is increasing as awareness of A.D.D. in adults grows.
- More than 80 percent of the prescriptions written for stimulants are for Ritalin or its generic equivalent.

Dexedrine (dextroamphetamine)

- It is approved for three years of age and over.
- This medication is given at about half the dosage level of Ritalin and may be used in younger children. The usual dose is one 5-mg tablet twice daily.
- The short-acting form lasts an hour or so longer than the short-acting Ritalin.
- Each dose may last about three to five hours.
- There is a longer-acting form of Dexedrine called SR, for slow release (the usual dose is 10 mg), which begins acting one to two hours after administration and acts for about eight hours. (In our experience, slow-release Dexedrine has a more reliable effect than slow-release Ritalin.)
- It probably acts by increasing dopamine and norepinephrine neurotransmitters.

Cylert (Pemoline)

- It is approved for six years of age and over.
- The effect lasts about seven hours (in adults about eleven hours).
- It may take four to six weeks to notice the effects, unlike the immediate effects of Ritalin and Dexedrine.
- The starting dose is 37.5 mg given once daily in the morning, and it is increased by 18.75 mg if necessary.
- Because this drug may produce changes in liver-function tests, they are done before the drug is begun and monitored at least every three months. The liver tests usually return to normal when the drug is stopped.
- It probably acts by influencing dopamine neurotransmission.
- Cylert is a completely different type and class of medication from Ritalin and Dexedrine. The DEA places no restrictions on prescribing Cylert.

Adderall

- It is approved for three years of age and over.
- It comes in 10-mg and 20-mg tablets. The starting dose for children age six and older is similar to Ritalin's.
- Initially it may be given twice a day at intervals of approximately four to six hours. This will vary with different individuals.
- It is an amphetamine with sympathomimetic properties, and it acts as a stimulant.
- It is not available in Canada.

Clonidine (Catapres)

Clonidine is used to treat A.D.H.D. children who also have behavior problems, such as those who are extremely aggressive or impulsive, showing explosive, often out of control, behavior. It may be used when a trial of a stimulant medication has not been effective. It is seldom useful for a child with A.D.D. without hyperactivity. This drug is often considered for children who primarily have a behavioral problem rather than a learning problem. While it has no direct effect on attention, it may indirectly improve learning in children who are hyperaroused to the extent that their impulsive behavior interferes with their learning.

- Since Clonidine is chemically similar to the neurotransmitter norepinephrine, it is thought to work by decreasing the release of naturally produced norepinephrine. The theory is that if children's impulsive behavior is caused by the hypersecretion of the neurotransmitter norepinephrine, Clonidine may slow down this release. Basically, it is thought to reduce the hyperarousal state of the brain or, in neurotransmitter jargon, reduce the background noise in the brain in the opposite way stimulant medications do, which are thought to increase the arousability of the brain, especially those areas involved in inhibiting behavioral impulses.

- The dosage range is 0.15 to 0.3 mg per day. Your doctor will begin with a very low dose and work up over several weeks. It is given in divided doses one to four times a day, and the effect of a single dose lasts three to six hours. It may also be administered at bedtime due to its sedative effect. It must not be withdrawn rapidly due to rebound hypertension (high blood pressure), sleep disturbance, irregular pulse, headaches, and agitation. If a stimulant is also being given, then the dosage levels of both medications are usually lowered considerably because deaths have been reported in children taking both Clonidine and stimulants if one is changed suddenly.

- Clonidine needs to be given for three to six weeks before an adequate evaluation of its effectiveness can be made.

- Sedation is a serious complication, particularly during the first few weeks of administration. Up to 15 percent of patients stop the medication due to this effect. Sedation is a serious side effect, since one of the prime difficulties with many persons who have A.D.D. is being underaroused.

- The side effects include constipation, dry mouth, and urinary retention. Some medications given for depression or for allergies may reduce its effectiveness. A decrease in blood pressure and pulse rate occurs. Dizziness, headache, digestive system symptoms, depression, and heart arrhythmias have all been reported.

- It is also available as a transdermal patch, which may work better in a child who is reluctant to take pills. Expect some local reddening and itching.

- Contraindications and precautions include combining with Ritalin (very serious toxicity has been reported, and great care must be exercised if this combination is contemplated), depression, heart disorders, and kidney disease.

embarrassment, is usually temporary. Once the child sees his own improvement and gets positive strokes from teachers and parents for improved grades and good behavior, he's likely to feel better about taking the pill.

Most schools have a policy that children cannot give themselves medicine while at school, but it's important to involve your child in his own medication monitoring. The information will be helpful to you, and he'll feel more in control of the situation. When you are filling out the medication effectiveness chart, periodically ask your child for help. Ask him specifically how he feels before and after the pill. What kinds of differences does he notice? Children from five to ten often have difficulty explaining the effects of the pill. You're likely to get behavior-based comments such as, "It helps me sit still." Many children are outcome-based evaluators: "It helps me get good grades."

GIVING THE PILL THE CREDIT

My child has experienced a complete turnaround since she started taking Ritalin. Will she think her success is due to the pill and not herself?

When a child misbehaves at school occasionally, teachers have been known to ask, "Did you forget your pill today?" This sends the message that the child is basically bad and can only behave with the help of a pill. Give credit where credit is due. Impress upon your child that she got the grades and she was the one who behaved well. The medicine only helped. She was the one who had to study for the tests, complete her homework, and do her jobs around the house. It was she who succeeded. Naturally, you praise your child and not the pill. When she is

---

The Problem with Pills

Pills tell children that something is wrong with them and that they need to take a pill to fix it. Children may feel that they do better because of the pill, not because of themselves. They attribute their success to the pill rather than to their own efforts. Children who are constantly on medications may label themselves as sick. It's hard to convince children that nothing is really wrong with them when they have to go to the doctor once a month to have their medicine evaluated, or when they are standing in line for their medicine at the school nurse's office while their friends are at the playground. You have to be sure that children do not feel they are bad, dumb, or sick when they need medication. When a child does succeed, reinforce the fact that *he* did it, not the pill. The pill only helped. The pill by itself cannot do anything. Only the child can make the good grade or hit the ball.

---

within hearing distance, avoid making comments like, "Since we started giving her the focus pill, she sure is a good child." Keep those thoughts to yourself. In our experience, children who succeed do believe it is themselves who deserve the credit, not whatever tools they used to build themselves up.

A possible problem with praising the pill instead of the child is that parents and teachers might then lessen their efforts in trying other behavior and learning strategies that could eventually get the child off the pill. Also, the child may begin to rely on the pill, so that he is less motivated to continue to put out his best efforts. Parents and teachers should continue to view the medication as one of many tools used to manage the child's A.D.D. symptoms. Yes, medication is a useful tool, but it is a temporary one.

TEACHER PRESSURE

I don't want to drug my child, but the teacher suggested he'd have to be on medication or he could no longer be in the regular class. How should I respond?

We wish we could say that we've heard this only once. Unfortunately, we have heard it a number of times. Even though this may not be exactly what the teacher said, this is what the mother thought the teacher meant. Teachers are careful never to recommend medication directly, because prescribing drugs is out of their jurisdiction. In fact, teachers are becoming more aware of child development, realizing that many normal seven-year-olds are not yet ready to sit still at a desk for hours at a time and at this age are better visual and hands-on students than lecture learners. However, teachers are in a position to compare your child's behavior with that of others of the same age, so their observations are important. Ask your child's teacher to write down precisely what difficulties your child is experiencing. Also ask what has been tried to improve the situation. Setting up a behavioral training system is labor intensive and will require teacher time, perhaps consultation from the school psychologist, and help from a teacher's aide. Children with A.D.D. do respond to behavior modification at home and at school, but sometimes teachers feel using medication is more expedient.

Objective reporting is a teacher's job. The decision concerning medication is a job for

you and your child's physician. Reassure the school that you will take this information to your doctor and the two of you will decide what to do.

Jane, age nine, had a very observant and careful teacher. She watched Jane carefully over the first two weeks in school and wrote down a list of exactly what Jane did that was disturbing to other children. She also wrote down exactly how frequently and how long these behaviors occurred and the responses Jane gave when she was corrected. She then set up an interview with Jane's parents and discussed her observations and gave them a copy of her findings. She suggested that they might wish to discuss these with the school psychologist or their own physician.

The teacher's information and suggestions were helpful to Jane's parents, who did discuss the problem with her pediatrician. The doctor decided to treat Jane with Ritalin temporarily. The parents later brought the teacher's observations to the attention of a psychologist, who added neurofeedback training to the overall management plan. The pediatrician was then able to gradually decrease the dose of Jane's medication. Within a short time she came off medication completely while improving in school to the degree that she moved from being at the bottom of the class to being in the top half.

It's important for parents to realize the teacher's point of view and for the teacher to be able to put herself behind the eyes of the parents. Here are some points for both sides to consider:

The teacher's dilemma. Your child's teacher may be required to teach thirty children or more, and the teacher is responsible to the parents of all those children. The teacher is placed in a difficult position when helping one child keep up with the rest or when one child constantly disturbs the others, so that no one gets much done.

The parents' dilemma. Parents are responsible for the health and well-being of their child and only their child. From the parents' perspective, it is the school's job to figure out how to meet the needs of all the children in the classroom. The parents know that it's important for their child to have friends, to feel good about himself or herself, and to do well in school, and that moving a child into a special-education class may compromise these goals. Parents are the ones who must manage any side effects from medication and who are ultimately responsible for the child's long-term health and well-being.

How can all these adults who are so important to the child work together better? Parents and teachers must live up to their own responsibilities, communicate regularly, be open to each other's ideas, and keep the child's welfare foremost. The best solutions for the child will involve commitment from everyone.

SEIZURE DISORDERS

My child has a seizure disorder. Since he has been taking medications for his seizures, his A.D.H.D. symptoms have become much worse. What can we do?

Some medications used to control seizures, such as Dilantin, Phenobarbital, and Mysoline may increase the symptoms of A.D.D. Also, stimulants given to a child with an underlying seizure disorder may lower the seizure threshold and increase the frequency and severity of the seizures. When your child has both A.D.D. and a seizure disorder, he will need careful professional management of the dosage levels of the stimulant and anticonvulsant. Children with seizure disorders are particularly helped by neurofeedback (see chapter 8), which could help you avoid this balancing act altogether. Research has demonstrated a decrease in the intensity and frequency of grand mal and partial complex seizures following neurofeedback therapy.

GENERIC MEDICATIONS

We are on a tight budget, and my child will probably need to be on stimulant medication for a long time. I've heard generics are cheaper but don't work as well. Is this true?

Generic drugs are often less costly than brand-name drugs, but in some children they may be less effective. Government regulations require generic medications to be equivalent to brand-name medications, but equivalent does not mean identical. Some generic tablets contain as little as 80 percent or as much as 120 percent of the active ingredient when compared to brand-name equivalents. The variability from pill to pill allowed by federal guidelines for generic tablets may be greater than the variability in pills regulated by the brand-name manufacturer. It is our practice to begin with a brand name and continue to adjust the dosage and timing to the desired effect. Then, if cost is a consideration, we try a generic, and try to be objective when evaluating if it works as well.

10

Feeding the Child with A.D.D.

Healthy nutrition is important for all children; it is doubly important for a child with A.D.D. Yet, ask most scientists about the influence of diet on A.D.D. and they are likely to say "little effect." Nearly every well-controlled scientific study has come to this conclusion, but ask most mothers and they will tell you stories about peeling their children off the wall after drinking a Mr. Freeze. As parents and professionals, we certainly believe in the food-mood connection in some children. Even though in the majority of children diet is not the cause of the behavior or learning problem, it can certainly contribute to it.

HOW NUTRITION AFFECTS BEHAVIOR AND LEARNING

Regardless of what double-blind, placebo-controlled studies claim, the common sense that has come out of grandmothers' kitchens says that the better you feed the brain, the better it works. Body organs seem to have a nutritional pecking order. The most vital organs get first pick of available nutrients entering from the bloodstream, and the brain gets prime pick. It stands to reason that unhealthy

nutrition can lead to diminished brain function. Here's how. The brain is composed of billions of nerve cells called neurons. Thought, memory, actions, and all brain functions depend on how these cells interact with each other. Transmission of thought and action processes occur by rapid transmission from one cell to another. To facilitate the transmission of signals from one cell to another, chemicals called neurotransmitters act like biological bridges between these cells. Nutrition can affect the health and function in three areas of the brain's nerve cells.

- The *nerve cells* themselves need proper nutrition to carry on their metabolism, just like other cells in the body.
- The *myelin sheath* is a fatty substance that covers the branches of the cells like insulation covers electrical wires. It speeds the transmission of electrical signals within the nervous system.
- The *neurotransmitters* (e.g., seratonin, dopamine, and norepinephrine) carry messages from one cell to the other and are thought to be the biochemical basis for changes in concentration, behavior, and mood.

Each one of these three parts of the nervous system needs specific nutrients to enable the whole circuit to function properly. If any part is deficient in nutrients, the circuit, like a defective electrical wire, misfires. New insights suggest that the neurobiological basis of A.D.D. may be an imbalance in the neurotransmitters. Providing the child with a diet rich in nutrients that encourage a healthy neurotransmitter balance could, theoretically, improve learning and behavior, and providing a diet deficient in nutrients essential for neurotransmitter function could hinder behavior and learning.

Another theory is that A.D.D. children may repeatedly subject themselves to stress as a way of producing their own neurotransmitters. Yet when they get overstressed, they deplete themselves of neurotransmitters and get out of control. This could explain why active, energetic children cross the line into A.D.D. when their neurotransmitters get out of balance. So, a child with a behavioral tendency toward A.D.D. needs a diet rich in the nutrients that continually replenish neurotransmitters.*

BEST BRAIN FOODS

It's not only the type of food, but when and how you eat it, that affects brain function. Here is some food for thought on how parents can encourage their children to eat a brain-friendly diet:

Carbs that calm. Some carbohydrates cool behavior, others excite it. The brain is a sugar

hog, a carbo craver, utilizing 20 percent of the body's carbohydrate supply. Yet it's a smart hog, being selective in what types of sugars it craves and how it processes them. The nutritional key word is "steady." When the brain receives a steady supply of sugar for fuel, it functions more steadily. But when the blood sugar fluctuates up and down, the sugar entry into the brain is also unsteady, resulting in behavior and learning that also show ups and downs. Feed your child sugars that enter the brain steadily instead of in spurts, and your child's learning and behavior is more likely to be steady.

To help you understand which sugars are brain-friendly and which are not, here are some sweet facts about sugars that you should know. The rate at which a sugar enters brain cells (and other cells of the body) is called the "glycemic index" (GI) of a particular food. Foods with a high glycemic index stimulate the pancreas to secrete a lot of insulin, which causes the sugar to quickly empty from the blood into the cells and is responsible for the ups and downs of blood sugar, and, consequently, of behavior. Foods with a low glycemic index do not push the pancreas to secrete so much insulin, so the blood sugar tends to be steadier with fewer peaks and valleys. Feeding your child carbohydrate foods with the lowest glycemic index is one way of smoothing a child's behavior and performance. Here is a list of the best brain sugars.

- *fruits.* Grapefruit, apples, cherries, oranges, and grapes have a low glycemic index.
- *cereals and grains.* Oatmeal and bran have the lowest GI. Avoid sugar-coated cereals, which have a higher glycemic index. Favorite grains with a favorable GI are spaghetti and rice.

---

* *A valuable resource for understanding the biochemical basis of the connection between food, mood, and learning is* Feeding the Brain: How Foods Affect Children, *by Keith C. Conners (Plenum Press, 1989).*

Breakfasts for Smarter Brains

"Breakfast" means just that, breaking the overnight fast. Eating breakfast allows your child to restock the depleted overnight stores of energy and begin the day with a tank full of the right fuel. Sending your child to school without breakfast is like driving your car to work with either the wrong fuel in the tank or not enough of it. If you want your child to rise and shine rather than limp along sluggishly at school all morning, give your child the best nutritional start to his day.

Breakfast basics. Throughout the brain, biochemical messengers called neurotransmitters help the brain make the right connections. Food influences how these neurotransmitters operate. The more balanced the breakfast, the more balanced the brain function. There are two types of proteins that affect neurotransmitters: 1) neurostimulants, such as proteins containing tyrosine, affecting the alertness transmitters dopamine and norepinephrine, and 2) calming proteins that contain tryptophan, which relaxes the brain. A breakfast with the right balance of both stimulating and calming foods starts the child off with a brain that is primed to learn and more likely to behave. Eating complex carbohydrates along with proteins helps to usher the amino acids from these proteins into

the brain, so that the neurotransmitters can work better. Complex carbohydrates and proteins act like biochemical partners for enhancing learning and behavior. This biochemical principle is called synergy, meaning that the combination of two nutrients works better than each one singly, sort of like 2 + 2 = 5. If you don't refuel your child's body in the morning after an overnight fast, throughout the rest of the morning the child has to draw fuel from his body's own energy stores. The stress necessary to mobilize these energy reserves may upset behavior or learning or leave the child feeling irritable and tired.

Breakfast research. If your hectic household resembles morning rush hour, as it does in our homes, sleepy kids and hurried parents don't always have time for healthy breakfasts. Yet here is what breakfast studies show:

- Breakfast eaters generally make higher grades, pay closer attention, participate more in class discussions, and manage more complex academic problems than breakfast skippers.
- Breakfast skippers are more likely to be inattentive, sluggish, and make lower grades.
- Breakfast skippers are more likely to show erratic eating patterns throughout the day, eat less nutritious foods, and give into junk-food

- *vegetables and legumes.* Legumes, such as soybeans, kidney beans, chick peas, and lentils, have the lowest glycemic index of any food.
- *dairy products.* Milk and yogurt have low glycemic indexes — slightly higher than

legumes, but lower than fruits. Plain yogurt has a lower glycemic index than fruit-filled preparations.

The company a food keeps also affects its glycemic index, or how fast and steady is the cravings later on. Children may crave a sugar fix because they can't wait until lunch.

- Some children are more vulnerable than others when they skip breakfast, and the effects on behavior and learning as a result of missing breakfast or eating a non-nutritious breakfast vary from child to child.
- Children who eat a breakfast containing both complex carbohydrates and proteins in equivalent calories tend to show better learning and better performance than children who eat primarily a high-protein or high-carbohydrate breakfast. Exclusively high-carbohydrate breakfasts seem to sedate children rather than stimulate their brain to learn.
- Children who eat high-calcium foods for breakfast (e.g., dairy products) show enhanced behavior and learning.
- Morning stress increases the levels of stress hormones in the bloodstream, which can affect behavior and learning in two ways. First, stress hormones themselves can bother the brain. Second, stress hormones, such as cortisol, increase carbohydrate craving throughout the day, which may affect behavior and learning in children who are sensitive to the ups and downs of blood-sugar levels. Try to send your child off to school with a calm attitude.

Breakfast also sets the nutritional pattern for the rest of the day. If your child misses breakfast to save time or to cut calories, she is a candidate for erratic bingeing and, possibly, overeating throughout the rest of the day.

Best breakfasts. Here are examples of breakfasts with balanced complex carbohydrates and proteins:

- granola cereal, yogurt, and a sliced apple
- scrambled eggs, toast, and orange juice
- veggie omelet, bran muffin, and fruit-flavored yogurt
- whole-grain pancakes or waffles topped with berries and/or yogurt, and a glass of milk
- breakfast "pizza": a large whole-grain pancake topped with fruit or fruit preserves and orange or banana slices, and a glass of milk
- whole-wheat zucchini pancakes topped with fruit, and a glass of milk
- french toast topped with fruit, orange juice, and a glass of milk
- A Healthy Smoothie — see page 266.

Of course, it's not what you say but what you eat that impresses a child. By treating yourself to a healthy breakfast, you both give yourself a smart start to the day and model to your children that eating a healthy breakfast is important.

sugar's supply to the brain. Whole fruit has a lower glycemic index than juice, because the fiber in the fruit steadies the absorption of sugar from the intestines. So a whole apple will be more brain-friendly than apple juice; a whole orange better than orange juice.

Freshly made juice containing a lot of pulp is more brain-friendly than filtered juice.

If your child wants a food with a high glycemic index, such as juice, candy, or a sweet treat, it is better consumed with a meal, because the company of other foods

Lethargic After Lunch

Ever wonder why children's learning and behavior deteriorates after lunch? It's because some foods perk up the brain, while others put it to sleep. Here are some healthy lunch tips that can improve your child's attention and behavior for afternoon learning:

Have the right balance of proteins and carbohydrates. Whether your child learns well after lunch or dozes through afternoon classes can be influenced by the proteins in the lunch and the carbohydrate company these proteins keep. The two protein amino acids that have been shown to have the greatest effect on brain function are L-tryptophan, which sedates the brain, and L-tyrosine, which wakes up the brain. These amino acids affect different transmitters. L-tryptophan is a nutrient that helps make up the neurotransmitter seratonin, which slows down the brain and has a calming, sedative effect. Rich dietary sources of tryptophan are eggs, milk, bananas, dairy foods, sunflower seeds, and meat.

Combining a carbohydrate-rich meal with tryptophan-containing foods helps more tryptophan get into the brain and makes more of the sedating neurotransmitter seratonin. Carbohydrates usher tryptophan in to the brain by releasing insulin, which directs the amino acids that compete with tryptophan into muscle tissue, allowing more tryptophan to the brain. A high-calorie, high-carbohydrate lunch sedates the brain and reduces cerebral performance. The after-lunch sluggishness following a high-carbohydrate meal is biochemically a seratonin slump.

A lower-calorie, higher-protein lunch, on the other hand, makes the eater more alert after lunch. You can counteract the seratonin slump by adding protein to the carbohydrates. The main protein that perks up the brain is tyrosine, found in seafood, turkey, tofu, legumes, and tuna. So, a salad made up of legumes with tuna, tofu, or turkey (three T's that contain tyrosine) is an ideal lunch for your child if you want him to work and learn rather than drowse or sleep.

Encourage a light lunch rather than a heavy lunch. A healthy lunch for school-age children is between 600 and 800 calories, with a balance of complex carbohydrates, proteins, and a minimum of fats. A high-calorie, high-carbohydrate meal, such as pasta with a fatty sauce, is likely to diminish your child's academic performance after lunch. A high-fat diet diminishes mental alertness by diverting blood from the brain to the stomach to help digest a fatty meal. An example of a healthy lunch would be a tuna or turkey sandwich on whole-wheat bread with lettuce, tomato, mustard, and a low-fat mayonnaise made with canola oil; a side salad; a piece of fruit; and a glass of milk. Encourage your child to skip dessert after lunch and to save his daily dessert treat for after dinner.

Lobby for healthy school lunches. In many schools, the school lunch project is a nutritional failure. Because of the junk lunches that are served, many schools deserve the behavior they get from the children after lunch. Fast-food outlets are now competing for counter space in school cafeterias, where children are taught that the four food groups are McDonald's, Pizza Hut, KFC, and Burger King. Get involved in your PTA and make the topic of healthy school lunches a high priority. Also, monitor what is sold in the vending machine, emphasizing juice rather than heavily sugared, high-caffeine sodas. The same advice that we gave in "Breakfasts for Smarter Brains," pages 262 to 263, applies to lunches for smarter brains.

slows its absorption and steadies the entry of sugar into the bloodstream and, therefore, the brain. Indulging in highly sugared foods as a between-meal snack is more likely to hinder behavior and learning. Mixing highly sugared foods (those with a high GI) with foods that have a lower GI steadies the blood sugar effect of the fast-acting sugars.

Sugar. Most scientists discount the relationship between sugar and A.D.D., but try explaining this to a mother whose child goes wild after eating a Twinkie. In a 1995 paper published in the *Journal of the American Medical Association,* researchers analyzed sixteen studies of children who were challenged with sugar meals and compared them with a placebo group. The researchers concluded that sugar had no impact on behavior or thinking. This research finding is at odds with some mothers' observations. The reason for this, researchers believe, is that parents have been conditioned by media reports and hearsay to expect their children's behavior to deteriorate after a high-sugar meal. If a mother comes into one of our practices and tells us that every time her child has a certain soft drink or eats a candy full of red dye he becomes a wild man for the next hour, we believe her. A research study on one hundred children who have A.D.D. might not show the substance she complained about was a statistically important factor, but that is simply a statistical finding. Her child may be the one in a hundred who gets squirrelly after eating red jelly beans. One study that achieved front-page prominence in a national newspaper concluded that sugar had no effect on behavior, yet the study included only twenty-five children each in the placebo and sugar diet group.

So we're back to the "science" of common sense. Not all sugars are created equal. Differ-

ent sugars act differently on the brain, and it is only logical to conclude that some sugars can adversely affect the thinking and actions of some children. These "junk sugars" include glucose, dextrose, and sucrose, found in table sugar, candy, icings, syrups, and frostings. These sugars enter the bloodstream quickly and in high doses, which triggers the release of insulin, the hormone needed to escort the sugars into the body's cells. This sugar is used rapidly, and when it's all used up, the blood sugar level plunges to a sugar low, leading to the condition known as hypoglycemia, or "sugar blues." The low blood sugar triggers the release of stress hormones that squeeze stored sugar from the liver, sending blood sugar levels back up. The roller-coaster effect is likely to carry some children's moods and concentration up and down. High blood sugar can stimulate neurotransmitter imbalance, causing the child to feel fidgety, irritable, inattentive, and even sleepy.

Children need energy, and that comes mainly from sugar and what are called complex carbohydrates, or what grandmother termed starches. These and fruit sugars (fructose) do not cause the roller-coaster mood swings that the junk sugars do. The molecules in these foods are long, so they are slower to be absorbed through the intestines. They provide a time-release source of energy rather than a sudden surge followed by a sudden drop. A breakfast high in protein and complex carbohydrates provides steady energy to the brain for the whole morning.

Proteins that perk up. Like carbohydrates, proteins affect brain performance, primarily by their effect on neurotransmitters, the biochemical messengers that carry signals from one brain cell to another. The better you feed these messengers, the more efficiently they deliver the goods. Proteins are the prime nutritional foods for neurotransmitters. Some proteins spark the brain; others sedate it.

Protein foods that jumpstart the brain are ones that contain the amino acid L-tyrosine (e.g., seafood, beans, tofu, lentils, poultry and meat). *Foods that relax the brain* are tryptophan containing foods (e.g., eggs, milk, bananas, dairy, and sunflower seeds).

Feeding your child proteins from both of these groups seems to provide a balance of both stimulating and relaxing the brain. Also, eating carbohydrates along with a protein meal (see explanation under "Breakfasts for Smarter Brains," pages 262 to 263) improves how the brain utilizes the nutrients from proteins.

Fats that feed the brain. In addition to carbohydrates and proteins, the fat content of a meal can influence how a child thinks and behaves. Be careful about translating the adult low-fat craze into a child's eating habits. Instead of thinking low fat when you feed your child, think *right* fat. Children need fat for their nervous system to grow and function properly. In fact, for a healthy diet, children need 25 to 30 percent of their daily nutrition in the form of healthy fats. Brain cells and the myelin sheath around each nerve depend on an adequate nutritional supply of healthy fats and essential fatty acids found in foods.

Avoid fake fats. The nutritional bad words that parents should shun are "hydrogenated" and "partially hydrogenated." These biochemically altered fats are present in many packaged foods, such as potato chips, and are made by injecting the natural fats with hydrogen, which prolongs their shelf life and may give the food a more appealing taste. These fake fats enter the cells of the central nervous system and may compete with the action of natural fats, with the result that the healthy fats are not able to perform their cellular function, possibly causing the nerves of the brain to malfunction. Fake fats also disturb normal cholesterol metabolism. They raise LDL (the bad cholesterol) and lower the HDL (the good cholesterol).

Feed your child healthy fats. The healthiest fats for children (and adults) are those from seafood and vegetable sources, such as vegetable oils, salmon, nuts, soybeans, avocados, and flaxseed. This is why we advise adding one or two tablespoons of flaxseed oil to a child's daily diet (see "School-Ade," in the box below). Studies have shown that some children with A.D.D. actually have insufficient essential fatty acids (EFAs) in their

---

School-Ade

Here is a Sears family recipe for a healthy smoothie we give our children (and ourselves) every day:

- *4-8 oz. plain yogurt*
- *6 large, frozen strawberries, sliced*
- *1 sliced frozen banana*
- *½ cup frozen blueberries*
- *1 scoop of Juice Plus lite (French vanilla or Dutch chocolate)*
- *1 tbsp. flaxseed oil*
- *1 tbsp. honey (optional)*
- *lecithin, 1 serving*
- *any nutrient or supplement that child needs but won't otherwise take*
- *Milk, juice, or rice or soy beverage*

Mix ingredients and blend until smooth. Add liquid to get desired consistency. Blend again. Serve immediately after blending, while the mixture still has a bubbly, milkshake texture.

diet. Seafood and vegetable oils are valuable sources of nutritious fatty acids.

EFAs may be deficient in diets that are too high in sugar, refined flour, or hydrogenated vegetable oils, such as those found in margarine and some snack foods. Proponents of the EFA theory promote the use of such EFA supplements as oil of evening primrose or flaxseed oil. Signs of an EFA deficiency are excessive thirst, dry flaking skin, brittle fingernails, and eczema. The use of EFAs in the treatment of A.D.D. has not been proven effective, but dietary common sense tells you it's a good idea to eliminate or greatly reduce the junk food in your child's diet and increase healthy fats.

Eat more iron. Insufficient iron in a child's diet can contribute to A.D.H.D. symptoms, such as inattention, aggression, and irritability. When children who are iron deficient are given iron supplements, they learn and behave better. A sufficient amount of iron is necessary for proper brain neurotransmitter activity. The behavioral effects of low blood-iron levels can occur before the problem is detected by a hemoglobin test or diagnosed as anemia. In other words, the brain can be tired before the blood shows it's tired. Discuss the possibility of iron deficiency with your child's doctor.

Iron deficiency is particularly prevalent in adolescent females due to the combination of a generally poor diet, frequent fast-food meals, menstruation, and indulgence in foods that actually interfere with iron absorption, such as the caffeine in coffee, tea, colas, and chocolate. Best iron foods that children are likely to eat are soybeans, iron-fortified cereals, fish, beef, barley, lentils, clams, beets, tuna fish, and raisins. Eating or drinking foods high in vitamin C, such as orange juice, with meals enhances the iron absorption from foods.

Milk and caffeine-containing foods decrease the absorption of iron from foods.

If you or your child's doctor even suspects that your child's diet is deficient in iron, it is best to do a blood test. Start with a simple finger-stick hemoglobin test in your doctor's office. But don't be fooled if the result is normal. Blood iron can be low enough to affect brain function but not low enough to be reflected in the hemoglobin test. A more sensitive test detects the *serum ferritin level.* This test needs to be done at a laboratory on blood drawn from a vein. A serum ferritin level test is a necessary part of a medical evaluation of a child with possible learning or behavior problems, especially if the child's diet is suspected of being iron deficient. If the serum ferritin level is low, your child should be given extra iron in his diet and, possibly, iron supplements for at least two months after the level returns to normal.

Care about calcium. Calcium is important not only for building growing bones but for feeding growing brains as well. Studies have shown that some hyperactive children had lower calcium intakes in their diet than less hyperactive children. Children with calcium deficiency may show impaired behavior and learning. Studies show that some schoolchildren who were in the habit of skipping breakfast behaved better when given milk in the morning.

VITAMINS AND SUPPLEMENTS

Scientifically controlled studies have shown that megavitamin therapy does not help in the management of A.D.D. Moreover, children may develop skin rashes in reaction to megadoses of vitamins, especially niacin. However, the following minerals and other

Grazing

Even if scientific studies fail to confirm mothers' testimonies about the food-mood connection, sometimes we must rely on the "science" of personal observations and plain common sense. In our families, and in our professional practices, we have noticed how children's behavior often deteriorates in the late morning and late afternoon, or three to four hours after the previous meal — whether they have A.D.D. or not. The child has simply run out of fuel. When blood-sugar levels go down (hypogyclemia), stress hormones kick in to increase automatically the blood sugar, but this can cause behavior problems and diminished attention. To smooth out the blood-sugar mood swings, try the fine art of grazing. Let your child nibble, or graze, on nutritious foods throughout the day. Make them easily accessible in a lunch pack at school or away from home. While at home, keep a readily available supply of healthy grazing snacks in the pantry or refrigerator. If you shorten the spacing between feeding, you are less likely to have spacey children.

For the preschool child, here's a trick from the Sears family kitchen. Prepare a nibble tray: an ice cube tray, a muffin tin, or a compartmentalized plastic dish containing bite-size portions of colorful and nutritious foods. Tag these nutrients with childlike names, such as avocado boats (a quarter of an avocado sectioned lengthwise), banana or cooked carrot wheels, broccoli trees, cheese blocks, little O's (O-shaped cereal), canoe eggs (hard-boiled eggs cut lengthwise in wedges), moons (peeled apple slices, thinly spread with peanut butter), or shells and worms (different shapes of pasta).

And don't forget that children love to dip. Reserve one or two compartments in the tray for your child's favorite nutritious dips, such as yogurt or guacamole (without the spices). Encourage the child to sit and nibble from the tray frequently throughout the day, especially late in the morning and mid- to late afternoon, when the fuel from the previous meal begins to wear off. Smart parents send healthy snacks to school or day care and take along a grazing bag on family outings or shopping trips. Smart teachers allow even upper-grade children to have a mid-morning snack.

---

supplements have some scientific basis or at least make sense, for helping children learn and behave.

- *Zinc.* A deficiency of this essential mineral has been shown to affect children's behavior and learning. Rich sources of zinc include whole-grain bread, eggs, seafoods, meat, nuts, and seeds.
- *Calcium.* As mentioned above, a calcium deficiency can interfere with learning.
- *Iron.* See page 267.
- *Pycnogenol.*® This pine-bark extract has been shown to improve behavior and learning in some children with A.D.D.
- *Lecithin.* This nutrient is a source of choline (which helps build neurotransmitters). It is found in nuts, seafood, soybeans, and in cruciferous vegetables. It can also be given as a supplement. (See "A Healthy Smoothie," page 266.) Other supplements that may improve learning are antioxidants,

carotenoids, vitamin E, selenium, chromium, manganese, vitamin B-complex, magnesium, L-glutamine, L-taurine, folic acid, and vitamin C.

Regarding vitamin supplements, it would make sense for any child with A.D.D., especially if his or her general diet is suspect, to take a daily multivitamin. Studies have shown that schoolchildren whose diets are supplemented with adequate vitamins and minerals of at least the recommended daily allowance show improved learning and score higher on intelligence tests.

Giving nutritional supplements to children should not be a do-it-yourself home treatment. If not administered properly, supplements may harm rather than help your child's learning and behavior. Because you may be inclined to want to try anything that might help your child, always remember to ask yourself if nutritional supplement recommendations make sense. For example, if you hear about hair analysis as a way to detect mineral deficiencies, don't fall for it. Hair analysis will not give an accurate measure of mineral levels in a child's body, since hair can be affected by shampoo, diet, and the rate of growth. It is best to consult your child's physician or a nutritionist who is knowledgeable about the effect of diet on learning and behavior or a doctor of naturopathy (N.D.)

AN ELIMINATION DIET

One bright spot in the food-mood controversy is the *oligoantigenic diet,* a so-called pure diet that eliminates the foods to which the child is most likely to be sensitive. In the past ten years, two studies of this diet on hyperactive children showed beneficial results. In one study, seventy-six children were placed on a pure diet (ie., free of foods likely to cause an allergic reaction), and their behavior was evaluated. The foods to which the children were most likely to be sensitive were gradually reintroduced in order to identify those most likely to cause deteriorating behavior. Behavior in the diet group was compared with behavior in a control group. Eighty-six percent of the children in the study showed improvement in manageability at home and school; 29 percent were judged as behaving normally. Researchers identified forty-eight foods that were most likely to promote hyperactivity. The most common were artificial colorings and preservatives. In another study, researchers eliminated from the diets of children with A.D.D. artificial colorings, preservatives, chocolate, monosodium glutamate, caffeine, and any other substances suspected by the family. Forty-two percent of children in this study exhibited an improvement in behavior. The general conclusion was that in some children, behavior is affected by multiple food sensitivities and that behavior improves when these foods are identified and eliminated.

How to tell if food affects your child's behavior. To detect hidden food sensitivities that may affect your child's behavior or learning, first develop an objective mind-set. Remember, in your desire to find a cause (and therefore a cure) for your child, it's easy to pin the problem on a food sensitivity. This may not only be nutritionally unwise but may keep you from trying other alternatives that will produce better results. Try this step-by-step way of tracking down hidden food sensitivities:

1. Make a list of what your child eats for a week and, using a little detective work (read lots of labels), see if you can pinpoint the

Artificial Sweeteners

Feed your child artificial sweeteners and you may increase the risk of artificial thinking and behavior. It is safe and somewhat scientific to say that artificial sweeteners have no place in the diets of growing children, especially those who already have problems behaving and learning. The large volume of studies trying to show a food-mood connection with artificial sweeteners have been so confusing and conflicting that parents are back to relying on their common sense. Artificial sweeteners (e.g., Nutrasweet, Equal) were originally developed as a sugar substitute for diabetics, but the manufacturers discovered a huge market in a calorie-conscious society that has been misfed a lot of hype about the hazardous effects of sugar. Consider these sweet facts: A teaspoon of artificial sweetener contains four calories, while a teaspoon of table sugar has sixteen calories. A saving of twelve calories per teaspoon is not worth the biochemical uncertainty and possible food-mood connection of artificial sweeteners.

Despite statistical studies showing no conclusive food-mood connection, nutritionists are concerned about some biochemical quirks of artificial sweeteners. Sugar is sugar, while aspartame is basically a combination of two amino acids. Sugar and amino acids have different effects on the brain. In natural foods, the sugars enter the brain in company with other naturally occurring amino acids. Nutritionists are concerned about the unnatural chemical effect amino acids may have on the brain's neurotransmitters. Theoretically, it is also possible that the amino acids in the artificial sweeteners compete with the natural amino acids in the foods to throw the brain's neurotransmitters out of balance. The natural conclusion is that feeding the brain an unnatural substance may cause it to perform unnaturally.

most likely offenders. High on the list of likely triggers are junk food, red dyes, food preservatives, high-sugar drinks, corn syrup, artificial colors, and food additives.

2. Do a food-mood connection. When your child eats a certain food, do you notice a difference in his behavior within the hour?

3. If you are unable to detect a few possible offending foods to eliminate, put your child on a "pure" diet for a week. For a week, use no processed foods and no foods containing dyes, artificial colors, or preservatives. Stress high-protein foods and complex carbohydrates (e.g., turkey, lamb, baked or boiled potatoes, sweet potatoes, rice and millet, squash, pears, rice beverages, and diluted pear juice). This bland diet will require some marketing and some creative flavoring, but your child should be able to try anything for a few days to a week. At the end of the "pure" diet week, objectively evaluate your child's behavior or learning problems. (A good way to do this would be to use the charts for evaluating medication found on pages 234 and 245. Be sure to do a "before" evaluation, so you have something with which to compare your results.) If eliminating foods has had a positive effect, gradually add a new food each day to see if the symptoms recur. This way you should be able to pinpoint the offenders.

Pure Children

Throughout twenty-five years in pediatric practice, Dr. Bill has been struck by the connection between how children are fed and how healthy they are. Mothers who consistently do not allow any unhealthy food to pollute the bodies of their children have healthier children. These children have fewer office visits and fewer colds, and when they come for periodic checkups, they seem more settled and better behaved. These "pure children" seem to get tagged with fewer labels, such as "A.D.D." or "learning disability." And even when these children do warrant such tags, they seem to cope better with their behavioral and learning differences, which also seem less severe.

To increase compliance, involve your child in the detective work. Fabricate a game, "Find the Food," using a fancy game-board chart.*

A general rule regarding food sensitivities: In our experience, a child who truly has a food allergy or sensitivity will experience multisystem symptoms (usually gastrointestinal, respiratory, or dermatological) in addition to the behavioral effects of the food. However, in an occasional child, a nutritional sensitivity may produce only behavioral changes — no runny nose, diarrhea, stomachache, headache, or rash. In this situation, parents must be objective observers, as well as meticulous record keepers.

Many children who are raised on a steady diet of nutritious foods will eventually make their own food-mood connections. They will often even label foods (with a little reminding) as "feel-good foods" and "feel-bad foods." If A.D.D. is, at least in some children, due to a neurotransmitter imbalance, since food affects neurotransmitter activity, it follows that foods could influence the severity of this condition. So, even though the scientific literature itself will be confusing and conflicting, parents of a child with A.D.D. should pay attention to their child's nutrition, using their own observations and a pinch of common sense.

---

* *A useful reference to help you track down food sensitivities is* Detecting Your Hidden Allergies, *by William G. Crook (Professional Books, 1988).*

Understanding A.D.D. Laws

Parents, you may be pleasantly surprised that when it comes to getting your child the help you think he needs, the A.D.D. laws are on your side. The legal system protects your child's rights to receive educational benefits appropriate to his individual style of learning. To ensure that your child gets all the laws allow (and to get through the tangle of school district evaluations and conferences), you need to know what the law provides, whether your child is eligible, and how the system works.

The laws discussed in this chapter apply in the United States of America. In Canada there is not yet federal legislation governing A.D.D. There are provisions for children who are deemed to be "exceptional" (that is, requiring special programming to meet their needs), and this may be on the basis of learning disabilities, behavior problems, physical handicaps, or intellectual differences. There is no uniform agreement across provinces, or even across school boards within a province, as to whether A.D.D. is a learning disability.

The law is on your side, but just because the laws exist does not mean they are always obeyed by every state and every school system. It's up to you to know the educational resources to which the laws allow your child

access, and it's up to you to be sure your child gets them.

You may meet with some resistance from the school about providing special-education resources for your child, because not every school board, teacher, or professional educator believes that A.D.D. has a neurobiological cause. They may attribute a child's behavior or difficulty to learn to the child's being poorly disciplined, lazy, or unmotivated, or to a difficult home situation — more of a psychological basis than a neurophysiological basis. However, both scientific research and previous court cases are on your side; the prevailing medical and legal opinion concerning A.D.D. is that it is primarily a neurological, and not a psychological, problem.

To help you wade through the confusing sea of the legal and educational systems, here's a step-by-step approach to help you become your child's advocate and get the most out of the systems.

STEP 1: DOCUMENT THE DIAGNOSIS

In order to get what the laws allow, you must have documentation from a professional that your child has A.D.D. (Your child also has a right to an evaluation paid for by the school district, even though it may not come up with the diagnosis of A.D.D.) Obtain a letter, preferably from the A.D.D. specialist who evaluated your child. The specialist's report should contain the following:

- the diagnosis of A.D.D.
- the criteria for making this diagnosis in your child
- specific recommendations for behavioral and learning strategies that parents and school should consider for the child

If the professional whom you have consulted for A.D.D. has performed any behavioral or academic tests, be sure you have the results of those tests and that you understand their meaning. Even before you approach the school, formulate a plan in your own mind in consultation with your A.D.D. professional. Write down the specific educational suggestions from any assessments done by independent psychologists or learning centers. Remember, the stronger your documentation, the stronger is your case that your child needs special-education resources, and the more likely school officials are to take you seriously.

STEP 2: KNOW WHAT THE LAW ALLOWS

Parents of children with A.D.D. need to know what benefits the law provides and, most important, how to interpret the laws to fit their child's individual needs.

IDEA

In 1975 the U.S. Congress enacted the Education for All Handicapped Children Act, now called the Individuals with Disabilities Education Act, or IDEA. The purpose of this law was to ensure that "all children with disabilities have available to them . . . a free, appropriate public education . . . which emphasizes special education and related services designed to meet their unique needs . . . and to ensure that rights of children with disabilities and their parents or guardians are protected."

Under the provisions of this act, funds are provided to local school systems for the education of children generally between the ages of three and twenty-two who have special needs, and local schools are required to comply with the act and its implementing regulations as a condition for receiving the funds. The problem in this law is the word "handicap," and the controversy is whether A.D.D. itself is a handicap and therefore qualifies for special-educational services and funding.

As a further elaboration of this law, U.S. Code (USC) 1401 defined "children with disabilities" as children with mental retardation, hearing impairments, deafness, speech or language impairments, visual impairments, serious emotional disturbance, orthopedic impairments, autism, traumatic brain injury, other health impairments, or specific learning disabilities. The basic controversy is whether or not IDEA applies to persons who have A.D.D. but no accompanying learning disability as diagnosed by educational performance tests. This question was addressed in the Department of Education's Office of Special Education and Rehabilitative Services in a memorandum issued on September 16, 1991. In it the Department of Education (DOE) confirmed that A.D.D. can be considered within the scope of IDEA, depending on circumstances, qualifiable under the code as "other health impairments" or "serious emotional disturbance" or "specific learning disabilities." The DOE determined that A.D.D. fits most naturally into the category of "other health impairments." The DOE concluded the term "other health impairments" includes chronic or acute impairments that result in limited alertness, which adversely affects educational performance. Thus children with A.D.D. should be classified as eligible for services under the "other health impaired" category in instances where the A.D.D. is a chronic or acute health problem that results in limited alertness, which adversely affects educational performance. The DOE stated that "Children with A.D.D. . . . may be considered disabled under . . . IDEA."

The law seems clear in its interpretation, but parents may have to become their child's advocate to be sure that the school district classifies the child's A.D.D. under "other health impairments" so that the child can receive special resources. This is the letter of the law, not a loophole. The child has certain rights under this provision.

Parents will have more difficulty if they use "specific learning disability" as the phrase under which they feel their child has a right to special-education resources. The DOE ruled that "children with A.D.D. are also eligible for services under . . . IDEA if the children satisfy the criteria applicable to 'other disability' categories." The crucial point in this is how USC 1401 defines learning disability: "Those children who have a disorder in one or more of the basic psychological processes involved in understanding or in using language, spoken or written, which disorder may manifest itself in imperfect ability to listen, think, speak, read, write, spell, or do mathematical calculations." While problems with attention may certainly influence these skills, the law does not include them specifically, so it may be more difficult to obtain services under this provision of the law.

Another phrase in the law is "seriously emotionally disturbed," about which the DOE concluded: "Children with A.D.D. are also eligible for services under IDEA if the children satisfy the criteria applicable to other disability categories . . . for example . . . the 'seriously emotionally disturbed' category," which they defined as "the inability to learn, which cannot be explained by intellectual, sensory, or health factors . . . an inability to build or maintain satisfactory interpersonal relationships with peers and teachers . . . inappropriate types of behavior."

Eligibility. Under the IDEA, every child with a disability does not automatically get special-education resources. The child must meet two criteria for eligibility: The first criteria for the child to be eligible under the law is that the child must meet the law's diagnostic categories. It is important for parents to understand that under the law, "limited alertness" or "inattention" qualifies as a health impairment. Secondly, the child's disability must interfere with educational performance. This is where schools and parents often run into a conflict. The school may not consider the child eligible for service unless it can be proven that A.D.D. is interfering with the child's education; and to prove this, school officials may look for a documented learning disability. One rule of thumb that is sometimes used as a working definition for interfering with educational performance is how far behind grade expectations a child is. A child who is functioning within a year of his grade placement is considered average. If the child is two or more years behind, this is evidence that something is interfering with learning.

There are two sides to this ongoing battle. The educators worry that because A.D.D. is not as concrete a diagnosis as other "disabilities," such as deafness or blindness, it could become overused, draining the already over-burdened school system of its resources. The worry is that eventually demands for special education will get out of hand, so that children needing special resources may outnumber those who do not. Parents, on the other hand, aren't interested in statistics, trends, or the future financial health of the school system. They just want the best education for their child and believe they have a right to it.

STEP 3: DETERMINE IF YOUR CHILD IS ELIGIBLE FOR SPECIAL-EDUCATION RESOURCES

Don't be put off by the red tape in both the educational and legal systems. The IDEA (along with Public Laws 101-476 and 94-142) is simply an educational bill of rights for your child. Simply stated, your child is eligible for special-education resources if the following apply:

- he has any condition that interferes with his learning
- you can prove that his academic performance is significantly impaired because of this condition

If your child has a condition that limits his alertness (inattention) and this is hindering his educational performance, he is certainly eligible for special resources.

STEP 4: SET UP A MEETING WITH SCHOOL PERSONNEL

Set up a meeting with your child's teacher and any other school personnel who may be involved with your child. Be diplomatic, yet assertive. Don't walk in waving a flag, demanding your legal rights. According to federal law, the school is legally obligated only to provide "minimum" educational requirements, and if you come in quoting the law, you may get only what the law says — minimum resources. If you have done your homework and are armed not only with the letter of the law but also the spirit of the law, as well as a sympathetic understanding of your child's difficulties in the classroom, school personnel are likely to take your requests more seriously. Be prepared for some resistance, as some educators still do not believe that A.D.D. should be categorized as a learning disability. This meeting is an informal one in which you want to accomplish the following:

- convince the school that your child is eligible for special-education resources
- learn what your child's teachers and other educators suggest for giving your child extra educational help
- lay the groundwork for the next and most important meeting — the setting up of an individual educational program (IEP) for your child

During this initial meeting you may ask, or the teachers may offer, to have your child tested to determine if your child has a specific learning disability. These tests may be necessary for two reasons: to help the school know what specific educational resources your child needs and to be certain your child truly is eligible for special resources. The school is unlikely to accept just the child's performance records or vague and subjective criteria, such as "he gets poor grades," "he can't pay attention in school," or "he doesn't understand his homework." Yet, the results of the educational tests themselves should not be the only criteria used for judging whether or not your child qualifies for special-educational resources. The school psychologist's report should also consider the child's A.D.D. traits. The teacher should evaluate and document the child's performance in the classroom. The school may interpret the letter of the law to mean that your child must be shown to have a learning disability before qualifying for special-education resources. But you can challenge the school on this point, remembering the "other health impairments" category and the spirit of the law. (Find out what specific criteria and tests are used to come to a decision that a child's educational performance is impaired.)

After these tests, if necessary, are performed, you have a right to copies of the results and a full explanation as to what they mean. Be sure the teachers interpret the meaning of the tests to you in language you can understand. Don't be put off by educators' jargon and bureaucratic paperwork. Ask them to explain to you exactly what the tests mean, how accurate they are, and what they are going to do with the results. If you do not understand the results of the tests, especially if the results do not "support" your child's need for services, and you feel your child truly does need special-educational resources, you may want to discuss the test results with your A.D.D. specialist or another learning specialist.

STEP 5: SET UP A MEETING TO REVIEW YOUR CHILD'S IEP

When a child is eligible for special resources, according to the IDEA law and USC 1400 and 1401 (which interpret the IDEA), the school is required to provide an individual educational plan (IEP), designed to meet the student's unique needs. The law requires that the IEP be put together by a team, including parents, possibly the child, when appropriate, the child's teacher, designated specialists, and a representative of the public agency qualified to supervise the IEP. In putting together the IEP, you should look for the following components:

- a statement of the present educational performance level of the child
- a statement of short-term educational objectives and annual goals
- a statement of specific educational services to be provided to each child and how the child will be able to participate in the regular or mainstream education programs
- an indication of when these services will be initiated and how long they will be provided
- evaluation procedures for determining whether the preset instructional objectives are being achieved

These are the general components of any individual educational plan. Specifically, you should be sure the IEP is tailored to meet your child's needs, so it should have some specific components pertinent to A.D.D. The teachers and other significant persons dealing with the child in school should be educated about A.D.D. and about specific teaching and behavioral management techniques to use with your child. The IEP should talk about such things as where the child is seated in the classroom, about frequent breaks to allow the child to focus better, and other issues, including specific discipline techniques. It should also include adjusting the test-taking environment. Sometimes allowing extra time for an exam is all that is needed. In other instances, some tests might need to be done in an oral rather than written format. As a parent, you know your child best. To help your child's teachers, use the IEP process as a chance to share with them what behavioral strategies you have found work best, what your child's quirks are, and the best ways to work around them.

In an ideal world, every child in every class would have an IEP in order to truly help each child develop his or her fullest academic potential. But this is not economically possible, and most children seem to do okay with a generalized curriculum. For children with A.D.D., however, an IEP is not only more frequently necessary, it is their legal right. And the law requires the school to involve parents in each step of formulating the IEP. Parents should also be aware that the child has a right to be educated in "the least restrictive environment," which simply means that children have a right to learn in an environment appropriate to their individual needs. For some children, this means being educated with their peers or mainstreaming; for other children, it would be in their best interests to be in a special class; for some children, a combination of both a mainstream class and a "special-resource" class is the best strategy. For parents, you can interpret the spirit, if not the letter, of the law to mean that children have a right to an educational environment where they feel comfortable.

According to the law, parents must be kept fully informed at every stage of the child's IEP. The parent has a right to view all school records, test results, and participate in all IEP meetings. Another important bit of information that parents should know is that if you disagree with the types of tests, the method, or with the conclusions based upon the test results, you have a right to an independent second opinion provided at the school's expense.

An IEP meeting can be intimidating for parents. There may be half a dozen or more professional educators in the room and only one or two of you. The language being used is familiar to all of them but may be confusing to people who don't speak the jargon. You can bring along anyone you want to an IEP meeting. This might include your A.D.D. specialist, other people significant in the child's life, or a friend who can provide moral support and another perspective on what is said. Parents have been known to pay a lawyer just to sit in the room with them so that they can be sure their concerns will be addressed. The IEP paperwork will require your signature, but you don't have to sign it until you're happy with it. You also have a right to call an additional meeting at any time to change the IEP.

QUESTIONS YOU MAY HAVE ABOUT A.D.D. LAWS

LEGAL RIGHTS

I know my child needs special help at school, yet the school insists, based upon the test results, that he doesn't have a learning disability and therefore doesn't qualify for special-educational resources. How can I get him the resources that I know he needs?

If you disagree with the conclusions of the school district on your child's eligibility for special resources or on what resources the school will provide, you are legally entitled to a "due process hearing," in which an impartial hearing officer will hear your appeal.

In the event that parents feel their state is not providing services at the level specified by law, federal law states that the parents may challenge the state's decision in a state or federal court, especially if they are dissatisfied with the IEP or how it's being carried out. At this point, you'll need a lawyer.

Remember, in most instances you do not want to have to refer to the letter of the law. Parents and school personnel should be natural allies with a common goal of providing an optimal learning environment within the resources that are available.

MAINSTREAMING

The school wants to put my child in a special-resource class, but his friends are all in the regular class, and I'm afraid they'll start calling him lazy or dumb. I don't want him singled out. His self-esteem is already so low, and I don't want him getting these labels. I really believe he will do better in his regular class. What should I do?

According to the law, children have the right to be educated in the "least restrictive environment" appropriate to meet their individual needs. This has been interpreted to mean that the child must be placed in regular classes (mainstreaming) to the maximum extent possible. In addition to the regular class, the child may receive extra services in what is termed a resource room or resource services. It's up to you to make the case that your child will be better off in the regular class. A successful educational alternative that has kept many children with A.D.D. in the regular classroom is the concept of "team teaching," where a special-resource teacher comes into the regular class and spends extra time with children who have A.D.D. or other difficulties. So that your child is not regarded as "dumb" by his peers, sometimes the regular teacher spends extra time with your child while other teachers give special attention to the other children. Peer tutoring, or peer

helpers, is another method for managing children of varying abilities within the same classroom. Remember, in the eyes of students, needing more teacher attention equates with being less smart. Above all, you want to avoid the "dumb" label. A creative, flexible teacher will be able to find ways for your child to receive special help without being singled out, especially if the teacher's efforts are supported by the availability of teacher aides and other resources. It may boost your case if you point out that all the children in the class will benefit from these classroom interventions.

PRIVATE SCHOOLING

Our school district just can't provide the special resources my child needs, yet we can't afford a private school or private tutoring. Am I entitled to some financial help?

Yes. According to the law, your school district is required to pay for private resources, but only if you can prove that the resources within your public school district cannot appropriately meet your child's educational needs. Remember, a public school system is not required to pay for private resources just because they are superior to those provided in the public school or just because you prefer to have your child in a private school. You must demonstrate that your school cannot provide what your child needs. The spirit of the law seems to suggest that you are entitled to private resources at public expense only if it can be shown that "there is no public school equivalent" to those resources available privately.

In most cases, if you choose a private school you will be deciding to make the investment yourself. The advantages cited by

Dealing with Schools

For the benefit of your child, you want to get the school system and the teachers on your side. Below, some parents share their tips on how to work diplomatically with the school system to get the best education for children with special-education needs.

In our IEP meeting, we approached the teachers as team members, not adversaries. They were impressed that we had done our homework and that we knew our legal rights. We didn't want to put them off by pulling out the legal stuff unless we really had to, but we went prepared to do so. We wanted them to like having our child in the class, not to do it just because the law made them.

Parents should not just accept and sign the IEP that the teachers give them. Parents must have their input. The school teaches to the level of the IEP. If it contains a lower level of academic expectations than you feel your child is capable of, it's important to point that out.

We insisted that our child be in a full-inclusion class, that is, a regular class with typical kids. When he was mainstreaming, he didn't feel like he really belonged in the regular class. Mainstreaming was token inclusion; we wanted full inclusion.

Full inclusion prepares her better for real life. When she grows up, she will be work-ing with regular people, so she needs to learn to get along with regular kids in school. She wasn't learning that in the special-ed class.

Because our child had behavior and learning problems, the school wanted to place him in the special-ed class rather than fully include him in the regular class. The teachers felt the extra time and energy spent on our child would not be fair to the typical students. We kept insisting on full inclusion in the regular class with extra assistance for our child from the teacher's aid. We believe that full inclusion benefits not only the special student, but the typical students as well. It gives these students greater sensitivity to individuals who are different and helps them to respect all people.

We didn't let the school intimidate us. The teachers wanted to give our child an IEP and place him in a special-ed class. We wanted him fully included in a regular class as a regular kid with an IEP. It helped to present this idea to the IEP team as an experiment, and we said we would take full responsibility for the experiment. We knew our child would do better in the regular class with typical kids and "special" help than in the special-ed class. We believed that the expectations of his achievements would be lower in the special-ed class, a sort of dumbing down of his requirements.

parents who choose an independent school for their child with A.D.D. are usually smaller classes, greater accountability for academic results, and closer monitoring of homework.

If you can't find the special resources you need in a private school, home schooling offers an alternative. Although states vary in how willing and able they are to provide resources to home schoolers, you may be eligible for financial assistance for special tutoring. Many children with unique learning styles have been successfully taught at home, where their teacher is the person who knows them best, loves them the most, and will most likely be the best advocate they will ever have. Remember that children with A.D.D. are not going to be as easy to teach as their non-A.D.D. peers. Make sure you have the required patience, energy reserves, and expertise before choosing this option.

Other Approaches

Endless numbers of interventions for A.D.D. attest to how desperate parents are to improve the quality of life for their child and themselves — and how creative they can be. Alternative therapies are just that: other ways of managing A.D.D. The term "alternative" has picked up some other meanings that are unfair, especially the idea that anything out of the mainstream must be in the snake oil category of remedies. Actually, many of the scientifically respected methods of managing A.D.D. began with the simple observation by a parent or investigator that something worked. Stimulants were first tried in the 1930s, yet it took almost forty years for them to become mainstream A.D.D. treatment.

Just because some method or technique hasn't been scientifically proven doesn't mean it won't help your child. Most methods undergoing scientific scrutiny are judged statistically. In the number (usually small) of children studied, a technique or drug is found to help or not help. The conclusion is a statistical one, which should generalize, that is, apply to other children outside of those studied. Yet your child is an individual, not a statistic. Statistical studies are a starting point for professionals to offer parents their opin-

ion on the validity of a certain therapy, but for an individual child, the testimonies of observant parents can be more meaningful than the conclusions of a million-dollar scientific study.

IS A CONTROVERSIAL TREATMENT WORTH TRYING?

The Parents' Dilemma

Love and the desire to give their child every opportunity to be successful in life make parents vulnerable to claims that a certain therapy will fix their child. It is understandable that well-meaning parents, intent on helping their child and family, are tempted to try anything that promises good results, scientifically validated or not. They may be almost afraid not to try a new therapy, for fear of depriving their child of some chance to improve. But they also don't want to waste time, energy, and money on a questionable therapy when these resources could be better spent on proven techniques. And they certainly don't want to try something that may prove to be harmful.

Advice and decisions on whether or not to

try a certain alternative are rarely black and white; the judgments are more likely to be shades of gray. This means that parents and the professionals they consult for guidance must use an extra degree of discernment in evaluating alternative approaches to helping the child with A.D.D.

Before trying any alternative, ask these questions:

- Does the way the treatment is advertised to work make physiological sense?
- Does the professional I am consulting for advice have personal experience with this therapy? Does this professional have appropriate credentials to critique this therapy?
- What does it cost?
- Am I prepared to spend the time, energy, and money to carry out this intervention?
- Is it safe? What are the risks, if any, of trying the treatment? Is there a risk to not trying it?
- How long will it be before I can expect to see results?
- What are objective ways that I can use to evaluate whether or not a certain treatment is helping my child and our family?
- Are there safer, quicker, less costly, more effective alternatives that we haven't yet tried?

Finally, keep an open mind and proceed with caution. It may be helpful to ask other people who have a child similar to yours to share their experience with a new method of treatment. This may reassure you, but remember, your child is unique. Another family's positive experience is not a guarantee that the method will work for your child. In this chapter, we present some of the more common alternatives and some practical ways to help you evaluate whether they might work or should even be tried with your child.

A.D.D. Fads

Parents, remember that love for your child and the desperation you feel to help your child behave, learn, and feel better makes you vulnerable to unproven claims of quick fixes. Buyer beware. This caution is especially true concerning A.D.D., which is the disorder of the decade. A problem springs up, a catchy label gets pinned on it, and, in the American spirit of free enterprise, a whole industry gets rolling to support its popularity. And parents dole out lots of time, energy, and money in a desperate effort to do something for their child.

Be discerning. Before buying into a questionable treatment method, ask yourself:

- Does the method make sense, given what we currently know about A.D.D.?
- Are the claims reasonable? Consult someone knowledgeable and unbiased about this method, and whose wisdom you trust.
- Is it applicable to *my* child?

The Professional's Dilemma

The family doctor, pediatrician, or specialist in A.D.D. realizes that parents come to them for advice and direction. The professional is supposed to have the knowledge and experience to direct parents toward treatment methods known to work and to help steer them away from those that are unproven. As a result, the professional tends to suggest only treatment methods well established in the scientific literature, but this approach has some limitations.

Professionals are taught in school that, ideally, treatments should be tested with placebo-controlled, double-blind studies (see page 223). Yet, the professional realizes that some treatments simply do not lend themselves easily to this medical model of evaluation. The effects of pills are easy to evaluate by this method; more interactive strategies, such as sensory-motor integration and neurofeedback training, must often be studied in other ways. Thus, these strategies may not carry the same scientific seal of approval as drug studies. A professional may be more reluctant to recommend these treatment methods, though they may be very effective. Also, parents should remember that every professional is human and vulnerable to quirks of human nature. He or she may not be familiar with the latest studies of every technique advertised to help the child with A.D.D. It's a vast subject. Or a professional may be so enamored with the one or two techniques that they may have researched themselves or in which they have a lot of experience that they are unable to be objective about alternative methods.

Another reason that both parents and professionals have difficulty judging whether an alternative method is worthwhile is the human element, or placebo effect, found with nearly every form of treatment. In many interventions, especially those that require a lot of focused attention on the child, it's hard to tell if the child gets "better" because of the treatment or because of all the extra attention he receives.

THE FEINGOLD DIET

In his 1974 book *Why Your Child Is Hyperactive,* pediatrician Benjamin Feingold connected hyperactivity to food additives and proposed a diet for children with A.D.H.D. that was free of artificial colorings, preservatives such as BHT and BHA, and foods containing natural salicylates (found in peaches,

oranges, raisins, apples, berries, tomatoes, and almonds). Some followers claimed dramatic improvement in their children on the diet. Even though scientific studies have since discounted the effectiveness of the Feingold diet, an organization and its loyal followers still exist. For additive-free food lists, contact The Feingold Association (P.O. Box 6550, Alexandria, Virginia, 22308, 800-321-3287). Researchers on the Feingold diet caution parents that the diet may be low in vitamin C and possibly other nutrients found in the forbidden fruits and vegetables. The general conclusion in the scientific community about the Feingold diet is that its primary benefit is the extra attention the child receives while being on this diet. It is a time-consuming and difficult diet to begin and follow, and because the parents are devoting so much time and energy to the diet, and indirectly to their child, the parent's expectations are high, and the child may be picking up more positive messages from the parents.

SENSORY-MOTOR INTEGRATION

Sensory-motor integration (SMI) may prove to be helpful in a specific subgroup of children who have A.D.D. and sensory-motor integration problems. "Sensory" refers to sensory input from various sources, such as vision, hearing, touch, pain, motion, position, balance, taste, smell, and temperature. "Motor" refers to the ability to control movement of all parts of the body, such as limbs, fingers, eyes, and the muscles necessary for vocalization. The key word is "integration." It refers not only to the ability to organize the sensory information but also to coordinate that information with motor abilities.

An SMI therapist carefully defines the child's particular sensory-motor integration problem and designs exercises to help overcome it. For example, a child who may be uncomfortable and fidgeting due to a sensitivity to light touch may be given activities that gradually increase the ability of that child to tolerate the kinds of stimulation to which he has been overly sensitive. For children who have signs of difficulties with motor awkwardness or sensory sensitivities, it makes excellent sense to use approaches that may help them improve.

This is not, however, the kind of problem usually found in children who have A.D.D. Indeed, some children with A.D.D. are incredibly artistic, athletic, and demonstrate superior abilities in areas that involve sensory-motor integration. There is no scientific evidence that the sensory-motor problems are at the root of A.D.D., although sensory-motor disorders may have symptoms that include decreased attention span and distractibility. There is no scientific evidence that SMI therapy will help learning disorders or A.D.D., though it does have effects on motor coordination. However, this does not mean that some children with A.D.D. cannot be helped by SMI. It isn't necessary to establish that a sensory-motor integrative problem is the cause of A.D.D. in order to justify trying these exercises. There is anecdotal evidence accumulating that they do help selected children. It is important to evaluate before-and-after behaviors objectively.

MORE CONTROVERSIAL APPROACHES

There are additional approaches to treating A.D.D., such as the following.

The Inner Ear

Dr. Harold Levinson has popularized looking at inner-ear dysfunction as a factor in a wide range of problems, including A.D.D. He believes that the vestibular (balance) system is central to understanding and treating A.D.D. Persons who follow this line of thinking believe that disturbances in this system have major effects on the ability of the brain to integrate sensory information. They also believe that this system regulates body energy levels. Unlike persons who use sensory-motor integration therapies, however, Dr. Levinson uses medications including anti-motion-sickness drugs, stimulants like Ritalin, antihistamines, antipsychotics and antidepressants, and nutritional supplements.

We recommend that persons who have difficulties that could be associated with the known functions of the vestibular system (balance, feeling light-headed, dizziness) or difficulties with central auditory processing, see a neurologist or an ENT (ear, nose, and throat) specialist and have the appropriate testing carried out. It is not surprising that persons having a specific vestibular difficulty might secondarily experience some difficulty with attention. If you suspect your child has such a problem, treat it and then reevaluate for A.D.D.

Optometric Vision Training

Research to date demonstrates a clear association between language delay and reading disabilities. Research does not support a causative connection between visual function and A.D.D. On the other hand, tracking exercises (exercises to improve how the eyes work together, change focus, and fixate on a series of changing objects) could all reasonably be expected to help a child improve his attention span. As with sensory-motor integration therapies, it isn't necessary to say that a vision problem is the cause of A.D.D. in order to try visual exercises for helping a person who has both difficulties. It is important to demonstrate improved attention after completion of the exercises. Conclusive research on this question is still to be done.

Chiropractic Techniques

This is another approach that focuses on how sensory messages are received by the brain. Specifically, malalignment of the sphenoid bone and the temporal bones is said to cause unequal pressure on different parts of the brain. In addition, body reflexes are said not to be synchronized. Manipulation of the spine is supposed to correct the problems. There is no scientific evidence to support this treatment for A.D.D., and this therapy is apparently not practiced by most of the chiropractic profession. There are some cases, however, where chiropractic treatment reportedly has helped a child with A.D.D. symptoms. The question remains as to which children might be helped and which symptoms might respond to what treatment.

Irlen Lenses

Followers of this theory believe that A.D.D. symptoms could be caused by what they call Scotopic Sensitivity syndrome. This is said to cause difficulties with perception. They believe that people who have this difficulty see the printed page differently from the way other people do. This will lead to fatigue and secondarily to attention difficulties. They recommend tinted lenses or filters to reduce certain wavelengths of light. More conventional groups, such as optometrists and ophthalmologists, have apparently objected and suggested that the problems seen are due to ordinary problems with vision and should be addressed with conventional methods such as proper glasses. Despite opposition and the lack of studies supporting this approach, there are anecdotal reports of good results by some individuals. We do not know of any harm that can be done by using color overlays or wearing tinted glasses, but if you are going to try it, we recommend you first have your child's eyes examined by a professional and have appropriate glasses prescribed if they are necessary. When Irlen lenses do work, it is perhaps because the child had a specific perceptual problem and not A.D.D.

Light and Sound Machines

You may have seen advertisements showing a person wearing headphones and dark glasses that promise a change in your mental state. Stimulation of the brain through closed eyes by flashing colored lights (tiny lights are built into the frames of the glasses) and through the ears by a pulsing tone has been found to "entrain" brain waves. This means that the brain waves (which can be picked up by electrodes placed on the head) show a preponderance of waves at the same frequency as the flashing lights and pulsing tones. This type of light and sound presentation has been used mainly to assist people to relax. The light is made to flash at slow frequencies, which are the normal brain wave frequencies for people who are meditating or daydreaming. Theoretically, this same procedure might be used to entrain brain waves to the faster frequencies associated with concentrating and problem solving and thereby give a person a feeling for being in a brain state associated with concentrating. Using light and sound for relaxation is more common than for treating A.D.D. These units have been designed for adults rather than children. It is not known if the light and sound stimulation might have any long-term negative effects on children's more sensitive vision and hearing. Future research will have to demonstrate whether this stimulation works for A.D.D.

Putting It All Together:
A Case Study

To help you digest everything you've read in this book, we are going to follow twelve-year-old Robert's progress from the time when the need for diagnosis and action became apparent until there was successful intervention and management of his A.D.D. Every child is unique, and there are endless variations on A.D.D., so your child will be different from Robert in many ways. Robert's story does, however, illustrate many of the characteristics most commonly found in children with A.D.D. and their families.

Features of A.D.D.

When twelve-year-old Robert was "advanced" rather than promoted to seventh grade, his parents knew they had to take further action. He had always required an inordinate amount of supervision at home for everything from getting dressed and keeping his shoelaces tied to doing his homework. In the morning he had trouble with routines. He would wander around rather than getting ready. Mother finally made up a schedule that was posted on the refrigerator to help him manage his time and get the tasks done so he could be ready to leave on time. Robert also frequently forgot things. Sent to do something, he would get sidetracked and forget what he was supposed to be doing. He would regularly forget his homework. When he did remember to bring the work home, he would put off doing it. Written work was the biggest challenge, and he showed great resistance to getting words down on paper, though he could dictate great stories for his mother to type out.

Though Robert could not learn his multiplication tables, he could easily memorize bits of dialogue from favorite movies and television shows. He could also focus in on his artwork. Though generally squirmy, he would sit very quietly while drawing and would not even notice if his little brother bumped into him.

He was good with his seven-year-old brother, Sam, and other younger children and liked to make them laugh. He still enjoyed building with Lego with Sam, who was more focused and organized than Robert in many ways. Sam could be told to do something, and he would follow through independently. For Robert to complete his homework, his parents might have to sit with him for three hours. Despite the frustrations, his parents tried to be positive. In the morning Father sometimes called from work to wish Robert a good day and remind him to stay focused.

Robert was good with animals and loved being outdoors and spending time at the summer cottage. He had not done well in soccer or hockey, since he did not really understand the games. His parents invested in hockey day camp to build up his skills, but Robert did not try as hard as the other boys. Individual sports required a lot of extra practice with his father, because what he learned in class just did not seem to sink in. He was made to do more push-ups than the other boys in karate class because of his inattentiveness, and he lost interest. He liked swimming for fun and was good enough for a swim team, but he was not motivated to take lessons and earn his certificates.

Father was sympathetic to Robert because he felt he had had a similar style and remembered being bored in school. In college he had definitely had to work harder than others to earn good grades. He could be very intense about things that interested him and he was very successful in a sales career. Mother was a teacher, and she felt some embarrassment

that she could not seem to motivate her own child. She had certainly done a lot of individual work with Robert to ensure that he could read well, but he had little interest in books, though he had always enjoyed being read to. His parents worked hard to avoid problems with self-esteem, knowing how important it was that Robert feel successful.

School Struggles

Robert's lack of academic progress was a major concern. His parents felt that attentional problems were interfering with his learning. He had never been disruptive in school, but a friend was moved to another part of the classroom because he and Robert were talking too much. Though not hyperactive, Robert was often restless and would fidget with his hands, make faces, or bite his lip. He had trouble sticking to his work and might get up and sharpen his pencil and then break it and sharpen it again. As a young child, he was known to wander away from the group during circle time, preferring to play with the big hollow blocks. Robert said that often his mind wandered, and he might find himself making up weird riddles instead of catching what the teacher was saying. He said he did not remember half of what the teacher said but was reluctant to ask her to repeat something. Then he would just sit and doodle because he had not caught the instructions.

Although everyone considered Robert bright, he was not getting the work done. As a preschooler he had done well in a Montessori setting and had picked up information readily. As work at a desk in a regular classroom increased in the primary grades, he began having trouble. In third grade he regularly brought home a *Must Do* homework book, which was mainly work he had not finished in class. The teachers had all been good

A Dozen Steps to Successful Management of A.D.D.

Here is a step-by-step outline that you can follow to ensure that you have covered all the bases in working out the best approach for your child. Since every child with A.D.D. requires an individual management program, not every step is needed for every child. Nor are all these steps exclusively A.D.D. interventions. Numbers 9 to 11 zero in on A.D.D. The others are part of optimal parenting of any child. The sections in the book that will help guide you through this checklist are shown in parentheses.

Step 1: Educate yourself about A.D.D. (chapter 1)

Step 2: Identify your child's individual needs. What are the main problems in behavior and/or learning?

- Complete the A.D.D.-Q. (pp. 42–43)
- Assess the severity of the problems. (p. 40)
- Interview teachers and other caregivers. (p. 41)
- What are your child's special qualities? Which ones work to his advantage or disadvantage?

Step 3: Tune up family functioning.

- Reread chapter 6. (pp. 139–171)
- Take a Family Functioning Inventory. (pp. 141–142)
- Review family organization and time management techniques. (pp. 143–156)

Step 4: Review your child's extracurricular activities. Which ones work to his advantage, and which ones are detrimental to his behavior or self-esteem?

- Sports. Is your child in the right sport and in the right position on the team? (pp. 150–151 and 162)
- Is your child involved in appropriate school activities (choir, band, dramatics, debating, art, photography, etc.)?
- Assess your child's friends. Which ones mesh with his personality? Which ones clash? Guide your child toward friendships that bring out his best qualities and discourage those that bring out his worst.

Step 5: Support your child's school success.

- Reread chapter 7. (pp. 172–204)
- Interview the teacher and visit the classroom. (pp. 173 and 176)
- Try various learning strategies. (pp. 188–201)
- Improve your child's organization and attention skills. (pp. 178 and 183)
- Improve your child's memory and motivation. (pp. 199 and 202)
- Request psychological, behavior, intelligence, and any other tests that the school can provide, which may indicate your child's specific style of learning and give recommendations to improve areas that need help. Save a copy of those tests for your appointment with the A.D.D. specialist.
- Consider tutoring/supplemental education to boost your child's skills and confidence.

Step 6: Develop strategies for improving your child's behavior.

- Reread chapter 5. (pp. 89–138)
- Based on the suggestions in this chapter, develop your own behavior-improving strategies that work for you and your child.

Step 7: Assess your child's nutrition.

- Reread chapter 10. (pp. 260–271)
- In consultation with a nutritionist, perform a nutritional analysis. (p. 269)
- Try an elimination diet to exclude food sensitivities (p. 269)
- After identifying possible nutritional deficiencies, work out a daily nutritional supplement program. (p. 267)
- Feed your child a healthy breakfast and lunch for a good nutritional start each day. (pp. 262–264)

Step 8: Get your child a complete medical checkup.

- Have your child's vision and hearing checked.
- Have your child's iron level checked.
- Discuss with your doctor any possible medical condition that may be affecting your child's behavior and learning.
- Ask your doctor's opinion on whether or not medication would be helpful for your child. Remember that medication may be used in addition to all the other strategies and should not be the only intervention.
- Ask your doctor to recommend an A.D.D. specialist, learning specialist, or behavior specialist as needed.

Step 9: Get an evaluation by a specialist in A.D.D.

- Review the strategies you have been using—what works, what doesn't.
- Bring along medical records, school records, teacher assessments, and the A.D.D.-Q checklist that you have filled out. (p. 42–43)
- Ask the specialist for an opinion on other management strategies in which the specialist has had both training and experience (e.g., stimulant medication, neurofeedback, nutritional supplement therapy, etc.).
- Review the results of the school tests (step 5, above) with the A.D.D. specialist
- Work out an overall management plan.

Step 10. Consider neurofeedback training to help your child learn self-regulation.

- Reread chapter 8. (pp. 205–227)
- Consider whether your child is a candidate for neurofeedback. (p. 219)
- Set realistic goals and chart your child's progress during neurofeedback.

Step 11: Consider medications to help your child with A.D.D.

- Especially when hyperactivity is extreme, consider medical management that includes medication.
- To educate yourself about the drugs used for A.D.D., reread chapter 9. (pp. 228–259)
- Chart the effects of medication on your child. (p. 234)

Step 12: Monitor your child's progress.

- Have periodic checkups with your child's doctor and/or A.D.D. specialist.
- Repeat the A.D.D.-Q every few months to track changes.
- Stay in touch with your child's teachers.

- Keep a diary to track what is working, what isn't, and which areas still need improvement.
- Give yourself a pat on the back for all the work you are doing. Remember that even though things may not be perfect, they are better due to your effort.
- Take time to enjoy your child.

---

about keeping in touch with Robert's parents, and various suggestions had been tried in the junior grades: dropping him off early so he could get work done before school started, having him skip the school bus and be picked up later by his mother so he could do homework after school. His teachers wanted him to take more responsibility, but this just seemed impossible. He described his frustration this way: "Sometimes my mind goes blank. I'm doing my math and I don't see it. My brain goes fuzzy." He made more and more comments about school being boring.

Early History

Robert's mother's pregnancy had been normal, but Robert arrived three weeks early, and he was delivered by forceps. He was a bit colicky, but this cleared up once an allergy to milk was discovered; if mother drank milk, Robert reacted. Robert was breastfed for seven months exclusively and partially for seventeen months, and eventually he grew out of his milk allergy. He generally slept and ate well, though he was a rather picky eater and did not like to try new things. Robert would be moody if he did not get enough sleep. His parents watched his diet carefully and avoided foods that seemed to make him

more restless or irritable, such as candy that had a lot of artificial color.

Milestones were early for both motor skills and language development. He was quite active, and Robert's parents could not turn their backs on him. At eight months of age he was found on top of a wall unit. Fortunately he was coordinated and did not hurt himself. It was also helpful that Robert had a big backyard. Mother said she could not have raised him in an apartment.

Though generally healthy, Robert was prone to ear infections from an early age, and antibiotics were frequently prescribed. Finally, when he was four, tubes were inserted, and eventually his ear infections stopped. Father wondered if he had gotten used to not paying attention when people spoke because, with his ears blocked so often when he was little, it had required too much effort to catch what people were saying.

Assessments

During a conversation with his sixth-grade teacher at the end of the year about how inconsistent Robert had been in his work, the teacher pointed out that the time Robert spent on his work did not depend on the level of difficulty but on his level of interest and degree of focus. It broke Mother's heart when the teacher asked, "Does Robert ever smile?" She had not been aware of how unhappy Robert was at school. Mother asked the school to do an assessment.

The school administration, though sympathetic, would not allow the school psychologist to do the assessment because Robert was not that far behind in terms of achievement and there were other needier children. Robert's parents had a psychoeducational assessment done at a private clinic that specialized in learning problems. Mother and Father filled out questionnaires, and Robert underwent two days of testing. Mother and Father were not surprised to hear that Robert's ability level was above average, but they were shocked to hear that he was only at the fifth percentile on the subtests most affected by distractibility. No specific learning disabilities were found, and his basic skills were average, except for his written language. The clinic recommended family counseling and that Robert's parents discuss medication with their doctor.

After eliminating hearing and vision problems and checking thyroid function, their family doctor referred Robert to a pediatrician who dealt with children with A.D.D. She was willing to prescribe Ritalin and said that Robert might require medication for the rest of his life. A lot of time was spent discussing how they would do a trial of the drug at different dosages and get back reports from the teacher on how it was working. Robert, however, did not want to take medicine and be different from the other kids.

After Robert was diagnosed with A.D.D., his parents considered their alternatives. Robert had been upset by the diagnosis, but his parents had reassured him that A.D.D. was a correctable or controllable problem and that they would let him help make the decisions about how to handle his treatment.

Even though Mother was a teacher, she felt A.D.D. was outside her area of expertise, so she searched the Internet to research treatments and read as many books as she could find at the library. There seemed to be a lot of controversy around neurofeedback training, but it was an option worth considering. Mother and Father felt medication could be kept in reserve as a backup if nondrug intervention did not work.

Interventions

The results of Robert's first visit to the neurofeedback center indicated that he was a good candidate for neurofeedback training. A history and questionnaires and the assessment already done at the private clinic all contributed to his initial evaluation. Robert found the computerized continuous performance test quite challenging, but he tried hard, and his results fell just within the normal range (that is, not in the bottom 2 percent for his age). His reaction time, however, was on the slow side, and it was quite variable. Sometimes he was quick, hitting the button as soon as he saw a target, but other times there was a delay. This variability mirrored his inconsistency in everyday life.

The assessment of his brain wave pattern showed that he did produce more slow wave activity and less fast wave activity than one would expect for his age. This is typical of attentional problems that are neurologically based. Robert tended to tune out with bursts of theta waves (4 to 8 cps) even when he was trying to concentrate on reading. The tests finally got interesting for him in the practice neurofeedback training session, when he got to try games such as moving a fish through a maze. He thought it was neat to be playing a computer game using only his brain power and without moving. He figured out very quickly that his score was better when he did not fidget. Robert was ready to start right away.

Since it was still summer vacation, Robert began with three training sessions a week. Once school started, this was cut back to two sessions. During each hour-long session, Robert worked with an enthusiastic trainer who let him know he was doing a good job learning to balance his brain waves to produce good concentration. As he got better, the levels could be set a little harder. Robert felt good about exercising his brain.

When Robert's attention span began to increase, his trainer also coached him in strategies that would help him be more efficient in his schoolwork. Robert had to maintain his concentration while he practiced new strategies. He learned ways to study his spelling words and started getting close to or even perfect on his weekly tests. He became a more active reader and actually started reading on his own at home rather than watching as much TV (though he still would not miss his Saturday morning cartoons and was better than ever at remembering lines that he heard). He even memorized his multiplication tables, having first built his confidence by learning the nine-times table using finger math.

Robert's parents began noticing changes after the first couple of months. Robert was more aware of what was going on around him and was remembering tasks. There was also more participation in family discussions. By the end of forty sessions of training, the biggest change was described as "growing up a lot." He showed more mature work habits, and he was less down in the dumps according to his father. He even seemed to have more energy in his sports. He could also be relied on to finish his homework and chores. Mother beamed when the teacher called to

say Robert was laughing and participating in class discussions. His parents began to look forward to his first report card. When it came, the E's had changed to C's and D's, and the other grades were A's and B's. More important were the comments, which did not mention lack of participation or incomplete work.

A formal reassessment confirmed Robert's parents' observation that he had changed. Now all his scores on the computerized continuous performance test were actually better than average for his age. Compared with his first test, he was less impulsive, more attentive, and had a faster and steadier reaction time. His IQ score had shifted significantly from the bright range (eighty-first percentile) to the superior range (ninety-sixth percentile). His academic scores for reading, spelling, and math had moved from the lower end to the high end of the average range. As well, his EEG pattern looked more mature: there had been a shift toward less slow wave and more fast wave activity. This was important because such a shift in the brain wave pattern indicates that the good results of neurofeedback can be expected to last. Best of all, his parents felt that Robert was a happier child.

A Final Word

Not every child shows such a dramatic improvement as Robert did. He had many advantages, including being bright and having very supportive parents who took a lot of time to organize him, monitor his diet, exercise, and sleep needs, and build his self-esteem. His schoolteachers also tracked his progress carefully and let his parents know when there were concerns. They also called to report good news. Everyone worked hard to set Robert up for success. But what made the biggest difference in Robert's case was that he learned to self-regulate his mental state using neurofeedback. Once his ability to concentrate improved, he could make use of all the other resources around him at home and school and in the community. With other children, the change might come with the use of medication, a change in school environment, new behavior management techniques, changes in diet, extra tutoring, relaxation techniques, sensory-motor integration training, or some combination of interventions.

The future looks bright for Robert and, indeed, for other children who have A.D.D. People are starting to recognize the positive side of A.D.D., and there is a wider range of interventions than ever before. Resourceful parents continue to educate themselves and do not give up until they find the combination that works best for their own special child.

A.D.D. Resources

U.S.A.

ADDA (Attention Deficit Disorder Association)
P.O. Box 972
Mentor, OH 44061
800-487-2282

Association for Applied Psychophysiology
    and Biofeedback
10200 West Forty-fourth Avenue
Suite 304
Wheat Ridge, CO 80033-2840

This organization maintains a list of researchers
and clinicians using biofeedback in a variety of ap-
plications. If you send a stamped, self-addressed
envelope with your request, they will provide the
names of practitioners in your local area.

CH.A.D.D. (Children and Adults with Attention
    Deficit Disorder)
499 N.W. 70th Avenue
Suite 101
Plantation, FL 33317
954-587-3700
954-587-4599 (fax)
800-233-4050 (U.S. only)
Internet address: www.chadd.org

Learning Disabilities Association of America
4156 Library Road
Pittsburgh, PA 15234
412-341-1515

CANADA

CH.A.D.D. (Children and Adults with Attention
    Deficit Disorder)
835 Carling Avenue
Ottawa, ON
K1S 2E7
613-722-8482

Learning Disabilities Association of Canada
323 Chapel Street
Suite 200
Ottawa, ON
K1N 7Z2
613-238-5721
613-235-5391 (fax)
e-mail: ldactaac@fox.nstn.ca

Index